Wills of
Chester County
Pennsylvania

1748-1766

Based on the Work of
Jacob Martin

HERITAGE BOOKS
2007

HERITAGE BOOKS
AN IMPRINT OF HERITAGE BOOKS, INC.

Books, CDs, and more—Worldwide

For our listing of thousands of titles see our website
at
www.HeritageBooks.com

Published 2007 by
HERITAGE BOOKS, INC.
Publishing Division
65 East Main Street
Westminster, Maryland 21157-5026

Copyright © 1994 F. Edward Wright

All rights reserved. No part of this book may be reproduced or transmitted in any form or by any means, electronic or mechanical, including photocopying, recording or by any information storage and retrieval system without written permission from the author, except for the inclusion of brief quotations in a review.

International Standard Book Number: 978-1-58549-363-0

INTRODUCTION

The wills of Chester County were first abstracted by Jacob Martin of Marshallton, Pennsylvania and indexed by the indefatigable Gilbert Cope.

The abstracts done by Jacob Martin appear to be accurate and complete. Some minor corrections have been added. Recently it was noted by the Chester County Historical Society that the abstract of the will of James Whitaker was in error in that Martin had incorrectly given Whitaker's son's name as Edward Clayton which during mid 1700s would have suggested that Edward was a son-in-law and husband to daughter Ann Clayton. An examination of the original will showed Edward Whitaker to be son of James Whitaker while daughter Ann Clayton is mentioned as having a husband, but unnamed. This error occurs in our earlier volume for the period, 1713 through 1748. This volume was also checked against the original volume with only a few corrections noted. Nevertheless, the reader is cautioned that the original should be examined whenever possible. All the wills covered by this volume are available on microfilm through Family History Centers (LDS).

The first date given is normally the date that the will was written; subsequent dates are usually dates on which witnesses appeared to attest to the validity of the will or the date the court proved the will. Dates are frequently given numerically in the following order: month, day and year. Prior to 1752, March 25th (Feast of the Annunciation) was the first day of the new year by traditional acceptance of the ecclesiastical calendar. Later as the Gregorian calendar was being accepted the double dates were used from January 1st until March 25th.

Basic information on the records of administration was included in Martin's work along with data gathered by him from deeds and other court records, all of which has been included here. Information on administrations can be especially helpful when no will exists (died intestate). Martin uses the phrase, "Adm. to ---" to indicate the name of the administrator/administratrix to whom the administration was assigned. The first name appearing in each entry, will or administration, is always the name of the deceased.

                                                      F. Edward Wright
                                             Westminster, Maryland 1994

GEORGE, GEORGE. Radnor. Yeoman.
February 20, 1747. April 20, 1748. B. 264
To my sister Jane, wife of John Evans, the Plantation containing 204 acres during life, subject to maintenance of mother Amey as my Father's will directs. Personal estate to be sold, 1/2 given to Mother and remainder as follows. To brother Richard George £20, to Amey, daughter of sister Jane and John Evans £10 and remainder to children of my 2 brothers, Richard and John. Plantation at sister's death to George, son of brother Richard, with reversion to brother John's son, George and failing him to brother Richard's son John. To be buried at St. David's Church near his father.
Executors: Cousin Richard George of Merion [in Philadelphia] and brother John George.
Wit: Susanna Williams, Edward H. George.
A deed on record in Delaware County shows that Richard's son, John, inherited the land.

BROWN, SAMUEL. West Nottingham.
1/16/1747/8. April 22, 1748. B. 265.
Wife Elizabeth to have real estate until eldest son Samuel is 21. To son Samuel the house and 200 acres of land where we live. To sons Joseph and William remainder of land. Remainder of personal estate to my 6 children: Hannah, Mary, Katherine, Samuel, Joseph and William Brown, in equal shares, boys at 21 and girls at 18.
Executors: Wife Elizabeth and Henry Reynolds.
Wit: John Gartril, Timothy Kirk, William Knight.

HARRIS, WILLIAM. West Nottingham.
1/22/1747/8. April 22, 1748. B. 266.
To son John all my land on North side of Octoraro Road. To son Richard 50 acres of land off the East corner of my land, also 50 acres more after wife's decease. Provides for wife Elizabeth including house and remainder of land during life. At her decease the land to sons, John and Richard. To son and daughter, Thomas & Mary Slycer, 1 shilling and no more. To daughter Elizabeth Brown 1 shilling. Remainder of movables to 4 daughters: Sarah, Susanna, Rachel and Hannah Harris.
Executors: Henry Reynolds and son, John.
Wit: John Gartril, Thomas Coulson, William Reynolds.
Account filed, names daughter Hannah Smith.
*Deed 5-10-1713, James King to William Harris of Abington, 245 acres in Nottingham for £21-15.

READING, MATTHEW. Vincent.
April 4, 1748. April 27, 1748. B. 267.
To Jane Adams £20 at 18. For repairing the Valley Church £2 and to the minister £2. Remainder to wife Jane.
Executors: Wife Jane and her cousin, Anthony Prichard.
Wit: Robert Watkins, John Evan, Francis Bridges.

CLARK, HENRY. Darby.
December 8, 1742. April 28, 1748. B. 267.
To wife Mary all estate, also Executor. Friend Henry Lewis to

assist her.
Wit: William McClelen, John McClelen.

PACKER, JOHN. Of Moorton in parish of Thornbury in
Gloucestershire. Yeoman.
March 25, 1726. April 5, 1750. Died 9/25/1749. B. 268.
Names cousin Edward Gregory, son of William and Mary, his wife.
Brother William Packer. John and Martha, children of William
Gregory. Cousins Daniel and John Weare. William and Israel
Roach. All living in England. To John, son of William and Jane
Brenton of Birmingham in Pennsylvania 1/2 of my lands in said
Province he paying to his brothers and sister £10 each. To Mary,
daughter of John Wyeth of Birmingham, 100 acres of land in said
Province. To William Brenton and son Joseph, all my lands in
Kennett Township in Trust for the use of the poor of the Quakers
of Concord Monthly Meeting. See Pemberton Papers, Penna. Hist.
Soc. Vol. 65.
* John Gregory of Cleve in parish of Yatton, County of Somerset,
carpenter, heir at law to John Packer late of Pennsylvania.
Executed power of attorney March 8, 1749 to Joseph Williams and
John Harrison of Concord. Deed Book G. 645. Original in
possession of Philip P. Sharpless 2/20/1879.

KING, GEORGE. East Nottingham.
March 4, 1747/8. April 29, 1748. C. 1.
To wife Sarah all estate until son James is 21 and then equally
divided between them.
Executors: Wife and William Bean.
Wit: Robert Young, James Hutcheson.

YEARSLEY, JOHN. Thornbury. Yeoman.
April 19, 1748. April 30, 1748. Died 21st. C. 2.
To son Isaac the plantation that he lives on in Thornbury
containing 105 acres, also the 10 acre field, he paying his
sister, Elizabeth wife of John Heald, £12. To son Jacob the
plantation he lives on in Westtown containing 100 acres. To son
Thomas the plantation he lives on in Westtown containing 100
acres. To son Nathan the plantation I now live on containing 230
acres, also stock, subject to provision for wife Sarah. To
Joseph Williamson 1 shilling. To grandson John, son of Thomas
£5.
Executors: Wife Sarah and son Nathan.
Wit: Ann Vernon, John Taylor, John Townsend.

FREEMAN, JOHN. West Bradford.
2/25/1748. May 4, 1748. C. 5.
To wife Elizabeth all estate, she paying legacies. To son
Nathaniel, Bible and articles of wearing apparel. To son John £5
in cattle. To son Samuel wearing apparel. To son in law
Jeremiah Barnard, my hand saw, and to his wife my daughter,
Judith an auger and broad axe. To William Lee and Sarah Keetch
at expiration of apprenticeship, one ewe each. To William Keech
in right of his deceased wife my daughter, Sarah, 5 shillings.
Executrix: Wife Elizabeth.

Wit: Susanna Stanson, John McCarty, Thomas Edmunds Sr., Thomas
Edmunds Jr.
[Codicil: 2/26/1748.]

RIGG, ROBERT. Uwchlan.
March 14, 1747/8. May 5, 1748. C. 7.
Provides for wife Elizabeth including profits of real estate
until son Richard is of age and married, for bringing up 3
youngest children, viz., Richard, Ann and Mary. To son Clement 1
shilling. To daughter Sarah £5. To daughters Ann and Mary £10
each at 18. To grandson Robert Rigg £3 at 21. To son Richard my
land when he is 21 and marries a wife.
Executors: Wife Elizabeth, son Clement, and brother in law
Richard Richison.
Wit: Peter Aston, Elizabeth Aston, Hannah Aston.

JAMES, THOMAS. Whiteland.
July 29, 1747. May 14, 1748. C. 10.
To my cousins, viz., Joseph James, Mary Earl, Thomas, Aaron,
Jonathan, Martha and Hannah James 5 shillings each. To cousin
Elizabeth, daughter of Joseph Lewis bed and bedding. To cousin
Elizabeth, daughter of Samuel James riding horse. To cousin
Joseph Talkinton my lott in Wilmington and £5. To Griffith John
my Welsh Bible. Remainder to cousin Samuel James of Whiteland,
also Executor.
Wit: Llewellin Parry, Thomas Guest, Richard Thomas.

ALLISON, ALEXANDER.
April 9, 1748.
Adm. to Christian Allison.

ROSWELL, JOSEPH.
April 26, 1748.
Adm. to John Mather.

WILLIAMS, THOMAS.
April 11, 1748.
Adm. to Catherine Williams.

BAKER, JOSEPH.
May 1, 1748.
Adm. to John Taylor, Esq.

HAYES, JOSEPH.
April 23, 1748.
Adm. to Jane Hayes.

DELL, THOMAS, JR.
May 2, 1748.
Adm. to Joseph Garrett.

HENDRICKSON, JOHN.
April 26, 1748.
Adm. to Catherine Hendrickson.

MADDEN, JOHN.
May 5, 1748.
Adm. to Daniel Pritchard.

COLLINS, MARY, widow of Joseph. Goshen.
12/10/1742/3. May 14, 1748. C. 12.
To eldest son John Collins, £12. To son Joseph, 1 shilling. To
son Henry, 1 shilling. To daughter Sarah Mallan and to
granddaughter Mary, daughter of John Collins articles of
household furniture. To grandson Joseph, son of John Collins £6.
To granddaughter Elizabeth, daughter of Thomas Mallan articles
named. To grandson Joseph Mallen the £7 his father owes me. To
daughter in law Ann, wife of John Collins remainder of clothes.
Remainder to grandson John, son of John Collins.
Executor: Son John Collins.
Wit: Samuel James, Isaac Sevill.

MARSH, JOSHUA. East Nantmell. Yeoman.
6/18/1747. May 17, 1748. C. 15.
To son John 5 shillings. To sons George and Peter 5 shillings each. To daughter Deborah McMullen 5 shillings. To daughter Abigail Atherton 5 shillings. To son Jonathan my plantation in E. Nantmell and remainder of personal estate. Also to said son my farm in Belenacar in Clanbrasel Co. of Armagh, Ireland, containing 33 acres.
Executor: Son Jonathan.
Wit: David Davies, Richard Davies, Ellis Davies.

BARTON, JOSEPH. Willistown.
April 28, 1748. May 19, 1748. C. 17.
To eldest son James, a young filly. To wife Mary, all remainder of estate. Letters to widow Mary Barton.
Wit: Abraham Thompson, Thomas Grifin, Thomas Rowland.

MC DONALD, JEREMIAH. Kennett. Weaver.
April 9, 1748. May 20, 1748. C. 18.
To my brother Thomas, wearing apparel when 21. To friend John Pyle, remainder of goods and chattels for the use of my Mother when she calls for it.
Executor: John Pyle.
Wit: Thomas Houlden, William Cooper, Jane Houlden.

WYLLEY, WILLIAM. Kennett.
May 12, 1748. May 31, 1748. C. 19.
To John Harper a heifer. Remainder to wife Katherine and sons, William and James, and daughter Abigail, in equal shares.
Executors: Wife Katherine and Joseph Buffington of E. Bradford.
Wit: John Long, Gabriel Clark.

BRINTON, JOHN. Kennett. Yeoman.
June 20, 1747. June 1, 1748. C. 21.
Provides for wife Hannah including plantation in Kennett containing 195 acres until son John is 21 and then I devise said land to him, he paying legacies. To sons Jacob and David, £60 each. To daughters Lydia and Hannah £30 each, also a legacy "to the child my wife is now big with."
Executors: Wife and brother Edward.
Wit: Samuel Bettle, Joseph Williams, John Taylor.

EVANS, EVAN. Uwchlan. Yeoman.
May 13, 1748. June 1, 1748. Co. 25.
To brother Thomas all my land except 40 acres of the eastern end, also stock. To mother £6 and remainder of stock. To brother Richard, the 40 acres reserved as above. To sisters Martha Hopps, Mary Cleton, Margaret Todhunter and Susanna Sorel, 1 shilling each.
Executor: Brother Thomas Evans.
Wit: Peter Aston, Joseph Beeler, Cadwallader Jones, Jr.

PHILLIPS, JOHN. Tredyffrin. Labourer.
November 25, 1746. June 3, 1748. C. 27.
To John Davis of Plymouth and James Davis £50 for support of

Baptist Congregation in Tredyffrin. To John Davis minister at Tredyffrin £10. To Thomas Jones minister at Tulpehocken £10. To Owen Thomas minister at the Welsh Tract £10. To Thomas Davis minister at Long Island £3. To cousin Esther, wife of Robert William, £10 and to her 2 daughters £5 each. To John Lewis, tanner, all interest due me. To Thomas Reece now at French Creek the interest due me. To John, son of Richard Thomas £4 interest due me. To David Thomas of Charlestown the money due from him. To Mary Lloyd £1.16. To Elizabeth Parry £2.10. To James Davis £5. To my relations in Wales, brothers John and Thomas, sisters Joan and Jennett and John and Grace, children of Griffith Phillips £60. Remainder to brother Owen Phillip who with James Davis are executors. Mentions land of Thomas Davis in Charlestown.
Wit: Edward Jones, Jr., Samson Davis, Margaret Davis.

OARR, SAMUEL. New London. Weaver.
May 30, 1748. June 13, 1748. C. 32.
To brother Aaron Craford all estate.
Executor: Friend Peter Higet.
Wit: William Clinton, clerk, Seret Ciddell.

CASSEDY, BRYAN.
May 6, 1748.
Adm. to Samuel Grubb.

BLUNDELL, ROBERT.
May 9, 1748.
Adm. to John Little

BOSS, JOHN.
May 14, 1748.
Adm. to Adam Buckley.
Bentley.

CULLIVER, RICHARD.
May 16, 1748.
Adm. to Joseph Garrett.

HEALD, SAMUEL.
May 16, 1748.
Adm. to Rachel Heald.

WRAY, JAMES.
May 18, 1748.
Adm. to John Mackentyre.

BENTLEY, JOHN.
May 31, 1748.
Adm. to Jeffrey & John

MICKLE, ROBERT.
May 31, 1748.
Adm. to Aaron Watkin.

KEY, MOSES. Aston. Yeoman.
April 19, 1746. June 14, 1748. C. 33.
To wife Elizabeth all estate except as devised and after her decease to son Robert for his maintenance during life. To son William 20 shillings. To son Moses smith tools and 10 shillings. To daughters, Lettice Vernon, Elizabeth Morgan and Rebecca Pattin 10 shillings each. To daughter Ann Key furniture. To granddaughter Hannah Sharpless 5 shillings.
Executors: Wife and son in law Thomas Morgan.
Wit: John Bezer, Jane Cummings, Elinor Petters.

DICKIE, JOHN. New London. Yeoman.
June 11, 1748. June 16, 1748. C. 35.
To daughter Elizabeth 5 acres of land in Londonderry. To wife Elizabeth 1/3 of all estate during life; remainder to daughter.
Executors: Wife Elizabeth and Joseph Smith of Londonderry.

Letters to wife, Smith renouncing.
Wit: Abraham Emmit, Robert Finney, Robert McClenachan.

BEATY, ABRAHAM. Fallowfield. Yeoman.
May 11, 1748. July 15, 1748. C. 37.
To son David and his son Abraham, wearing apparel. To son Robert apparel and to his son, Abraham a heifer or £2. To son Robert Kerson 6 shillings. To son George Menaugh £3. To daughter Rebecca Beatty the plantation provided she marries with consent of executors, subject to maintenance of wife Agnes. Robert May to be overseer.
Executors: William Beatty of Octoraro and David Beatty of E. Caln. Wit: Robert May, David Beatty, Robert Beatty.

MASSEY, MORDECAI. Marple.
4/9/1748. July 22, 1748. C. 39.
Provides for wife, Rebecca. To daughter Hannah the plantation in Marple, subject to her mother's life interest with reversion to brothers, James and Thomas Massey and sisters, Esther Pearson, Mary Fell and sister Hannah's children Jesse and Alice Maris. Also £5 each to above named brothers and sisters. Also £5 to Friends of Springfield Meeting.
Executors: Wife Rebecca and brother Thomas Massey.
Wit: George Maris, John Rhoads, Mordecai Taylor.

CARTER, MARY. East Bradford.
April 15, 1748. July 29, 1748. C. 42.
To brothers George and John Carter £10 each. To sisters, viz., Rachel wife of Abraham Marshall and Elizabeth, wife of Samuel Worth, £10 each. To half brother James Jefferis £10. To half brother Emmor Jefferis. To half sister Abigail Jefferis £10 and wearing apparel. To mother Elizabeth Jefferis, my right in plantation in East Bradford left by my father, George Carter.
Executors: Elizabeth Jefferis and Thomas Worth.
Wit: Samuel Dunkin, Benjamin Jefferis, James Porter.

WOODWARD, JAMES. West Bradford. Yeoman.
May 23, 1748. July 19, 1748. C. 44.
To son Joseph part of my land on south side of great road where John Kirgan lives, except 10 acres at west end - at age 21. To son Robert at 21, 40 acres on north side of road and 10 acres reserved above. To other two sons, William and James, at 21 remainder of land; James to have buildings. Wife Ann to have use of real estate until sons are of age. To daughters Jane and Ann Woodward, £30 each at 18.
Executors: Wife Ann and brother William Woodward.
Wit: Edward Clayton, James Milleson, Benjamin Hawley.

BULGER, RICHARD.
June 2, 1748.
Adm. to Thomas Hyatt.

BARNES, EMANUEL.
June 2, 1748.
Adm. to James Miller.

MATSON, JOHN.
July 16, 1748.
Adm. to Hannah Matson.

DAVID, JENKIN.
July 22, 1748.
Adm. to James Rhoads.

MC DOWELL, JOHN.
June 8, 1748.
Adm. to Catherine & William McDowell.

MONTGOMERY, ROBERT.
July 26, 1748.
Adm. to Michael Montgomery.

DOUGHERTY, RICHARD.
June 15, 1748.
Adm. to Mary Dougherty.

EDMESTON, JOHN. West Nottingham.
March 26, 1748. April 12, 1748.
Plantation and all other estate to be sold and proceeds divided in equal shares between wife Jane, and daughters Martha and Mary, allowing to son William, £2.6.
Executors: David Edmeston, Hugh Edmeston and John Steel to be overseer. Will not recorded, but account filed March 22, 1749.
Wit: Joseph Mc Neely, James Gorrell, Robert Hynman.

WILLSON, JAMES. Londongrove.
June 28, 1748. August 17, 1748. C. 46.
Provides for wife Martha including use of plantation until son John is 21. To sons John and James my plantation containing 200 acres to be divided when 21. Also to John a lott in Newport. To daughter Sarah £100 when James is 21.
Executors: Wife and son John.
Wit: Richard Flower, Thomas Bryan.

DEAN, WILLIAM. Nantmill. Minister.
July 7, 1748. August 23, 1748. Died July 9, 1748. C. 48.
To wife Sarah 1/3 of estate. Remainder equally divided among my 5 children, viz., Joseph, William, John, Sarah and Benjamin Dean. Gives to wife use of plantation to maintain and educate the children. Mentions that "I expect my brother, Alexander Dean, from Ireland this summer."
Executors: Wife and brother Alexander Dean.
Wit: John Hamilton, William Leslie.

MYLLS, HENRY. East Caln. Labourer.
July 21, 1748. August 30, 1748. C. 51.
To son George my chest and wearing apparel. Remainder for use of 3 children that is in Ireland whose names are, Jean, William and Mary Mylls.
Executor: Thomas Downing.
Wit: John Boggs, Andrew Nox, Martha Boggs.

RILEY, EDWARD. Goshen. Yeoman.
March 30, 1748. September 10, 1748. C. 53.
To daughter Rebecca, wife of John Taylor, £45 when she is 55, to receive the interest in meantime and in case of her decease to grandson, Thomas Taylor, now apprentice to Nathan Matlock. Also to said grandson £45. To son in law John Taylor 5 shillings. To my housekeeper, Sarah Field, £12 at 55. Mentions having sold to Robert Eachus his plantation containing 50 acres and authorizes executors to make title to same. Also gives to John Eachus, brother of Robert, 2 years interest on his debt of £123-11-6.

Executors: Friend Henry Collins and his brother Joseph Collins.
Wit: Daniel Hoopes, James Walter, Richard Jones.

SIMPSON, JOSIAS. North Providence.
August 5, 1748. September 13, 1748. C. 56.
To wife Mary 1/3 of personal estate and use of real estate of about 200 acres during life and afterward equally divided between 2 daughters, Sarah and Rebecca.
Executors: Wife and Matthew Cowden.
Wit: John McMichell, James McCullough.

ROGERS, THOMAS. West Nottingham. Husbandman.
March 7, 1744/5. September 20, 1748. C. 58.
Provides for wife Elizabeth. To daughter Hannah Brooks £5. To sons William and Rowland 20 shillings each. To daughter Elizabeth Knight 20 shillings. To son John £30. To daughter Deborah Ruddell 20 shillings. To daughters Priscilla Rogers and Susanna Rogers £20. Remainder real and personal to son Thomas.
Executors: Wife and son Thomas.
Letters to Thomas, the widow renouncing.
Wit: John Baley, John Robinson, Joseph Richards.

THOMAS, JOSEPH. Willistown. Yeoman.
7/9/1748. October 1, 1748. C. 60.
Provides for wife Jemima including plantation on which I live until son Samuel is 21 and then she shall dispose of it to my sons, Nathan, Abraham, Joseph and Samuel. To daughter Priscilla £2-10. To daughter Tamer £30 at 21. To daughter Dinah £30 at 21.
Executor: Wife and friend Nathan Lewis.
Wit: Elizabeth Thomas, Elizabeth Norbury, Thomas Massey.

THOMAS, ANN. Uwchlan.
March 8, 1748. October 1, 1748. C. 63.
To son William Thomas 5 shillings. To daughter Margaret Phillips 5 shillings. To daughter Ann Thomas £2 per year for 10 years and household goods. To son Evan Thomas riding mare. To grandson Isaac Thomas a cow. To grandson William Phillips £4 at 15. To grandson Evan Phillips a heifer at 15. To sons Morris and Evan Thomas, my tract of land and all other estate. Also executors.
Wit: Jonathan Pugh, John Benson.

BEAN, NATHAN.
August 24, 1748.
Adm. to Mary Bean.

MOWBERRY, WILLIAM.
September 1, 1748.
Adm. to Barbara and Robert Mowberry.

PYLE, JAMES.
September 20, 1748.
Adm. to Saray Pyle.

CLAYTON, WILLIAM, JR.
September 24, 1748.
Adm. to Mary Clayton. Francis Routh and Daniel Brown Sureties. Widow married Isaac Marshall of N. Bradford and on 27 January 1786 was "lately deceased."

BLAIR, WILLIAM.
September 26, 1748.
Adm. to James Blair.

VERNON, JACOB.
September 23, 1748.
Adm. to Elizabeth Vernon.

THOMAS, NATHAN.
October 1, 1748.
Adm. to Jemima Thomas.

CRAWFORD, JOHN.
September 23, 1748.
Adm. to John Crawford.

HOLLINGSWORTH, SAMUEL. Birmingham.
August 30, 1748. October 1, 1748. C. 65.
To wife Hannah all estate during life. What remains at her decease to my 4 children, viz., Enoch, John and Samuel Hollingsworth and daughter, Betty Green.
Executors: Sons Enoch Hollingsworth and Henry Green.
Wit: Robert Kilpatrick, Joseph Pyle.

MENDENHALL, JOSEPH. Kennett.
7/25/1748. October 18, 1748. C. 67.
Provides for wife Ruth. To son Isaac the tract of land where William Smith lived containing 66 3/4 acres and 50 acres of the west end of tract where I live. To son Joseph lott of ground in Wilmington, Del. adjoining the lot where the house stands in which he lives. Also lott on High Street and 1/3 of a piece of marsh, he paying to son Jesse £20. To son Benjamin the remainder of my plantation containing about 200 acres. To daughter Hannah Mendenhall £65 and furniture. To daughter Ann Mendenhall £70 at 18. To son Stephen my house in Wilmington, Delaware where son Joseph lives and 1/3 of the marsh at 21, paying to his brother, Jesse £25. To son Jesse 1/3 of the marsh and £85 when 21. Remainder to wife.
Executors: Wife Ruth and sons, Isaac, Joseph and Benjamin.
Wit: William Harvey, Jr., Samuel Levis, William Levis, Thomas Carleton.

JACKSON, JAMES. New Garden. Weaver.
8/18/1748. October 26, 1748. C. 72.
To my father in law James Miller £20. To cousin Ann Gibson my pacing filly. To my father Isaac Jackson remainder of estate.
Executor: Brother William Jackson.
Wit: John Clark, James Miller.

SMITH, ROBERT. New London.
September 21, 1748. October 27, 1748. C. 73.
To wife Jean 1/3 of estate real and personal. To my children, viz., Jonathan, James, Robert, William, Jenah and Jean all remainder of estate at discretion of executors for the bringing up of the small children. Executors to sell plantation I now live on. Friends James Cochran and John Smith, Overseers and guardians. Executors: Wife and brother James Smith.
Wit: William Gillespy, Humphrey Risk.

VANLEER, JOHN GEORGE. Marple. Gentleman.
July 27, 1748. November 8, 1748. C. 75.
To son Bernhard 5 shillings. To grandson George Vanleer a lott of land in Philadelphia. To wife Rebecca all remainder of

estate, also executrix.
Wit: James Crozer, William Fell, Jonathan Maris.

BROWN, WILLIAM, blacksmith. W. Nottingham.
September 29, 1748. November 12, 1748. C. 78.
Provides for wife Phebe including use of plantation until son Jacob is 21. To son Jacob all my land when 21. To dau Margaret, £20 at 21.
Executors: wife Phebe and Friend Joshua Brown.
Wit: Richd. Francis, Richd. Stedman, Jacob Brown.

DAVID, EDWARD. Easttown. Yeoman.
7/14/1748. November 12, 1748. C. 80.
Provides for wife, not named including 75 acres of land during widowhood. To son Samuel the above 75 acres after expiration of his mothers interest. To daughter Esther £10. To daughter Priscilla £50. To daughters Sarah and Phebe £10 each. To grandson Edward Moore £1. Friends, Thomas Thomas, Joseph Williams and William Thomas, Trustees.
Executrix: Wife Jenness.
Wit: David Morgan, Margaret Philip, William Thomas.

BARBER, SUSANNA.
October 6, 1748.
Adm. to Joseph Richards.

SMYLEY, WILLIAM.
October 10, 1748.
Adm. to John Smith.

TRAVERS, ARTHUR.
October 22, 1748.
Adm. to Moses Dickie.

MC FADNER, JAMES.
October 27, 1748.
Adm. to Samuel Hill.

EDGAR, ROBERT.
November 7, 1748.
Adm. to Margaret Edgar.

KENNEDY, BRYAN.
November 19, 1748.
Adm. to Charles Crosley and and Isaac Lea.

BLACK, HENRY.
November 19, 1748.
Adm. to Sarah Black.

TAYLOR, SARAH. Widow of Isaac. North Providence.
9/14/1748. November 26, 1748. C. 82.
To eldest son Isaac £8. To son John £10 and to his wife Elizabeth £2 and to his daughter Sarah £3. To sons Joseph and Josiah £3 each. To son Benjamin 5 shillings. To daughter Mary Thomas £3. To daughter Sarah, wife of Thomas Massey £5. To daughter Elizabeth, wife of James Sharpless £5. To granddaughter, Sarah Dicks £4. To granddaughter Mary Sharpless £3 at 18. To granddaughter Rebecca Sharpless £3 at 18. To grandsons James, Joshua, Job and Nathaniel Sharpless £2 at 10 years of age. To sons in law James Sharpless and Thomas Massey small legacies. To Priscilla, wife of James McMichell £10. Remainder to son John.
Executor: Son in law Thomas Massey.
Wit: John McMichell, George Miller, Joseph Vernon.

DAVIS, LEWIS. East Nantmell. Yeoman.
June 26, 1748. November 29, 1748. C. 86.
To brother John Davis £9 which he owes me and to his daughter
Mary articles named. To Mary Mills (who now keeps my house) £10
and articles named. To John Gwin wearing apparel, horse and £10.
Also gives other legacies to 3 legatees above named and divides
remainder equally among them.
Executors: Brother James Davis, Mary Mills and John Gwin.
Wit: Hannah Stephen, David Stephen, Samuel Meredith.

IRWIN, GEORGE. West Nantmell. Farmer.
April 13, 1748. November 29, 1748. C. 88.
To wife Jane 1/3 of estate real and personal during widowhood.
To son Jerret a part of my plantation. To son Alexander the
remainder of plantation. To son George £10. To son John £20.
To daughters Sarah, Mary, Mercy and Letitia Irwin £20 each. To
sons William, Robert and Archibald £5 each. Legacies to be paid
to sons, Jerret and Alexander.
Executors: Wife Jane and brother Robert Irwin.
Letters to Jane, the other renouncing.
Wit: James Porter, James Mitchell, William Porter.

ARCHER, GERTRUDE. Ridley.
November 9, 1748. November 29, 1748. C. 91.
To son Jacob Archer the remainder of a bond of John Crosby,
Esquire. To daughter Mary Sketchley all the money and effects
she now has in her hands. To daughter Catherine Peterson £8. To
son in law John Sketchley £4. To granddaughter Mary, daughter of
son Adam Archer £10 out of my thirds of his estate and grandson
Jacob and granddaughter Martha Archer £5 each out of same. To
grandson John Morton bed and furniture. To children of son,
Jacob and daughters, Ellen Jones and Elizabeth Simcock the
remainder of son Adam's estate if recovered.
Executors: Son Jacob and grandson John Morton.
Wit: John Burston, Anne Catherine Flemen.

TAYLOR, CHRISTOPHER. (Tinnecum) Ridley. Yeoman.
December 8, 1748. December 24, 1748. C. 94.
To cousin John, son of brother Thomas Taylor my tract of land
where I dwell, also 20 acres of woodland. To cousin David
Sanderlin tract of land on Tinicum Island, also my share of Long
Hooks Island. To cousins Thomas Taylor and Christopher Elliot
and Gerall Elliot remainder of tract on Tinicum. To brother
Thomas' eldest son by his last wife named Joseph, tract of land
in Greenwich, West New Jersey containing 100 acres. To cousin
Sarah Taylor, daughter of Thomas tract in West New Jersey
containing 300 acres. To brother Benjamin £50. To cousin Sarah,
wife of Oliver Thomas £50. To sister Dinah Cartman £50. To
sister Hannah Lloyd £50. To sister Elinor Molloy £50. To sister
Sarah Baily's two daughters, Hannah and Mary £25 each. To
Raccoon Church £2. To brother Samuel Taylor 5 shillings. To
Mary Shield, Thomas Taylor, Sr., George Pooleg and William Smith
1 shilling each. To Mary and Elizabeth, daughters of Joseph
Armitt £50 each at 21 or marriage. To my nurse, Deborah Blake

£5. Household goods to cousin Sarah Taylor. Mentions that his deceased wife made a will without his consent and that some of above legacies in deference to her wishes.
Executors: Brother Benjamin and brother in law Enoch Elliott.
Wit: Samuel Bunting, William Thompson, William May.

PUGH, HUGH. Uwchlan. Yeoman.
December 26, 1748. January 6, 1748/9. C. 98.
Executor to sell all of the estate. To youngest son Hugh £20 at 21. Remainder in 4 equal shares to son, Enos 2 shares at 21, and to daughters, Dinah and Rebecca one share each when 18. Directs that eldest son Enos be placed with cousin John Pugh of Radnor until he is 16 and that youngest daughter Rebecca be put to Margaret, wife of Nathan Lewis of Newtown until she is 18. Mentions Sarah Cadwellader "the girl that now lives with me," £5.
Executors: Brothers in law, John Edward and Cadwallader Jones Jr.
Wit: Thomas Martin, John Williams, Aubrey Roberts.

SIMPSON, WILLIAM. Chester.
7/13/1748. January 20, 1748/9. C. 102.
To sister Lydia Barton her living in the house I bought of brother Zebulon in Chester, also my tools of the ship carpenter's trade. To brothers George and Zebulon my house in Chester. To my friend John Mather all remainder of estate for the use of sister, Lydia Barton.
Executors: John Mather and Thomas Cummings.
Wit: Jo. Parker, John Baldwin, Benjamin Pumroy.

COMMONS, JAMES.
November 19, 1748.
Adm. to Thomas Bryan.

HOLMAN, CHARLES.
November 19, 1748.
Adm. to Eleanor Holman.

FLOWER, RICHARD.
November 9, 1748.
Adm. to Abigail & Richard Flower.

INGLISH, MATTHEW.
November 22, 1748.
Adm. to Jonathan Vernon.

STINSON, ROBERT.
November 29, 1748.
Adm. to Francis McConnell.

ROMAN, JACOB.
December 1, 1748.
Adm. to Mary Roman.

HENDERSON, ALEXANDER.
December 8, 1748.
Adm. to Daniel Henderson.

WALLACE, THOMAS.
December 10, 1748.
Adm. to Sarah Wallace.

REYNOLDS, RICHARD.
January 3, 1748/9.
Adm. to Joseph Cloud.

MC KOWNE, DANIEL.
January 9, 1748/9.
Adm. to George Curry.

TURNER, ELIZABETH.
January 13, 1748/9.
Adm. to Benjamin Howell.

MARSH, JONATHAN.
January 19, 1748/9.
Adm. to Mary Marsh.

OGDEN, SAMUEL.
January 25, 1748/9.
Adm. to David Ogden.

DARLINGTON, JOSEPH.
February 28, 1748/9.
Adm. to Mary Darlington.

PETTERSON, ROBERT. Upper Providence. Husbandman.
July 29, 1748. January 30, 1748/9. C. 103.
To son in law William Meclemons, my servant lad, Charles Blakely till he is of age. To son James £14.10. To daughter Isabella Petterson £14.10. To daughter Jane £14.10. To daughter Mary Petterson £19.10, £5 for schooling her.
Executors: Friends Matthew Cowden and William Caldwell.
Letters to Caldwell, the other renouncing.
Wit: William Moore, Michael Johnston.

CUMMIN, WILLIAM. Londonderry. Yeoman.
January 28, 1748/9. February 2, 1748/9. C. 106.
To friend Matthew Porter the tract of land now in my possession and all other estate, also executor. Name is spelled Common in inventory.
Wit: William Porter, Henry Russell.

MC COLLOCK, WILLIAM. London Britain.
January 30, 1748/9. March 4, 1748/9. C. 107.
Provides for wife Martha including use of plantation during life and £75 to dispose of by will. To son in law and daughter Nathaniel and Margaret McGee the plantation where I live, paying above £75 and 5 shillings to my daughter Isabella in Ireland and to my granddaughter Mary McCollock £10. Also £10 to a granddaughter in Ireland, the daughter of William and Isabella McCollock. To George McCleave all wearing apparel.
Executors: Francis Alison and George Curry.
Wit: William Love, James Kennedy, Samuel Snoddy.

MC COLLOCK, MARTHA. London, Britain.
February 11, 1748/9. March 14, 1748/9. C. 109.
To John Stewart my son in Ireland 5 shillings. To son in law William Betty's child in Virginia all remains of estate being £75 and movables as mentioned in my husband's will, to be equally divided. Only George and Martha are to have £10 each above the rest.
Executors: Francis Alison and son in law William Betty.
Codicil mentions daughter Martha in Virginia and servant, Eve Margaret Giger and gives to Francis Alison "my husband's gun, sword and new hat." Letters to son in law William Betty, Alison renouncing.
Wit: James Donnel, William Clinton.

FREEMAN, ELIZABETH. West Bradford.
11/27/1748/9. March 20, 1748/9. C. 112.
To Susanna Freeman a tract of land containing 12 acres purchased of Thomas Stubbs. To Nathan Freeman the right of the plantation he now lives on until such time as the heirs mentioned in Peter Collins' will shall come and demand the same. To brother, William Buffington £15. To John Freeman £5 in cattle. To sister Hannah Dean, to cousin Mary Dean, sister Lydia Martin, cousins Mary and Betty Martin, sisters Mary Turner, Phebe Buffington, Susanna Hanson and Damson Quaintance, articles of wearing apparel. Directs executors to assign William Lee to James Wickersham until he is 16. To Samuel Freeman a bed. To Jude

Barnard, George Fox's Doctrinal Books.
Executors: Nathaniel Freeman and Thomas Sheward.
Letters to Freeman, Sheward renouncing.
Wit: Isaac Vernon, James Marshall, Ealse Buffington.

COOK, WILLIAM. Fallowfield. Glazier.
January 23, 1749. March 23, 1748/9. C. 115.
All estate to be converted into cash and sent to my friends, William Park and John Nizbet of Cloghogan, County of Derry in Ireland, to be disposed of as follows: To wife Catherine one English Guinea and a mourning gown, the remainder to daughters Jean and Elizabeth in equal shares.
Executors: Joseph Park and John Boyd.
Wit: James Cochran, David Cochran, Stephen Cochran.

CULIN, JONAS.
March 16, 1748/9.
Adm. to Daniel Culin.

GREAG, THOMAS.
March 27, 1749.
Adm. to Dinah Greag.

DUTTON, JOHN.
March 21, 1748/9.
Adm. to Elizabeth & Richard Dutton.

HALE, FRANCES.
April 3, 1749.
Adm. to John White.

STEADWELL, EBENEZER.
March 27, 1749.
Adm. to Michael Rambo.

CULBERTSON, SAMUEL.
May 15, 1741. April 3, 1749. C. 117.
To wife, not named, £60. To son William £300. To son John £300. To daughter Kettren £100. To grandson Samuel £5. To Cattrin Doagrey £10.
Executors: Wife and son William.
Letters to son William, wife being deceased.
Wit: William Keyl, William Boyd.
Catharine married William Finley. Another daughter, Jane married John Daniel. (Deed Book 62, 245)

ENGLISH, ANDREW. New London. Tyaler.
March 13, 1749. April 3, 1749. C. 119.
To wife Elizabeth 1/3 of all lands and movables. To the child the mother is now with, 1/3 of estate and to Andrew my youngest son the other 1/3 part. To Margaret Larken my oldest daughter bed and bedding. To John my oldest son 5 shillings. To James my second son 3 shillings. To Jane and Elizabeth my 2 youngest daughters a note of 40 shillings due me. Letters C.T.A. to the widow.
Wit: Alexander Morrison, William Cry.

SPLAN, MORRIS. Fallowfield.
March 26, 1749. April 7, 1749. C. 120.
To James McCormick all estate, also Executor.
Wit: John Carrithers, James Carithers.

PETERS, JOHN. Wilmington. Fuller.
March 7, 1748/9. April 15, 1748/9. C. 122.
To daughter Elizabeth Weldon my house and lot in Wilmington during life and afterward to her children. To grandson Reese Petters large copper kettle which my son, John took from Radnor. To Hannah Parkins 10 shillings. Remainder real and personal to my 4 children, viz., William and John Peter, Ann Kerlin and Mary Harman in equal shares.
Executors: Sons William Peters and John Kerlin.
Wit: James Lindsey, William Baldwin.

OLDHAM, ROBERT. Nottingham. Joyner.
August 3, 1742. April 17, 1749. C. 124.
To son Edward and daughter Mary Good 5 shillings each. To daughter Eleanor Williston one cow. To son Robert my plantation I have lived on containing 150 acres, he to maintain wife Mary during her life.
Executor: Son Robert.
Wit: John Boggs, Robert Whitker, Samuel Thomson.

TORTON, ANDREW. Ridley.
April 5, 1749. April 18, 1749. C. 137.
Provides for wife Susannah including profits of 1/2 of real estate below the Kings Road during widowhood. To son Hans the other 1/2 of said real estate. To eldest son John 1 shilling. To grandson Daniel Torton all my other real estate where John Torton now dwells. To daughter Rodde Torton £50. To granddaughter Rebecca Cox £5. To granddaughters Mary and Ann Torton £5 each when 18. To grandson Andrew Torton £10. To granddaughter Martha Torton £5. Letters to Gruntum, the other renouncing.
Executors: Friends Charles Grantum and George Culin.
Wit: Hans. Torton, Daniel Torton, George Grantum.

ENGLISH, ANDREW.
April 3, 1749.
Adm. to Elizabeth English.

WOODWARD, RICHARD. East Bradford.
October 9, 1747. October 19, 1748. C. 126.
To son Henry 20 shillings and Dr. Everards works. To son John 20 shillings. To son Richard £30. To son Thomas 5 shillings. To daughter Deborah Bennett 20 shillings. To daughter Mary Strode 20 shillings. To daughter Alice Ash £5. To grandson Henry Woodward son of Henry £5. To grandson Richard Woodward son of John £5. To grandson Richard Strode £5. To granddaughter Mary Bennett £3. Remainder to wife Mary, also executrix.
Wit: George Strode, George Strode, Jr., Benjamin Hawley.

WOODWARD, MARY. East Bradford.
December 21, 1748. January 21, 1748/9. C. 132.
To son Henry £60. To sons John, Richard and Thomas, £20 each. To daughter Deborah, wife of William Bennett £20. To daughter Mary, wife of John Strode £30. To daughter Alice, wife of Joshua Ash £20. To grandson Henry Woodward, son of Henry £10 at 20 and

to his sister Mary £5 at 18. To granddaughter Mary Bennett £5.
To granddaughter Mary Strode £5. Remainder to 3 sons and 3
daughters.
Executors: Son Henry and son in law William Bennett.
Wit: John Stephenson, Grisel Stephenson, Thomas Worth.

SALKELD, AGNES. Chester.
January 7, 1748/9. January 17, 1748/9. C. 129.
To daughters Agnes, wife of Thomas Minshall and Jane, wife of
Moses Minshall the plantation where John Richey dwells in Chester
Township, they paying to each of my son David's 2 children, viz.,
William and Agnes £5 when 21. To daughter Mary Shaw 12 acres of
land next to Concord road. To son Thomas 25 acres on north
side of said Kings road. To son David Salkeld £2.13. To son
John Salkeld remainder of my land. Household goods to 3
daughters.
Executors: Son John Salkeld and son in law Thomas Minshall.
Wit: Isaac Lea, Thomas Morgan, Jo. Parker.

SMITH, JOHN. Chichester. Husbandman.
January 13, 1748/9. January 24, 1748/9. C. 135.
Provides for wife Rebecca. To daughter Hannah Smith a colt. To
son James the tract of land lately purchased of Benjamin ____ in
Concord after youngest son Joshua comes of age. To 3 children,
Hannah, Tristrin and Joshua the profits of said land until
youngest is 21, also 2/3 of personal estate. To friends John
Hughes and Benjamin Moulder wearing apparel. Provides for a
possible posthumous child.
Executors: Friends John Hughes and Benjamin Moulder.
Wit: William Wright, Samuel Hewes, James Dalziel.

THOMSON, JOHN. Londonderry.
April 18, 1749. May 23, 1749. C. 139.
Provides for wife Esther and the child with which she is now
pregnant. To daughter Martha 1/4 of real and personal estate.
To son William when of age the whole plantation paying to the
other 2 children their share of the value, but wife to have the
profits during widowhood.
Executors: Wife and William Armstrong.
Wit: William Brown, James Gilliland, Edward Lettemore.

ROBESON, SAMUEL. East Nottingham.
April 7, 1749. May 30, 1749. C. 141.
To wife Jean Robson £10. To sister Genet Robinson £10. To
sister Mary Robeson £17. Will reads, "I constitute and appoint
him sole executor. All lands, messuages, freely to be ordered."
The word "him" in will was made by the evidence to be Robert
Miller the nearest of kin to deceased. [Note by Register]
Letters to Miller.
Wit: Finley McGrew, Gilbert Buchanan.

JOHNSON, HUMPHREY. Chester Township.
September 22, 1748. June 10, 1749. C. 143.
To son Francis £20. To daughter Elizabeth Lamplugh £5. To
daughter Ann Johnson £5. To daughter Rachel Johnson £5. To son

David 1 shilling. Remainder of estate real and personal to son Humphrey.
Executors: Brother Francis Ruth and son Humphrey.
Letters to son, the other renouncing.
Wit: Aubrey Bevan, B. Davis, William Jones.

HARRISON, SARAH. Chester Township.
December 24, 1743. June 28, 1749. C. 144.
To husband Thomas Harrison the messuage where I now dwell in Chester and all personal estate, also Executor.
Wit: William Clayton, Mary Clayton, John Power.

EDWARDS, JOHN. Middletown. Yeoman.
10/13/1744. July 31, 1749. C. 146.
Provides for wife Mary. To son John, daughter Mary Baker, daughter Elizabeth Lawrence, son Nathan, daughter Hannah Harvey, son Moses and daughter Phebe Worrall 2 shillings 6 each. To son Amos £50 at 21. To son Joseph my plantation where I live in Middletown containing about 200 acres, paying debts and legacies.
Executors: Sons Nathan and Joseph.
Wit: George Smedley, Mary Smedley, Cadwallader Evans.

COATES, SAMUEL.
May 1, 1749.
Adm. to Elizabeth Coates.

VERNON, ABRAHAM.
May 2, 1749.
Adm. to Lydia Vernon

THOMSON, MOSES.
May 15, 1749.
Adm. to Mary Thomson.

THATCHER, ZERUBABLE.
June 2, 1749.
Adm. to Sarah Thatcher.

YARNALL, SAMUEL.
June 9, 1749.
Adm. to Sarah Yarnall.

CULLIVER, BENJAMIN.
July 17, 1749.
Adm. to Catherine Culliver.
Signed KC. Sureties John Palmer & Henry Peirce.
Inventory Jan. 30, 1749 by Joseph Chamberlin and William Trimble. Expenditures £44.14.9.

KIRK, WILLIAM.
June 2, 1749. Adm. to John Kirk "eldest son and heir at law," the widow having renounced.

MENDENHALL, ANN. Widow. Concord.
5/2/1749. August 1, 1749. C. 149.
To son Robert Mendenhall £200 and to his wife Phebe £5. To son in law Peter Grubb 5 shillings and to his wife, my daughter Hannah £20 and mentions "her 7 children that she had by her first husband, Thomas Marshall." To son in law John Bartram 5 shillings and to his wife, my daughter Ann £40. To each of the children of son Benjamin, viz., Mary, Hannah, Samuel, Martha and Lydia 20 shillings and to daughter in law Lydia Mendenhall 20 shillings and to Joshua, youngest son of Benjamin £5 at 21. To Esther, wife of son Samuel my spinning wheel. To children of son Joseph, viz., Isaac, Joseph, Benjamin, Hannah, Ann, Stephen and Jesse, sons £5, daughters £1, each at 21 and to daughter in law

Ruth £1. To each of the children of son Moses, viz., Alice and
Phebe £1 and to daughter in law Alice £1 and to Ann widow of
grandson Caleb £1. To each of children of daughter Hannah by her
first husband, Thomas Marshall, viz., Ann, Benjamin, Thomas,
Hannah, John and Mary 20 shillings and to Martha £5 when 21. To
each of children of daughter Ann Bartram 20 shillings at 21. To
children of son Robert, viz., Philip, Ann, Rebecca, Moses,
Nathan and John £5 each at 21. Test signed.
Executor: Son Robert.
Wit: Caleb Peirce, Ann Vernon, Mary Peirce.

PORTER, WILLIAM. Chester County.
April 4, 1749. August 3, 1749. C. 153.
Provides for wife Mary including benefit of plantation until son
William is of age. To 3 sons, William, Reese and John the
plantation. Personal estate equally divided between daughters
Elizabeth, Ann, Mary, Violet and the young one.
Executrix: Wife Mary.
Brother Hugh Porter and brother in law Reese Price, Overseers.
Wit: A. Barry, William Price, John Porter.

PATTERSON, ELIZABETH. Widow. Goshen.
3/27/1748. August 29, 1749. C. 155.
To youngest son Samuel 20 shillings. To 3 eldest sons, viz.,
John, William and Thomas all remainder of estate at interest and
paid them at 21.
Executor: Friend and neighbor Francis Mechem.
Wit: John Jarman, Samuel Phipps, Richard Jones.

PARKE, REBECCA. Widow of Thomas. East Caln.
6/19/1749. August 31, 1749. C. 156.
To son Thomas Parke my largest Bible and other articles. To son
Jonathan £5. Remainder as follows: 1/2 to daughter Rachel, wife
of William Robinson and other 1/2 to daughters Mary Valentine and
Rebecca Stalker.
Executors: Sons Thomas and Jonathan.
Letters to Thomas, the other renouncing. Test signed X.
Wit: Phinehas Lewis, William Purdy, William Pim.

WORRALL, PETER, being aged. Marple. Yeoman.
April 23, 1747. September 22, 1749. C. 158.
To son John 5 shillings. To sons Jonathan, Peter, James and
Joseph 2 shillings each. To daughters Mary Moore and Patience
Powell 2 shillings each. Remainder of land I have not deeded to
go to sons James and Benjamin, each to have the land adjoining
the houses where they now live. Provides for wife Elizabeth.
Executors: Friends Robert Taylor and William Fell.
Wit: Robert Caldwell, Jonathan Maris, Benjamin Talbot.

DUTTON, JACOB.
August 15, 1749.
Adm. to Hannah Dutton.

SALKELD, THOMAS. Chester. Cordwainer.
September 15, 1749. September 23, 1749. C. 160.

To my 3 sisters, viz., Mary Shaw, Agnes Minshall and Jane
Minshall £5 each. To brother Daniel Salkeld 8 acres of land
until his son William is 21 and then to said son. Remainder of
estate to brother John Salkeld, also Executor. Test signed T.
Wit: John Oliver, H. H. Graham.

WILLSON, JAMES. East Nottingham.
May 31, 1749. September 30, 1749. C. 162.
To son Matthew £40. To daughter Mary £80. To sons Robert and
James the plantation I live on and all remainder of estate. Test
signed j.
Executors: Sons Matthew and Robert.
Wit: Finley McGrew, John Smith.

THOMSON, JAMES. New Londonderry.
February 3, 1748/9. October 2, 1749. C. 163.
Provides for wife Ruth. To sons Alexander, Samuel, James, Robert
and William my plantation to be divided when youngest is of age.
Executors: Brother John Thomson and wife Ruth.
Samuel Steel and Francis Alison, Overseers.
Wit: John Meas, Thomas Miner, Hugh McLean.

DAVID, STEPHEN. Tredyffrin. Yeoman.
July 12, 1749. October 2, 1749. C. 165.
Provides for wife Hannah including disposal of all estate until
son David is 21 when he is to have possession of the real estate
on which I live. To eldest daughter Ann £80. To daughter Mary
£80 when 20. To son Samuel £80 at 21. To daughter Hannah £70 at
20. To son Stephen £70 at 21. To youngest son Thomas £70 at 21.
To wife Hannah all tenements in Wilmington. Test signed SD.
Executors: Wife and son David.
Wit: Elizabeth Anderson, Enoch Walker, Henry Atherton.

BLUNSTON, PHEBE, widow. Darby.
6/6/1746. October 9, 1749. C. 169.
To cousin Rebecca Minshall of Philadelphia, widow, £10. To
cousin Rebecca Blackham of Philadelphia £20. To Isaac and Samuel
Minshall, sons of Rebecca aforesaid £5 each. To cousin Sarah
Minshall of Middletown, widow, £10 and to her sons, Thomas, Moses
and John Minshall £5 each. To cousin Margaret, wife of Henry Cam
£20. To cousin Elizabeth Roads, widow, £30. To cousin Sarah,
wife of Samuel Bunting £20. To cousin Rebecca, wife of John
Griffith £20. To cousin Hannah, wife of Thomas Pearson, Samuel
Bunting, John Griffith, cousin Samuel Levis and Mary Hinds
legacies of £5 to £20. To Hannah Burgess of Bucks County,
formerly my servant, one pistole. To Mary, sister of John
Griffith, John Pyott and wife Deborah, John Bunting, Rachel wife
of John Moore and William Horne of Darby, small legacies.
Executors: Cousins Samuel Levis and Samuel Bunting.
Wit: John Davis, John Hunt, Abraham Bonsall.

DAVIS, JOHN. Darby.
August 14, 1749. October 9, 1749. C. 174.
Provides for wife Rebecca. To son Joseph £50 and 1/2 of looms.
To sons Lewis and John a tract of marsh and £20 and other 1/2 of

looms. To daughter Mary Davis £60. To daughter Sarah Davis £60.
To daughter Hannah Smith £50. Remainder to sons, Joseph, Lewis
and John, daughters Rebecca, wife of John Levis, Ann wife of
William Parker, Mary and Sarah Davis.
Executors: Wife and sons Joseph, Lewis and John.
Wit: Nathan Garrett, Joseph Scothorn, William Horne.

BURKE, PATRICK.
August 18, 1749.
Adm. to John Lyann.

ASH, JOHN.
October 2, 1749.
Adm. to Anne & Joshua Ash.

MC LAUGHLIN, LAWRENCE.
August 19, 1749.
Adm. to Dennis McLaughlin.

HIBBERD, ANNE.
October 2, 1749.
Adm. to Jacob Hibberd.

LAWRENCE, THOMAS.
September 16, 1749.
Adm. to Sarah Lawrence.

THOMAS, PHILIP.
October 2, 1749.
Adm. to David Thomas.

KILLCREASE, JAMES. September 19, 1749.
Adm. to Elizabeth Killcrease.

SCOTT, ABRAHAM. West Nottingham. Farmer.
September 21, 1749. October 17, 1749. C. 177.
Provides for wife Jane. To daughter Grisel Poak £10. To
daughter Elizabeth Tidbal £10. To daughter Elizabeth Cunningham
a horse and such furniture as my other daughters had that is
married, and £5. To son Abraham my plantation where I dwell, he
paying to each of his younger brothers, viz., Hugh, Josiah,
Samuel and Thomas £10 when 21. Remainder sold and divided into 6
shares to wife, sons Hugh, Josiah, Samuel, Thomas and daughter
Sarah Scott.
Executors: Son Abraham Scott and William Buchanan.
Wit: James Barclay, William Denny.

HARRISON, THOMAS. Chester. Yeoman.
October 17, 1749. October 23, 1749. C. 180.
To Rachel, daughter of Thomas Coeburn £10. Remainder whether
real or personal to my friend Thomas Coeburn, also Executor.
Test signed.
Wit: James Mather, Jonathan Martin, Abraham Martin.

MARSHALL, JOHN. Darby. Yeoman.
October 1, 1749. October 25, 1749. C. 181.
Provides for wife Eleanor including use of real estate until son
John is 21. To son Thomas, fulling mill and 9 3/4 acres in
Darby, 50 acres adjoining in Blockley when certain debts are
paid. To son Abraham 20 shillings, having already provided for
him. To son John a brick house and lott in Newport, New Castle
County, also 10 acres of marsh and other lotts. To 4 daughters
Johanna, Martha, Mary and Susanna £30 each at 21. Names
daughters Sarah and Margaret "already married," refers to "former
wife." To daughters in law Hannah and Rachel Shenton 20
shillings each.
Executors: Brother in law Lewis Thomas and friends Thomas and

Isaac Pearson.
Wit: John Sellers, John Thomas, John Hays.

KILGREIST, ELIZABETH. Tredyffrin.
November 21, 1749. November 28, 1749. C. 187.
Directs her burial in Baptist graveyard. To son Francis Stinson living in North Britain £31. To John Davis Baptist minister in Tredyffrin, £5. To James, son of Maris David £5. To Thomas Godfrey of Tredyffrin £5. To Samuel John, Isaac Walker, David Davies, blind man, and David Hacket of Merion £5 each. To landlord Daniel Walker £35, "I owe nothing but rent since the 1st of May last." Test signed.
Executors: Stephen Evans and Thomas Water both of Tredyffrin.
Wit: John Moore, Rees Moore, Richard Moore.

HOPE, JOHN. Kennett. Yeoman.
October 27, 1749. December 7, 1749. C. 189.
To son Thomas, 250 acres whereon he now dwells being part of a tract my brother Thomas Hope left me by will. To son John the plantation whereon he now dwells and part of plantation where I dwell (described), 31 1/2 acres, in all 181 1/2 acres. To son Amos remainder of plantation containing 318 acres when 21. To son in law Stephen Hayes and wife Sarah 5 shillings each. To son in law George Harlan and wife Elizabeth 5 shillings each. To daughter Susanna Fred 50 acres of land in possession of John Fred. To grandson John Hayes lott of ground in Wilmington, Del. Provides for wife Elizabeth.
Executors: Wife and son Amos.
Wit: Samuel Harlan, Thomas Harlan, Mary Cummings.
* Mentions John Way, William Temple and Aaron Harlan as owning adjoining lands.

MARSHALL, JACOB.
October 2, 1749.
Adm. to John Marshall.

HARLAN, SILAS.
October 7, 1749.
Adm. to David Harlan.

FINLEY, JOHN.
October 14, 1749.
Adm. to Margaret Finley.

HASSELETT, ROBERT.
October 19, 1749.
Adm. to David Kennedy.

CRAWFORD, JAMES.
October 25, 1749.
Adm. to Mary Crawford.

PACKER, JOHN.
November 20, 1749.
Adm. to Nathaniel Jenkins.

HASELGROVE, JOHN.
December 16, 1749.
Adm. to Francis Reynolds.

MC CULLOUGH, JAMES of Chester.
December 30, 1749.
Adm. to Martha McCullough
m. 2nd William Evans, Orphans Court.

HUTCHISON, ROBERT. Chester County. Weaver.
January 20, 1748/9. December 11, 1749. C. 192.
"To dear and related" Uncle Robert Wilson £5 and best hat. To my Uncle James Hutchison remainder of estate.

Executors: Isaac Johnson and David Evans.
Letters to Evans.
Wit: Archibald M. Sparran, William McDowell, Benjamin Robison.

TOWNSEND, JOSEPH. East Bradford.
December 2, 1749. December 12, 1749. C. 194.
Provides for wife Lydia. To son Francis my sawmill in East Bradford with 60 acres of land adjoining when 21. To my other 2 surviving sons, the other part of my plantation containing about 152 acres, son Benjamin to have the dwelling house. To daughter Esther £50 at 18. Also provides for a child yet unborn.
Executors: Wife Lydia, father Joseph Townsend and brother in law John Hoopes.
Wit: Benjamin Cock, Robert Jefferis, John Taylor.

MOORE, REBECCA, widow. Charlestown.
November 23, 1749. January 1, 1749/50. C. 196.
To my 2 granddaughters Rebecca and Susanna, daughters of eldest son John Moore £25 each. To son Thomas Moore £100. To daughter Rebecca Evans £100. To son Daniel £100. Remainder to son William, also Executor.
Wit: Phineas Bond, Patrick Archibald, Alice Devonshire.
Directs burial at St. Peter's Churchyard in Great Valley.

CLIFFE, BENJAMIN. Darby. Shop keeper.
10/28/1749. January 18, 1749/50. C. 198.
To Benjamin Lobb, my sister's son, a tenement and lot of land in Darby. To Elizabeth Loo, my sister's daughter, £5. To Rachel Caster, my sister's daughter, £5. To Mary Shaw £2. Remainder to Benjamin Lobb, who is also Executor.
Wit: John Brinnan, Abraham Bonsall, James Hinde.

PYLE, SAMUEL. Kennett.
December 18, 1749. January 26, 1749/50. C. 200.
Provides for wife Sarah including house and land belonging during widowhood. Afterward land to be sold and proceeds as also proceeds of sale of my share of grist and sawmill equally divided among all children, viz., Nicholas, John, Edith Harlan, Sarah Ann and Betty Pyle.
Executors: Wife Sarah and son Nicholas.
Wit: Thomas Evan, Jacob Heald, Joseph Heald.

HEWES, ISAAC. Birmingham. Tanner.
January 4, 1749/50. February 2, 1749/50. C. 202.
Provides for wife Lydia and a child that may yet be born. In case child should not survive, gives to brother John Hewes £50. To brother Samuel £40. To brother Caleb £40. To Aaron Hewes, son of brother William £30. Remainder to mother Mary Hewes.
Executor: Brother John.
Wit: Joseph Brinton, Edward Brinton, James Dilworth.

DAVID, JOHN. Radnor.
January 10, 1749/50. February 8, 1749/50. C. 204.
To eldest son Joshua the tract of land where he now dwells in Radnor containing about 50 acres. To son Samuel tract of land

where he dwells in Radnor containing about 60 acres, he paying to
executors £23-10. To son Edward remainder of land I live upon
when 21, subject to provision for wife Bridget during life and
paying to each of his sisters £10 and to his brother John £30.
To daughter Mary by my first wife 5 shillings.
Wit: Samuel Morgan, Thomas Thomas 1st, Thomas Thomas.
Letters to son, wife deceased.
Executors: Wife Bridget and son Edward.
Kinsman Evan Evans and son Samuel, trustees.

LONG, FRANCIS. West Nantmell. Yeoman.
December 4, 1749. February 27, 1749/50. C. 206.
Provides for wife Rebecca including use of land during widowhood
for schooling the children and maintenance of my mother and
brother John Long. Sons John and William to be put to trades
when fit for it and estate divided between them when of age, they
paying to their sister Agnes £60 when she is of age. Test
signed.
Executors: Andrew Willson and John Colberson.
Wit: Thomas Green, John Henders, William Darlinton.
Mentions brother Joseph Long.

PAINTER, THOMAS. Birmingham. Cordwainer.
December 22, 1749. March 9, 1749/50. C. 209.
To wife Hannah all she brought with and £30. To my daughter
Betty Painter all that her mother Grace brought with her.
Provides for a child yet unborn. Remainder to daughter Grace.
Executors: Wife Hannah and brother Samuel Painter.
Letters to Samuel, the widow renouncing.
Wit: George Gilpin, Jonathan Thatcher, Richard Thatcher.

CROSLEY, CHARLES. Middletown. Yeoman.
January 14, 1749/50. March 26, 1750. C. 211.
To wife Hannah £50. To son Samuel £150. To son John £5. To
grandson James Crosley £10. To daughter Elizabeth Malin £5 and
£10 to grandson Jacob Malin.
Executors: Wife Hannah and sons Samuel and John.
Trustees: John Newland of Concord and son in law William Malin.
Wit: Charles Linn, Mary Linn, George Deeble.

TURNER, JOHN. Upper Providence. Laborer.
April 24, 1750. May 22, 1750. C. 213.
To Ann Johnston Jr. 5 shillings. To cousin Mary Johnston 3
shillings. To cousins John Johnston Jr. and Andrew Johnston 5
shillings each. To John Johnston Sr. of Upper Providence all
clothes. To daughter Jean Turner all other estate, also
Executrix. John Johnson, Sr. renouncing.
Wit: Alexander Withrow, William Dean, George Deeble.

VAUGHAN, JOHN. Uwchlan. Yeoman.
December 30, 1749. May 30, 1750. C. 215.
Provides for wife Emma including profits of plantation for
support and schooling of 3 younger children, viz., Margaret,
Joseph and Isaac. When youngest son Isaac is 21 estate to be
divided among 6 children, viz., John, Joshua, Jonathan, Margaret,

Joseph and Isaac.
Executor: Wife Emma.
Trustees: Richard Thomas and Samuel James of Whiteland.
Wit: James Rees, Thomas Evans, Samuel John.

SANKEY, WILLIAM.
January 20, 1749/50.
Adm. to Giles Sankey.

PIGGOTT, SAMUEL.
January 27, 1749/50.
Adm. to John McAdow.

PUGH, SAMUEL.
March 1, 1749/50.
Adm. to Joseph Pugh.

HARLAN, GEORGE.
March 10, 1749/50.
Adm. to Elizabeth Harlan.

HOPE, THOMAS.
February 21, 1749/50.
Adm. to Mary Hope.

KING, GEORGE.
March 27, 1750.
Adm. to Rees Price.

WALL, JOSEPH.
April 2, 1750.
Adm. to John Wall.

EVANS, JOHN.
April 14, 1750.
Adm. to Jane Evans.

OLDHAM, THOMAS JR.
April 20, 1750.
Adm. to Mary Oldham.

ROBERTSON, JOHN. New Londonderry. Weaver.
December 5, 1749. June 6, 1750. C. 217.
Provides for wife Isabel. Divides clothes between sons William
and Thomas. I appoint my sons William and Thomas to bury me at
their expense.
Executrix: Wife Isabel.
Wit: Nathaniel Ramsey, David Allen, David Ramsay.

HIGHET, PETER. New London.
March 17, 1749/50. June 14, 1750. C. 219.
To wife Frances 1/3 of estate and articles named. Remaining real
and personal to be sold and the 2/3 divided between my 3
daughters, viz., Agnes Allen, Mary Thompson and Margret Clinton
to be divided among their children except 5 shillings each.
Executors: Wife Frances and William Clinton (son in law).
Will not signed but proven by consent of legatees.

HIBBERD, JACOB. Darby. Yeoman.
December 29, 1749. June 26, 1750. C. 221.
Provides for sister Ann Ash during her widowhood, she to have the
care and education of daughter during her minority. To my 3
brothers John, Benjamin and Isaac £10 each. To Hezekiah, son of
brother Joseph deceased, £10 at 21. To friend Martha Dicken £10.
To Mary, wife of Henry Comston £10. To Henry Frederick, my late
servant lad, £2. To only child Esther the plantation where I
dwell in Darby when 21 with reversion to brothers and sisters
children excepting Elizabeth Bonsall, daughter of brother Joseph,
who shall have no share. Also sister Sarah's child from whose
share £30 shall be given to brother Benjamin's son, Jacob.
Executors: Brother Benjamin and Isaac Pearson.

Wit: Enoch Bonsal, Joshua Ash, Isaac Bonsal.

THATCHER, JONATHAN. Thornbury. Yeoman.
10/21/1747. July 7, 1750. C. 224.
To son Richard 20 shillings. To daughter Jane, wife of Martin Brooks 20 shillings. To daughter Mary, wife of George Hogson 20 shillings. To daughter Deboroh, wife of James Rennolds 20 shillings. To daughter Martha, wife of Thomas Long 20 shillings. To daughter Elizabeth, wife of James Campbell 20 shillings. To grandchildren, viz., John, George, Ann, Hannah, Richard and Sarah Bate, 5 shillings each. Remainder to son Jonathan, also Executor.
Wit: William Brinton, Isaac Widdow, Samuel Bettle.

WOOD, GEORGE. Darby. Innholder.
February 25, 1748/9. August 16, 1750. C. 226.
Provides for wife Hannah. Remainder of estate to be sold. To 2 sons Jonathan and George £10 each and remainder to them and the rest of my children equally. 2 daughters Jane and Sarah accounting for what they have received. Also provides for daughter Ann while unmarried.
Executors: Wife, son in law John Pearson, daughter Ann and son George.
Wit: Charles Grantum, Richard Lloyd, Joseph Bonsall.

HEWES, MARY, widow of William. Chichester.
4/29/1748. August 20, 1750. C. 229.
To son William Hewes 5 shillings. To daughter Hannah Hewes articles named and remainder of time [time of service] of Mary Stannings. To Mary, wife of son John Hewes articles named. To granddaughter Sarah Moulder 20 shillings at 18. Remainder to my 7 children, viz., John, Samuel, Isaac and Caleb Hewes, Lydia and Rebecca Grubb and Hannah Hewes in equal shares. Test signed M.
Executor: Son John Hewes.
Wit: John Riley, James Dellzel, Thomas Cummings.

FLEMING, HENRY.
May 1, 1750.
Adm. to Sarah Fleming.

PENNELL, THOMAS.
May 8, 1750.
Adm. to Mary Pennell &
John Fairlamb.

HURDMAN, JOHN.
May 23, 1750.
Adm. to William Young.

FREDD, NICHOLAS.
May 29, 1750.
Adm. to Joseph Fredd.

WEBB, MARY.
June 18, 1750.
Adm. to Daniel Webb.

KING, MIRICK.
August 30, 1750.
Adm. Jeremiah Starr.

THOMPSON, ARTHUR.
July 7, 1750. Adm. to
Samuel Kimson & Susanna
his wife who was the widow of
the decedent.

MC GUIRE, HUGH.
June 7, 1750.
Adm. to Richard Clark.

DELL, THOMAS. Ridley. Yeoman.
October 31, 1749. August 27, 1750. C. 231.
To wife Mary my houses and plantation where I dwell during life
and afterward the said premises to my grandsons, viz., Thomas and
Samuel Swaine for the term of 25 years and then to my
granddaughters Sarah and Mary Dell, children of son Thomas
deceased. To wife Mary all personal estate during life and what
remains at her decease as follows, to granddaughter Anne Swaine
£15-3 and remainder to all the children of daughter Elizabeth
Swaine deceased.
Executrix: Wife Mary.
Trustees: Caleb Harrison and John Sharpless.
Wit: Benjamin Ring, Jo. Parker, H. H. Graham.

MOORE, JOHN. West Nottingham.
March 8, 1749/50. August 28, 1750. C. 233.
Provides for wife Rachel. To son Robert, a part of my plantation
whereon he now dwells. To daughter Jane Walker £10. To daughter
Margaret Moore £50 in money and goods. To daughters Rebecca and
Rachel Moore the remainder of plantation after wife's decease.
Executors: Wife Rachel and cousin James Evans.
Wit: Hugh Kirkpatrick, David Edmeston, John Alexander.

BOWLS, WILLIAM. Kennett. Cooper.
August 29 in 23rd year of George II. September 10, 1750. C.
236.
To wife, not named, £20. To son Thomas £13. To grandson John
Bowls £10 at interest until he is of age. To 4 daughters, viz.,
Mary, Ann, Elizabeth and Jane £5 each. To daughters Barbara and
Kety 5 shillings each and to "another of my daughters living in
Ireland" Eleanor Bowls 50 shillings.
Executors: Wife and son Thomas.
Letter to Thomas, the widow Mary renouncing.
Wit: Richard Dillon, Robert Davis.

YOUNG, MARGARET. East Nottingham.
May 9, 1750. September 25, 1750. C. 237.
To grandson Robert Ross £10. To son Robert Young £12. To
grandson James Adams £28-13-6. To my other grandson Robert Adams
£30 at interest till he comes of age. To daughter in law Mary
Adams all wearing apparel and other articles. Test signed M.
Executor: Son Robert Young.
Wit: Charles Moore, Thomas Scot, James Steel.

SHEERER, DAVID. West Nantmeal.
July 21, 1750. September 27, 1750. C. 239.
Provides for wife Ann including all estate during widowhood. To
son John the South end of plantation and to son William the North
end. To each of 2 young sons David and Francis £100. To
daughter Mary £70. (Children all young.)
Executors: Samuel Allen, John Culberson, Ann Sheerer.
Letters to Ann the widow, the other renouncing.
Wit: John Sheerer, John Gardner, James Gardner.

MUCKLEDUFF, JOSEPH. West Nantmeal. Yeoman.
September 9, 1750. September 29, 1750. C. 240.
To brother Samuel Muckleduff the 200 acres of land I live on in the Manor of Springton. To my mother £100. To Rev. Adam Boyd £5. To Susana Armstrong £5. Brother Samuel to cause Black Jack to be baptized and set him free at 30. William and Sarah McConall to be free at 12. To James Lipard of Necked Creek in Virginia my beaver hat and wigs, and to his son Andrew my gun and to Andrew Liperd in Nottingham articles named and to James his son my books. Remainder to brother Samuel, who is also Executor.
Wit: Samuel McClain, John Darlinton, William Darlinton.
* Gives £5 to congregation if they build a new Meeting House where the old one is in Springton Manor.

BACKHOUSE, RICHARD.
September 1, 1750.
Adm. to Anne Backhouse.

LEVIN, WILLIAM.
September 3, 1750.
Adm. to James Bennett.

JAMES, JOHN.
September 3, 1750.
Adm. to Anne James.

BARRON, RICHARD.
September 4, 1750.
Adm. to Jacob Carter.

KILCREASE, JAMES.
September 18, 1750.
Adm. d.b.n. to Stephen Evans and Thomas Walter.

MOORE, THOMAS, JR.
September 18, 1750.
Adm. to Joseph Pratt

LOTTY, MATTHEW.
October 2, 1750.
Adm. to Robert Young.

THATCHER, SARAH, widow. Kennett.
6/8/1750. October 1, 1750. C. 242.
To grandson David Thatcher £30 at 21. To cousin Phebe Pritchett, a bed. Remainder to son Richard Thatcher, also Executor.
Letters to son, Thomas Carleton renouncing., Test signed.
Executors: Son Richard and Thomas Carleton.
Wit: Thomas Harlan, John Thompson.
*Mentions daughter in law Abigail Thatcher.

LLEWELLYN, DAVID. Haverford.
August 3, 1750. October 1, 1750. C. 245.
To son William the plantation I live on in Haverford containing about 150 acres and all personal estate. To son in law William Young and my daughter Ann his wife, the plantation adjoining to Patrick Millar and John Humphrey containing about 150 acres. Mentions having already provided for son David. Test signed.
Executor: Son William.
Wit: Thomas Cornock, William Cornock, Mary Boucher.

ALBIN, JAMES. West Marlborough. Yeoman.
September 1, 1750. October 11, 1750. C. 245.
Died September 29th, aged 41.
To wife Jane 1/3 of personal and 1/2 of real estate during life, the other 1/2 to be sold and money divided between my sister

Elizabeth's 3 children, viz., Mary, Hannah and James. To cousin
Elizabeth Bennett the 1/2 of real estate and 1/3 of personal.
Directs burial in Churchyard at Concord near where my sister is
laid and that gravestones be erected.
Executors: James Hunter of Newtown and James Bennett of
Middletown.
Wit: Ann Miller, Elizabeth Nicols, William Reed.

CROSBY, JOHN. Ridley. Yeoman.
September 22, 1750. October 15, 1750. C. 247.
Directs his burial at Friends Burying place at Chester. To
eldest son John the tract of land I now live on containing 200
acres, also 200 acres of the tract of 500 acres on the other side
of Plum Creek. To son Richard remainder of above tract. Also to
son John my 1/2 of forge and utensils. To grandson Richard
Crosby, granddaughter Susanna Crosby and grandson Samuel Crosby
articles named. To sister Catharine Fairlamb £5. To cousin John
Fairlamb my watch. To daughter in law Eleanor Crosby wife's
wearing apparel. To cousin Susanna, daughter of Robert Dutton,
£5 at 18 or marriage. To cousin Hannah daughter of Robert
Dutton, £5 at 18 or marriage. Remainder to sons John and
Richard, also Executors.
Trustees: Thomas Cummings and John Riley.
Wit: Jacob Carter, John Modlen, John Riley.

THOMAS, WILLIAM. Vincent.
September 18, 1750. November 1, 1750. C. 249.
To son Benjamin the tract of land in Coventry containing 100
acres. To only daughter Sarah £100 at 18. To eldest son William
the plantation on Pikesland and 1/2 of profits of the plantation
where I live. Gives £8 for use of St. Peters Church and 10
shillings for use of Charlestown Meeting house. Remainder to
wife Mary during widowhood, who is also Executrix.
Wit: Richard Richison, John Cuthbert, John Rees.

ROBERTS, MARY, widow of Roger. Widow 1st of Abel Roberts.
Radnor.
5/21/1748. December 8, 1750. C. 251.
To granddaughter Ruth Taylor £5. To granddaughters Hannah and
Mary Evans £3 each. To granddaughters Rachel and Lea Evans £2
each. To grandsons John and Amos Evans £2 each. To
granddaughter May Lewis, alias David, £5. To granddaughter
Rachel Lewis £3. To granddaughter Elizabeth Lewis £1-10. To
grandsons Abel Lewis £10, Samuel Lewis £2-10, John and Evan Lewis
30 shillings each. To cousin Joan, wife of William Williams of
Uwchlan, wearing apparel. Remainder to 2 daughters Katherine and
Rachel including tract of 100 acres of land bequeathed me by late
husband. Katherine to pay 1/2 value thereof to Rachel.
Executors: Daughters Katherine Lewis and Rachel Evans.
Wit: Thomas Thomas, Thamar Thomas, Margret Ellis.

BETTY, JANE (JEAN). New London.
October 18, 1750. November 8, 1750. C. 253.
To cousin Robert Betty's daughter, Jean a gown and one to her
sister Margaret. Remainder equally divided among my cousins'

children at Monockesey. Also mentions cousin Agnes Betty, daughter of brother John Betty at Monockesey and Susanna, wife of Edward Betty.
Executor: James Moore of New London.
Wit: Patrick McCay, John Moor, John Porterfield.

MARSHALL, ABRAM. West Bradford. Yeoman.
September 21, 1750. November 12, 1750. C. 254.
To wife Rachel all personal estate except £60 and profits of plantation until son Samuel is 21. To daughters Elizabeth and Mary £30 each to be at interest until they are 18. To son Samuel my plantation when 21, he paying to youngest daughter Hannah £30.
Executors: Wife Rachel and brother George Carter.
Wit: Samuel Sellers, John Battin, James Marshall.

DAVIS, JOSEPH. Darby. Yeoman.
8/15/1750. November 15, 1750. C. 255.
To brother Lewis Davis and brother John Davis £50 each. To sisters Rebecca Levis and Ann Parker £50 each. To sister Hannah Smith £3 per year during her life. To sister Mary Davis £50. To sister Sarah Davis £50. To Joseph Scothorn £5. Remainder real and personal to mother Rebecca Davis.
Executors: Brothers Lewis and John, brothers in law John Levis and William Parker.
Wit: Samuel Bunting, William Booth, Elizabeth Horner(?).
* Directs land in Marlborough to be sold.

FRAIZER, ALEXANDER. Kennett.
8/31/1750. December 18, 1750. C. 256.
To son Moses 1/2 plantation where I live (200 acres), the west end. To son John, £30 and 1/2 of plantation. To son Aaron 100 acres, part of a tract of 200 acres west of Susquehanna River. To son James the other 100 acres of said tract and 12 acres of another tract. To son Alexander the remainder of last tract, he paying to daughter Mary Garrettson £15. To daughter Miriam Frazer, a mare and other articles provided "she behave well and marry among the people called Quakers." Remainder including lotts in Newport and Wilmington to be sold and divided among children, Sarah Rich, Miriam Frazer, Moses and John.
Executors: Friend Samuel Levis and sons Moses and John.
Wit: James Hollingsworth, Joshua Harlan, Thomas Carleton.

BOYD, JOHN.
October 2, 1750.
Adm. to Lettice & Robert Boyd.

EDGE, GEORGE.
October 6, 1750.
Adm. to Anne Edge & Robert Pennell.

KELLEY, JAMES.
October 15, 1750.
Adm. to Charles McMichael.

MORRALL, MARY.
November 13, 1750.
Adm. to John Maxwell.

JAMES, AARON, JR.
November 21, 1750.
Adm. to Hannah James.

CONNER, CHARLES.
December 1, 1750.
Adm. to Samuel Neave & Atwood Shute.

OTTEY, PHILLIP.
October 30, 1750.
Adm. to Sarah Ottey &
Nehemiah Baker.

FLEMING, GEORGE.
November 10, 1750.
Adm. to James Fleming.

ARCHER, JACOB.
December 8, 1750.
Adm. to John Sketchley.

WILLIAMS, JOSEPH. Concord. Yeoman.
9/15/1750. December 20, 1750. C. 259.
Plantation in Newlin containing 77 acres purchased of Thomas Gilpin to be sold and all estate divided among the mother and children according to the Acts of Assembly. Daughter Mary only named.
Executors: Caleb Peirce, Edward Brinton, John Taylor.
Letters to Peirce and Brinton, Taylor renouncing.
Wit: John Gest, Joseph Cloud, Micajah Speakman.

MORRIS, WILLIAM. Willistown.
December 17, 1750. January 3, 1750/1. C. 260.
Provides for wife Mary including the plantation in tenure of Joseph Sill during widowhood. To son Richard my plantation in Willistown and Edgmont containing 260 acres at 21, with reversion to kinsman Benjamin Hampton. Also to said Hampton £30. To 2 sons in law John Moor and William Moor £10 each at 21. To Martha Stapleton £5.
Executors: Friends Joseph Pratt and Cadwallader Evans.
Wit: David Westherby, George Harris, William Clark.
* William Morris married widow of William Moore. See Orphans' Court records.

RHOADS, ABIGAIL. Marple.
June 1, 1750. February 1, 1750/1. C. 264.
To eldest son John and youngest son James Rhoades, granddaughter Elizabeth Powell and her sister Abigail, articles named. To each of her 15 grandchildren £5, granddaughter Jean Rhoades named. To daughter Rebecca Massey £5. Remainder to her 5 children, viz., John and James Rhoades, Rebecca Massey, and children of Mary Powell and Benjamin Rhoades. Test signed A.
Executors: Sons John and James.
Wit: Mordecai Morris, James Batten.
* Mentions son Robert Powell.

GIHON, THOMAS. Concord.
January 14, 1750/1. February 5, 1750/1. C. 265.
To wife Elizabeth my land in Concord on which I live being the 1/2 of 125 acres and all personal estate and Executrix. Test signed.
Wit: Elias Neeld, Nathaniel Newlin.

HARVEY, JOB. Darby. Yeoman.
January 4, 1750. February 26, 1750/1. C. 266.
Provides for wife Rebecca including all grants, privileges

mentioned in certain deeds made before our marriage. Mentions having done considerably for son Josiah in hopes of reformation with little hopes of amendment hitherto. Yet gives him £50 if he should reform. The same mention of son Joseph. To son Job £50 under same restrictions as his brothers. To daughter Mary Hunt £6 yearly unless she comes to a reformation, when she is to have £50. To grandson Job Harvey, son of Benjamin deceased £100 at 21 and to his brother Isaac and sisters Elizabeth and Margaret £50 each at 21. To Darby Monthly Meeting £30 for graveyard wall and to said Meeting £20 in trust for keeping up repairs. To son Job the southwest part of my tract of land in Charlestown during life and afterward to his 2 sons. Mentions his brother Joseph and brother in law Isaac Kirk. Remainder of land to be sold on decease of wife and divided among daughter Mary Hunt and grandchildren then living.
Executors: Samuel Buntin and Isaac Pearson.
Wit: Thomas Pearson, James Barry, William Linville.
* Mentions daughter in law, Mary Harvey, widow.

MASCALL, WILLIAM.
January 2, 1750/1.
Adm. to Elizabeth Mascall.

BEZER, JOHN. Chesterborough. Shopkeeper.
9/7/1749. March 26, 1751. C. 270.
To Judith Hollingsworth, my sister Susanna's daughter £40. To the children of Tobias Hendricks, son of my sister Frances £40. To cousin Sarah Grove £10 and to her daughter Martha £8. To Ruth, widow of George Chandler £10 and to her daughter, Ruth Chandler £8. To the children of my former wife's sister, Elizabeth Devonish in Kent County, Md. £40. To brother Richard Bezer £5. To Jacob, son of Nathaniel Lamplugh of Chichester £25 and to his brother John £25 and to their 2 sisters £5 each. To Samuel, son of Jacob Lamplugh late of Chichester £25 and to his brother William £25. To the 2 sons of cousin Edward Bezer £20 each. To friend Joseph Pyle and his children by Sarah, daughter of John and Mary Pennell £40. To friend Thomas Cummings of Chester £20 and to his wife Alice £10 and to their 2 children, Thomas and Elizabeth, £10 each. To Ann Meres, Mary Cummings, Elizabeth Cummings and Hannah Cummings, my wife's 4 sisters £10 each. To wife Jane all remaining real and personal.
Executors: Wife Jane and Thomas Cummings.
Wit: William Pennell, Jacob Howell, Joseph Hoskins.

MARSHALL, JOHN. West Bradford. Yeoman.
October 4, 1750. April 9, 1751. C. 273.
To wife Hannah all estate, real and personal absolutely. She to bring up the children until able to do for themselves and pay to 3 sons, Joseph, John, Abraham £10 each at 21 and pay daughters, Ruth, Ann, Mary and Hannah £5 at 18.
Executrix: Wife Hannah.
Wit: Humphry Marshall, James Marshall, Ann Caldwell.

KIRGAN, JOHN. Whiteland. Weaver.
February 1, 1751. April 15, 1751. C. 274.
To wife Sarah during life tract of 100 acres of land in East
Bradford and after her decease said land to son Jacob. To son
William 5 shillings. To son Hugh weavers loom. To daughters
Ann, Sarah and Mary Kirgan 5 shillings each.
Executors: Wife Sarah and Benjamin Hawley.
Letters to widow, Hawley renouncing.
Wit: Thomas Prise, John Todhunter.

REGESTER, DAVID. Edgmont. Yeoman.
January 13, 1750. April 24, 1751. C. 276.
To son Robert 5 shillings and to his son David my large Bible.
To daughters Mary Jackson, Lydia Baker and Ann Baker 5 shillings
each. To grandson David, son of Jesse Baker £5 at 21. To
grandchildren Nathan and Lydia Scott £7 due from their father,
John Scott. To son William wearing apparel and household goods.
To son John my plantation in Edgmont where I live containing
about 100 acres and all other estate.
Executor: Son John.
Wit: Abel Green, Jonathan Howell, Cad. Evans.

TORTON, HANS. Ridley. Yeoman.
January 3, 1750/1. April 27, 1751. C. 277.
Provides for wife Letitia. To daughter Rebecca, wife of Lawrence
Garrett that tract of land where John Grant now dwells containing
50 acres and 1/2 of meadow. To son Daniel my dwelling plantation
and remainder of personal estate. To daughter Margaret Torton my
upper plantation with my land adjoining and £40 at 18. Test
signed.
Executors: Wife Letitia and son Daniel.
Wit: John Morton, Charles Grantum, Daniel Culin.

EDWARDS, THOMAS.
January 11, 1750/1.
Adm. to Robert Hamilton.

COLLINS, ANDREW.
April 17, 1751.
Adm. to Hannah Collins.

LOAGUE, JAMES.
January 25, 1750/1.
Adm. to James Willson.

MAYES, WILLIAM.
April 29, 1751.
Adm. to Jane Mayes.

CHANDLEE, SARAH.
April 10, 1751.
Adm. to Cotty Chandlee.

RAFESNIDER, FREDERICK.
April 15, 1751.
Adm. to Arnst Rafesnider.

CONN, SAMUEL.
April 13, 1751.
Adm. to Edward Whiteker.

GOHEEN, ANNE.
May 28, 1751.
Adm. to John Goheen.

FILLSON [Felson], JOHN. Fallowfield.
September 3, 1748. April 29, 1751. C. 279.
Provides for wife Jane. To son Davison my land where I now dwell
containing about 200 acres. To son William 10 shillings. To
daughter Margaret 2 cows. To Martha Peoples if she remain in my
house at my death, a heifer. To my 3 grandsons John and the 2

Robert Filsons, a pocket Bible each. Remainder equally to sons John and William.
Executors: Sons John and Davison Filson.
Letters to Davison, John being deceased.
Wit: Francis Boggs, Joseph Davis.

FINNEY, WILLIAM. New London.
January 12, 1748/9. April 30, 1751. C. 281.
Provides for wife Jane including plantation during widowhood, afterward lands in Faggs Manor, about 90 acres, to be sold and all other land and divided among children who are not named. Letters to widow, the other renouncing.
Executors: Robert Finney of Thunder Hill and wife Jane.
Wit: John Meas, John Patterson.

CARTER, ROBERT. Kennett. Yeoman.
November 29, 1750. May 20, 1751. C. 283.
To son John 1 shilling. To daughter Hannah Harlan £6. To sons in law Caleb Pusey and Joseph Cobourn 1 shilling each. To granddaughters Anne Harlan and Susanna Doyle £5 each. To grandson Isaac Harlan £5. To granddaughter Lydia Cloud £5. To granddaughter Susanna Harlan article named. To my other grandchildren 1 shilling each. Remainder to grandson Thomas Harlan, also Executor.
Wit: Daniel Webb, Abraham Parker.

BEVERLY, SAMUEL. East Marlborough.
12/2/1747/8. May 29, 1751. C. 284.
To grandson Samuel Beverly the plantation I dwell on containing about 200 acres with stock, paying to wife £8 per year during life. To granddaughter Mary Beverly articles named. To my daughter Mary's 4 children, viz., Anne, Sarah, John and Jane Mickle £5 each when of age. To wife Jane all remainder of estate. Test signed.
Executors: Friends Richard Blackshall and James Miller.
Letters to Miller, the other renouncing.
Wit: Isaac Jackson, John Hackett, William Farlow.

JACKSON, ISAAC. Londongrove. Weaver.
1/20/1749/50. May 29, 1751. C. 286.
To son Thomas £10. To son John and 2 daughters Alice Gibson and Mary Windle £32 each. To my 7 grandchildren, viz., Anne Moore and Isaac, Jeremiah, Moses, Alice, Rebecca and Mary Starr £5 each. To son William's 2 sons Isaac and James mare and colt and to his wife Catherine, bed. To son William remainder of estate real and personal, also Executor.
Wit: Samuel Morton, John Clark.

TANNER, PHILIP. East Nottingham. Cloathworker.
January 26, 1750/1. June 3, 1751. C. 287.
To son Philip 20 shillings. To son Joseph 5 shillings. To daughters Hannah, wife of William Henry, Rachel, wife of John Dickey and Rebecca, wife of John Crosier 20 shillings each. To son James when 21 the fulling mill and 100 acres adjoining. Remainder of land and stock to wife Mary, also Executrix.

Mentions servant man William McWheny.
Wit: John Hathorn, David Wharry, Zachariah Butcher.

BOAKE, AMOS. East Caln.
October 9, 1750. November 2, 1750. C. 289.
Provides for wife Sarah including lotts of ground in Philadelphia she was possessed of at time of her marriage with me. To brother Abel Boake £20. To daughter Ann Boake all lands and remainder of personal estate.
Executors: Wife Sarah and brother Abel.
Wit: Jason Cloud, Thomas Parke.

MOORE, JOHN. Thornbury.
October 29, 1750. December 29, 1750. C. 290.
To Nathaniel Evenson £10. To John Townsend of Westtown all remainder of estate, real and personal, in trust, income to be applied "to nursing and bringing up of a child that one Hannah Otty of Thornbury is supposed to be a breeding of, provided she is delivered of said child within 230 days of the above date." If said child lives to 21, to have remainder of estate, otherwise to my brother.
Executor: John Townsend.
Wit: Joseph Gibbons, Nathan Yearsley, Sarah Yearsley.
* Mentions brother James Moore.

LITTLE, WILLIAM. Darby. Yeoman.
July 23, 1751. August 2, 1751. C. 292.
To only child William at 21 the plantation whereon I dwell in Darby. To kinswoman Mary, wife of William McClennan a silk gown which was my former wife's. To wife Ann the 1/3 of income of plantation during life and 1/3 of personal estate. Test signed.
Executors: Friends Robert McMullan and John Lewis.
Wit: Isaac Collier, James Serrill, James Collier.

SMITH, WILLIAM. Uwchlan.
January 21, 1752. March 24, 1752. C. 342.
To wife Anne 1/2 of all I possess and the other 1/2 I give to son Samuel, he to be in charge of my father John Smith. If son should die £5 to be given my mother Margaret Smith and £6 to my wife's daughter Anne Freed (Freece). Test signed.
Executrix: Wife Ann.
Trustees: Father John Smith and John Todhunter.
Wit: Robert Smiley, Rees Gatlive, James Gatlive.
Account filed December 16, 1760 by Anne Allcot. Treece in original will book, see page 235.

JAMES, THOMAS. Willistown. Yeoman.
January 4, 1752. April 30, 1752. C. 344.
To son in law Richard Battin the plantation whereon I live containing 100 acres, he paying to my wife Mary £12 yearly during life and other provision for her, including £20 to be disposed of by will. To each of my sons, viz., Thomas, Joseph and Benjamin, 1 shilling and to each of my grandchildren 1 shilling. Test signed.

Executors: Brother in law Thomas Goodwin and Benjamin Hibberd.
Wit: Joseph Lewis, Richard Jones, Lawrance Cox.

HUNTER, ALEXANDER. Middletown. Yeoman.
October 12, 1751. May 11, 1752. C. 348.
Provides for wife Hannah. To grandson Joseph Baker the
plantation where I now dwell containing 150 acres. To sons in
law Henry Pierce and Charles Moore £10 each. Remainder to wife.
Test signed.
Executors: Sons in law Henry Peirce and Charles Moore.
Wit: Isaac Howell, Thomas Grisell, Joseph Talbot.
* Mentions 16 grandchildren besides Joseph Baker (no names).

SHARPLESS, WILLIAM. Concord.
3/24/1750. August 9, 1751. C. 294.
To wife Abige £200, "all the putter she brought with her" and 1/2
of profits of my leased land in Sadsbury. Remainder of estate to
son Abraham and child expected when of age.
Executors: Wife Abigail and brother Samuel Sharpless.
Wit: Joseph Chamberlin, William Trimble, Nathan Sharpless.
* Mentions brothers Jacob and Abraham and sister Jane Pyle.

BLAIR, SAMUEL. Londonderry. Minister.
March 30, 1751. August 13, 1751. C. 296.
To wife Frances 1/2 of all estate real and personal and
management of other 1/2 while unmarried with authority to devise
the same by will among children if she die unmarried. If she
marries again £20 to be given to each of daughters Elizabeth,
Mary, Hannah, Sarah, Francina, Martha and Susanna when 21 and
remainder to sons Samuel, William Lawrence and Isaac.
Executors: Wife Frances and Job Ruston and David Ramsay.
Wit: Samuel Finly, John Brown, James Gilliland.

NAYLE, DEBORAH, widow. Thornbury.
October 5, 1750. August 28, 1751. C. 299.
To Nathan Dix, son of Esther Dix £20. To Esther wife of Francis
Swain £20. To Joseph Maddock, son of Nathan £20 and to his
daughter Deborah £10. To Phebe daughter of Simeon Taylor £5. To
Jonathan, son of Jonathan Thatcher, Jr. £5. To Nayle, son of
John Woodward £20. To the Quakers of Birmingham Meeting £5. To
Henry, son of Henry Peirce £5. To Mary, wife of Jonathan
Thatcher Jr. £5. To my negro woman, Bella £30 to free her, also
£25 and many articles named. To Hannah, wife of John Dilworth
£10. To Sarah Pyle, granddaughter of Esther Dix £5. To Nathan,
son of Sarah and Peter Dix, £5 and to Joseph, son of Sarah and
Peter Dix, £5. To Esther, daughter of Sarah and Peter Dix,
articles named. To Abraham Darlington and his daughter Elizabeth
articles. To John, son of John Woodward £10 and to Ann, daughter
of John Woodward and to Henry, son of same, to Amos son of same,
£5 each and to Richard, son of same, £2.10. To Rebecca
Darlington £5. Test signed D.
Executors: Abraham Darlington and Edward Brinton.
Wit: Isaac Davis, David Gorman, Benjamin Hawley.
* Mentions Rachel Darlington.

HIETT, THOMAS. New Garden. Yeoman.
5/31/1751. September 14, 1751. C. 303.
To son in law Thomas Hutton £10. To granddaughter Hannah Hutton
£5. To daughter Ann £30. To daughter Sarah £40; if she dies
under 21, £5 to go to her sister Katherine and remainder to her
mother. To wife Elizabeth, remainder of estate, also Executrix.
Wit: John Hutton, James Miller.

PYLE, JOB. Marlborough. Yeoman.
7/3/1751. September 19, 1751. C. 305.
To sons Amos and Caleb my plantation I now live on in Marlboro.
To daughter Anne Pyle £150 at 18. Remainder to above 2 sons and
daughter.
Executors: Friends and brethren Joseph Bennett and Robert Brown
of Kennett.
Wit: John Pyle, Jacob Bennett, Thomas O'Connor.

JENKINS, NATHANIEL. New Garden. Merchant.
Nov. 1737. September 24, 1751. C. 306.
"Being about to take a voyage to Great Britain." To wife Jane
the messuage and land I dwell on in New Garden containing 100
acres during life and after her decease to my son James. To
daughter Hannah (Joannah) Jenkins £100 at 18. To father and
mother Rowland and Ann Jenkins £8 yearly during life. To New
Garden Meeting for building a new house £5.
Executrix: Wife Jane.
Trustees: Michael Lightfoot, John Packer.
Wit: Jonathan Packer, Benjamin Fred, John Allen.
* Died between 2/27/1751 and 3/25/1751, see Meeting minutes.

MOODE, ALEXANDER.
June 29, 1751.
Adm. to Rebecca Moode.

POWELL, DAVID.
August 6, 1751.
Adm. to Susanna Powell.

OWENS, OWEN.
July 22, 1751.
Adm. to Richard Thomas.

RHOADS, JOHN. Marple.
August 23, 1751.
Adm. to Elizabeth Rhoads &
Randal Malin.

MC SPARRAN, ARCHIBALD.
August 2, 1751.
Adm. to James McSparran.

MC COMONS, ROBERT.
August 27, 1751.
Adm. to Elizabeth McComons.

WILLSON, JOSEPH. West Fallowfield.
June 19, 1751. October 1, 1751. C. 308.
Directs that mills and lands bought of Moses Dickie be sold. To
wife Janet 1/3 of estate real and personal. To daughter
Margaret, wife of William Dickie £10. To daughters Jean,
Elizabeth, Catherine Willson £30 each when of age. To brother
Gideon Willson £40. To sons Thomas, Hugh, John and Joseph
remainder of estate real and personal to be divided when Joseph
is of age. To son in law Abraham and daughter Anne Smith 4 ewes.
Executors: Wife Janet, brother Gideon Willison and son Thomas.
Letters to widow and son, the other renouncing.

Overseers: Father in law William McCrea and Andrew Sterling.
Witnesses: William Boggs, Robert Hamill, Andrew Sterling.

HUNTER, JOHN. Whiteland. Tanner.
July 30, 1751. October 1, 1751. C. 312.
To eldest Son James at 21 the tanyard and plantation where I live paying to his mother £6 yearly during life. To youngest son John at 21, 100 acres of land bought of John Chads, also house and lot of 7 acres. Provides for wife Ann including real estate until sons are of age. To daughters Hannah, Margaret, Elizabeth, Ann and Mary £60 each at 18.
Executors: Wife Ann and brothers William and James Hunter.
Wit: Andrew Buchanan, William Hudson, Malachi Jones.
* Elizabeth Hunter married William Jones whose brother Malachi married Hannah Hunter.

PHILSON, JOHN, JR. Fallowfield. Yeoman.
May 2, 1750. October 1, 1751. C. 314.
Gives one acre of land for use of the congregation where the Meeting House now stands. To father John Philson, Sr. all estate real and personal, also Executor. Letters C. T. A. to Davison Filson, Executor named being deceased.
Wit: Robert May, George Leggett.

CHAMBERLIN, MARY, widow. Concord.
11/21/1750/1. October 31, 1751. C. 315.
To daughter Susanna, wife of John Pyle £15 and to her children, viz., Jacob, William, Ebenezer, Stephen and Israel 10 shillings and to her daughters Mary, and Susanna 20 shillings each. To the 5 children of son Robert, viz., to Robert £3, to John 20 shillings, to Susanna, wife of Jacob Yearsley, 50 shillings. To granddaughter Mary, wife of Joseph Sharpless £6. To granddaughter Susanna, wife of John Griste £5. To granddaughter Hannah, wife of Robert Pennell articles named. To grandson Benjamin Chamberlain 20 shillings. To granddaughter Mary Baker £3 and to her brother John Chamberlain 50 shillings and to her other 2 brothers William and Isaac £3 each and to their sister Ann 5 shillings. Remainder to son Joseph Chamberlain, also Executor. Test signed M.
Wit: John Newlin, William Trimble, Samuel Sharpless.

GRIFFITH, DAVID. Charlestown. Yeoman.
October 5, 1751. October 31, 1751. C. 317
Provides for wife, not named (Mary). To Hosea, son of son Daniel deceased £30 at 21 and to his brother Daniel £20 at 21. To Mary, daughter of son John the big brass kettle. To son John carpenter tools and farming utensils. To son Timothy remainder of estate, also Executor.
Trustees: Llewellyn David and Joseph Williams.
Wit: David Davis, Daniel Beaton, John Rees.

COWAN, JAMES. Chester County.
September 29, 1751. November 4, 1751. C. 319.
To sister Jean £10. To my father, clothes. To brother Joseph my

pocket Bible. Remainder to wife Keatren and such children as she may bear.
Executors: Father Hugh Cowan and Thomas Hope Hoapp.
Wit: John Russell, James Leard.

HOLLINGSWORTH, SAMUEL. Birmingham. Yeoman.
October 2, 1751. November 11, 1751. C. 321.
Estate to be sold and equally divided between wife and 2 children, viz., Samuel and Jacob when 21. Sons to be apprenticed to brother in law Henry Green to learn trade of carpenter.
Executor: Brother Enoch Hollingsworth.
Wit: William Smith, Jehu Hollingsworth.

HOWELL, HOWELL. Easttown.
November 6, 1750. November 20, 1751. C. 323.
Provides for wife Elizabeth including use of plantation until son Joseph is 21. 50 acres of land to be sold. To sons David and Joseph remainder of land when Joseph is 21. To son Reece £70. To daughter Ann Howel £30.
Executrix: Wife Elizabeth.
Trustees: Kinsman Joseph Jones, John Samuel and David Thomas.
Wit: Reece Howell, James Hodgskins, Edward Jones.

HUGHES, JOHN. West Nantmeal.
August 30, 1751. November 20, 1751. C. 325.
To wife Margaret 1/3 of estate. To son Alexander £10 in addition to his equal share with the other children, viz., John, Jean and Rebecca and the child my wife is now with.
Executors: Wife Margaret and brother James Hughs.
Wit: Samuel Allen, William Graham.

SWAIN, FRANCIS. Chester County. Yeoman.
October 31, 1751. November 21, 1751. C. 327.
To sons Caleb and Joshua the tract of land where the saw mill stands, they paying £120 to my wife. To wife, not named, the tract of land where I reside, her heirs and assigns. To daughter Sarah a mare. To daughter Deborah £30 at 20. To daughter Nancy £30 at 20. Test signed F.
Executors: Wife Esther and son Joshua.
Witnesses: James Way, George Sinkler, William Brown.

PIN, WILLIAM. East Caln.
8/26/1751. December 17, 1751. C. 329.
Provides for wife Ann. To son Richard the 200 acres of land where I dwell, paying legacies as follows: To daughter Sarah Mendenhall £40. To daughter Hannah Paine £30. To grandson William, son of Thomas Pim £10 at 21. To grandson William Paine £5. To sister Susanna Purdy £5. To son Thomas my watch, who is also Executor.
Wit: Phinehas Lewis, Thomas Parke, Jane Parke.

MONEY, NEAL. East Marlborough. Yeoman.
9/9/1751. November 26, 1751. C. 331.
To son Samuel £5. To son Joseph £55. To son in law Henry Neal £16. To son James's 6 children £10 to be divided. To wife Ann

all remainder of estate. Test signed.
Executors: Wife and Henry Neal.
Wit: Francis Windle, Robert Wickersham, James Miller.

BRINTON, WILLIAM. Birmingham. Yeoman.
4/29/1750. January 3, 1752. C. 333.
To wife Jane the profits of plantation I now live on and all household goods. To daughter Ann, wife of Samuel Bettle £100. Mentions that the rest of children had received their full shares. Mentions sons Joseph and Edward Brinton. Remainder to wife Jane, also Executrix. Test signed W.
Wit: Daniel Gest, Agnes McLone, Caleb Brinton.

LEWIS, NATHANIEL.
September 23, 1751.
Adm. to Robert Lewis.

WILLIAMS, AMOS.
October 1, 1751.
Adm. to James & Joseph Williams.

HARDING, FRANCIS.
October 11, 1751.
Adm. to Jonas Chamberlin.

BOGGS, JOHN.
October 28, 1751.
Adm. to Margaret Boggs.

STEVENS, ROBERT.
October 29, 1751.
Adm. to Elizabeth Stevens.

MCKEAN, ANNE.
October 29, 1751.
Adm. to William McKean.

RAFESNIDER, FREDERICK.
December 17, 1751. Charlestown.
Adm. to Elijah Davis.

BRINTON, JOSEPH. Thornbury. Esquire.
10/13/1751. January 3, 1752. C. 334.
Provides for wife Mary. To son George the plantation whereon I live in Thornbury containing 210 acres, also 25 acres adjacent purchased of Samuel Bettle when 21. To son John a tract of land in Birmingham containing 36 purchased of John Bennett, also my 1/4 part of water corn mill called Gilpins in Concord. To son Caleb my plantation in Thornbury containing 200 acres purchased of brother William. Executors to sell 250 acres of land in Lampeter Township, Lancaster County, and divide money to daughters Ann Cock, Mary Jones, Jane Temple, Hannah and Phebe Brinton. To brother Edward £5. Sons James and Moses are mentioned.
Executors: Wife Mary and brother Edward.
Wit: James Dilworth, Daniel Gest, Richard Jones.
* Mentions deceased father, William Brinton, and sisters Mary Corbit and Ann Bettle.

OWEN, JOHN. Chester. Yeoman.
January 14, 1752. January 23, 1752. C. 339.
To son George house and lott on Market Street, Philadelphia. To daughter Elizabeth, wife of James Rhoads the back messuage on Church Alley, Philadelphia. To daughter Rebecca Owen the messuage where Matthew McLoghlin lives in Chester, also to

daughters Susanna and Rebecca Owen certain lotts and articles named on condition that they pay to daughter Jane West £6 yearly during life. To grandson Isaac West £40 when of age and to the rest of my grandchildren £5 each.
Executors: Son George, James Rhoads and Aubrey Bevan.
Letters to son and Rhoads.
Wit: B. Davis, Samuel Davis.

DEAN, JOSEPH.
January 13, 1752.
Adm. to Joseph Wilkinson.

BEATTY, WILLIAM.
January 16, 1752.
Adm. to William & Francis Beatty.

POWER, ROBERT.
January 21, 1752.
Adm. to Jane Power.

JENKINS, JONATHAN.
February 4, 1752.
Adm. to William Jenkins.

NICKLIN, JOSEPH, JR.
February 12, 1752.
Adm. to Mary Nicklin.

HOLLINGSWORTH, JACOB.
March 16, 1752.
Adm. to Susanna Hollingsworth.

TREGO, PETER.
March 25, 1752.
Adm. to Anne Trego.

SILL, JOHN.
March 27, 1752.
Adm. to James Sill.

NICKLIN, GEORGE.
March 30, 1752.
Adm. to Edward Bennett.

PYLE, JOHN. Thornbury. Yeoman.
April 14, 1752. July 20, 1752. C. 349.
To son Jacob 15 acres of my land in Thornbury including house where he now dwells during life and after his decease to my son Ebenezer. To wife Susanna my plantation in Thornbury containing 165 acres during widowhood, afterwards to son Ebenezer, he paying to my son Stephen £30. To son Israel my 55 acres of land in Concord. To son Moses, son William and daughter Sarah, wife of Henry Philips 5 shillings each. To daughters Mary and Susanna £10 each.
Executors: Wife Susanna and brother Joseph Pyle.
Letters to widow, the other renouncing.
Wit: John Peirce, Abraham Sharpless, Ann Sharpless.
* Mentions son William.

COLLETT, JEREMIAH. Upper Chichester.
June 8, 1752. August 8, 172. C. 352.
To daughter Jane Bazella £40. To sons Jeremiah and William 10 shillings each. To son James a tract of land containing 63 acres probably in Chichester and £5. To son Joseph the land I live upon with provision for daughter Jane during widowhood. To Esther Hopton 40 shillings.
Executors: Hugh Linn and John Hopton.
Wit: Hugh Blackwell, Joseph Booth, James Hunter.
* Mentions Mary, wife of son Jeremiah.

FREDD, BENJAMIN. New Garden. Yeoman.
7/12/1752. August 10, 1752. C. 354.
To wife Deborah, plantation where I dwell containing 300 acres
during life. To cousin John Fred, plantation where Robert Boyes
lives containing 200 acres. To cousin Joseph, son of Nicholas
Fred, plantation I now live on, at wife's decease, he paying to
his 3 sisters Mary, Sarah and Katherine £100. To sister Rachel's
children £170, that is James Miller £25, to Jesse Miller £25, to
Sarah Jackson £25, to Deborah Sharp £20, to Thomas, Benjamin and
Katherine Miller £25 each. To Rachel, daughter of Sarah Jackson
above named £10. To Sarah, daughter of Joshua Hadly £20. To
brother in law James Miller £20. To sister in law Ann Fredd £6.
Executors: Wife Deborah and brother in law James Miller.
Wit: Robert Halliday, Samuel Miller, Jacob John.

POWELL, JOSEPH. North Providence. Wheelwright.
May 2, 1752. August 15, 1752. C. 357.
To sons Edward and David 5 shillings each. To son John all
wearing apparel, remainder to wife Katherine.
Executors: Wife and John Sharpless.
Wit: Abraham Ashton, John Day, Joseph Vernon.

EVANS, JEAN. West Nottingham.
August 26, 1751. August 20, 1752. C. 358.
To son Robert Evans the plantation where he dwells. To son James
Evans the plantation he now dwells on. To son John Evans the
plantation he now dwells on. To daughters Isabel and Margaret
Evans, my clothes and negro woman and boy. Test signed.
Executor: Son Robert Evans.
Wit: James Kidd, Robert Kyll.

JOHN, DAVID. Charlestown.
September 7, 1751. September 16, 1752. C. 360.
To sons Daniel, John, David and daughter Margaret 1 shilling each
having given them their share. To daughter in law Mary Richards
of Coventry, all estate real and personal, she to provide for
self and wife, who is not named, during life.
Executrix: Mary Richards.
Wit: Llewellyn David, Patrick Collins. James John.

JENKINS, MARY.
April 21, 1752.
Adm. to James Davis.

EWING, ALEXANDER.
July 21, 1752. Nottingham.
Adm. to Anne & John Ewing.

WOODROW, SIMEON.
May 25, 1752. E. Nottingham.
Adm. to Jane Woodrow.

RUSTON, JAMES.
July 25, 1752. Goshen.
Adm. to Anne Ruston.

HUNTER, THOMAS.
June 5, 1752.
Adm. to Mary Hunter.

BLACK, SAMUEL.
July 27, 1752. Middleton.
Adm. to Elizabeth & James
Black & James Lindsay.

WICKERSHAM, THOMAS.
June 17, 1752.
Adm. to John Wickersham.

HOLLINGSWORTH, ENOCH. Birmingham.
August 11, 1752. September 18, 1752. C. 362.
Provides for wife Betty and refers to "her former husband." To
son Jehu my plantation in Kennett, he paying to my daughter
Abigail, wife of William Harlan, Jr. £25. To son Enoch my
plantation in Birmingham when 21, he paying to my daughter
Hannah, wife of John Moore £25.
Executor: Brother in law John Chads.
Wit: Elianor Pyle, Hannah Thatcher, Thomas Harlan.

PEIRCE, JOSHUA. East Marlborough.
8/23/1752. September 23, 1752. C. 365.
Provides for wife Rachel. To son George 5 shillings. To son
Joshua the plantation I purchased of Daniel Harry, containing 177
acres. To son Joseph, a lot in Wilmington containing 31 perches,
also 5 shillings. To son Caleb that part of my plantation I now
live on containing 189 acres. To son Isaac at 21, the remainder
of plantation containing 122 acres being the north part thereof.
To daughters Mary Cloud and Ann Mendenhall £40 each.
Executor: Son Caleb.
Wit: Ann Caldwell, Ann Mercer.

MOORE, THOMAS. Newtown.
May 30, 1752. October 2, 1752. C. 368.
Provides for wife Susanna including profits of plantation whereon
I live until son Nathan is 21, she to bring up younger daughters
Elizabeth and Sarah. To daughter Mary Batten £5. To son James
£20. To son William £80 until 21. To son Joseph that part of my
plantation bought of John Jones whereon I live containing 75
acres. To son Nathan the other part of plantation purchased of
John Reece. To daughters Elizabeth and Sarah £20 each and
remainder of personal estate.
Executors: Son James and brother in law Nathaniel Grubb.
Wit: Nathan Lewis, Jonathan Hughes, John Smith.

DAVIS, METHUSELAH. Tredyffrin. Yeoman.
December 27, 1750. October 2, 1752. C. 372.
"Being about removing out of this province," to daughter Sidney
1/2 of estate. The other 1/2 to the child my wife Elizabeth is
now pregnant with. If both said children should die, estate to
be divided between the children of my sister Anne, wife of
William Owen of Whiteland and children of Thomas Harris late of
Robeson Township, Lancaster Co. except £30 I give to Mary,
daughter of Isaac Davis, Esq.
Executors: Friends Joseph Bonsall, Esq. and Israel Davis.
Letters to Davis.
Wit: John Malchor, Jacob Davis, Isaac David.

JESSE, WALTER. Uwchlan.
January 14, 1752. October 2, 1752. C. 374.
To friend Charles Moore, books. To relation Edward Goff saddle
and wearing apparel. To Sarah, daughter of Edward, and Mary Goff
£50 and all furniture at 18 and to Mary, daughter of said Edward
and Mary £50 at 18 and to Frances, daughter of Edward and Mary,
£50 and to their daughter Anne £40 when 18. To Sarah, daughter

of Philip and Elizabeth Davies £1. Remainder to Edward, John and
William, the sons of said Edward and Mary when 21.
Executors: Charles Moor and Edward Goff. Letters to Goff.
Wit: Humphrey Lloyd, David Davies, Myrick Davies.

HENDRICKSON, MAUDLIN, widow of John. Amosland in Ridley.
October 19, 1742. October 11, 1752. C. 376.
Directs her burial at Swedes Church at Wickaco by her husband
John Hendrickson. To son Andrew £12 and to his daughter a bed
and to his daughter Susanna articles named. To son Israel negro
girl Sarah, also cattle. To grandchildren Matthias Hendrickson
and son Israel's eldest daughter, my still. To grandson Ebenezer
Stedwell a mare. Test signed.
Executors: Sons John and Israel.
Letters to Israel, John being deceased.
Wit: John Crosby, Margret Hubbard, Mary Helem.

SHELDON, RICHARD. Marple.
October 18, 1751. October 27, 1752. C. 378.
To wife Ann all estate during widowhood. At her death land to
descend to son Joseph during his life and then to his eldest son
William and to continue to the eldest of the male line forever.
To grandsons William and Jonathan Sheldon, articles named. To
daughter Mary remainder of household goods.
Executors: Wife Ann and son Joseph.
Wit: Jonathan James, Joseph Sill, William Quin.

WILLIAMS, MARY, widow, being antient. London Britain. Widow.
September 27, 1752. October 30, 1752. C. 379.
To brothers William, Simeon, Levi and sister Ann 5 shillings
each. Remainder of estate to Baptist Congregation of London
Britain for the use of their poor.
Executors: John Evans and William Chambers.
Wit: George Evans, Joseph Hall.

JONES, THOMAS.
August 28, 1752. Vincent.
Adm. to Isaac Davis.

WILKINS, RICHARD.
September 15, 1752. Kennett.
Adm. to William Dilworth.

PRICE, JOHN.
September 26, 1752. E. Bradford.
Adm. to Thomas Price.

LOGAN, JOHN.
September 27, 1752. New London.
Adm. to Alexander Reynolds.

GRIZELL, EDWARD.
September 29, 1752. Middletown.
Adm. to Mary & Thomas Grizell.

HARRIS, GEORGE.
October 2, 1752. Willistown.
Adm. to George Harris.

PILKINTON, EDWARD.
October 14, 1752. Middletown.
Adm. to Thomas Pilkinton.
William Smedley charges 18th,
9 mo 1752 for making E. P.'s
coffin £1.

PYLE, EBENEZER.
October 17, 1752. Thornbury.
Adm. to Susanna Pyle.

MC ADOW, JOHN. West Nottingham.
November 16, 1751. November 2, 1752. C. 381.
To son Andrew of Cecil County, £10. To son in law William
Hutchman of said county, £10. To son John of same county, £10.
To son in law Robert Creswel of Nottingham £10. To Margaret
daughter of Robert Porter deceased one bed. To wife Agnes my
plantation and all personal estate and to her heirs and assigns.
Executrix: Wife Agnes.
Wit: Andrew Leper, John Gartril.

WILSON, BARBARA.
September 21, 1752. November 10, 1752. C. 383.
Nuncupative will. Being at the house of Robert Wilson in
Concord, leaves house and lott in Charlestown to her mother if
she be alive, if not to her 5 cousins, viz., Robert Wilson, Jr.,
Nicholas Wilson, Cathrine Wilson, Ann Smart and Hannah Wilson.
Letters to Robert Wilson, Jr. and Nicholas Wilson.
Wit: John Gest, Jean Gest.

WOODWARD, RICHARD. West Bradford. Yeoman.
6/30/1748. November 17, 1752. C. 385.
Provides for wife Martha. To son William, daughter Esther wife
of Thomas Wilson, daughter Jane Hayes widow, daughter Sarah wife
of Evan Jones, daughter Elizabeth wife of John Young, daughter
Mary wife of George Entrikin, daughter Hannah wife of Joseph
Underwood, daughter Grace wife of James Milleson 5 shillings
each. To daughter Deborah £20. To son Richard a tract of land
adjoining where I now live containing about 230 acres. To son
John the plantation where I now dwell.
Executors: Sons William and John.
Wit: Thomas Worth, Susanna Worth, Ebenezer Worth.

COLLINS, HENRY. Goshen. Yeoman.
October 5, 1748. Codicil 10/3/1752. November 18, 1752. C. 388.
Provides for wife Hannah including profits of plantation for the
bringing up and schooling of my daughter and the child "she goes
ensent with." If said child should be a son, devises the
plantation where he lives containing 125 acres to him at 21 and
to daughter Mary plantation of 85 acres.
Executors: Wife Hannah and friend Joseph Gibbons.
Codicil mentions having 3 young daughters and no son, gives said
plantation of 125 acres to 2 of said daughters, they paying her
equal share of valuation to the other. Daughters names are Mary,
Ann and Charity.
Trustees: Brother Joseph Collins and Isaac Hains, Jr.
Account filed September 16, 1767 by Nathaniel Moore and wife
Hannah.
Wit: Thomas Evans, Richard Jones, Joseph Collins, Alexander
Bane.

NICKELSON, JOHN. New London. Yeoman.
September 1, 1752. November 21, 1752. C. 393.
To cousin Alexander Walker all estate real and personal as
follows: To Robert son of above Alexander Walker £10 when of
age. Test signed.

Executors: Cousin Alexander Walker and William Clinton.
Wit: John Menough, Richard White.

PARKER, ABRAHAM. Kennett. Yeoman.
October 21, 1752. January 23, 1753. C. 395.
All estate real and personal to be sold. To wife Eleanor 1/3 of estate and £10. To son John 2 shares of remainder when 21. Remainder to my 4 daughters, viz., Mary, Elizabeth, Lydia and Kezia in equal shares when 21.
Executors: Brothers in law Samuel Gilpin and John Chads.
Wit: Ann Caldwell, Ann Mercer, Thomas Harlan.

STUART, JAMES. Londonderry. Gentleman.
February 26, 1752. February 7, 1753. April 15, 1752. C. 397.
Wife Margaret to her living on plantation while a widow. To sons John and Robert the plantation and to daughters Agnes, Jean and Mary £25 each. Test signed.
Executors: William Stuart and Matthew Young.
Letters to Young, Stuart renouncing.
Wit: Richard Daucharty, William Stuart.

KERLIN, MATTHIAS.
November 14, 1752. Concord.
Adm. to John Kerlin.

DOAKE, HENRY.
December 20, 1752. West Caln.
Adm. to Mary Doake.

RUSSELL, ALEXANDER.
November 17, 1752. E. Nantmeal.
Adm. to Matthew McDougall.

DILWORTH, JOHN.
January 22, 1753. Birmingham.
Adm. to Hannah & James Dilworth.

LOW, JOHN.
December 18, 1752. Ridley.
Adm. to Jennett Low.
No. 1464. Sureties Thomas Low & Aubrey Bevan. Bond £200.

NEWLIN, JOHN.
February 10, 1753. Concord.
Adm. to Mary Newlin.

SKETCHLEY, JOHN. Ridley.
January 29, 1753. February 16, 1753. C. 399.
To wife Mary my house and plantation and all stock and household goods, to her and her heirs and assigns. To Mary daughter of Adam Archer the lot I purchased of Adam Archer containing about 2 1/2 acres with reversion to Jacob son of John Morton. To my brother Richard Sketchley in England £100. To John Morton my wife's son, my share in the Darby Library, my books and surveying instruments. To Sketchley and Jacob 2 of the sons of John Morton remainder of estate. Mentions plantation bought of Andrew Torton.
Executors: Wife and her son John Morton.
Wit: Joshua Thomson, Abel Janney.

KIMBER, RICHARD. West Bradford.
2/15/1753. February 26, 1753. C. 401.
Directs plantation and all other estate to be sold and debts paid and of the remainder 1/2 to wife not named and the other 1/2 to all children when of age and directs son Predy to be put to

weaving(?) till he is 20 and Sarah to be left in care of her
mother.
Executors: Thomas Edmonds and Robert Chaffin.
Wit: Henry Heastings, Sr., Henry Holis.

GLEAVE, JOHN. Springfield.
June 17, 1751. March 3, 1753. C. 402.
Provides for wife Elizabeth. To son Isaac the plantation where I
dwell in Springfield, he paying legacies after wife's decease.
To granddaughter Elizabeth, daughter of John Crosier £10. To
granddaughter Mary, daughter of James Crosier £10 with reversion
to her brother John. To daughter Esther, wife of John Crosier
£40. To daughter Rachel, wife of James Crosier £40.
Executors: Wife Elizabeth and son Isaac.
Wit: Benanuel Lownes, William Fell, Isaac Pearson.

VOGEN (VOGAN), JAMES. West Fallowfield.
January 22, 1753. March 26, 1753. C. 405.
Provides for wife Jean. To son in law Joseph Smith 5 shillings.
To grandson Joseph Smith, Jr. a cow. To son in law John Watson
horse and cows. To son William the improvement I now live on,
also Executor.
Guardians: Samuel Irwin and Samuel Patterson.
Wit: Samuel Entriken, Mary Entriken, Samuel Irwin.

JOHN, WILLIAM. Uwchlan. Farmer.
February 2, 1744/5. April 2, 1753. C. 407.
To grandson William John, son of Owen John deceased, my
plantation in Uwchlan containing 193 acres, he paying to my 4
grandchildren of Owen John, viz., Thomas, Evan, Rebecca and Sarah
John 50 shillings each. To the child my daughter Jane Reess is
now big with £5. Remainder to daughter Jane Rees and her
children. Mentions daughter in law Sarah John (widow of Owen).
Test signed W.
Executors: Daughter Jane Rees, son in law John Rees assistant.
Letters to John Rees, daughter Jane being deceased.
Wit: Griffith Evans, Evan Evans, Henry Hockley.

MARIS, GEORGE. Springfield. Yeoman.
April 23, 1753. May 17, 1753. C. 410.
Provides for wife Jane including all lands on southwest side of a
certain line until my grandson George Taylor comes to age and
then to said grandson, he paying to his sister Hannah Taylor £50.
To grandson George Owen all land on northeast side of aforesaid
line except 120 acres to my 3 granddaughters, Elizabeth Rhoades,
Susanna and Rebecca Owen, they paying to their sister Jane West
£3 per year during life. Test signed.
Executors: Wife, cousin George Maris and James Rhoades.
Wit: John Hall, William McCay, James Maris.

OGELBAY, JAMES. Nottingham. Farmer.
September 28, 1752. May 22, 1753. C. 413.
Provides for wife Sarah. To daughters Margaret Boggs and Violet
Porter 5 shillings each. To granddaughter Margret McWhorter 7
shillings 6, when of age. To grandson James Porter £1 and to

grandson John Porter 15 shillings. To my children John, Sarah
and Jean Ogelbay remainder of personal estate. To son John the
whole of the plantation at death of his mother. Test signed.
Executors: Wife Sarah and son John.
Wit: James Harris, Samuel Galt, Samuel Thomson.

PIERSOL, RICHARD. West Nantmeal. Yeoman.
May 7, 1753. May 24, 1753. C. 416.
Provides for wife Bridget including 100 acres of plantation where
I live during life and after her decease to my son Richard, he
paying legacies. To daughters Rachel, Elizabeth, Martha and Mary
£5 each, also to daughter Martha £50 due on bond of Francis
Morgan if she marries with consent of her mother. To servant
Elizabeth Harmon £3. To 3 daughters that are married, viz.,
Rachel, Elizabeth and Mary a bond of £14.15.
Executors: Wife Bridget and Robert Brown.
Wit: John Piersoll, Sr., Joseph Trego, John Bishop.

WEBB, WILLIAM. Kennett. Esquire.
August 26, 1749. May 28, 1753. C. 418.
Provides for wife Rebecca including plantation whereon I live
during life and £500, she to provide for grandson William Webb
until he is 21. To son William the plantation whereon he dwells
which I bought of Samuel Pyle. To grandson William, son of
William the plantation whereon I dwell and other life estate of
wife at her decease, also to said grandson £200. To grandson
Stephen Webb £20. To granddaughter Rebecca Webb £100 at 21 or
marriage. To grandson Ezekiel Webb £10 at 21. To sister Esther
Bennett of Kennett £5. To friend Dr. Samuel Pyle my best suit of
clothes.
Executor: Son William Webb.
Wit: William Cooper, George Miller, Thomas Harlan, Samuel Pyle,
Samuel Grubb, Mary Grubb.
* Mentions brother Daniel Webb deceased, also land rental to
Elizabeth McNeil.

URIAN, ANDREW.
February 14, 1753. Darby.
Adm. to Margaret, Benjamin
& Andrew Urian.

FINLEY, JOHN.
March 2, 1753. Nottingham.
Adm. to George McCullough.

LEWIS, SAMUEL.
April 9, 1753. Haverford.
Adm. to John Lewis.

BISHOP, CHARLES.
April 13, 1753.
Adm. to Patience Bishop.

DUTTON, EDWARD.
April 16, 1753. Aston.
Adm. to Hugh Linn & Hugh
Trimble.

DOUGLASS, JAMES.
May 15, 1753. Radnor.
Adm. to Adam Douglass.

IDDINGS, RICHARD. Newtown. Yeoman.
March 16, 1753. June 5, 1753. C. 423.
Provides for wife Margaret including 160 acres of land in Newtown
during life and after her decease 1/2 of same to daughter
Priscilla during her life and after her decease to her daughter

Elizabeth Wayne, and the other 1/2 of said land to said granddaughter after wife's decease. Also to said granddaughter Elizabeth Wayne, tract of land in Tredyffrin containing 100 acres after wife's decease.
Executrix: Wife Margaret.
Trustees: Kinsman Thomas Thomas of Radnor, Philip Thomas of French Creek, David Thomas of Newtown.
Wit: John Meris, Jacob Thomas, David Thomas.
* Mentions daughter Elizabeth Wayne. See Iddings in next will.

OTTEY, ANN, widow. Tredyffrin.
December 5, 1737. April 16, 1753. C. 425.
To son Thomas Ottey £3. To son Philip Ottey £5. To son Richard Ottey £5. To son Christopher Ottey £5 and remainder of estate. To Ann Ottey daughter of Christopher £6 and to his other children John, Jane and Sarah £4 each when of age. Test signed.
Executor: Son Christopher.
Trustee: Richard Iddings.
Letters to Humphrey Wayne, executor named being deceased.
Wit: John Jones, Mary Plain, David Thomas.
Richard Iddings writes, "This will was left under my care by Ann Ottey when she went from this Province to Carolina and she is now dead and the money sent for."

ELLIS, BENJAMIN. Easttown.
3/5/1753. July 20, 1753. C. 427.
To wife Ann plantation where I live and all other lands with stock until son Ellis Ellis is 21 for maintenance of herself and children. To son William part of my land as described containing 29 acres. To eldest son Ellis the remainder of land where I live when 21. To son Thomas the messuage now in possession of Isaac Hughes. To daughter Rebecca £25. To my other 3 daughters, viz., Mary, Rachel and Hannah £20 each at 18. To John Brooks £6 and mare.
Executors: Wife Ann and friends Thomas Macy and Thomas McKean.
Wit: William Silleker, Elizabeth Brooks, William Lewis.

MOORE, ANDREW. Sadsbury (Sattsbury).
February 1, 1753. August 14, 1753. C. 430.
To son James £5 and to his son Andrew £5 when 21. To daughter Mary Carson £50. To daughter Margaret Love £5 and to her son Andrew Love £40 at 21. To son William £5 and to his son Andrew £5 at age 21 years. To son Andrew the tract of land containing 170 acres known as the Gillmor place when 21, also £20. Provides for wife Rachel including income of mills and plantation for maintenance of herself and 5 of my youngest children, viz., Robert, John, David, Rachel and Sarah until son John is 16. To son Joseph 91 acres of land on south side of this I now live on when 21. To son Robert £200 at 21. To daughters Rachel and Sarah £100 each at 20. To son John 1/2 of mill and 200 acres of land. To son David the other 1/2 of mill and land.
Executors: Wife Rachel and son James.
Wit: Samuel Miller, Samuel Williams.

HEWES, WILLIAM. Chichester. Yeoman.
August 4, 1753. August 18, 1753. C. 434.
Provides for wife Rebecca including profits of real estate during
life. To son Aaron my tract of land in Chichester which I hold
as Tenant in Common with John Kerlin at 21, with reversion to
Chichester Meeting for establishing a school. Orders gravestones
for Father and Mother, wife and children. Remainder for
education of son Aaron.
Executors: Brother John Hewes and brother in law Richard Dutton.
Wit: Richard Flower, John Padrick, John Rawson.

STEEN, JOHN. West Nantmeal. Farmer.
April 10, 1749. August 24, 1753. C. 437.
Provides for wife Jane including plantation to raise and school
the children for 14 years. To son James £100 at 21. To son John
the plantation I live upon at 21. To daughters Sarah and Mary
£40 each at 18, also £60 to the child yet to be born.
Executors: Wife Jane and brother in law John Moor.
Letters to Jane, John Moor being out of the Province.
Wit: James Graham, John Hanna, Hugh Morrison.

ARMSTRONG, WILLIAM. New Londonderry. Yeoman.
February 24, 1745. August 24, 1753. C. 439.
To 2 sons William and John the improvement and survey I live upon
and all moveable goods, paying £10 to son Lancelot when "he is
fit to set up at his own hand."
Executors: Brother James Armstrong and son John Thoptson.
Letters to Armstrong, the other being deceased.
Wit: George McCullough, James Carson.

MC CANDLIS, JAMES. New London.
June 7, 1751. August 27, 1753. C. 449.
To wife Elizabeth all real and personal. The real estate at her
decease to son James, he paying to my 3 grandchildren, the
children of Robert and Elizabeth Kelton, viz., Margaret, Nancy
and James £5 each when of age. To son in law and daughter,
Robert and Elizabeth Kelton 5 shillings each. Test signed.
Executor: Son in law James Kelton.
Wit: George Correy, John Ross.

CROXSON, SAMUEL.
May 19, 1753. Willistown.
Adm. Mary Croxson & Francis
Smedley.

REGISTER, ROBERT.
May 25, 1753. Edgmont.
Adm. to Jane Register.

CHANDLER, JOHN.
July 23, 1753.
Adm. to Susanna Chandler &
William Chandler.

WEATHERMAN, WILLIAM.
July 28, 1753.
Adm. to Joseph Hunt.

BROWN, WILLIAM.
August 22, 1753. Londonderry.
Adm. to Sarah Brown.

ROBERTS, AWBREY.
August 28, 1753. Uwchlan.
Adm. to Ruth Roberts.

BARNES, JOSEPH. West Nottingham.
August 12, 1751. August 29, 1753. C. 451.
Provides for wife Mary including real estate at appraised value
if she choose, otherwise to be sold. To daughters Frances and
Mary and son James 5 shillings each. Remainder equally divided
among wife and rest of children who are not named.
Executors: Wife and son in law John Peak.
Letters to the widow, Peak renouncing.
Guardians: James Porter, Samuel Scott, William Maxwell.
Wit: David Patton, John Brally.

STARR. ISAAC. Goshen.
6/8/1753. September 1, 1753. C. 454.
To wife Margaret 1/3 of all estate. Remainder to all children in
equal shares. Eldest son Thomas, sons John, Isaac, William and
daughter Mary, sons Samuel and Moses, real estate not to be sold
until necessary in judgment of Executors.
Executors: Wife Margaret and her brother Samuel Lightfoot.
Wit: Benjamin Lightfoot, Thomas Parvin.

THOMAS, EZEKIEL. Newtown. Blacksmith.
7/30/1753. October 1, 1753. C. 456.
Directs that 120 acres of land in Nantmeal be sold. To wife
Phebe 1/3 of all estate real and personal except above. To son
Samuel remainder of land in Nantmeal at 21. To son Ezekiel all
land in Newtown when 21.
Executrix: Wife Phebe.
Trustees: Father in law Samuel Wells and brother David Thomas.
Wit: John Jones, Joseph William, Joseph Jones.

HOWELL, THOMAS. Chichester. Yeoman.
November 4, 1753. November 13, 1753. C. 458.
To son William 5 shillings, he having been provided for. To son
Samuel 5 shillings. To son Isaac £25, also to son Samuel my
riding mare and saddle, he paying to my 5 children, viz., Isaac,
Jacob, Daniel, Mary Williamson and Susanna Howell £4 each.
Executor: Son Samuel with authority to sell all remainder of
estate real and personal and divide proceeds equally among above
5 children except £30 to be paid daughter Rachel Grubb.
Wit: John Kerlin, Andrew Tybout.

WALN, MARY, wife of Richard. Norrington, Philadelphia Co.
10/18/173. November 27, 1753. C. 460.
To my 2 daughters Hannah Pennell and Ann Lennon all wearing
apparel. To son Jonathan Lewis, Bible and Concordance. To son
in law Joshua Pennell 5 shillings. To granddaughter Mary,
daughter of son Mordecai Lewis deceased 5 shillings. To 3
children Jonathan, Hannah and Ann all household goods.
Executors: Son Jonathan and Joseph Maris with authority to sell
all real estate and 1/3 of proceeds given to James Bartram in
trust for use each of daughters Hannah and Ann and remainder 1/3
to son Jonathan.
Letters to Lewis, Maris renouncing.
Witnesses: John Morris, William Lewis, Ann Yarnall.

* Mentions son in law Thomas Lennon.

JOHN, GRIFFITH. Tredyffrin. Yeoman.
July 31, 1753. November 29, 1753. C. 462.
To son Samuel 5 shillings. To grandson Griffith, son of son William deceased the 100 acres of land that formerly belonged to my brother Henry John deceased at 21, with reversion to my son Samuel. To son Thomas the 176 acres of land purchased of the Proprietor. To daughter Margaret, wife of Evan James 5 shillings (married June 8, 1739). To son John the house and land whereon I live containing 150 acres. Test signed.
Executors: Sons Samuel and Thomas.
Wit: Nathaniel Miles, Enos Miles, James Davis.

PIM, ANN, widow. Westtown.
11/22/1753. December 18, 1753. C. 465.
To son Joseph Gibbons £160 and to his 7 children, viz., James, John, Joseph, Abraham, Mary, Ann and Jacob £120 to be divided at 21. To Jane, widow of son James £20 and to their son James £5. To granddaughter Jane Gibbons £20 at 18. To grandsons William and Thomas Gibbons £20 each at 18. To Rebecca McClure £5. To Sarah Blowit £3. To Mary Wentworth £3. To Edward Brinton £20. To son Joseph Gibbons all remainder of estate.
Executor: Son Joseph.
Guardian: Brother in law Edward Brinton.
Wit: Caleb Peirce, Thomas Mercer, Francis Hickman.

WILLIAMS, EDMUND. Darby.
October 9, 1753. January 14, 1754. C. 467.
To my cousin William Williams my plantation whereon I dwell except as excepted. To cousin Ann Williams house in Philadelphia, also a lott called the Lower Orchard of plantation devised as above and £10. To cousin Thomas Williams house in Philadelphia and a lott adjoining to Ann Williams. To cousin Mary Williams the remainder of said Orchard lott and £20. To William Williams, my brother's son, £50 and remainder of money left in Bristol. To 3 cousins Thomas, Rachel and Mary Williams £10 each. To sisters Elizabeth and Ann. To negro man Harry his freedom, £5 and tract of land during life. Test signed.
Executor: Cousin William Williams.
Wit: Jacob Webber, William Parker, Benjamin Pearson.

SHARPLESS, MARY.
October 1, 1753. Upper Providence.
Adm. to James Sharpless.

SHARP, JOHN.
November 19, 1753.
Adm. to Nicholas Pyle.

NOSSETT, PETER.
October 1, 1753. Birmingham.
Adm. to Jane Nossett.

ROBINSON, MICHAEL.
November 28, 1753.
Adm. to Mary Robinson.

PEARSON, ROBERT.
October 15, 1753. Marple.
Adm. to Abel Janney.

JACKSON, JOHN.
December 17, 1753. East Marlborough.
Adm. to Jonathan Jackson.

ELLIOTT, JAMES.
November 8, 1753. West
Nantmeal.
Adm. to Margaret Elliott.

VANAMAN, JOHN.
November 13, 1753.
Adm. to Benjamin Ford.

ROBINSON, JOSEPH.
Sept. 16, 1753. New Castle
County.
Adm. to Richard Robinson.
Copy of letters issued in
New Castle County.

WILLIAMS, JOHN. West Caln. Yeoman.
9/29/1746. January 28, 1754. C. 470.
Provides for wife not named including use of plantation during widowhood. To son Samuel the plantation I live on containing 136 acres at wife's decease or marriage, he paying to daughter Elizabeth Carson £1.
Executrix: Wife.
Trustees: Son Samuel and Aaron Musgrave.
Letters to wife Lettice.
Wit: Moses Musgrave, John Musgrave.

ROGERS, JOSEPH. Vincent.
February 9, 1750. February 19, 1754. C. 471.
To son Joseph and daughter Mary 1 shilling each. To daughter Hannah £15. To wife Mary all remainder of estate, also Executrix. Test signed.
Wit: Garrett Brownback, Samuel Harris, Samuel Meredith.

MC CLASKEY, JOSEPH. Chester County. Farmer.
April 24, 1753. February 26, 1754. C. 472.
Provides for wife Barbara. To daughters Jane Kerk, Martha Kimmings and Jennett Dutton 20 shillings each. To daughters Mary and Elizabeth McClaskey £5 each. To son Joseph part of my plantation containing 60 acres adjoining that I gave him a deed for. To son James the remainder of land, about 112 acres, also stock.
Executors: Sons Joseph and James.
Wit: John Wharton, James Lindsey.

WILSON, ANDREW. Uwchlan.
October 19, 1753. March 20, 1754. C. 475.
To eldest son John 3 sheep and articles of wearing apparel. To daughter Margery 3 sheep. To daughter Jean £1. To daughter Margaret one sheep. To daughter Mary one heifer. Remainder in 4 parts. Wife Jennet to have 3 and 2 youngest children Joseph and Elizabeth the other parts. The improvement to wife and son Andrew equally.
Executors: John Bell and Thomas Willson.
Wit: Robert Wilson, James Wilson.

PYLE, JOSEPH. Concord. Yeoman.
3/18/1754. April 8, 1754. C. 476.
To son Robert best suit with silver buttons, he having been well provided for by his grandfather. To son Joseph £150. To 2 sons Isaac and Adam my tract of land in Bethel and New Castle County containing 354 acres when 21. Remainder to 6 daughters, viz.,

Sarah, Rachel, Ann, Hannah, Esther and Martha Pyle at 18.
Executor: Friend William Peters.
Wit: Robert Green, John Peters, Robert Green, Jr.

WHIGAM, JOHN. West Nantmeal.
January 31, 1754. April 17, 1754. C. 479.
To wife Hannah all estate real and personal, also Executrix.
Test signed.
Wit: Robert Brown, Jacob Cochran.

THOMAS, THOMAS. Newtown. Yeoman.
7/20/1752. May 13, 1754. C. 480.
To daughter Sarah Thomas £10 and articles named. To daughter Priscilla £18 in household goods. To Joseph Dickinson and wife Margaret 15 shillings. To sons Jacob and William £5 each. Directs Executors to provide for son Solomon during life "and not suffer him to be abused by an means." To son Hezekiah my plantation whereon I live in Newtown containing about 150 acres with stock.
Executor: Son Hezekiah.
Trustees: Brother in law Edward Woodward and William Lewis.
Wit: Thamar Thomas, Sarah Miles, Thomas Thomas.

GIBSON, JOHN. Birmingham. Miller and Farmer.
March 9, 1754. May 16, 1754. C. 482.
To son Thomas all real estate, mills, mill lands subject to provision for wife Christian. To granddaughter Elizabeth Chandler £100 at 20. To friend John McKee 40 shillings. Remainder to wife.
Executors: Wife Christian and son Thomas.
Wit: James Chandler, John Slack, John Pritchet.

LEWIS JOSEPH. Willistown.
4/6/1754. May 30, 1754. C. 484.
Nuncupative will. To daughter Jane 5 shillings besides what she has already received and remainder equally to the other 5 who are not named.
Executor: Benjamin Hibberd.
Wit: Joseph James, Daniel Yarnall, Abraham Hibberd.

SIMONS, RICHARD. Sadsbury.
August 22, 1753. June 18, 1754. C. 486.
To eldest daughter Elinor £20. To youngest daughter Susanna £20. To Jean Edmunson £5. To son William the plantation where I live with stock, also Executor.
Wit: John Hamill, James Whithill, Rosanne Edmonson.

EAVENSON, JEMIMA.
December 25, 1753. Thornbury.
Adm. to Richard Eavenson.

CATHCART, ROBERT.
January 4, 1754. Birmingham.
Adm. to Elizabeth Cathcart & Thomas Gray.

ROBINSON, SARAH.
March 11, 1754. Chester.
Adm. to John Riley.

JAMES, SAMUEL.
March 22, 1754.
Adm. to Joseph James.

HALL, JOHN.
January 19, 1754. Goshen.
Adm. to Hezekiah Hall.

EWING, JOHN.
March 6, 1754. Nottingham.
Adm. to Susanna & Robert
Ewing.

HAINES, DAVID.
April 24, 1754. Goshen.
Adm. to Mary Haines &
Joseph Burgoin.

HARLAN, EZEKIEL.
May 13, 1754.
Adm. d.b.n. to Daniel
Calvert.

SELLERS, SAMUEL. Darby.
May 27, 1745. June 22, 1754. C. 487.
To daughters Anne Tustin and Sarah Harrison 1 shilling each. To sons Thomas, Luke and William 1 shilling each. To wife Esther all remainder of estate, except £5 which I desire her to give to my son William when she thinks proper.
Executors: Wife and Lewis Thomas.
Wit: Moses Hibberd, John Talbot, Sarah Hibberd.

WEIRE, GEORGE. West Marlborough. Cooper.
December 3, 1750. July 11, 1754. C. 488.
Provides for wife Elizabeth including profits of plantation during life, afterward to be sold. To daughter Jane Webb, wife of Samuel, and grandchildren, viz., William, Constant, Jane, Faithful, George and Samuel Webb, after wife's decease all estate to be divided among them at 21 and 18 years. William to have £20 more than the others. To Elizabeth Webb, alias Hall, my granddaughter 5 shillings and no more. To Samuel Haselet £10 when 18. Test signed.
Executors: Friends Aaron Baker, John Pusey and Joshua Pusey.
Wit: John Williams, Henry Hayes, Thomas Maguire.

LEWIS, MARY. Londongrove.
10/13/1753. July 11, 1754. C. 491.
To my 2 grandsons William and Thomas Baldwin £12 each at 21. To my 3 granddaughters Mary, Lydia and Hannah £10 each at 18. My daughters in law, viz., Elizabeth Baldwin and Mary Pusey, to make equal division of my wearing apparel among 3 granddaughters above named.
Executor: Friend John Pusey.
Wit: Joshua Pusey, Joshua Johnson.

PYLE, ANN. Concord.
4/9/1754. July 27, 1754. C. 492.
To my 2 brothers, viz., Robert and Joseph Pyle 5 shillings each. To my 2 sisters, viz., Sarah Hatton and Rachel Romano 5 shillings each. To 2 brothers Isaac and Adam Pyle £4 each at 21. To sisters Hannah, Esther, and Martha Pyle articles named. To Martha, daughter of Moses Palmer 1 shilling.
Executor: Friend William Peters.
Wit: John Gest, John Peters, Catherine Toilly.

HUEY, WILLIAM. Westtown. Yeoman.
May 21, 174. August 14, 1754. C. 494.
Provides for wife Gennett including a plantation purchased of

Mordecai Maddock containing 125 acres until children are 21. To son James when 21 the above plantation with reversion to daughter Mary. Personal estate to wife and daughter Mary.
Executrix: Wife Gennett.
Wit: John Taylor, Mary Hunt, John Dely.

ELLIS, MARGARET. Haverford. Spinster.
July 25, 1754. August 16, 1754. C. 495.
To my brother Humphrey Ellis, 2 shillings 6. To brother Sublimus Ellis £4 which he owes me and £6. To my sister Rachel Kerk a gown. To nephew Thomas Ellis £3 and Bible. To nephew David Ellis £1.10. To nephew Jesse Ellis £1.5. To nephew Jonathan Ellis £1.5. Remainder to brother Jeremiah Ellis and sister Mary Kerk, who are also Executors. Test signed.
Wit: Thomas Vaughn, John Vaughan, William Lewis.

WEBSTER, WILLIAM. East Marlborough. Yeoman.
7/11/1754. August 28, 1754. C. 497.
Provides for wife including the yearly annuity of £3.6.8 during life being in lieu of her thirds of the real estate of her former husband Evan Harris. To son John a tract of land in Marlborough described containing 120 acres, also my scales for weighing gold and silver coin. To son William £5. To son Thomas the remainder of plantation described containing 75 acres when 21.
Executrix: Wife Elizabeth.
Trustee: Friend Joshua Pusey.
Wit: Edward Swayne, Edward Swayne, Jr., T. Woodward.

BOYD, HUGH. West Nottingham.
9/16/1754. September 30, 1754. C. 500.
Provides for wife Margaret. To daughter Rose McCord £5. To daughter Jean Findly £5. To daughter Anne Meak £5. To son Francis, plantation I have already given him, which I bought of Wm. Mckim; also £5. To daughter Mary Boyd £80 when of age. To son Alexander the place where I live being 200 acres when of age.
Executors: Son Francis and son in law Robert Findly.
Wit: James Scott, William Mershel, Jean Rowland.
* Mentions land bought of William McKim.

HARVEY, WILLIAM. Kennett. Yeoman.
6/3/1750. October 1, 1754. C. 503.
To son William my plantation whereon I live except 5 acres, he paying to daughter Hannah, wife of Jacob Way £60. To son James several tracts of land in Kennett bought of James Few, Richard and Mary Fletcher, and Stephen Hayes, also the 5 acres above mentioned containing in all 182 acres. To 3 sons William, Isaac and Amos a lot of land in Wilmington.
Executor: Son William.
Witnesses: Edward Brinton, James Dilworth, John Newborough.

MORGAN, ROBERT. West Nottingham.
September 3, 1754. October 1, 1754. C. 505.
To son in law Richard Sidwell (sadler) tract of land in Orange County, Virginia, which I formerly bought of him, he paying to

Executors £30. To brother John Morgan the money he borrowed of me, 5 shillings. To brothers Joseph, Moses and David Morgan 5 shillings each. To son in law Henry Sidwell all the money he owes me. To son in law Abraham Sidwell £10. To sons in law Hugh Isaac and Jacob and Joseph Sidwell £10 each. To daughters in law Anne and Mary Sidwell £10 each. To 2 daughters Sarah and Susanna Morgan my tract of land on Deer Creek in Baltimore County, Maryland, and my tract called the Island in Susquehanna River when of age. To wife Anne that 50 acres of land I bought of John Sidwell, Jr. Remainder to wife and 2 daughters.
Executors: Brother David Morgan and son in law Abraham Sidwell.
Wit: John Crawford, John Marshall, Samuel Reynolds.

SEED, EDWARD. East Bradford. Yeoman.
August 2, 1754. October 1, 1754. C. 508.
Provides for wife Abigail including plantation during widowhood for maintaining the children who are not named. Test signed.
Executors: Wife Abigail and brother Joseph Buffington.
Wit: William Bennett, Evan Jones.
* March 1, 1758 on petition of Joseph Buffington, Court approved James Trimble and James Marshall guardians of children, Abigail, Adam, Richard, George, James and Mary Seed.

FLOWER, THOMAS. Londongrove. Yeoman.
August 15, 1754. October 1, 1754. C. 509.
Directs tract of land on Elk River containing about 173 acres to be sold. To mother Abigail Flower 1/3 of proceeds of said sale. To brother Richard the tract whereon I dwell containing 100 acres. To sister Mary Starr £30. To sister Dinah Flower £30. Provides for mother during life. To cousin Caleb Harlan £10. To cousin Stephen Harlan £15 in case he live with Richard to age of 15.
Executor: Brother Richard Flower.
Wit: John Gregg, Thomas Bryan, Thomas Harlan.

THOMAS, RICHARD. Whiteland. Yeoman.
September 23, 1754. November 7, 1754. C. 511.
To eldest son Richard 1/2 of the tract of land whereon I live as described, also the right which my father left me of the land and money in Flintshire, Wales, one lott in Philadelphia when 21, he paying to his sister Lydia £100 when 25 and to his sister Hannah £100 at 25. To youngest son George the western 1/2 of my land as described when 21, he paying to his sister Grace £100 at 25. Provision made for wife Phebe.
Executrix: Wife Phebe.
Wit: Samuel James, Randal Malin, John Todhunter, Henry Atherton.

WOODWARD, EDWARD. Newtown. Yeoman.
5/15/1754. November 12, 1754. C. 515.
Provides for wife Elizabeth. To son George my plantation in Newtown whereon I dwell containing about 200 acres as the same was conveyed to me by my former wife and Robert Tippin with stock, he paying legacies as follows: To daughter Jane Woodward £60. To daughter Margaret, wife of Aaron Vernon £5. To daughter

Abigail, wife of Moses Vernon £5. To daughter Hannah, wife of William Hunter £5. To grandchildren of daughter Margaret Vernon 10 shillings each. To grandson Edward Woodward, son of Edward deceased, old Bible my mother gave me. To all other grandchildren 10 shillings each. To Joseph, son of Peter Taylor deceased, £5 at 21. To Margaret McLone the woman who now lives with me £5. To John Bradley the boy that now lives with me £5 if he lives with George till he is 21.
Executor: Son George.
Trustees: Son in law William Hunter and William Levis.
Wit: John Williamson, William Levis, George Smedley, Jr.

VERNON, THOMAS. North Providence. Yeoman.
December 27, 1752. November 21, 1754. C. 519.
To eldest son Thomas and sons Jonathan and Mordecai 5 shillings each. to daughters Esther, wife of Abraham Ashton, and Hannah, wife of John Calvert, 5 shillings each. To Nathaniel Ring who married my eldest daughter Lydia 5 shillings and to their son Benjamin Ring 5 shillings. To granddaughter Hannah, wife of Thomas Gibson 20 shillings. To wife Lydia the remainder of my land in Marlborough, also lot in Chester to be at her own disposal, also profits of house and land in Providence during life. To son Nathaniel my plantation in Providence containing 95 acres at wife's decease.
Executrix: Wife Lydia.
Trustees: Caleb Cowpland and Peter Dicks.
Wit: John Sharpless, William Swaffer, Joseph Vernon.

MEREDITH, DAVID. Whiteland. Yeoman.
April 20, 1754. December 13, 1754. C. 521.
Provides for wife Sarah. To son Joseph £20. To son William part of my tract of land as described. To children David, Rebecca Jenkins, Hannah Guest, Rachel Connoly and Mary Bane 5 shillings each. To son John remainder of estate real and personal. Test signed.
Executors: Son John and Samuel James.
Letters to son John, Samuel James being sick and unable to come.
Wit: William Lewis, Samuel Lewis.

ARNOLD, MARY.
May 20, 1754. West Bradford.
Adm. to Sarah Arnold.

KERR, DANIEL.
May 30, 1754. Sadsbury.
Adm. to Robert & Thomas Kerr.

WHITE, THOMAS.
July 31, 1754. L. Chichester.
Adm. to Eleanor White.

RIDDLE, JOHN.
August 28, 1754. London Britain.
Adm. to John Porter.

MC ILHENNY, MARY.
Nov. 1, 1754. East Bradford.
Adm. to James McIlhenny.

SHEWARD, SAMUEL.
November 4, 1754. Kennett.
Adm. to Ruth Sheward.

DAVIS, DAVID.
November 7, 1754. Goshen.
Adm. to Jane Davis.

HOLTON, NATHANIEL.
Nov. 29, 1754. Marlborough.
Adm. to Martha & Saml. Holton.

STARR, ISAAC.
October 1, 1754.
Adm. to Mary Starr.

LEWIS, WILLIAM.
December 9, 1754.
Adm. to Hannah Lewis.

TAYLOR, PHILIP.
October 14, 1754. Thornbury.
Adm. to Mary Taylor.

JAMES, SAMUEL. Whiteland.
November 17, 1754. January 20, 1755. C. 523.
To son Samuel my plantation whereon I live and saw mill containing 150 acres, also 2 small tracts "Contagious," also tract described containing 34 acres when 21. Remainder of lands to be sold and proceeds divided among 5 daughters, viz., Elizabeth, Rachel, Magdalen, Sarah and Hannah James. To wife Rachel the profits of plantation for bringing up children until son is 21.
Executors: Brother Joseph James of Willistown and brother in law David Lawrence of Haverford.
Wit: Thomas Morris, William Beale.

DAVIES, RICHARD. Goshen.
11/25/1754. January 28, 1755. C. 527.
Mentions that his father David Davis died intestate and disposes of his part being a double portion thereof as follows: To my mother £20. To brother Ellis £5. To brother Jonathan £50. To brother Amos £100. To sister Hannah Ashbridge £5. To sister Jane Pratt £40. To sister Susanna Hoopes £30. To sister Priscilla Ashbridge £40.
Executor: Brother in law Joseph Ashbridge.
Wit: Josiah Haines, William Eachus, Jr., Richard Jones.

EVANS, MARY, daughter of William. Willistown.
February 8, 1755. February 25, 1755. C. 528.
To brother Richard Evans £5. To sister Magdalen Morgan £5. To brother William Evans £1. To sister Sarah, wife of John Wayne £10. To sister Hannah Evans £1. To brother Joel Evans £6. To brother Joshua Evans £5. To Sarah, daughter of Samuel Morgan, £3 and to Eleanor, daughter of Samuel Morgan, £3. To Eleanor, daughter of Samuel John, £3. To Elias, son of Samuel John, £2. Test signed.
Executor: Brother in law John Wayne.
Wit: Lewis Reece, Thomas Treviller, George Smedley, Jr.

JONES, PETER.
February 11, 1755. Darby.
Adm. to Andrew Urian.

WAY, JAMES.
February 13, 1755.
Adm. to Mary Way.

MORTON, MARGARET, widow. Ridley.
July 4, 1754. March 26, 1755. D. 1.
To daughter Letitia Torton 5 shillings. To Charles Grantum, late husband of my daughter Catherine 5 shillings. To daughter Lydia, wife of Morton Morton 5 shillings. To grandson Daniel Torton 5 shillings. To granddaughter Rebecca, wife of Lawrence Garret 5 shillings and to her 2 daughters Mary and Lydia £5 each at 18.

To granddaughter Margaret Torton £40. To granddaughter Margaret, wife of Thomas Thompson 5 shillings. To grandsons George, Jacob and Charles Grantum 5 shillings each. To grandchildren Margaret, Andrew and Rebecca Morton all remainder of estate when eldest is 18. Letters to Grantum, the others renouncing.
Executors: Daughter Lydia Morton and grandson George Grantum.
Wit: Morton Morton, George Culin, Jr., Susanna Longaur.
* A daughter Ellin married Adam Archer and died without issue. Rebecca perhaps unmarried.

NUTT, SAMUEL. Coventry.
September 25, 1737. March 9, 1737/8. D. 2.
To wife Anna all my right to the Furnace and forge and the 1/2 of the land whereon the Furnace stands, also 120 acres on north side of French Creek and another tract as described and house and lott that Samuel Nutt, Jr. bought at Lancaster. To son in law Samuel Savage wearing apparel. To friend John Blaufoy of Evesham in Worcestershire, England £150. To the heirs of Thomas Crook of Hay Park in Yorkshire £50. Remainder of estate to son in law Samuel Nutt and Rebecca his wife.
Executors: Wife Anna and son in law Samuel Nutt. Friend Jonathan Robeson, Esq. to assist.
Wit: Joseph Phipps, Nathan Phipps, John Phipps.

MC CLUSKEY, DAVID. Londonderry.
June 21, 1754. April 22, 1755. D. 4.
All estate real and personal to son David, he paying legacies. To daughters Elizabeth and Mary 20 shillings each. To daughter Ester £15. To daughter Jean £10. To grandson Joseph £5. The real estate to son David for life and then to his son David. Test signed.
Executor: Son David.
Wit: William Corsby, William Boyd.

LOCKHART, PATRICK. East Caln. Yeoman.
May 8, 1751. May 6, 1755. D. 5.
Provides for wife Jean including profits of real estate until son Robert is 21, she paying £10 each to my daughters, viz., Elizabeth, Mary, Margaret, Susanna and to child yet unborn if a daughter and to said child if a son that part of my land purchased of brother Jacob being 111 acres during life and then to his heirs. To son Robert remainder of real estate at 21 during life and then to his heirs. Mentions his mother as living without naming her.
Executor: Wife Jane.
Wit: Theophilus Irwin, Robert Darlinton, Joseph Wilkinson.

WOODWARD, MARTHA, widow. West Bradford.
September 28, 1753. May 28, 1753. D. 7.
To son Thomas Heald 20 shillings. To granddaughter Martha Key best apparel. To son John Heald bed and furniture. Remainder to son John and daughter Phebe Yearsley, also executors. Letters to John Heald.
Wit: Ebenezer Worth, Susanna Worth, Thomas Worth.

SHARPLESS, NATHAN. Goshen. Yeoman.
5/13/1755. June 11, 1755. D. 8.
To wife Hannah plantation where I live, purchased of William Dean
containing 200 acres, but to son William at age 21, he paying his
sisters Martha and Hannah £5 each.
Executors: Wife Hannah and brother John Townsend of East
Bradford.
Wit: Joseph Chambers, Jacob Sharpless, John Taylor.

PATTEN, ROBERT. Sadsbury.
May 15, 1755. June 4 and 14, 1755. D. 9.
Executors to sell all estate. To daughter Sarah 5 shillings. To
son John 7 shillings 6. To daughter Rebecca £3. To daughter Jean
£5 when of age. Remainder in 6 equal parts to wife, son Andrew,
daughter Elizabeth, sons Robert, Thomas and Joseph. 3 last named
sons to be put to trades when of proper age.
Executors: James Blelock, E. Fal., and John Woods, Hanover,
Lancaster County.
Wit: John Kirkead, John McPherson.

MC KNIGHT, WILLIAM. Rowan County, North Carolina.
November 8, 1759. (November 15, 1759) January 1760. D. 10.
To eldest son Charles the north 1/2 of plantation on Caddle
Creek. To son Thomas 1/2 of plantation whereon I dwell. To son
William all my tract in the lower settlement. To son James
remainder 1/2 of land on Caddle Creek. To son Hugh the tract of
land purchased of William Watson. To son John the remaining 1/2
of plantation where I live. To son David £80. Mentions nieces
Jane and Isabella Heoy *(Hevy or Heuy?)*. Executors to sell 326
acres of land in Chester County, now in care of Alexander Rogers
and proceeds divided between sons Charles, John, William, James,
Hugh, Thomas, David and daughters Jennett Kerr and Margaret
Young.
Executors: Son in law John Kerr and son Charles.
Letters to Kerr and William McKnight, Charles McKnight
renouncing, in favor of his brother. *Will proven in North
Carolina.*
Wit: John Latta, William Sim, Francis Beatey.

WAYNE, ANTHONY.
March 25, 1755.
Adm. to Elizabeth & Humphrey
Wayne.

MELCHIOR, WILLIAM.
April 7, 1755. Tredyffrin.
Adm. to Elizabeth Melchior.

JONES, BENJAMIN.
April 15, 1755. Tredyffin.
Adm. to Esther Jones.
Sureties Webster, David Jones,
Morris Evans. Inv. April 11,
1755 by Samuel Richards and James Davis.

DAVIS, MARY.
May 2, 1755.
Adm. to David Davis.

RAIN, JOHN.
May 30, 1755.
Adm. to Mary Rain.

BATTIN, SAMUEL.
June 7, 1755.
Adm. to Rachel Battin &
John Martin.

LLOYD, RICHARD. Darby. Miller.
5/9/1755. August 19, 1755. D. 13.
All estate real and personal equally divided between wife Hannah and 2 sons Isaac and Hugh, sons share to be in hands of brother Robert Lloyd and brother in law John Hunt as guardians until they are of age.
Executors: Wife Hannah and son Isaac.
Letters to Hannah, son being under 17 years of age.
Wit: John Paschall, John Rudulph, John Otlay (Quaker).

PAINTER, SAMUEL. Birmingham.
January 31, 1753. August 23, 1755. D. 15.
To son Samuel the tract of land in Bradford purchased of William Hudson, he paying to his cousin Patience Painter £40 at 21. To son John the plantation he now lives on in Birmingham, also 13 acres of that where I dwell. To wife Elizabeth the plantation I live on during life and after her decease the southern 1/2 of same to daughter Ann and the northern 1/2 to daughter Mary and granddaughter Elizabeth Painter.
Executrix: Wife Elizabeth.
Wit: James Dilworth, Richard Eavenson, Richard Thatcher.

HAMILTON, JOHN. Londonderry. Farmer.
May 31, 1755. August 29, 1755. D. 16.
Provides for wife Jean. Plantation and other estate to be sold and proceeds divided between 3 children James, John and Catherine when of age. To youngest son John a plantation and fulling mill in Cumberland County, son to be in care of Josiah Scott of Lancaster County until 21.
Executors: Dr. Robert Thompson of Lancaster County and Alex Johnston of New London and Robert Allison of Charlestown, Maryland.
Wit: Robert Finney, John Morrison, Thomas Minor.

SCOTT, PROVIDENCE. Birmingham. Yeoman.
February 26, 1753. September 26, 1755. D. 18.
To wife not named 1/3 of estate. To sister in law Ann Scott £5. Remainder real and personal to be sold and proceeds divided into 3 shares, 2 of which I give to grandson Levi Low when 21 and the other share to son in law Obadiah Bonsall and wife Rebecca and their children.
Executor: John Chads.
Wit: Amos Harvey, Kezia Harvey, Jonathan Thatcher.
* Joseph Davis, Londongrove Meeting, complained of 7/5/1766 as executor of Providence Scott.

SPEAR, JOHN. West Marlborough.
November 13, 1754. October 2, 1755. D. 19.
To daughter Mary £3 when of age. Remainder equally divided among my wife and my other 6 small children who are not named.
Executrix: Wife Ann.
Overseers: David Ramsey and William Boyd.
Wit: John Daysart, William Daysard, William Boyd.

CALLWELL, JAMES. East Nottingham. Farmer.
September 5, 1755. October 2, 1755. D. 20.
To wife Ann £120 and the further sum of £80 now in the hand of her brother Andrew Simm. To John Calwell, son of brother William in Scotland £30. To John Calwell son of brother Abram in Ireland £10. To John Calwell, son of brother Dann. £20. To John Tarbert, son of sister Elinor £10. To James McCullough, son of sister Agnes £20. To Robert Tweed and wife Agnes the black horse. To sister Martha and her children £34. To George, son of sister Agnes £20. To Ann Wharrey £20. To Robert Williamson £2.
Executors: William Edmiston, James Wharrey and wife Ann.
Wit: James Gilles, James McCullough, James Petterson.

STARR, MARGARET. Chichester.
10/8/1755. October 25, 1755. D. 22.
To sons Thomas, John, Isaac and William Starr 25 shillings each. To son Jacob 20 shillings. To executors household furniture and other articles in trust for daughter Mary Parvin. To sons Samuel and Moses all remainder of estate when 21.
Executors: Cousins Thomas Lightfoot, Jr. and Samuel Lightfoot, Jr.
Wit: John Riley, Richard Riley.

BOYD, MARY. East Nottingham.
October 7, 1755. December 23, 1755. D. 23.
To cousin Samuel Jackson all lands and moveable effects, also Executor. Test signed.
Wit: John Cooper, William Ross.

MC CLURE, JAMES. Chester County. Yeoman.
September 29, 1755. November 5, 1755. D. 23.
To wife Mary 1/3 of all estate and to daughters Esther and Jean 1/3 of estate each at 18. To brother Robert McClure wearing apparel.
Executors: Brother Robert McClure of East Nantmeal and John Lewis of Uwchlan.
Wit: John McClure, David Denny, Samuel McClure.

BUTCHER, ZACHARIAH. East Nottingham. Yeoman.
August 18, 1754. December 4, 1755. D. 25.
To daughter Sarah Butcher £8. To daughter Rachel Oldham 40 shillings. Executors to sell real and estate and divide proceeds among all children, viz., Mary, Elizabeth, Margaret, Susanna, Rachel, Hannah and Sarah.
Executors: Son in law Robert Oldham and daughter Mary.
Wit: Samuel Gilpin, Joseph Gilpin, Samuel Gilpin, Jr.

SHANKS, SAMUEL.
June 19, 1755. W. Nottingham.
Adm. to Sarah Shanks & William Cuming.

ALLEN, JOHN, JR.
June 25, 1755.
Adm. to Phebe Allen.

GREGORY, WILLIAM.
August 26, 1755.
Adm. to Margaret Gregory.

MC KEE, ROBERT.
October 1, 1755. New London.
Adm. to Alexander Johnston.

MC DOWELL, JOSEPH.
July 23, 1755.
Adm. to Nicholas Pyle.

MC CRACKEN, ARCHIBALD.
November 25, 1755. Kennett.
Adm. to Hannah McCracken.

MOORE, CHARLES.
February 24, 1756. Marple.
Adm. to Elizabeth Moore.

HACKETT, JOHN.
July 31, 1755. New Garden.
Adm. to Elizabeth Hackett.
June 18, 1765 John Black and Samuel Sharp appointed guardians of Mary, Elizabeth (over 14), John and Agnes Hackett, children of John, deceased.

MEREDITH, DAVID. Whiteland. Yeoman.
February 19, 1755. December 12, 1755. D. 26.
Provides for wife Eleanor. Executors to sell real estate and remainder of proceeds to children, viz., Ann, Esther, Hannah, Daniel, George, Sarah, Elijah and Alice Meredith when of age, sons to be put to trades at 16.
Executors: Brothers in law Thomas and William Garrett and wife. Letters to wife and Thomas Garrett, the other renouncing.
Witnesses: William Meredith, Henry Atherton.

RICHARDS, JOSEPH. Aston.
January 10, 1756. February 5, 1756. D. 27.
To wife all real estate in Aston during life and at her decease to son Jonathan. To sons Joseph and John £5 each. To daughter Mary, daughter Roday and Margaret Collen £5 each.
Executors: Wife Lydia and son Jonathan.
Wit: Hugh Linn, Edward Bennett.

CLAYTON, THOMAS. Chichester.
November 30, 1752. February 12, 1756. D. 28.
To wife Hannah all estate real and personal during life and at her decease to son Adam except following legacies. To daughter Hannah Clayton a lot of ground and £50. To grandson Thomas Neals a lot of land where Richard Leanard now lives. To grandson John Neals 5 shillings. To daughter Rachel Rain 5 shillings. Test signed.
Executors: Wife Hannah and son Adam.
Wit: William Hewes, David Clayton, John Riley.

JONES, DAVID. London Britain. Farmer.
February 4, 1756. February 18, 1756. D. 29.
To friend Rev. David Davis in New Castle County £5. To the poor of our Church 40 shillings. To sister in law Ann Evans the young mare on account of her care of my child. Remainder to brother Rev. Jenkin Jones in Philadelphia. Test signed.
Executors: Morris Thomas, Chester County, Hugh Evans and John Thomas, New Castle County.
Letters to Morris and John Thomas, Evans renouncing.
Wit: William Clinton, clerk, John Short.

WILLIAMS, ELLIS. Goshen. Yeoman.
5/14/1754. February 25, 1756. D. 30.
To eldest son Robert 20 shillings. To son Ellis farming
implements. To son Isaac articles named and all he owes me
except £5 which he shall pay to my grandson George Garrett and 20
shillings he shall pay to grandson Ellis Garratt. To daughter
Mary, wife of Thomas Garrett household goods. To granddaughter
Mary Williams articles named. To granddaughters Esther and Ruth
Garrett Williams. Remainder to 3 sons, Robert, Ellis and Isaac
and daughter Mary Garrett. Test signed.
Executors: Son Isaac and brother in law John Meredith.
Letters to Isaac, Meredith renouncing.
Wit: Lewis Williams, Richard Jones, Ann Parker.

BRINTON, JANE, widow. Birmingham.
10/10/1752. February 26, 1756. D. 32.
To son William Brinton £5. To 2 daughters Mary Corbet and Ann
Bittle all household goods and remainder of estate.
Executor: Son Edward Brinton.
Wit: James Dilworth, Daniel Gest, Joseph Peirce.

HARVEY, JOSEPH. Ridley. Carpenter.
January 9, 1754. March 2, 1756. D. 33.
To daughter Alice my plantation in Ridley, she paying as follows:
To daughter Susanna £200 and to granddaughter Mary Harvey £100.
To wife Mary 1/2 of estate during life. Remainder to wife and
grandchildren living at my decease.
Executors: Wife Mary, son in law John Lewis, Joseph Maris and
John Cruckshank.
Wit: William Davis, Mordecai Thomson, Samuel Levis, Jr., John
Davis.
* Mentions a mill and malt house.

OLDHAM, THOMAS. East Nottingham.
2/3/1750. March 2, 1756. Died 2/15/1756. D. 35.
To wife Rachel 1/3 of estate real and personal. To Mary, widow
of son Thomas and to their son Thomas 5 shillings each. To
Sarah, widow of son William and to Lacy Rowles, husband of
daughter Mary deceased 5 shillings each. To daughter Martha,
wife of James Scivington 5 shillings. To daughter Deborah, wife
of Joshua Litter 5 shillings. To daughter Susanna, wife of
Daniel Brown and daughter Hannah, wife of Thomas Barrett all
remainder of estate real and personal. Test signed.
Executors: Son in law Thomas Barrett and friend William
Churchman.
Letters to Barrett, the other renouncing.
Wit: William Churchman, James Hamill, George Churchman.

DAVID, LLEWELLYIN. Charlestown. Yeoman.
February 27, 1756. March 8, 1756. D. 36.
To son Isaac my tract of land in Charlestown whereon I live
subject to provision for wife Margaret and daughter Ruth while
unmarried. To daughter Ann Williams £5. To daughter Magdalen
Howell £10. To daughter Ruth David £35 at 22. To grandson

Daniel Griffith £5 at 21. To granddaughters Margaret and
Elizabeth Williams £5 each at 21. To grandson Ezekiel Howell £10
at 21. Remainder to son Isaac who is also Executor. Test
signed.
Wit: John Griffith, Joseph Williams, David John.

WELSH, GEORGE. West Nottingham.
January 30, 1756. April 5, 1756. D. 39.
To wife Mary and 2 children William and Robert Welsh the
plantation I lately bought of William Cuming and the Widow
Shanks. Also household goods. Mentions having made over to
eldest son John 1/2 of plantation whereon I live. To son James
£20 and horse, also the £30 I let him have formerly to go to
Carolina. Remainder of land and estate to 3 children George,
Jane and Mary Welsh. Test signed.
Executor: Son John.
Wit: Jean Stephenson, John Gartril, William Allen.

PUSEY, CALEB. East Marlborough. Yeoman.
1/30/1753. May 3, 1756. D. 40.
To son Robert 20 shillings. To son David the land which I call
Wantage containing 152 acres, he paying to his sister Margaret,
wife of John Perry £30. To son in law William Swayne, my desk.
To Margaret widow of son Caleb and to his 4 children, viz.,
Thomas, Prudence, Elizabeth and James £30. To son Thomas all
remainder of estate real and personal, he paying to his sister
Ann, wife of William Swayne £30.
Executor: Son Thomas.
Wit: Hannah Brown, T. Woodward, Benjamin Leonard.
* The will of Margaret Pusey of the town of New Castle, widow,
dated December 28, 1769, proved March 5, 1771, gives all estate
equally between her three beloved children, Thomas, Prudence and
Elizabeth and appoints Thomas executor. Made her mark.

JACKSON, THOMAS. West Marlborough. Yeoman.
6/5/1751. May 3, 1756. D. 42.
To son John £20. To son Jonathan £50. To daughter Ann Jackson
£40 and all household goods. To daughter Judith Ivory £16. To
daughter Mary Wright £20. To daughter Elizabeth Chalfant £16.
To grandson Thomas Jackson, son of Jonathan a colt. To the
children of son Thomas deceased £24. To all grandchildren 20
shillings each. Remainder real and personal to be sold.
Executors: Sons John and Jonathan.
Letters to Jonathan, John being deceased.
Wit: Robert Johnson, Moses Pyle, T. Woodward.

HALL, RICHARD. Marple.
May 4, 1756. May 13, 1756. D. 43.
To mother £6 she going to live with her daughter Jane Ross or
Elizabeth Kerns. To wife 1/3 of estate, the other 2/3 to be
divided between children, viz., Alice, Jane, Alexander and
Richard and child that may yet be born.
Executors: Wife Rose and John Gilbraith of Springfield.
Wit: John Hemphill, Mordecai Taylor, Elizabeth Kerns.

BROWN, GEORGE. Chester County. Gentleman.
April 10, 1756. May 28, 1756. D. 44.
Provides for wife Mary. To daughter Jean £60 and her maintenance
till she is of age. To youngest daughter Mary same. To 2 sons
Alexander and William the remainder of estate when Alexander is
of age.
Executors: Wife Mary and William McCamant.
Wit: James McCamant, Isaac McCamant.

TAYLOR, THOMAS of the Island of Tinicum. Ridley. Gentleman.
April 23, 1756. June 10, 1756. D. 45.
Provides for wife Mary including my plantation in Pilesgrove
containing about 100 acres. To son John 1/2 of my marsh. To son
Thomas part of the plantation I live on as described, also 1/2 of
marsh. To daughter Elizabeth 1/2 of a tract in Pilesgrove, part
of which came to me by my second wife Mary containing 270 acres.
To daughter Mary the 1/2 of said tract. To daughter Sarah the
bond of £53 I have on Thomas Wilkins. To daughters Elizabeth and
Mary £150 each at 18 or marriage. To son Joseph the plantation
whereon Charles Smith lives being part of my dwelling plantation,
also part of Tinicum Island. To the child yet unborn £20 at 21.
Executors: Sons John and Thomas and friend Lewis Davis.
Codicil revokes appointment of son John as Executor.
Wit: John Morton, Daniel Ries, Elizabeth Holston.

BEVERLY, JANE, widow of Samuel. East Marlborough.
12/23/1752. August 4, 1756. D. 48.
To grandson Samuel Beverly my plantation in East Marlboro
containing 200 acres on which I dwell. To granddaughter Mary
Beverly £15 at 20 or marriage. To my grandchildren Mary Mickle's
children, viz., Ann McFarlin, alias Mickle, John, Sarah and Jane
Mickle 5 shillings each (being children of Robert Mickle).
Remainder to grandson Samuel Beverly, also Executor.
Witnesses: Richard Blackshall, James Miller, Jesse Miller.

HOUSE, JAMES. Kennett.
February 18, 1756. August 14, 1756. D. 50.
To son Amos the plantation in Kennett purchased of William Andrew
containing about 150 acres when 21. Plantation whereon I live
containing 5 acres and that purchased of Daniel McPherson to be
sold. Provides for wife Mary. Remainder equally divided among
children when 21, none named.
Executors: Wife Mary and brother in law John Chads.
Letters to widow Mary, Chads renouncing.
Wit: Joel Baily, Jr., Thomas Harlan.

PEIRCE, HENRY. Concord. Yeoman.
July 18, 1756. August 31, 1756. D. 51.
Provides for wife Sarah. To 3 sons, viz., Henry, William and
John my plantation and 2 tracts of land in Concord containing 250
acres to be divided when youngest is 20. Younger children to be
maintained on plantation until they are 16. Remainder equally
divided among wife and all children.
Executors: Wife Sarah and son Henry.
Wit: Ann Hoe, Caleb Perkins, John Hannum.

MC WILLIAMS, WILLIAM.
February 25, 1756. E. Nottingham.
Adm. to Sarah McWilliams &
Robert Young.

HOWELL, OWEN.
March 8, 1756. Willistown.
Adm. to Magdalen Howell.

MC CONNELL, FRANCIS.
March 9, 1756. W. Nottingham.
Adm. to James McAdow.

"Whereas a Certain Instrument purporting to be the Last Will and Testament of John Taylor late of Chester County, Gentleman, deceased, was Exhibited into the Register General's office at Chester for probation thereof in due form of Law, but several Caveats having been filed in the said Office against the proving the same and it being Suggested and insinuated that the said Writing purporting to be the Will of the said John Taylor was obtained by Fraud and also that the said John was not of sound and disposing mind and memory at the time of Executing the same, and the Register's Court upon hearing the matters aforesaid having ordered and decreed that the Facts above suggested be tried at Common Law upon a feigned issue to be joined between the parties and that in the mean time during the Contention about the said Writing Letters of Administration of all and singular the Goods Chattles Rights and Credits of the said John Taylor be Committed unto you the said Edward Brinton and John Hannum," &c. 10th of March 1756.

TAYLOR, JOHN.
March 10, 1756. Thornbury.
Adm. dep. litae to Edward
Brinton & John Hannum.

STRODE, WILLIAM.
March 19, 1756. E. Bradford.
Adm. to Deborah Strode.

HARKNESS, DAVID.
April 6, 1756. E. Nottingham.
Adm to John Hathorn.

TOMLINSON, OTHNIEL.
July 20, 1756. Concord.
Adm. to Mary Tomlinson

CRANSTON, ELIZABETH. Chichester.
August 1, 1751. September 1, 1756. D. 53.
To son John Balden 5 shillings. To daughters Ann Welsh and Elizabeth Armour wearing apparel. Remainder equally divided among children, viz., James Bond, Ann Welch, Elizabeth Armour, Mary Clark, William Cranston and Hannah Bankson. Executors: Jacob Bankson, Richard Clark.
Letters to Clark, the other renouncing. Wit: Richard Flower, Benjamin Mounder, John Riley.

SIMSON, ALLEN. Londonderry. Yeoman.
January 22, 1754. September 2, 1756. D. 54.
Provides for wife Margaret. To son David all my lands. To sons John, William James and Robert and daughter Cataren Simson 5 shillings each. To grandchildren Allen and Ellis Simson £5 each.

Executor: Son David.
Overseers: Friends Joseph Smith and John Simson.
Wit: Archibald McDowell, James Simson, William Little.

BACKHOUSE, ALLEN. Queen Anne's County, Maryland. Yeoman.
June 5, 1756. September 29, 1756. Codicil: August 10, 1756.
D. 55.
To brother Richard all my rights to 1/3 of mill house and tract
of land on Choptank River in Queen Anne's County, at 21; until he
is of age the profits to go to my mother, Anne Backhouse.
Remainder to Mother, also Executrix. Mentions sister Isabella
Backhouse.
Wit: Elizabeth Cummings, Thomas Cummings.

MC CALL, JAMES. West Nottingham.
12/14/1755. October 1, 1756. D. 57.
Directs debts and funeral expenses to be paid but gives no
legacies. Test signed.
Executor: Friend Henry Reynolds.
Wit: William Reynolds, Benjamin Bowen.

WHITE, JOHN. East Caln.
August 19, 1756. October 1, 1756. D. 58.
To father John White £15. To brother Samuel White £20. To
sister Hannah Love £5. To sister's son Samuel £7.10 and to her 2
sons William and James £7.10 to be divided. To cousin Thomas
White £4. To cousin John White a coat. To brother in law Samuel
Love cloth jacket. To cousin Jane McBride £3.
Executors: Brother in law Samuel Love and brother Samuel White.
Wit: John Campbell, Thomas Boyd, John McCune.

FEARNAN, EDWARD. London Britain. Taylor.
September 20, 1756,. October 22, 1756. D. 59.
To wife Margaret 1/3 of estate real and personal. To brother
Francis wearing apparel. To daughter Margery, son Solomon,
daughter Elizabeth, and son Edward all remainder of estate in
equal shares. Test signed.
Executors: Wife Margaret and James Kennedy.
Wit: Thomas Patten, John Huey.

PENNELL, JOSEPH. Edgmont. Yeoman.
September 16, 1756. October 26, 1756. D. 60.
To daughter Ann wife of Cadwallader Evans part of my land in
Edgmont as described containing 340 acres. To daughter Mary,
wife of Moses Meredith part of my land in Edgmont as described
containing 165 acres. To granddaughter Rachel Jordan £10. To
son in law Joseph Jackson £5. To each of my grandchildren 20
shillings. To son in law Cadwallader Evans all remainder of
estate, he paying above legacies.
Executors: Cadwallader Evans and Moses Meredith.
Letters to Evans, Meredith renouncing. Test signed.
Wit: Joseph Pratt, John Hoare, Richard Jones.

BELL, JOSEPH. Uwchlan.
August 27, 1756. November 4, 1756. D. 62.
To my mother Jean Bell, articles named. Remainder equally
divided between my wife and children "being 3 now living and my
wife great with child."
Executors: Wife Mary and her brother Andrew Wilson of Uwchlan.

Witnesses: Richard Bell, Robert Robinson.

WILSON, THOMAS. Uwchlan.
September 29, 1756. November 4, 1756. D. 62.
To eldest son Joseph a double portion of land and chattels. To each of my daughters being 4 in number £15, at 18, not named. Remainder in 3 equal shares to wife Mary and sons George and Thomas.
Executors: Wife Mary and brother Robert Wilson.
Wit: Andrew Wilson, Frederick McCaskey.

PEIRCE, GEORGE.
October 1, 1756. Goshen.
Adm. to Mary Peirce & John Townsend.

HENDERSON, JOHN.
October 1, 1756. W. Nantmeal.
Adm. to Janett Henderson & Francis Alexander.

CALDWELL, WILLIAM.
October 2, 1756. Springfield.
Adm. to Jane & John Caldwell.

MORGAN, JOHN.
October 22, 1756. E. Caln.
Adm. to Lydia Morgan.

MC CLINTOCK, MARY.
October 26, 1756. Kennett.
Adm. to William Harvey.

JACKSON, SAMUEL.
Oct. 29, 1756. E. Marlborough.
Adm. to Isaac Baily.

RAMSEY, WILLIAM. Sadsbury.
November 10, 1756. November 15, 1756. D. 63.
To wife Susanna all my land and moveable estate, also Executrix.
Wit: Joseph Moore, John Scott, James Boyd.

PRATT, JOSEPH. Edgmont. Yeoman.
11/16/1756. November 30, 1756. D. 64.
Provides for wife Mary. To son Joseph the plantation where I now live. To son in law Randal Malin my watch. To son in law Amos Davis my Dutch servant boy, Jacob Trustle. Remainder of estate to wife and 4 daughters, viz., Rose, Sarah, Alice and Ann.
Executors: Son Joseph and son in law Randal Malin.
Trustees: Son in law Lewis Lewis and William Lewis.
Wit: William Griffith, Edward Farr.

MORGAN, SAMUEL. Chestertown.
November 15, 1756. December 6, 1756. D. 66.
To brother Thomas Morgan 1/3 of all estate real and personal. To sister Mary Morgan the other 2/3 of estate.
Executors: Sister Mary Morgan and friend Samuel Howell.
Wit: Thomas Pedrick, Elisha Price.

PRICE, THOMAS. East Bradford. Husbandman.
October 6, 1755. December 9, 1756. D. 67.
All real and personal estate to be sold and provision made for wife, not named, during life, after her decease to Sarah, daughter of Joseph Burgoin £5 and to Joseph, Tamer, James, Susanna and John, other children of Joseph Burgoin £5 each. To Alice and Sarah, daughters of Thomas Thornborough £5 each. To Hannah and Sarah, daughters of son John £5 each. To Hannah

Jefferis, my housekeeper, £5.
Executors: Son in law Thomas Thornborough and friend Benjamin Hawley.
Witnesses: Robert Johnson, Cathrine Johnson, Dorcas Few.

MINSHALL, SARAH, widow. Middletown.
12/20/1748. January 11, 1757. D. 68.
To son Moses Minshall £20. To daughter Sarah, wife of Griffith Minshall £5. Remainder to my 4 children, viz., Thomas, John, Moses and Sarah in equal shares.
Executors: Son John Minshall and son in law Griffith Minshall.
Wit: Aaron Minshall, George Turner.

WOODWARD, GEORGE. Newtown.
12/13/1756. January 20, 1757. D. 69.
To sister Jane Woodward my plantation I now live on as it was given me by my father, subject to interest of my mother in law, Elizabeth Woodward. To sisters Margaret, Abigail and Hannah £5 each. To cousin Edward Woodward silver watch. To Nathan Vernon, sister Abigail's son £5. To John Bradley, my servant boy, £5 at 21. Test signed.
Executors: Sister Jane Woodward and friend William Lewis.
Wit: Richard Fawkes, Martha Bittle, George Smedley, Jr.

BEZER, RICHARD. Chichester. Yeoman.
January 31, 1757. February 7, 1757. D. 71.
To Jacob, son of Nathaniel Lamplugh deceased, £5. To William, son of Jacob Lamplugh deceased £80 and household goods. To Samuel, son of Jacob Lamplugh £30. To John, son of Nathaniel Lamplugh £40 and to the 3 daughters of said Nathaniel, viz., Mary, Susanna and Martha £20 to be divided. To the 2 sons and 2 daughters of Tobias Hendricks, late of York County deceased, £100 to be divided. To Thomas and Isaac, the 2 eldest sons of Thomas Hollingsworth of Christiana Hundred, deceased, £50 each and to his 2 youngest sons £40 each and to Judith his daughter £40. To Abigail, widow of Nathaniel Lamplugh, and her son William, Mary, widow of Jacob Lamplugh, and her youngest son John 1 shilling each. To John and William, sons of Edward Bezer £20 each. To Ruth, widow of George Chandler, and her daughter Ruth £15 to be divided. To Friends of Chichester Meeting £5. To William, son of Jacob Lamplugh, the messuage whereon I live. Remainder of real estate to be sold.
Executors: Cousin Judith Hollingsworth and her sons Thomas and Isaac.
Letters to Thomas and Isaac, the mother renouncing.
Wit: John Cloud, John Hewes, John Power.

LLOYD, WALTER. Willistown.
February 6, 1757. February 22, 1757. D. 74.
To daughter Margaret Meredith £5. To William and Jonathan Bowen, children of my step daughter Mary Bowen 5 shillings each. To John Bowen, son of step daughter in law Anne Bowen 5 shillings. To my neighbour Susanna Phillips 10 shillings. To step sons in law William and Jonathan Evans, sons of my wife Anne, sheep. to step daughter in law, the wife of Ezekiel Bowen, mare and colt.

Test signed.
Executors: Friends Lewis Rees and Thomas Lloyd.
Wit: James Lloyd, Thomas Jones.

O'SKILLEN, MORRIS. Pikeland.
August 15, 1755. February 24, 1757. D. 75.
To wife, not named, 1/3 of clear estate. Remainder divided among children now living and one yet unborn. Test signed.
Executors: Wife Hannah, Bartholomew Tool and Samuel Lightfoot. Letters to the widow and Tool, Lightfoot renouncing.
Wit: John Kissick, Samuel Lightfoot, Jr.

DAVIS, MARY, widow. Charlestown.
September 29, 1753. March 9, 1757. D. 76.
To son John Davis 5 shillings. To son Thomas Davis £6. To Jane, wife of Thomas David of Charlestown (her daughter) £2.7.6 and to her 7 children, viz., 6 daughters and 1 son £28 to be divided. To grandson Samson Davis £6. To great grandson Abner Davis £3. To Sarah and Jacob, children of John Morgan £1. Remainder to son John Davis, also Executor.
Wit: George George, Susanna Oneal, James Davis.

EDMESTON, JAMES. West Nottingham.
September 12, 1753. March 16, 1757. D. 77.
Provides for wife Margaret. To daughter Elizabeth Edmeston £100 and goods to value of £40 when 20. To sons William and John all lands and saw mill to be divided when of age. (Appears to have been other daughters who are not named.) Test died before will was signed.
Executors: Wife Margaret and son William
Wit: Abraham Scott, Robert Moore.
* Mentions brother Hugh.

RAPSON, HENRY.
November 8, 1756. Chester.
Adm. to William Swaffer.

BENNING, SAMUEL.
November 23, 1756. Oxford.
Adm. to Edward Latimore.

PETERSON, JONAS.
November 27, 1756. Darby.
Adm. to Susanna Peterson
& George Grantum.

MORGAN, THOMAS.
December 22, 1756. Chester.
Adm. to Joseph Ashbridge &
John Taylor.

GILPIN, HANNAH.
January 19, 1757. Birmingham.
Adm. to George Gilpin.

HOWELL, JAMES.
February 25, 1757.
Adm. to Samuel Landers.

COLLIER, ISAAC.
March 3, 1757. Darby.
Adm. to Ruth & Isaac
Collier.

HOLLAND, JOHN, SR.
March 15, 1757. Whiteland.
Adm. to John Holland & John
Bowen.

HOLLINGSWORTH, VALENTINE. Kennett.
November 30, 1749. March 25, 1757. D. 80.
To son James the plantation I now live on, also a lott on

Brandywine Creek. To granddaughter Betty Hollingsworth £5 and to granddaughter Ann Hollingsworth £5 at 18. To granddaughters Sarah and Mary Harlan £5 at 18. To grandchildren Betty and Aaron Harlan £5 each at 21 and 18. To granddaughter Sarah Hollingsworth £5 at 18. To son Valentine 5 shillings. To daughter Rachel Hope 5 shillings and to the child she is now pregnant with 5 shillings when 21. To daughters Elizabeth and Sarah Harlan 5 shillings each. Remainder to son James, also Executor. Test signed.
Wit: Enoch Hollingsworth, John Heald, Henry Harvey.

VERNON, ISAAC. West Bradford. Yeoman.
4/8/1756. May 12, 1757. D. 81.
To sons Isaac and Nehemiah, daughters Susanna, wife of Henry Jackson, Rachel, late wife of Felix Fitzsimmons, Hannah, wife of Joseph Snargrass, Lydia, wife of James Walter, and Priscilla, wife of James Stephens 5 shillings each. To wife Mary 2 lotts of land in Wilmington, also about 10 acres of land in Blockley Township, Philadelphia County, and all personal estate for maintenance of youngest daughter Ruth Vernon during life.
Executors: Wife Mary and son Isaac.
Wit: John Battin, Hannah Wood, Richard Vernon.

MEARS, JAMES. New London. Farmer.
January 9, 1756. November 20, 1756. June 1, 1757. D. 82.
To wife Martha 1/3 of all estate. To son James the plantation bought of Roger Cook. To 3 daughters, Susanna, Mary and Hannah £20 each. To daughters Elizabeth Allison and Martha Crawford, one Celigo gown each. To son Samuel the plantation on which I live and remainder of personal estate.
Executors: Wife Martha and son Samuel.
Letters to son, the widow being deceased.
Wit: Josias Emmit, Abraham Emmit, Jr. (June 1, 1757), Abraham Emmit (Nov. 20, 1756).

RICH, JOSEPH.
4/28/1757. August 6, 1757. D. 84.
To son Joseph the 100 acres off my plantation which I formerly gave him. To son John the remainder of plantation. To Martha, wife of Tobias Lang 5 shillings. Remainder equally divided among my 13 grandchildren, viz., Elizabeth and Anne, children of son Peter deceased; Mary, Elizabeth, John and Sarah Rich, children of son John; Martha, Mary, Samuel, Sarah, Rachel, Hannah and Stephen Rich, children of son Joseph.
Executor: Joshua Brown Sr.
Letters to John and Joseph Rich, executor named renouncing.
Wit: William Glasgow, Robert Starret, John Gantril.

PATTERSON, ARTHUR. East Caln.
May 21, 1757. August 12, 1757. D. 85.
Provides for wife Charity including profits of real estate for maintaining and educating children. Remainder to 2 daughters, Mary and Isabella.
Executor: Friend John Culbertson.
Wit: William Sturgeon, Rachel McLean.

HIBBERD, DANIEL.
March 25, 1757. Darby.
Adm. to John Pearson who m.
Rachel Hibberd of Blockley by
N.J. license dated July 9 or
30th? 1735. Aaron Hibberd
was a bondsman.

BOON, SAMUEL.
April 6, 1757. Darby.
Adm. to Mary Boon &
William Donaldson.

SHARPLESS, JOSEPH.
May 19, 1757. Middletown.
Adm. to Joseph Chamberlin.

SINKLER, WILLIAM.
May 24, 1757. West Caln.
Adm. to John & George
Sinkler.

DICKIE, JOHN.
June 1, 1757. W. Nantmeal.
Adm. to James McCoskry.

RAMBO, MOSES.
August 2, 1757. Darby.
Adm. to William Donaldson &
Henry Fisher.

DAVIS, BETHELL.
August 2, 1757. Chester.
Adm. to Benjamin Davis.

BEATON, SAMUEL.
August 22, 1757. Pikeland.
Adm. to John Walker during
minority of the heirs.

PENNELL, WILLIAM. Chester Borough. Yeoman.
12/20/1756. Codicil 7/5/1757. September 9, 1757. D. 86.
Provides for wife Mary. To son Robert part of my land in
Middletown adjoining his deeded land. To son William the
remainder of said land in Middletown. To sons James, Robert and
William the house I now live in and land belonging in trust for
use of son Samuel during life and after his death to his
children. To daughter Hannah Ellis £25 in trust during her life
and at her decease to her son Jacob Halcombe. To daughter Ann
Edge £50 and to her 4 children, viz., Mary, John, Sarah and Ann
£1 each. To my daughter in law Mary, now wife of John Lea 5
shillings and to her 4 children, viz., Abigail, Joseph, John and
Mary £1 each. To grandson William, son of James Pennell, lot of
land in Wilmington. To my grandchildren Hamath, Edith, Rebecca,
James, Thomas, Ruth, Nathan and Timothy, children of son James £1
each. To grandchildren Mary, Joseph, Thomas, Susanna and
William, the children of son Robert, £1. To grandchildren
Abraham and Robert, the children of son William, £1. To
granddaughter Elizabeth, daughter of son Samuel, £1. To my
daughters in law Jemima, Hannah, Mary and Rachel 5 shillings
each.
Executors: Sons, James, Robert and William.
Wit: Thomas Cumings, John Lea, H. H. Graham.

LEWIS, LEWIS. Newtown. Yeoman.
2/18/1747. September 15, 1757. D. 89.
To son Lewis my plantation where I now live in Newtown containing
320 acres. To grandsons Phinehas and Gabriel, sons of son Jabez,
a tract of land as described containing 54 acres, son Jabez to
have the profits until sons are 21. To sons Phinehas and David 5
shillings each. To daughters Ann Massey and Lydia Garrett 5
shillings each. To grandchildren, viz., the children of John
Hibberd and daughter Deborah deceased, Abraham, Phinehas, Samuel,

John and Ann 5 shillings each. To Friends of Newtown Meeting 50
shillings for use of poor. Remainder of personal estate to
daughter Agnes Lewis. To daughters Mary Roberts and Elizabeth
Evans 5 shillings each.
Executor: Son Lewis.
Trustees: Sons Phinehas and David and kinsman Nathan Lewis.
Wit: William Lewis, John West, Richard Jones.

WILLSON, JOHN.
July 9, 1757. September 30, 1757. D. 90.
Devises his tract of land in Middletown Township, Cumberland
County to who ever of my brothers or sisters shall come first
from Ireland to take it.
Executor: Daniel Henderson of Sadsbury.
Wit: William Henderson, Richard Nicholson, Joseph Houston.

CHAPMAN, GEORGE. Chichester.
September 10, 1757. October 1, 1757. D. 91.
To wife Mary 1/3 of all estate. To son Gilley Chapman all
remainder of estate real and personal and if he dies before he is
21, £10 to be given to Lower Chichester Church and remainder on
wife's decease to brother and sisters children, viz., Jean,
George, John, Joseph, Thomas and William Chapman, deceased
brother William's children, and Thomas, Elizabeth (Lemon or
Pearass), Mary and William Lemon, my sister Lucy's children.
Executors: Wife Mary and Allen Robinett, Jr.
Wit: Allen Robinett, Sr., William Colgan, Benton Davis.

MC CADDON, RICHARD. Easttown.
August 8, 1757. October 1, 1757. D. 93.
To wife Ann £30. To daughters Elizabeth, Margaret and Mary £30
each at 18 or marriage. To son John £30 with interest for 6
years at 21. Remainder equally to wife and children.
Executors: Wife Ann and friend Isaac Wayne.
Wit: Thomas Massey, Isaac Massey.

DARLINTON, WILLIAM. West Nantmeal.
September 7, 1757. October 6, 1757. D. 94.
To wife Mary and sons Joseph and Robert all estate real and
personal except following legacies: To son John £300. To son
Meredith £300. To son William £20 if he ever comes personally to
demand it. Test signed.
Executors: Wife Mary and son Meredith.
Wit: James Culbertson, Joseph Park, Robert Brown.

WHITE, THOMAS.
August 16, 1757. No date. October 10, 1757. D. 95.
Matthew White to have £30. Son Robert to have £30 and Thomas £5,
the rest he allows to his wife and when she dies he allows her
not to forget Marget there is £10 more to be given to Matthew
which makes he part £40. Test signed.
Letters to Margaret White, Executrix, by implication.

REGESTER, JOHN.
August 25, 1757. U. Providence.
Adm. to Hannah Regester.

TEMPLETON, MATTHEW.
August 30, 1757.
Marlborough. Adm. to Jane Templeton.

LEWIS, WILLIAM.
August 30, 1757. Newtown.
Adm. to Susanna & William
Lewis.

HOWELL, ELIZABETH.
October 1, 1757. Easttown.
Adm. to David Howell.

TASSEY, MARY.
October 21, 1757. Marple.
Adm. to Alexander Tassey.

STEEL, ANNE.
October 1, 1757. Darby.
Adm. to James Steel.

READ, GEORGE.
October 1, 1757. E.
Adm. to Thomas Read.

LEWIS, JABEZ.
October 1, 1757. Newtown.
Adm. to Hannah Lewis.

BROWN, MARTHA.
Sept. 1, 1757. W. Nantmeal.
Adm. to Charles Brown.

CALDWELL, JOHN.
Sept. 27, 1757. Londonderry.
Adm. to Priscilla & Joseph
Caldwell.

HOWELL, WILLIAM. Chichester.
October 15, 1757. December 15, 1757. D. 95.
Provides for wife Hannah. To son Thomas the plantation where I
live in Chichester as described, he paying to daughters Mary and
Martha and the child my wife is now big with £50 to be divided at
21 and to daughter Sarah £50 at 21. To daughter Sarah that part
of my land leased to John Power as described. To daughters Mary
and Martha and the child unborn remainder of land. Mentions
having sold land to Thomas Parvin, John Rawson and Benjamin
Howell, but not conveyed the same.
Executors: Brother Samuel Howell of Philadelphia and John Power.
Wit: John Kerlin, John Pedrick, John Dutton.

IRWIN, THOMAS. East Nottingham. Yeoman.
September 13, 1756. December 22, 1757. D. 98.
To mother Mary Irwin my house and plantation her life time, after
her decease to brothers Samuel and William Irwin, to sister
Martha's children John, Thomas and Jean Lapsly £10 each at
interest till they come of age. To brother William Lapsly and
sister Martha Lapsly 5 shillings each.
Executors: Mother Mary and brother Samuel.
Wit: John White, Robert Macky.

CLAYTON, WILLIAM. Chichester. Yeoman.
October 28, 1757. January 9, 1758. D. 99.
To daughter Patience, wife of Henry Grubb £5. To children David,
Mary Carter, Lydia, wife of Abraham Carter and Prudence, wife of
John Ford 1 shilling each. To grandchildren, viz., Hannah,
Sarah, Margaret and William, children of son William deceased,
and Mary, Prudence, Jonathan and Ann, children of daughter Sarah,
late wife of John Phipps 1 shilling each when 21. Remainder to
wife Mary, who is Executrix.
Wit: William Linsey, John Power.

WRIGHT, WILLIAM.
October 4, 1757. January 10, 1758. D. 100.
Son William, his choice of the places in Carolina, James' excepted. To son James the place he now lives on. Son George next choice and Moses the other. The plantation in Caln and all movables to be sold and proceeds as follows to wife, not named, £50. To daughter Ann £50 and remainder to 4 sons.
Executors: Wife Hannah and son William.
Wit: Alexander Rogers, William Clingan, John Wall.

STRODE, GEORGE. East Bradford. Yeoman.
Being antient. May 9, 1757. January 16, 1758. D. 101.
To son Williams' 2 children, Richard and William £20 each at 14. To daughter in law Deborah Strode my negro girl, Hannah, during widowhood, afterward to be sold for benefit of her 2 children. To son George all other estate real and personal. Test signed.
Executor: Son George.
Wit: Thomas Douglass, Joshua Lewis, Thomas Curry.

REES, JAMES. Uwchlan. Yeoman.
April 17, 1752. January 17, 1758. D. 102.
Provides for wife Jane including that part of lands now leased to Thomas Marten during life and after her decease to daughter Elizabeth, wife of Daniel John of Uwchlan. Also all other real estate during life and then to her son James John. To Friends of Uwchlan Meeting £5. Discharges stepson John Roberts from all debts due from him. To daughter Elinor, wife of Thomas Evans, household goods after wife's decease and all other personal estate.
Executors: Daughters Elizabeth John and Elinor Evans.
Wit: Awbrey Roberts, Thomas Martin, Morris Rees.

CARSON, WILLIAM.
October 21, 1757. Ridley.
Adm. to John Caldwell.

COWPLAND, CALEB.
November 2, 1757. Chester.
Adm. to Sarah Cowpland.

DONALDSON, WILLIAM.
October 31, 1757. Darby.
Adm. to Margaret & Arthur Donaldson.

ROWAN, WILLIAM.
November 3, 1757. New Garden.
Adm. to Elizabeth & William Rowan. Sureties Jacob John and Joseph Fredd £500.

SCOTT, THOMAS.
October 31, 1757. E. Nottingham.
Adm. to Jane & John Scott.

WORRALL, JOHN.
November 5, 1757. Middletown.
Adm. to Hannah & John Worrall.

DENNIS, JOHN. Uwchlan.
January 23, 1758. February 8, 1758. D. 104.
(Nuncupative will). To wife £40 out of the hundred and daughter to have the remainder, who were not named.
Executors: Wife Jane and her father Samuel Culbertson.
Wit: Noble Butler, Humphrey Lloyd.

SHARP, ALEXANDER. Londongrove.
January 30, 1758. February 10, 1758. D. 104.

To my brother Andrew Sharp, son of Alexander Sharp of the Parish of Romone, County Antrim, Ireland, all my estate and in case he be dead, I leave it to my half brother Edward Sharp.
Executor: William Hanna.
Overseer: John Ross.
Wit: David Wiley, Jonathan Lindly, Samuel Young.

HAYES, JAMES. East Fallowfield.
November 26, 1757. March 1, 1758. D. 105.
Provides for wife Mary, she and son Nathan to maintain and school children till they are 16. To son Nathan the plantation whereon I dwell lying on Brandywine Creek, 1/2 at 21 and remainder at wife's decease. To son Henry the plantation on Doe Run formerly of William Rankin at 21. To my 4 daughters, viz., Sarah, Rachel, Hannah and Lydia £100 each at 21. To sister Ruth Heaney £10.
Executors: Wife Mary and son Nathan.
Wit: Joseph Davis, Joseph Fleming, Samuel Hayes.

PENNELL, SAMUEL.
November 9, 1757.
Chester.
Adm. to Rachel Pennell.

WELCH, WILLIAM.
November 29, 1757. Ridley.
Adm. to Robert & William Caldwell.

HARLAN, MICHAEL.
November 30, 1757. Londongrove.
Adm. to David Harlan.

PEARSOLL, JOHN.
December 13, 1757.
Adm. to Sarah Pearsoll.

LADELY, MARGARET alias Wallace.
January 25, 1758. L. Britain.
Adm. to William Alexander.

MERCER, THOMAS.
Jan. 28, 1758. Westtown.
Adm. to Danl. & Thos. Mercer.

CONNELL, GEORGE.
Feb. 27, 1758. Chichester.
Adm. to Elizabeth Connell.

SITTON, MATTHEW.
March 3, 1758. E. Nottingham.
Adm. to Job Ruston.

WHITE, JOHN. East Nottingham.
February 15, 1758. March 9, 1758.
To daughter Mary £50. To William Shields that is married to my daughter Mary, 1 shilling. To son Patrick Carson 1/2 of plantation I now live upon, the East end of it. To daughter Jean Carson chest of drawers. To daughter Agnes White the other half of plantation and furniture. To son Robert Croswell £50. To granddaughter Ester Carson £10. To granddaughter Elizabeth Shields £5.
Executors: Nephew John White of Oxford and son Patrick Carson.
Wit: Andrew Buyers, Samuel Buyers.

GLEAVE, ELIZABETH, widow. East Marlborough.
1/28/1758. March 21, 1758.
To son John Eachus 5 shillings. To son William Eachus 10 shillings. To son Robert Eachus 10 shillings. To son Enoch Eachus £5. To daughter Elizabeth Taylor £5. To daughter Alice Ogden £5. To son Daniel Eachus my riding mare. To daughter Ann Wickersham wearing apparel. Remainder equally divided between

son Daniel and Son in law James Wickersham, also Executors.
Wit: Thomas Carleton, Daniel Baily, Isaac Baily.

MC MICHAEL, CHARLES. Upper Providence.
1/31/1758. March 21, 1758.
All lands in Cumberland County to 6 children, viz., Walter, Elizabeth, Robert, Martha, Jane and Rebecca. To brother Walter silver sleeve buttons. To cousin Martha Miller same. Provides for wife Rebecca.
Executors: Wife and friend Hugh Trimble.
Wit: George Miller, Charles Linn, Samuel McClelan.

BUNTING, SAMUEL. Darby.
8/5/1756. March 21, 1758.
Provides for wife Sarah including "one large Bible given her by her Uncle Michael Blunston." To daughter Sarah Bartram £5. To granddaughter Mary Goforth £5 at 21. To daughters Martha and Hannah Bunting £100 each at 21. To son Josiah the West end of plantation on which I now dwell with buildings, also meadow by Darby Creek. To son Samuel, East end of plantation containing 50 acres, also one acre bounded by the High Street in Darby and mill race. To each of my daughters a Bible. To son Josiah all remainder of personal estate.
Executors: Wife Sarah and son Josiah.
Wit: John Bartram, Abraham Musgrave, John Moore.

SMEDLEY, THOMAS. Willistown.
7/30/1757. March 25, 1758.
Provides for wife Sarah. To eldest son Francis the plantation whereon he now lives in Township of Willistown containing 223 acres and to his heirs lawfully begotten to the third generation. To son John plantation whereon I now live containing 400 acres and to his heirs to the third generation, also stock and farming implements. To son Thomas plantation where he now lives purchased of Samuel Jobson containing 253 acres, also tract of 22 acres adjoining. To son George tract of land where he now lives in Willistown containing 255 acres. To daughter Sarah, wife of John Minshall £60. To grandson Abiah Taylor 5 acres of land in Whiteland Township, part of 25 acres purchased of William Kinnison, also £20 at 21. Mentions granddaughter Mary Minshall. Remainder to 4 sons and son in law.
Executors: Wife and 4 sons.
Letters to the sons.
Wit: Aaron Ashbridge, William Garrett, Richard Jones.

WILLIAMS, JOSEPH. Newtown.
4/2/1758. April 22, 1758.
All estate to wife Margaret during life except wearing apparel to friend Andrew Girey. Remainder after wife's decease to Elizabeth, daughter of John Jones of Newtown.
Executors: David Reece and William Hunter.
Wit: Edward Williams, John Smith.

COWPLAND, SARAH. Chester Borough.
2/11/1758. April 29, 1758.

To daughter Jane, wife of Thomas Parke £50. To son Caleb
Cowpland £300. To son Jonathan 5 shillings. Wearing apparel to
daughters Abigail Edge, Jane Parke and Agnes Lownes. All
remainder to daughter Agnes, wife of John Lownes.
Executor: Son in law Thomas Parke.
Wit: Caleb Stackhous, Rachel Lewis, Richard Jones.

HASTINGS, HENRY. West Bradford.
April 9, 1758. May 26, 1758.
Provides for wife Elizabeth. To daughter Rebecca 5 shillings and
privilege to remain in the house she now occupies. Refers to her
husband who is not named. To daughter Elizabeth 5 shillings. To
son Henry and daughters Hannah and Phebe 5 shillings each. All
remainder to son James on condition that "he doth marriage well."
Executors: Wife and Joseph Buffington of East Bradford.
Witnesses: George Martin, William Richardson, James Milleson.

HAYES, STEPHEN.
March 20, 1758. E. Fallowfield.
Adm. to Robert Lewis.

COWPLAND, CALEB.
April 4, 1758. Chester.
Adm. to Jonathan Cowpland.

YARNALL, JOSEPH.
April 15, 1758. Springfield.
Adm. to Mary & Daniel Yarnall.

CORREY, SAMUEL.
April 21, 1758. New London.
Adm. to John & Samuel Correy.

ROGERS, THOMAS.
April 22, 1758. W. Caln.
Adm. to Alexander Rogers.

TAYLOR, JOHN.
May 3, 1758. Thornbury.
Adm. to Edward Brinton &
John Hannum.

COWAN, ANNE.
May 30, 1758. Sadsbury.
Adm. to Henry Renick &
Catherine Renick.

PYLE, ROBERT. East Marlborough.
3/22/1758. June 12, 1758.
Estate divided between wife Deborah and daughter Ruth Pyle when
daughter arrives at age of 18 years.
Executors: Wife Deborah and neighbor Thomas Woodward.
Witnesses: Robert Johnson, Olive Leonard.

AILES, STEPHEN. Londongrove.
11/6/755. Codicil 1/20/1758. June 12, 1758.
To grandson William Ailes plantation I live on containing 200
acres, in trust, proceeds to be divided among the 4 children of
son William deceased, grandson William to have double what the
daughters have and the 5 children of son Stephen deceased,
grandsons Stephen and Amos to have double what the daughters
have. Daughter in law Ann, widow of son Stephen to have use of
plantation during her widowhood. To daughter Mary's 3 children,
viz., Mary, Hannah and Rebecca £5 to be divided. To
granddaughter Ruth Underwood £5.
Executors: Daughter in law Ann Ailes and relatives John and
Joshua Pusey.
Codicil mentions granddaughter Hannah Ailes. Letters to John.
Witnesses: Joshua Pusey, John Allen, William Jackson, Isaac

Jackson.

WOODROW, ISAAC. Fallowfield.
10/11/1756. June 22, 1758.
Provides for wife Mary. Estate to be sold when youngest child is 5 years old and proceeds divided among children who are not named except the 2 following. To son Simon narrow end of my lot in Burlington, New Jersey. To son Joseph broad end of same lot.
Executors: John Jackson and Thomas Woodward.
Witnesses: Moses Pyle, Thomas Pusey, Elizabeth Woodward.

COWAN, ESTHER.
May 30, 1758. Sadsbury.
Adm. to Henry Renick & Catherine Renick.

BROWN, THOMAS.
May 30, 1758. W. Caln.
Adm. to William Hamilton.

SEVILL, JAMES.
June 6, 1758. Darby.
Adm. to Alice Sevill & Abram Musgrave.

MILLER, JAMES.
June 12, 1758. New Garden.
Adm. to Rebecca Miller.

SAMUEL, JOHN.
August 4, 1758. Radnor.
Adm. to Hugh Samuel.

RICE, NICHOLAS.
August 15, 1758. Ridley.
Adm. to Daniel Rice.

MARIS, JOSEPH. Springfield.
8/28/1758. September 21, 1758.
To wife all estate until children attain age of 21 years. To son Jesse 200 acres in Springfield "being the old place where my father formerly dwelt." To 2 daughters Mary and Elizabeth all the remainder of land in Chester County. To son Samuel messuage and lot of land in Wilmington, Delaware. Executors to sell tract of land in Lancaster County, proceeds to son Samuel.
Executors: Wife Ann and William Fell of Springfield.
Witnesses: Matthew Hall, Seth Pancoast, James Rhoads.

ALLEN, JOHN. West Nottingham.
2/18/1758. October 2, 1758.
Provides for wise Ester. To son John plantation in West Nottingham and my part of the lot in Charlestown. To son Samuel place bought of Barbary Moobery where he now lives, also plantation bought of John Woodrof where William Armour now lives. To 2 sons plantation bought of John Gollifer to be divided by William Allen and John Gartril. To son James plantation whereon I now live when he comes of age. To my 3 sons John, Samuel and James all my land in York County. To daughter Tamer Coulson £10. To daughter Patience £30. Remainder equally divided among my 5 children. Mentions brother William Allen.
Executors: Wife Ester and son John.
Witnesses: Hannah Boon, John Gartril, William Allen.

THOMPSON, MORDECAI.
August 28, 1758. Ridley.
Adm. to Hannah Thompson.

CAM, HENRY.
October 2, 1758. Newtown.
Adm. to Margaret Cam.

SMITH, JOHN.
August 30, 1758. W. Nantmeal.
Adm. to James Scott.

MC KOWN, RICHARD.
August 31, 1758. W. Fallowfield.
Adm. to David Brookes.

DOUGHERTY, EDMUND.
October 11, 1758. London Britain.
Adm. to Mary Dougherty & Denis Sullivan.

VERNON, ANNE. Thornbury.
4/10/1754. October 2, 1758.
To daughter Hannah, wife of John Woodward of Thornbury £10. To daughter Sarah, wife of Vincent Bonsall of Wilmington £10. To grandson Jacob Brinton £5 at 21. To grandson Joshua Marshall £5 at 21. To daughter Mary, wife of Richard Parks plantation whereon I now dwell containing 150 acres (which my deceased husband Jacob Vernon devised to me), also all remains of estate.
Executors: Caleb Peirce and son in law Richard Parks.
Letter to Parks.
Witnesses: Joseph Gilpin, Mary Gilpin, John Pierce.

HARRY, WILLIAM. East Marlborough.
September 15, 1758. October 2, 1758.
Provides for wife Ester and "helpless daughter, Olive." To son William plantation I now live on containing 170 acres subject to legacies. To sons Amos, Hugh and Silas £5 each. To daughter Ester £20. To daughter Abigail Mendenhall 20 shillings. To daughter Dina £5. To daughter Olive 5 shillings. Son Silas to be bound an apprentice at 17.
Executor: Son William and nephew Evan Harry to be his assistant.
Witnesses: Richard Thatcher, Jeremiah Cloud.

LEVIS, SAMUEL. Springfield.
3/19/1758. October 6, 1758.
Provides for wife Hannah. To son John watch and smith tools and use of a field now in his possession during the life of his Aunt Elizabeth Shipley. To son Joseph 5 shillings having given him sufficient in my lifetime. To son Samuel plantation whereon I dwell together with that part now in the tenure of Jonathan Willis, also all remainder of personal estate.
Executors: Sons John and Samuel.
Witnesses: John Hall, George Hall, Mary Hall.

GAY, MATTHEW. Concord.
August 23, 1758. October 9, 1758.
To wife Margaret 1/3 of all estate. To son John 2/3 of estate except a horse which I bequeath to my stepson Alexander McConnell and cow to stepdaughter Jean McConnell.
Executrix: Wife.
Witnesses: Alexander Withrow, Ann Gregg.

MC LAUGHLIN, MICHAEL. East Nottingham.
June 2, 1757. October 2, 1758.
To eldest son William all real estate. To Walter Buchanon 5 shillings. To second son John £20. To 3rd son James £20. To

youngest daughter Ann McLaughlin £30.
Executors: Son William and Moses Ross.
Witnesses: James Petterson, John Hutchison.

LINN, MARGARET.
October 21, 1758. Bethel.
Adm. to Hugh Linn, Jr.

WAY, BENJAMIN. Birmingham.
March 27, 1758. October 25, 1758.
Provides for wife Mary. To eldest son Benjamin plantation in Kennett when he is 21 paying to his brother Isaac £100 when he is 21. Lands in New Castle County to be sold and proceeds to son Isaac. Reversionary legacies to wife's daughter Hannah Gilpin and Benjamin Way son of brother John.
Executors: Wife Mary and her brother Samuel Painter.
Letters to Mary Way.
Witnesses: James Dilworth, Richard Eavenson, Titus Bennett, Robert Chamberlin.

ELLIOTT, JOHN. West Nantmeal.
September 15, 1758. October 30, 1758.
Provides for wife Anne all estate during widowhood for maintaining of 3 children, Robert, Margaret and John. To daughter Margaret £50 at 18. Remainder between two sons.
Executors: Wife Anne, Daniel Henderson and Frances McConnell.
Letters to wife, the others renouncing.
Witnesses: Daniel Shields, John Culbertson.

CALDWELL, HENRY. Newtown.
September 14, 1758. November 1, 1758.
Provides for wife Elizabeth. To son in law James McClelan and his wife Martha all real estate subject to wife's life interest. At her decease to be divided among their children, his eldest son Joseph to have a double share. To congregation at Middletown £5.
Executors: Wife and James McClellan.
Witnesses: William Lindsay, Samuel McClelan.

MITCHELL, WILLIAM. Sadsbury.
October 2, 1758. November 6, 1758.
Provides for wife not named. To only son John now a captive with the French the remainder of estate with reversion in case he dies without issue as follows, real estate being sold. To my sister Jean's grandson Mitchell Black £15 and to her granddaughter Margaret Leckey £15. To George son of Joseph Park £15. To John Davidson Jr. £15. To Agnes Mitchell, widow of James Henry £15. To Elizabeth, widow of George Mitchell £15. To Margery, widow of Joseph Mitchell £10. To William, son of William Mitchell £15. To brother Samuel's grandson William £10. To brother in law William Waddel's children £10. To wife's sister's daughter, Margaret Johnston a cow. To Mary Evans now in her servitude to me 2 sheep. Remainder for support of the Gospel in this place.
Executors: Friends Mathew Shields and Joseph Park.
Witnesses: Andrew Sterling, Thomas Ker.

HUMPHREY, SOLOMON. Darby.
September 4, 1758. November 9, 1758.
Provides for wife Mary. Mentions mother in law Martha Harvey deceased. To son John lot of land in Darby having 50 feet front on Springfield Road at 21. To son Daniel, smith shop and also lot adjoining son John's, also tools. Also devises a lot of land to 4 children, Richard, John, Martha and Mary. All remainder to wife for bringing up children.
Guardians: Brother Edward Humphrey and brother in law William Parker.
Executrix: Wife Mary.
Witnesses: John Rudulph, William Wood.

HIBBERD, ABRAHAM.
November 27, 1758. Darby.
Adm. to John & Phineas Hibberd.

HATTON, PETER. Concord.
October 27, 1758. November 17, 1758.
To son John, east end of tract of land I now live on containing about 100 acres, also about 2 acres bought of Joseph Gilpin, also stock. To son Peter west end of plantation containing about 84 acres, he paying £10 to my grandchildren, Mary, Amos and Isaac Garrett. To son James tract of land whereon he now lives in Concord containing about 70 acres. To grandson Enoch, son of Isaac Garrett, lot of land in Newport, Newcastle County. To grand-daughter Elizabeth, daughter of James Hatton £5 at 18. Remainder between James and Peter.
Executors: Son Peter and son in law Isaac Garrett.
Overseer: Joseph Gibbons.
Witnesses: Thomas Evan, Benjamin Marshall, Micajah Speakman.

PARKE, THOMAS. East Caln.
10/15/1758. November 28, 1758.
Provides for wife Jane. To son Robert tract of land lying north of this I now live on, he paying to my son Jacob £200 at 21. To 3 daughters, Sarah, Rebecca and Hannah Parke £200 each at 18. To son Thomas all remainder of real estate, viz., the plantation I now live on, paying to my son Jacob £200. To son Jacob £100 at 21. All remainder to wife for bringing up children.
Executors: Wife, son Robert and Robert Valentine.
Letters to Jane Parke and Robert Valentine.
Witnesses: Phineas Lewis, Thomas Pim, Richard Pim.

BUCHANAN, DAVID.
November 28, 1758. Goshen.
Adm. to Elizabeth Buchanan & John Buchanan.

MC CLUGHAN, HUGH.
Nov. 30, 1758. E. Nottingham.
Adm. to Guyan Morrison.

SWAYNE, CALEB.
November 28, 1758. Londongrove.
Adm. to Joshua Swayne.

COLE, WILLIAM. Nottingham.
3/18/1758. July 4, 1758.

Provides for wife Prudence. to son William all title and interest in tract of land and 1/2 part of a grist mill where my dwelling is situated. To daughter Hannah, wife of James Murphy 5 shillings. To daughters Rebecca and Prudence £5 each. To son Ellis and daughter Lydia Coles 5 shillings each. Remainder to William, Rebecca and Prudence.
Executor: Son William.
Copy from the original, proven and recorded in Baltimore County, Maryland.
Witnesses: Joseph Taylor, Jonathan Hanson, Charles Gorsuch.

MERCER, JOSEPH.
December 14, 1758. E. Marlborough.
Adm. to Edward Swayne.

JONES, CADWALLADER. Uwchlan.
7/11/1758. November 30, 1758.
To son Evan Jones £80. To daughter Sarah, wife of Thomas Martin £20. To daughter Rebecca, wife of John Thomas £20. To my sister Given John £1. To sister Elizabeth Cater £1. To grandson Hugh Pugh 10 shillings and to all other living grandchildren 5 shillings each. All remaining real and personal to son Cadwallader, also Executor.
Witnesses: Samuel Lightfoot, Moses Cadwallader, John McCord.

YARNALL, PHILIP. Edgmont.
11/7/1758. December 6, 1758.
Provides for wife Mary. To son Philip 74 3/4 acres of land on the eastwardly side of my land. To son David plantation bought of George Hall containing 165 acres in Kennett paying to my executors £150. To son Abraham 5 shillings. To daughter Jane Yarnall £50. To daughter Elizabeth £50. To daughters Esther, Dorothy and Mary £50 each. To grandson Philip Bonsall £10 at 21. Remainder equally divided.
Executors: Wife Mary and son Philip.
Witnesses: Josiah Lewis, Moses Meredith.

PEDRICK, JOHN. Lower Chichester.
September 27, 1758. December 14, 1758.
Provides for wife Rachel. All remainder of estate real and personal to 3 children, John, Adam and Rachel Pedrick.
Executrix: Wife Rachel.
Witnesses: Mary Moulder, Thomas Pedrick, James Allen.

FAWKES, JOHN.
December 19, 1758. Newtown.
Adm. to Richard Fawkes.

STEEL, ANDREW.
January 8, 1759. Goshen.
Adm. to Sarah Steel.

TAYLOR, JOSEPH.
January 5, 1759. West Bradford.
Adm. to Hannah Taylor & Jesse Taylor.

WALTER, LYDIA. Darby.
November 20, 1758. December 21, 1758.
To sister Sarah £10. To sister Esther £10. To brother Abraham

Walter all remainder of estate, also Executor.
Witnesses: Abraham Lewis, Jr., James Maris.

ELLIOTT, PETER. Easttown.
July 26, 1754. December 25, 1758.
Provides for wife Sarah. To son Morris Elliott 5 shillings. To son James all my smith tools. To daughter Rachel Logan £5. To son James plantation containing 200 acres on death of wife.
Executors: Wife and son James res. legatees.
Letters to James.
Witnesses: John Havard, David Havard, John Havard, Jr.

CAMPBELL, CHARLES. New London.
December 9, 1758. December 29, 1758.
To wife Rachel one negro child named Ruth over and above what is mentioned in contract of marriage, also £20. To daughter Martha and son Michael 10 shillings each. To son James house and land in Conogogig, also negro woman Jane. To grandson Charles £10. Remainder to James and William, also Executors.
Witnesses: Alexander Geddes, Alexander McBeath.

CLOUD, ABIGAIL, relict of Mordecai. East Marlborough.
5/12/1757. January 5, 1759.
To son Isaac Baily clock and table. To daughter Abigail Cloud £83.10 at 21. To son Joseph Cloud £83.10 at 21. To daughter Sarah Harlan couch. To my Hannah Harlan all remainder of household goods. To son Abner Cloud colt. To granddaughter Abigail Harlan saddle. To my 3 daughters, viz., Sarah, Hannah and Abigail all wearing apparel.
Executor: Brother Robert Johnson.
Witnesses: William Cloud, Mordecai Cloud, T. Woodward.

KEY, ELIZABETH, widow of Moses. Aston.
10/15/1758. February 3, 1759.
To granddaughter Rebecca Key, daughter of my daughter Ann Key all household goods and £50 at 18. In case she dies before reaching that age, legacy to go to granddaughter Hannah Sharpless, daughter Lete's, grandchildren by Joseph Baker and son Moses. To son Moses bond I hold against him for £10. To granddaughter Mary, wife of Andrew McCoy 20 shillings. To granddaughter Rebecca, wife of Richard Patton 1 shilling. To grandson Allen, son of William Key 5 shillings. To great-granddaughter Lettice, daughter of Joseph Baker deceased 10 shillings. To son in law John Sharpless riding shay.
Executors: Son in law John Sharpless and James Lindsay.
Witnesses: David Johnson, Abraham Martin, John Lindsay.

MITCHELL, ISABELLA. Sadsbury.
October 30, 1758. November 6, 1758.
To Rachel Waddle, my sister's daughter horse and saddle. To John Brouster £2.10. To his wife Ann Brouster alias Erwin wearing apparel. To Mary Evans, my bound servant wearing apparel. To sister's daughter, Margaret Johnson all remainder of things bequeathed me by my husband. Letters to Margaret Johnston.
Witnesses: Andrew Sterling, Dorcas Sterling.

KNOWLES, JOHN.
January 12, 1759. Ridley.
Adm. to John Morton.

DUTTON, JOHN. Chichester. Cordwainer.
February 6, 1759. February 17, 1759.
Authorizes executor to sell tract of land in Chester Township containing about 20 acres. To brother Richard Dutton £5. All remainder to brother David Dutton and sister Sarah Power to be equally divided.
Executor: John Power of Chichester.
John Dutton died on 6th of February 1759 when about to sign the above will as appears by the depositions of William Lamplugh and Barnaby Sweney.

STROUD, JAMES. Chichester.
1/27/1759. February 26, 1759.
Executors to sell tract of land in Whitemarsh, Philadelphia County, to wife Rachel 1/3 of all estate and remainder equally divided between Thomas, Mary and Joseph, my children.
Executors: Wife and son Thomas.
Witnesses: Richard Moore, Benjamin Reynolds, William Linsey.

HEWES, JOHN. Chichester.
February 2, 1759. March 2, 1759.
To wife Mary tenement and tract of land in Chichester during life for maintaining and bringing up my children Christian and Jacob Hewes. Also all that tract of land in Douglass Township, Berks County, containing 200 acres purchased of Thomas Barnard until my children attain the age of 21, with reversion to brother William's son, Aaron Hewes and the sons of brother Samuel Hewes.
Executors: Wife Mary and Richard Dutton.
Witnesses: William Lamplugh, Samuel Lamplugh, John Power.
* Archibald Dick and wife Mary, and Richard Dutton file accounts 1764.

CLENDENIN, THOMAS.
March 5, 1759. E. Nottingham.
Adm. to Rowland Rogers.

KITLER, GEORGE.
March 6, 1759. U. Providence.
Adm. to John Moore.

HOWELL, ISAAC. Lower Chichester.
April 9, 1758. March 10, 1759.
Provides for wife Mary. All remaining real and personal to son Mordecai and a child expected, at age of 21.
Executors: Brother Jacob Howell and John Kerlin.
Witnesses: Benjamin Howell, John Hewes, Thomas Stroud.

TAYLOR SAMUEL. East Bradford.
1/24/1759. March 12, 1759.
Provides for wife Deborah including a certain piece of my plantation in East Bradford during widowhood, beginning at a gate on the southwest side of my barnyard and so bounded by a ditch on the south side and extends to Brandywine Creek and across said Creek and by a straight westerly line to a ditch that leads to

Thomas Worth's line and all the land to the N.W. of the above
mentioned to the land late of John Taylor until it comes to a
lane that leads from the house to the laid out road including an
orchard by the barn. To son Abiah part of my land containing 40
acres and 10 acres woodland. To son Samuel pacing horse. To 4
sons, Samuel, Abraham, John and Isaac all remainder of
plantation. Sons to be kept at school until of age to be put to
trades and division of land to be made when they come to age of
21. Remainder to 4 daughters, Mary, Deborah, Elizabeth and
Rachel at 18. To Mary certain articles that belonged to my
former wife.
Executors: Joseph Matlock of Goshen, and son Abiah.
Witnesses: Thomas Worth, George Carter, Ebenezer Worth.

COOK, JOHN. Londongrove.
12/27/1758. March 15, 1759.
Provides for wife Elinor. To son John £4. To daughter Mary Pyle
£4. To daughter Margaret Johnson £4. To daughter Hannah
Brabston £4. To daughter Phebe Plummer £4. To son Stephen
plantation I now live on and all remainder of personal estate
subject to legacies. Executors: Wife and son Stephen.
Letters to Stephen, the other being absent.
Witnesses: John Pusey, Isaac Jackson, Dinah Cook.

ROBINETT, ALLIN. Lower Chichester.
February 4, 1759. March 15, 1759.
To wife and son Joseph all estate except as follows: To daughter
Prudence £0.2.6. To son Allen £0.2.6. To daughter Rachel
£0.2.6. To son David £0.2.6. To daughter Lydia £0.2.6.
Executrix: Wife Lydia.
Witnesses: Richard Linard, Richard Derrick, Mary Tomlinson.

LEA, JOHN. Chester Borough.
April 7, 1759. May 1, 1759.
To brother Isaac Lea £12 worth of wearing apparel and all the
money he owes me. Executor to sell all real estate. Provides
for wife Mary. To son Thomas £150 at 21. Remainder to 3
children, viz., Hannah, Anne and Thomas Lea as they arrive at 21.
Executrix: Wife Mary.
Witnesses: Edward Russell, John Fairlamb.

WHITEKER, PETER.
March 26, 1759. E. Caln.
Adm. to Mary Whiteker.

JENKIN, JOHN.
April 5, 1759. Uwchlan.
Adm. to William Beale.

HATTON, JOHN.
April 2, 1759. Concord.
Adm. to Elizabeth Hatton.

PORTER, CHARLES.
April 6, 1759. W. Nottingham.
Adm. to Andrew Porter.

EDMONDS, THOMAS.
April 5, 1759. W. Bradford.
Adm. to Thomas Edmonds.

SHEPPARD, WILLIAM. East Nottingham.
1/8/1748/9. May 26, 1759.

Provides for wife Ann. To son Robert the land he now lives on, also wearing apparel and shoemaker tools. To sons William, Samuel and John 5 shillings each. To son James plantation I now live on with all the movables, also Executor.
Witnesses: Thomas Barrett, John Slater.

LAUGHLIN, JAMES. Kennett. Joiner.
March 8, 1759. June 12, 1759.
To wife Elizabeth all personal estate paying legacies. To son William 5 shillings. To son Hugh £5. To daughter Margaret Laughlin £3. To daughters Elizabeth Alford and Mary Passmore all my right of a tract of land bought of Jeremiah Chamberlain on Big Conewago, near Susquehanna containing 197 acres, paying to their mother Elizabeth £15 each.
Executrix: Wife Elizabeth.
Witnesses: James Hollingsworth, Thomas Carleton, Jr.

TOWNSEND, JOHN. Thornbury. Carpenter.
2/12/1759. June 20, 1759.
To wife Deborah use of real estate until twin sons John and James attain the age of 21 when I give the said real estate consisting of plantation of 155 acres in Thornbury to said sons. To daughter Rebecca £30 at 18 and £20 to a possible posthumous child.
Executrix: Wife Deborah.
Witnesses: Thomas Goodwin, Isaac Thomas, Richard Jones.

JONES, JOSEPH.
April 11, 1759. Radnor.
Adm. to John Jones.

CALVERT, DANIEL, SR.
May 1, 1759. Willistown.
Adm. to Daniel Calvert.

BRACKENRIG, DAVID.
April 16, 1759. Londongrove.
Adm. to John Brackenrig.

BOND, RICHARD.
May 26, 1759. U. Providence.
Adm. to Mary Bond.

HENZLEY, CHARLES.
April 21, 1759. Chichester.
Adm. to Jacob Howell.

DANIEL, JAMES. Londongrove.
June 5, 1759. June 26, 1759.
Provides for wife Hannah. To brother Hugh in Ireland £4 and to his children £30 to be divided. To sister Jean Mordoch's children in Ireland, to be divided. To brother John £1 and 10 shillings to each of his children "being 4 by this his last wife." To brother John's son, Samuel £10. To sister Mary £12. To father in law Samuel White £20. To Rev. Mr. John Blair £10. To the Session of Faggs Manor £10. Remainder divided among my brothers and sister Jean's children "at home in Ireland."
Executors: David Ramsey and William Boyd.
Letters to Hannah Daniel, executors named renouncing.
Witnesses: William Corsbye, William Robertson.

SALKELD, DAVID. Chester Township.
April 30, 1759. August 11, 1759.

Provides for wife Sarah including profits of real estate until son William comes of age, when Executor is to sell real estate proceeds to be divided 1/3 to wife and remainder to children to be equally divided, not named.
Executor: Brother John Salkeld.
Witnesses: Robert Russell, E. Price.

RAMSEY, SUSANNA. Sadsbury.
May --, 1759. August 28, 1759.
To nephew John Ramsey in Ireland £20. To niece Margaret, wife of George Brown £30. To nephew Robert Fullerton £20. To niece Agnes, wife of Robert Andrew £20. To my kinsman William McKnight if alive £60. To nephew William Fullerton £20. To my friend Dorcas, wife of Alex Allison £20. All remaining real and personal to nephew Humphrey Fullerton.
Executors: James Boyd and Daniel Henderson.
Witnesses: Daniel Boyd, Mathew Henderson.

ABRAHAM, NOAH.
May 29, 1759. E. Nantmeal.
Adm. to James Abraham.

CANBY, THEOPHILUS.
August 6, 1759. E. Bradford.
Adm. to Hannah Canby.

JACKSON, ANN.
May 30, 1759. E. Marlborough.
Adm. to Jonathan Jackson.

WILLSON, JOHN.
August 16, 1759. Vincent.
Adm. to Mary Willson.

YARNALL, THOMAS. Thornbury.
6/8/1759. September 1, 1759.
Provides for wife Margaret. All estate real and personal to be equally divided among all children when eldest son John arrives at 21. No other named.
Executors: Wife and brother Isaac Yarnall.
Witnesses: Thomas Cheyney, Christian Hill.

ALLEN, JOHN. East Marlborough.
8/30/1759. October 26, 1759.
To mother Esther Allen £40. To sister Tamer Colson £10. To sister Patience Allen £10. To brother James all my lands in York County and in or near Oxford, also my share of a lot in Charlestown paying to sister Patience £40. To Londongrove Meeting £10. To cousin John Woolman £5 and to Elizabeth Woolman £5. To East Nottingham Meeting £10. To uncle Isaac Allen my stone colt and saddle. To Mary Baker Jr. my printed books. Remainder to sister Patience. Letters to William Allen, executors named renouncing.
Executors: Joshua Brown and George Churchman, Jr.
Witnesses: William Swayne, Israel Taylor, Thomas Smith.

MC SWINE, JAMES.
August 29, 1759. New London.
Adm. to James Elder.

WAY, MARY.
September 19, 1759. Kennett.
Adm. to Joseph Pierce.

HAYES, ISAAC.
August 30, 1759. E. Marlborough.
Adm. to Hannah Hayes.

HEALL, THOMAS.
October 8, 1759. Goshen.
Adm. to Jonathan Davies.

ROBINSON, WILLIAM.
September 5, 1759. Haverford.
Adm. to Jane Dougherty.

EVAN, OWEN.
October 10, 1759. Kennett.
Adm. to Samuel Harlan.

JAMESON, DAVID.
September 14, 1759. New London.
Adm. to Evan Morgan.

HAYWOOD, MARY. Concord.
October 6, 1759. November 6, 1759.
To son Andrew McCoy £60. To son Abraham Barnett £60. To son William Barnet £60. To son in law James Wilson 5 shillings and to his wife, my daughter Martha £40, in trust during life of her husband. To son in law John Taylor 5 shillings and to his wife, my daughter Ruth £55 in trust as above. To grandson John, son of Abraham Barnett £10 and colt at 21. Wearing apparel to daughters Martha and Ruth. Remainder divided among the children of son Abraham Barnett at 21.
Executors: Ralph Pyle and Robert Mendenhall.
Witnesses: Peter Hatton, William Cullipher, James Morrison.

JONES, DAVID. Tredyffrin.
September 25, 1759. November 8, 1759.
Provides for wife Joanna. To son William Jones 1/2 of all my real estate in Tredyffrin including the buildings. To son Griffith Jones 1 shilling and 1/4 of all the books. To son Amos £100 and 1/4 of books. To son Levi the remaining 1/2 of my real estate with the new house thereon paying £40 to son Amos. To daughter Hannah Gwyn £20 and also the maintenance of her child since the death of her husband. To daughter Elizabeth Livering £10. To sons William and Levi all remainder of estate.
Executors: Sons Amos and Levi.
Witnesses: John Davis, Isaac Davis, John Johnston.

THORNBOROUGH, ROBERT. West Bradford.
November 4, 1759. November 21, 1759.
To mother Susanna Thornborough 1/3 of real and personal estate. To wife Ruth 1/3 of estate. To children Susanna and Ruth 1/3 of estate.
Executor: William Liggett.
Witnesses: John Smith, Sampson Davis, Daniel Gorman.

GREEN, ABEL, JR.
October 19, 1759. Thornbury.
Londongrove.
Adm. to Edward Green.

DANIEL, JOHN.
November 22, 1759.
Adm. to Isabella Daniel.

COCHRAN, ROBERT.
November 2, 1759. Oxford.
Adm. to Jennett Cochran.

ROSS, JOHN. Oxford.
August 11, 1759. November 27, 1759.
Provides for wife Margaret to have use of homestead formerly belonging to William Peney. To granddaughter Isabel Calbreath

cows and sheep to value of £17.6. All remainder to 2 sons John
and James Ross to be equally divided.
Executors: The said John Ross and Moses Ross.
Witnesses: John Black, Henry McCadden.

WAY, WILLIAM. West Caln.
November 6, 1759. November 29, 1759.
To cousin Robert, son of John Way £10. All remainder to mother
Mary Way including following tracts of real estate, tavern Sign
of Waggon and 100 acres bought of Caleb Swain, tract bought of
Gayen Moore and his son John containing 310 acres now in tenure
of James Wilson, also grist mill with 50 acres in tenure of John
and Francis Mechim.
Executors: Mother and friend Joseph Gibbons.
Witnesses: John Kerlin, William Clingan.

CARSON, GEORGE. East Marlborough.
5/16/1757. December 28, 1759.
Directs his only son George to be kept to school until 15 and
then put to a trade and all estate left to him at 21 with
reversion to brothers John, Richard and Robert Carson.
Executors: Brother Richard and George Passmore.
Witnesses: Richard Buller, Joseph Wilson, Henry Chalfant.

WARBURTON, ROBERT. Middletown.
December 21, 1759. January 9, 1760.
To wife Ruth plantation in Middletown containing 119 acres,
paying to son William £5. To wife 1/3 of personal estate,
remainder to son William.
Executor: Thomas Pilkinton.
Witnesses: Richard Noblit, Sarah Daily, Cadwallader Evans.

MILLER, BENJAMIN.   MARSHALL, THOMAS.
November 28, 1759. New Garden.   January 11, 1760. Concord.
Adm. to David Fream.   Adm. to Edith Marshall.

BIGGARD, WILLIAM.
June 5, 1758. January 15, 1760.
"Being listed for the Ohio Expedition" to my mother and 3
brothers all estate excepting £4.10 which I leave to cousin Hugh
Martine. John Fergus and Alexander Rogers to be Executors "until
such time as one of my brothers comes into this country."
Letters to John Fergus, the other renouncing.
Witness: Robert Hamilton.

PYLE, ADAM. Bethel.
January 11, 1760. January 15, 1760.
To Ann Tate £10. To Nathaniel Pyle, son of brother Isaac £33.
To brother Isaac, sisters Hannah, Esther and Martha 5 shillings
each. Remainder equally divided among brother and sisters.
Executor: Stephen Foulk.
Witnesses: James Bratten, Robert Barnett.

REYNOLDS, FRANCIS. Chichester.
January 3, 1760. January 19, 1760.

Provides for wife Elizabeth. To son Henry 1/2 of plantation on which I now live in Chichester containing about 198 acres. To son Francis the other 1/2 of said plantation with mansion house. To sons John and Samuel tract of land in Chichester containing 8 acres bought of Joseph Booth. Remainder to be sold and divided among all children, viz., Henry, Benjamin, John, Samuel, Francis, Lydia, Christiana and daughter Prudence Dutton's children.
Executors: Wife and sons Henry and Francis.
Witnesses: Hugh Linn, David Clayton, John Harding.

MARSH, GRAVENER. Sadsbury.
1/4/1760. February 13, 1760.
To cousin Gravener son of Henry Marsh 10 shillings. To cousins William and Gravener, sons of William Marsh 10 shillings. To Gravener son of Joel Baily 10 shillings. To brother James £5. All remaining to be sold and equally divided between my 3 daughters, Sarah, Elizabeth and Margaret. Provides for wife Mary. To only son Gravener all real estate.
Executors: Brothers Henry and William Marsh.
Witnesses: Thomas Truman, Amos Williams, William Dickey.

WEIRE, ELIZABETH. West Marlborough.
April 3, 1758. February 26, 1760.
To granddaughter Elizabeth Webb alias Hall £50 and wearing apparel. All remainder of my ready money to daughter Jane Webb and her children excepting Elizabeth Hall.
Executors: Aaron Baker, John and Joshua Pusey.
Letters to Baker, the others renouncing.
Witnesses: Aaron Baker, Jr., Mary Baker, Thomas Maguire.

WRIGHT, HANNAH. East Caln.
July 7, 1759. February 27, 1760.
To son Moses £20. To sister Ann Davis £10. To daughter Anne Walker wearing apparel. All remainder to be divided between 3 eldest sons, viz., William, James and George.
Executor: Friend William Clingan.
Witnesses: Robert Withrow, Ann Davis.

BABB, JOHN.
February 7, 1760. West Caln.
Adm. to Thomas Babb.

DONNALY, ARTHUR.
March 12, 1760. Kennett.
Adm. to Gabriel Clark.

GRANTUM, ELIZABETH.
February 27, 1760. Ridley.
Adm. to Charles Grantum, Jr.

DAVIS, MYRICK.
March 13, 1760. Radnor.
Adm. to Thomas Read.

SMITH, MARY. Darby.
June 20, 1759. Codicil: February 26, 1760. March 25, 1760.
To granddaughter Mary Davis lot of furniture. To 5 grandchildren, the children of daughter Rose deceased, viz., Nathan, Mary, Benjamin, Ann and Joseph £100 to be divided as they attain the age of 21. To granddaughter Rachel Smith, daughter of my son Samuel, furniture. To granddaughter Mary, daughter of my son Samuel, furniture. To granddaughter Rose Moore, daughter of my son Samuel. To daughter in law Elizabeth Smith clothing. To

son Samuel bond of £60 which he owes me. To daughter Elizabeth,
wife of Amos Moore £100 and remainder of household goods. Negro
man Summer to have his liberty and £30 given in trust as security
for the same. All remainder to be divided between son Samuel,
sons in law Lewis Davis and Amos Moore.
Executors: Son Samuel and John Davis of Darby.
Witnesses: Thomas Pearson, Jacob Webber, Isa Pearson.

WILLSON, WILLIAM. West Fallowfield.
February 23, 1760. April 5, 1760.
To children Elizabeth, Mary, Robert, Ann and Margaret Wilson all
estate to be equally divided. Jane Sanford to have an equal
share with my children in consideration of her keeping house for
me for some time past.
Executor: Joseph Davis.
Witnesses: William Hall, David Mathies, Samuel Floyd.

SWAYNE, JOSHUA.
March 31, 1760. West Caln.
Adm. to Thomas Fisher.

HOWELL, DAVID.
April 11, 1760. Whiteland.
Adm. to Griffith Howell.

INGHAM, THOMAS.
April 8, 1760. Willistown.
Adm. to Elizabeth Ingham.

BOWEN, JOHN.
April 12, 1760. Whiteland.
Adm. to Hannah Bowen.

DAVIS, THOMAS. Charlestown.
April 3, 1760. April 16, 1760.
Provides for wife Jane. To my 4 daughters already married, viz.,
Mary, Catharine, Elizabeth and Sarah £2 to be divided, also their
shares of legacies in the will of their grandmother Mary Davis.
To daughter Anne £50.10 to be paid her at time of her marriage.
To youngest daughter Rachel £50.10 at 18. To son David at 21 all
my land and plantation containing 340 acres.
Executors: Wife Jane and friend Sampson Davis.
Witnesses: John Davis, Margaret Davis, James Davis.

SINKLER, GEORGE. West Caln.
3/3/1760. April 21, 1760.
Provides for wife Ann. Remainder of personal to sons Samuel and
George. To son George plantation and tanyard in West Caln at 21.
To son Samuel plantation bought of Francis Hickman at 21. To
daughter Ann £150 when son George arrives at 21 years.
Executors: Wife and brother John Sinkler.
Witnesses: Evan Wilkison, Nathaniel White, Thomas Simrall.

O CUNNING, HENRY. West Fallowfield.
April 10, 1760. April 23, 1760.
To eldest daughter Agnes £5. To daughter Margaret £5. To son
John all remainder of estate real and personal.
Executors: Son John and James Glendinning.
Letters to John, the other renouncing.
Witnesses: George Copland, John Farton, John McLaughlin.

PIM, RICHARD.
April 5, 1760. East Caln.
Adm. to Hannah Pim.

SCOTT, THOMAS.
April 29, 1760. West Nantmeal.
Adm. to Eleanor Scott.

BENTLEY, MARY, widow, being very sick. Newlin.
March 22, 1759. April 26, 1760.
To Rev. Mr. Owen Thomas, minister of the Gospel at the Baptist
Church in Forks of Brandywine £5. To sons Jeffry and John
Bentley one crown each. To son in law Thomas Bayley and Sarah
his wife one English crown. To son in law Robert Chalfant one
English crown. All remainder of estate to grandchildren, that is
the children of Jeffrey and John Bentley and my 2 daughters, Ann
Chalfant and Sarah Bayley except £39 which my son in law Robert
Chalfant owes me and hath kept from me for many years.
Executors: Sons Jeffrey and John.
Witnesses: Samuel Worth, William Sorsby.

HAMBLETON, JAMES. East Fallowfield.
October 29, 1759. April 26, 1760.
Provides for wife Margaret. To son William best suit of clothes.
To grandson James Hambleton best hat. To son James all remainder
of estate real and personal, also Executor.
Witnesses: Jeffrey Bentley, Joseph Davis.

WYETH, JOHN. East Fallowfield.
4/4/1760. April 26, 1760.
To cousin Edward Dennis, son of Thomas and Sarah Dennis all
estate real and personal except legacies. To Thomas Dennis Jr.
£10. To Thomas and Sarah Dennis £5 yearly during their lives.
Whereas having a right to an estate in Old England and some
expectation of it being sent here to me if it should come I give
it to my cousins Edward and Thomas Dennis.
Witnesses: Joseph Bentley, Joseph Davis.

PUGH, JOHN. East Nottingham.
4/22/1760. May 12, 1760.
Provides for wife Agnes. Remainder equally divided among all
children living, viz., Mary wife of John Barrett, William and
John Pugh, Sarah wife of William White and Jane wife of John
Brown (in Philadelphia).
Executor: Son John.
Witnesses: John White, Hannah Bennett, George Churchman, Jr.

MC CUE, SAMUEL. Willistown.
April 27, 1760. May 19, 1760.
To brother Anthony McCue £30 and to his sons Thomas, John and
Abraham £10 each at 21. To Brother Anthony's 3 daughters,
Elizabeth, Mary and Ann McCue £5 each at 18. To father Samuel
McCue £30 for the use of my brother Thomas if he be living. To
brother in law James Farra and my sister Mary Farra £5 each and
to their 4 sons, William, Joseph, Samuel and Abraham £10 each at
21. To James and Mary Farra's 3 daughters Rebecca, Mary and
Sarah Farra £5 each at 18. To brother in law John Buttler and
his wife, my sister Hannah, plantation they now live on and £20.
To sister Hannah's son, Samuel Buttler £15 at 21. To kinsman

John Buttler Jr., £25 at 21. To sister Ann Harper £50 and to her
4 children £20 to be divided. To sister Alice McCue £100. To
cousin John Norton £7.
Executors: Father Samuel McCue and uncle Isaac Wayne.
Letters to McCue, the other renouncing.
Witnesses: Thomas Lloyd, Thomas Rowland, Samuel Hall.

ASHE, MATTHEW. Darby.
June 2, 1750. May 20, 1760.
To son Joshua Ash 5 shillings. To daughter Mary Ashe rents and
profits of my plantation where I now dwell during her life
providing she remains unmarried. To grandson Joshua, son of
Joshua plantation in Upper Darby paying legacies with reversion
to his brother Caleb. To Edward, Thomas and Samuel sons of my
son Edward deceased £20 to be divided at 21. To 2 youngest
children of daughter Sarah Councill deceased, John and Hannah £5
each at 21. To children of son Joshua, except the eldest, £10 to
be divided. To daughter Elizabeth Ashe £5, also all remainder of
personal estate.
Executor: Son Joshua.
Witnesses: Samuel Bunting, John Pearson, Isaac Pearson.

LLOYD, GRACE, widow. Chester Borough.
4/6/1760. May 22, 1760.
To brother Lawrence Growden 20 pistoles and to his daughter
Elizabeth Nicholson, 6 pistoles, and to his daughter Grace
Galloway, 6 pistoles and my clock. To sister Hannah Growden £10
worth of plate. To friend Rachel Pemberton silver cup. To David
and Grace, son and daughter of Humphrey Lloyd £5 each. To friend
Jane Hoskins silver porriger. To the overseers of the school of
the people called Quakers £200 in Philadelphia. To Mary, wife of
Charles Norris silver cup. Executors to pay £10 towards walling
in the grave yard of the Quakers in Chester. To Martha Pettel
£5. To Mary Little, widow, of Wilmington £5. To Sarah wife of
Robert Wade £3. To kinsman Joseph Richardson of Philadelphia
lott of ground in Chester, also £200 and to Patience Richardson
£5. Negro man Will to cousin Francis Richardson of Philadelphia.
Leaves lot of ground for burying place for negroes under the care
of Overseers of Friends Meeting in Chester. To Jennet Low widow
late of Chester £5. To Pennsylvania Hospital in Philadelphia
£25.
Executors: Israel Pemberton and Francis Richardson.
Trustee: Joseph Parker.
Letters to Richardson, the other renouncing.
Witnesses: Jane Bezer, Esther Bickerdike, John Eyre.

WOODWARD, RICHARD. West Bradford.
2/11/1760. May 24, 1760.
To son Joseph all land at 21. To daughter Rachel Woodward £100
at 18. To daughter Deborah £100 at 18. To wife Abigail all
remainder of personal estate, also use of real estate until son
Joseph is 17. Executors: Brother William Woodward and George
Carter.
Witnesses: Henry Hollis, Hannah Thornborough, Benjamin Hawley.

* Widow m. --- Bruce and her son for distinction was called
Joseph Bruce Woodward.

FEGON, GILES. Willistown.
May 15, 1760. May 27, 1760.
To wife (not named) 1/3 of estate and £25 "she being with child at this time." All remainder of estate to be in hands of Executor for clothing and bringing up my younger children not named.
Executor: Thomas Harris of Willistown.
Witnesses: Joseph James, Patrick Bruff.

PALMER, ISAAC.
May 22, 1760. Chichester.
Adm. to Henry Palmer.

DAVIS, ROBERT. Kennett.
April 29, 1760. May 27, 1760.
Plantation in Kennett containing about 150 acres bought of Executors of James House, to be sold. 1/3 of all estate to wife Dinah and remaining 2/3 equally divided among children who are not named. Said Executrix to be governed by the advice and counsel of friends Aaron Baker and Thomas Harlan.
Executrix: Wife Dinah.
Witnesses: Stephen White, Joshua Baker, Thomas Harlan.

WILLSON, JANET, relict of Joseph. West Fallowfield.
February 25, 1759. May 28, 1760.
To my married daughters Margaret Dickie and Ann Smith 10 shillings each. To 3 unmarried daughters Jane, Elizabeth and Catharine 20 shillings each. To son Thomas riding mare. All remaining to sons Thomas, John and Joseph Willson.
Executors: Sons Thomas and John.
Letters to Thomas the other being deceased.
Witnesses: Andrew Sterling, Robert Hamill, William Boggs.

SHEERER, HUGH.
May 28, 1760. West Caln.
Adm. to Elizabeth Sheerer.

CULIN, GEORGE. Ridley.
May 22, 1760. May 29, 1760.
Provides for wife Elizabeth. To sons Swan and George that part of my plantation lying south of the Kings road. To son Samuel that part of plantation north of said road, also 2 acres of meadow by Darby Creek. Remainder divided among sons William and Abraham and daughters Martha and Margaret.
Executors: Wife and sons Swan.
Trustee and Overseer: Brother Daniel Culin.
Witnesses: James Smith, Daniel Culin, Jr., John Morton.

STEEL, SAMUEL. Thunder Hill.
April 23, 1760. June 2, 1760.
To son Robert, daughters Ruth and Jean, and son Samuel £7.6 each.

To daughter Frances £20. To son Joseph £10. To son James horse and saddle. To son Ninian £10. To daughters Ann and Elizabeth £10 each at 20. Plantation to be divided between sons Samuel and James subject to life interest of wife Ann, who is Executrix.
Witnesses: Gilbert Bouchanon, James McCormick, Andrew Gamble.

SHIELDS, WILLIAM. Londonderry.
December 31, 1759. June 9, 1760.
To wife 1/3 of all estate. To son Joseph 1/2 of crop in the ground and £2. Remaining 2/3 to be divided among daughter Cathrin Shields, son Archibald, son Robert, son Thomas, daughter Hannah Shields, son William and daughter Martha Shields.
Executrix: Wife Martha.
Witnesses: William Kerr, Joseph Law.
* Daughter Katherine married James Ocheltree. See Deeds. Martha married Adam Reed.

SMITH, JOSEPH. Oxford.
May 22, 1760. June 12, 1760.
To sons Robert and John all estate real and personal subject to life interest of wife Isabel. To daughter Mary, wife of Robert Fulton £5. To daughter Elizabeth, wife of James Criswell £25. To daughter Isabel £30. To daughters Esther and Martha £40 each at 14. To son Joseph £100. To son Abram £60 at 18. To brother John Smith wearing apparel and to his son Joseph ewe and lamb.
Executors: Sons Robert and John.
Witnesses: Joseph Cowden, Robert Smith, Arthur McKisack.
* Daughter Isabel married John Ross?

GILLESPIE, WILLIAM.
December 14, 1759. June 13, 1760.
Provides for wife Mary. To son in law Thomas Sharp 10 shillings. To son in law James Rankin 10 shillings. To son William £20. To sons Samuel and David £20 each. To daughter Ruth Gillespie, a horse saddle. To sons John and Alexander all lands and remainder of personal estate, also Executors.
Witnesses: William Molly, John Alexander, Abraham Emmit.

SIMSON, JOHN. Oxford.
May 7, 1760. June 13, 1760.
Provides for wife, not named. To sons James and Allen all real estate paying legacies of £40 each to my other 5 children as they come of age, not named.
Executors: Friend David Ramsey and son James.
Witnesses: John Hayes, Martha Russell, William Boyd.

TRIMBLE, HUGH. Middletown.
May 19, 1760. June 16, 1760. D. 225.
Provides for wife Margaret. All estate real and personal to son James paying legacies. To son Thomas £100 to support him at learning. To son Samuel £100 at 21. To daughter Margaret her maintenance till of age and £60.
Executors: Wife Margaret and son James.
Letters to Margaret, the other being deceased.

Witnesses: Robert Smith, Thomas Slemons, Thomas Slemons, Jr.
* *James died before date of probate.*

BUFFINGTON, ISAAC. West Bradford. Cordwainer.
May 20, 1760. June 16, 1760.
All estate real and personal to mother Phebe Hadley, also
Executrix.
Witnesses: Dr. George Martin, Ruth Thornbury.

BENNETT, JAMES. Aston.
May 26, 1760. June 17, 1760.
Provides for wife. To daughter Mary Yarnall £15. To daughter
Elizabeth Hill £15. To daughter Hannah Grubb £15. Also to said
3 daughters house and lott in Wilmington. To grandson William
Hill £5 at 16. All remainder real and personal to son James
Bennett of Aston.
Executors: Wife Mary and son James.
Witnesses: John Burnet, John McMinn, William Griffith.

GRUBB, SAMUEL. East Bradford.
1/14/1760. Codicil 1/26/1760. June 20, 1760.
Provides for wife Mary. To nephew Curtis Grubb son of brother
Peter 1/2 of my lands in Lancaster County. To nephew Peter son
of Peter the other 1/2 of my lands in Lancaster County. To
sister Charity Beeson £20. To sister Phebe Hadley £20. To
brother Henry wearing apparel and £20. To nephew Samuel son of
brother John Grubb deceased all estate real and personal
bequeathed to me by my father, John Grubb. To Samuel Grubb son
of Samuel aforesaid £20. To Philadelphia Hospital £50. To James
Dilworth £50 towards building a Friends Meeting house in
Birmingham. All remainder to brother Nathaniel Grubb, also
Executor. Letters to Samuel Grubb and Joseph James, Executor
named being deceased.
Witnesses: Joseph Buffington, Nathaniel Jefferis, William Jones,
John Jones.

HARRY, HUGH. Kennett.
3/29/1760. June 24, 1760.
Provides for wife Elizabeth. To son James 10 acres of land to be
surveyed off plantation where I now dwell. To daughter Elizabeth
Harry £20 "at her first marriage." To son Stephen £5. To son
Jesse £5. To son Benjamin £5. To son Nathan £5. To son Thomas
£5. My 3 younger children, viz., Jesse, Benjamin and Nathan to
be put to trades at 16. All remainder of estate real and
personal to son Evan, also Executor.
Witnesses: Daniel Eachus, James Wickersham, William Lee.

CARTER, JOHN. Aston. Blacksmith.
June 19, 1760. July 1, 1760.
To son Joseph mare and cow. To son Samuel the wire loom. To
daughter Hannah, big Bible and brass kettle. To grandson Isaac
"to Book of Marters." Remainder between son Edward and grandson
Isaac.
Executor: Son Joseph.

Witnesses: Hugh Linn, Jacob Richards, Elizabeth Askew.

HICKMAN, BENJAMIN. Westtown.
November 1, 1756. July 5, 1760.
To son Benjamin plantation I now live on in Westtown containing 150 acres if he lives to 21. To daughter Ann Hickman £50, furniture and her mother's wearing apparel at 18. To son Francis all remainder of estate at 21.
Executors: Brothers John and Francis Hickman.
Witnesses: John Taylor, Thomas Hannaway, Ann Cheyney.

CRISWELL, ROBERT. Oxford.
June 25, 1760.
Adm. to Jane and James Criswell.

LINDLAY, SIMON. East Marlborough.
6/30/1760. July 10, 1760.
To father and mother Thomas and Ruth Lindley £40 to be divided. To brother James £20. To brother Thomas £5. To brother William all wearing apparel. All remainder to said brother William, Catharine, Ruth, John, Eleanor, Deborah and Jonathan Lindley to be equally divided as they arrive to the age of 21.
Executor: Uncle Robert Johnson of East Marlborough.
Witnesses: Henry Neal, T. Woodward.

LIGGETT, GEORGE. West Bradford.
October 1, 1758. July 29, 1760.
To son George plantation I now live on "which hath 2 deeds." To son John plantation in East Nantmeal. To daughters Rachel and Margaret plantation in East Fallowfield. To daughter Mary £50 when of age. Also to daughters Ruth, Ann and Rebecca Liggett and Elizabeth McKinley £50 each. To grandson George McKinley £10 at 21. Remainder to wife Elizabeth and sons George and John.
Executors: Wife and daughter Rachel.
Witnesses: John Davison, Samuel Filson.

VERNON, THOMAS.
July 10, 1760. East Marlborough.
Adm. to Abraham Ashton.

ASKEW, WILLIAM. Chichester.
12/1/1747/8. August 4, 1760.
Provides for wife Sarah. To son Joseph messuage where I now dwell containing about 90 acres, also tract recently bought of kinsman Dutton in Chichester containing 30 acres and all remainder of personal estate. To daughter in law Mabel Askew messuage where my son Lazarus lately dwelt containing 130 acres for 10 years from date of her husband's death for bringing up and schooling my 3 grandchildren at which time I give said plantation to my 3 grandchildren, the children of Lazarus deceased, viz., William, John and Lazarus Askew.
Executor: Son Joseph.
Trustees: Brother in law Joseph Parker and Edward Whittaker.
Witnesses: Edward Russell, John Baldwin, H. H. Graham.

CLAYTON, EDWARD. West Bradford.
June 20, 1760. August 9, 1760.
Provides for wife Ann (see will). To son John 5 shillings being already advanced. To son Joshua 5 shillings being already advanced. To daughters Elizabeth Strode and Hannah Green 5 shilling each being already advanced. To 3 youngest daughters Sarah, Ann and Susanna Clayton all remainder of my land lying on the northeast side of the road leading down to Evan Jones containing about 18 acres to be equally divided. To son William all remainder of plantation in West Bradford containing about 97 acres except 1/4 part of all mines on Mattaline Ores which son William shall dig on said premises which 1/4 part I give to my grandson Edward, son of John Clayton. Also to son William all land devised to wife Ann during life, at her decease paying to his 3 sisters Sarah, Ann and Susanna £10 each.
Executor: Son William.
Witnesses: William Woodward, Enoch Bradley, Joseph Buffington.

WILLIAMSON, JOHN. Newtown.
1/12/1759. August 14, 1760.
Provides for wife Sarah and gives £15 yearly out of rent of plantation to son Daniel yearly during his life and remainder of same to wife and son John at Daniel's death. Plantation to son John in fee, paying to my grandchildren then alive £200 to be divided among them. To daughter Mary Hoops £10 and her husband's bond for £20. To daughter Sarah Calvert £10 and her husband's bond for £35. To daughter Margaret Brinton £10 and her husband's bond for £20. To daughter Alice Lowns £10 and her husband's bond for £20. To daughter Esther Mendenhall £10 and her husband's bond for £20. To daughter Jane Green £10 and her bond when she was the widow Regester for £30. To each of my grandsons called John 20 shillings. Remainder equally divided.
Executors: Wife and son John.
Trustees: Kinsman George Smedley and Thomas Massey.
Witnesses: Samuel McClellan, Abel Green, Mordecai Moore.

EVAN, JOHN alias JENKIN. Vincent.
July 16, 1760. August 25, 1760.
To son David £3. To son James £3. To son John £100. To daughter Eleanor, wife of John Doddson £5. To daughter Ann, wife of Michael Doddson £5 (living in Maryland). To wife Ann and son William all remainder of estate real and personal, also Executors.
Witnesses: Robert Ralston, Humphrey Bell, Theophilus Thomas.

HOWELL, DAVID.
August 25, 1760. Whiteland.
Adm. to John Downing.

GATCHELL, RACHEL, widow of Elisha. East Nottingham.
2/17/1756. August 26, 1760.
To son Elisha Gatchell £20. To daughter Elizabeth Mitchell £20. To daughter Abigail Price £20. To daughter Esther Brown £20 and interest due on her husband Jeremiah Brown's bond. To daughter Hannah Brown £20 and interest due on her husband Joshua Brown's

bond, also to Joshua Brown £10. To daughter Ann Kirk £20 and interest due on her husband Timothy Kirk's bond. To granddaughter Sarah, daughter of Joshua Brown one heifer. To grandson Elisha Price mulatto boy Jack until he is 30 years old and to be taught to read and write.
Executors: 3 sons in law Jeremiah Brown, Joshua Brown and Timothy Kirk.
Letters to Joshua Brown and Timothy Kirk, the other renouncing.
Witnesses: Joseph Williams, William Knight, Benjamin Bowen.

COX, ANDREW.* East Caln.
June 12, 1760. August 26, 1760.
To son Andrew £20. To son John £10. To son Peter £10 at 21. To daughter Sarah Hughs 5 shillings. To 4 daughters Rebecca, Mary, Martha and Elizabeth Cox £3 each at 18. To wife Mary remainder of personal estate and use of real estate during widowhood. At her decease to be divided among the 7 following of my children, viz., Andrew, John, Peter, Rebecca, Mary, Martha and Elizabeth.
Executors: Wife Mary and cousin Joseph Bishop.
Letters to Mary Cox, the other renouncing.
Witnesses: Joseph Bishop, Mary Stanfield, George Larow.
* Andrew Cox married Mary Bishop Jan. 25, 1729/30 St. Paul's, Chester.

DAWSON, ABRAHAM. West Caln.
June 18, 1760.
To father Thomas Dawson Sr. £40. To mother Mary Dawson household goods. Mentions cousin Mary Montgomery. To cousin Abraham, son of Isaac Dawson my tract of land in Cumberland County, Pennsylvania. To cousin Jacob, son of Richard Dawson £20. To St. John's Church in West Caln £10. Tract of land on which Daniel Justice dwells to and for the use of the poor of West Caln. To brother Isaac negro girl Esther, also negro man Lonnon until he is 45 and then to be set free. To brother Thomas £40 who with Nathaniel White are Executors.
Witnesses: Richard Hope, James Sinkler.

BOYLE, ROBERT. West Fallowfield.
November 1, 1749. August 26, 1760.
To son Dorinton Boyle all stock and farming implements, also all utensils of tanning and currying and stock of tanned and raw leather bark. To daughter Mary, wife of Alexander Boyle £10. To daughter Elizabeth, wife of James Wilson 5 shillings. To daughter Margaret Boyle in Ireland £20. To daughter Abigail Boyle horse worth £20 and £100. Mentions a marriage settlement between Isabel Steel (my present wife) executed 29th November 1743 (she was the widow of Robert Steel). To son Dorinton messuage in West Fallowfield where I now dwell containing 363 acres, also Executor.
Overseers: James Whitehill of Lancaster County and John Miller.
Codicil: August 14, 1760 leaves an additional legacy to daughter Abigail Williams.
Witnesses: William Boyd, James Boyd, Daniel Henderson.

GRIFFITH, BENONI. Willistown.
3/5/1759. August 27, 1760.
To eldest son Nathan £5. To daughter Hannah Griffith £20 and
maintenance while unmarried. To youngest son Ezekiel piece of
land containing 7 acres being part of the land I live on. To 3
daughters who are married, viz., Elizabeth White, Sarah Morgan
and Rachel Randall 5 shillings each. To wife Catharine and son
John all remainder of estate real and personal. Granddaughter
Hannah Morgan mentioned.
Executors: Wife and son John.
Witnesses: Caleb Atherton, Henry Atherton, Jr., Henry Atherton,
Sr.

DIX, NATHAN. Chester.
August 19, 1757. August 29, 1760.
to wife Sarah 1/4 of all estate absolutely. To daughter
Elizabeth 1/4 of all estate. To daughter Mary 1/4 of estate. To
daughter Sarah 1/4 of estate. Daughters to have their portions
at 18 or marriage. Wife to have whole estate until that time.
Executors: Wife Sarah and William Swaffer of Chester.
Letters C.T.A. to Job Dicks, widow Sarah being deceased and the
other renouncing.
Witnesses: John McMichael, Jr., James McMichael.

CRAWFORD, WILLIAM.   GRIFFITH, DANIEL.
August 27, 1760. W. Nottingham.   August 28, 1760. Pikeland.
Adm. to John Crawford.   Adm. to John Griffith.

PUSEY, JOSHUA. Londongrove.
8/16/1760. September 1, 1760.
To son Ellis Pusey interest for 2 years on bond of £150 which I
have against him. To son William £400. To son Joshua 1/2 of my
mill and plantation where I now dwell containing about 140 acres,
also my right in a piece of London land adjoining thereto paying
to my wife £250. To wife the other 1/2 of said land for 12 years
after my decease at which time son Joshua is to have the whole
estate. To son Lewis £400 at 21. To daughter Elizabeth, wife of
John Smith £200. To daughter Mary £200 at 18. To daughters
Phebe, Hannah and Lydia £200 each at 18.
Executors: Wife not named and son Joshua.
Letters to Joshua, the other being deceased.
Witnesses: Joshua Johnson, Jonathan Morris, Isaac Jackson.

DICKS, PETER. Nether Providence.
10/31/1756. Codicil: August 21, 1760. September 3, 1760.
To eldest son Joseph plantation in Nether Providence containing
133 acres bought of James Ewing and his heirs "on the body of his
present wife Anne begot or to be begotten." To son Job 2 pieces
of land in Springfield bought of Benjamin Maddock, also piece of
land being a part of the tract I now live on. To son John
messuage and divers lotts of ground in Chester purchased of
Robert and John Barber. To youngest son Roger messuage where I
now dwell containing about 140 acres which I purchased of
Swaffers children. Son Abraham and brother in law William
Swaffer Executors, who are to sell all remainder of lands in

Chester and York County. Provides for wife Sarah. To daughter
Jane Dicks £100 at 21. Remainder divided among all children
except Nathan, "whom I exclude from any share unless he pay the
money now justly due me from him."
Witnesses: John Sharpless, H. H. Graham, Nathaniel Browne.
Codicil gives to Pennsylvania Hospital £50. Mentions £300 he had
put into Grubb's Iron Works.

BALDWIN, ANTHONY. Newlin.
June 9, 1753. September 5, 1760.
To wife Margery 1/3 of all estate real and personal and £40 more.
To eldest son William £5. To second son Joseph £5. To grandson
William Edwards £5 at 21. To daughter Elizabeth 5 shillings. To
brother Thomas Baldwin and wife the six acres of land they now
live on during their lives. Remainder of estate real and
personal to be divided among my youngest children, viz., Anthony,
George, John, Thomas, Martha, Hannah, Robert, Ann, Margery and
Sarah.
Executors: Wife and son Anthony.
Witnesses: Philip Taylor, Thomas Stubbs, James Trimble.

TAYLOR, ROBERT. Marple.
5/24/1759. September 12, 1760.
Provides for wife Jane. To granddaughter Mary Morris dwelling
house and lot of land where I now live at expiration of wife's
interest with reversion to granddaughter Phebe Morris paying to
her sister Hannah £10. To daughter Elizabeth, wife of John
Morris, rents of plantation in Marple whereon William McAffee now
lives during lifetime of her husband and so long as she continue
his widow. To grandson Robert Morris the above plantation at
expiration of his mother's right. To granddaughter Jane Morris
case of drawers. To step daughter Sarah Woolley £6. Remainder
divided between wife Jane and daughter Elizabeth Morris.
Executor: Son in law John Morris.
Witnesses: John Stringer, Mordecai Taylor, Anne Woolley.

HUSTON, HENRY. West Caln.
September 23, 1760. October 1, 1760.
To brother Levenees Huston 1/2 of estate and wearing apparel. To
sisters Jennet and Frances the other 1/2 of estate who are now in
Ireland.
Executors: John Kinkead, Sr. and John Fleming.
Letters to Fleming, the other renouncing.
Witnesses: William Fleming, John Loudon.

JOHN, ROBERT.
September 13, 1760. Uwchlan.
Springfield.
Adm. to Griffith John.

GRUBB, NATHANIEL.
September 15, 1760. Willistown.
Adm. to Samuel Grubb.

HALL, JOHN.
September 20, 1760.

Adm. to John Hall & Peter
Taylor

EVANS, WILLIAM.
October 1, 1760. Tredyffrin.
Adm. to Joshua & Joel Evans.

CRISWELL, ROBERT.
September 20, 1760. Oxford.
Adm. to George Criswell.

TRAYHORN, ADAM. Easttown.
7/9/1760. October 1, 1760.
Provides for wife Mary. To Friends of Newtown Meeting £2. To 4 grandchildren, viz., Mary, Elizabeth, Israel and Ruth 1 shilling each. Executors to sell real estate, of proceeds 1/3 to wife and remainder to 3 daughters, viz., Barshaba, Mary and Abigail at 21.
Executors: William Lewis and Joseph Lewis.
Witnesses: William Hunter, John Steel, Thomas Massey.

CRESWELL, JAMES. Oxford. Tanner.
May 7, 1760. October 16, 1760.
To nephew Joseph Creswell, son of brother Robert my land containing 150 acres. To nephew James Creswell, son of Robert £10. To niece Rachel Creswell alias Dysant £40. To niece Isabella Creswell, daughter of brother Robert £10. To niece Hannah, daughter of brother Robert £10. To niece Jane, youngest daughter of brother Robert £15. To sister Rachel Whitehill £10. To nieces Jane Clark and Rachel Creswell, daughters of brother John £5 each. To nephews James, John and Robert, sons of sister Mary Creswell £5. To niece Rachel Woodside £5.
Executors: Brother James Whitehill and nephew James Creswell, Jr.
Witnesses: George Miller, Robert Fleming, Rebecca Boggs.

JOHNSON, ABRAHAM.
October 1, 1760. Bradford.
E.Marlborough.
Adm. to Benjamin Orin.

OGDEN, STEPHEN.
October 1, 1760. Springfield.
Adm. to Hannah Ogden, John Lewis & James Day.

JACKSON, HENRY.
October 15, 1760. Thornbury.
Adm. to Daniel Calvert.

JOHNSON, ROBERT.
October 16, 1760.
Adm. to Henry Nayle.

EDWARDS, JOHN.
October 21, 1760. Uwchlan.

GEST, JOHN.
October 25, 1760. Concord.
Adm. to Simon Gest.

HOWARD, HENRY. Edgmont.
9/13/1758. October 27, 1760.
To son John plantation whereon he now dwells in Edgmont for 7 years from my decease, at expiration of which time I give the said plantation to my 3 sons John, Peter and Richard. To son Peter £20. To son Richard £30. To daughter Grace Kendal £5 and Bible. To daughter Mary Moss £20. To daughter Hannah Passmore £10. To daughter Rebecca Howard £20. To son James plantation where I now dwell and tract of meadow adjoining containing 6 acres, he paying legacies and provide for his mother Hannah Howard during her life.
Executor: Son James.
Witnesses: George Miller, Thomas Pritchett, William Pritchett.

ROWAN, ANDREW.
October 6, 1760. October 27, 1760.
[Nuncupative will, the subscribers being at the house of Rev.
James Finley on the 6th of October 1760 when Andrew Rowan of
Faggs Manor lay sick, he declared the following was his will.]
To Michael Rowan £50. To sister Mary £50. To my brother in
Ireland £20. To my sister in Ireland £20. To my sister's
children in Ireland £30. To my sister's 2 children in Virginia
£20.
Executor: None named.
Letters to Michael Rowan and Robert Ray, the husband of his
sister Mary.
Witnesses: Hugh Blackburn, William Read.

WORRALL, JOHN. Ridley.
December 9, 1748. October 28, 1760.
Provides for wife Ruth. To son Joseph 1 shilling sterling. To
son John plantation I now live on in Ridley. To son Thomas 130
acres in Upper Providence joining the school house. To son
Edward 130 acres in Upper Providence where Daniel Broom lived.
To daughter Ruth £70. To daughter Mary Worrall 50 acres in Upper
Providence adjoining Peter Taylor's. To daughter Elinor Worrall
50 acres in Upper Providence from the land Robert Patterson lives
on.
Executrix: Wife Ruth and John Sharpless, Sr., assistant.
Witnesses: Daniel Sharpless, Sarah Sharpless, Richard Haslam.
* Samuel Darke and Martha Worral married 12/6/1685 in Bucks
County, Middletown Monthly Meeting. Martha Darke of Falls
Township, widow, in will March 7, 1725/6 mentions brother John
Worrill of Chester County (shown to be Ridley).

ROBISON, JOHN.
September 4, 1760. October 29, 1760.
Provides for wife Janet. To son in law John Harper £3. To son
John 1/3 of whole estate. To son Charles 1/6 of all estate. To
son James 1/6 of estate. To son Alexander 1/6 of estate. Son
John to have "my place after being valued at a middling easie
rate."
Executors: Wife Janet and son John.
Witnesses: Alexander Rogers, John Campbell, Martha Thompson.

GRIFFITHS, GRIFFITH.
March 29, 1748. Codicil: July 3, 1754. November 7, 1760.
To eldest son Abel 2/6. To son Evan 2/6. To children William,
Dan, Amos, Levi and Rebecca Griffiths all remainder of estate.
Brother John Griffiths and David Stephens to be guardians over
minor children until of age to choose their guardian. To wife
Gwin 1/3 of personal estate absolutely and 1/3 real estate during
life, also household goods.
Executors: Wife and son William.
Letters to Dan Griffith, the other renouncing.
Witnesses: Thomas Atherton, Samuel John.
Codicil names son Dan as Executor in place of William.
Witnesses to Codicil: William Rogers, David Stephens.

EMMIT, JOSIAS. East Nottingham.
November 16, 1759. November 7, 1760.
To nephew Josias Emmitt, my oldest brother John's son, 50
shillings. To brother Abram 10 shillings. To brother Samuel's
heirs, viz., Samuel Beaty's children, 40 shillings. To brother
David, 40 shillings. To niece Martha, Zacheus Alexander's
daughter, 40 shillings. To nephew Josias, son of William
Porterfield, 40 shillings. To wife Rebecca all remainder of
estate and on her death 1/2 to be divided between my nephews,
viz., Josias, my elder brother's son and Abram, my youngest
brother's son.
Executrix: Wife Rebecca.
Witnesses: William Molloy, John Lawson

CHADS, JOHN. Birmingham.
10/10/1760. November 20, 1760.
To wife Elizabeth, tract where I now live, joining land of Isaac
Harvey, containing 40 acres; at her death to my cousin Joseph
Davis and his heirs, also £30. To cousin Sarah Chalfant £35. To
Hannah, wife of Joseph Davis 20 shillings. To cousin William
Baily, for use of his children, £30. To cousin Elizabeth Pugh
£20. To cousin Susanna Dougherty £10. To cousin Mordecai Cloud
£30. To cousin John Neils £30. To cousin Betty, alias Elizabeth
Painter £20. To cousin Mary Peterson £30. To cousin Joseph Pyle
£5. To cousin Eleanor Robinson £20. To cousin Mary Leard £5.
To cousin John Pyle £20. To cousin Sarah Pyle £20. To cousin
William Pyle £60. To cousin Ralph Pyle £650 and wearing apparel.
To Keziah, wife of Amos Harvey 1/2 of bond of about £90 which
said Amos owes me if he will pay it without compulsion, but no
suit at law to be brought against him for it. Executors to sell
tract of land in Marlborough, also tract in Birmingham containing
14 3/4 acres. Remainder to Joseph Davis and Ralph Pyle.
Executor: Joseph Davis.
Witnesses: Isaac Harvey, Henry Hayes, Ann Hayes.

BALDWIN, ELIZABETH. Londongrove.
9/-/1760. November 26, 1760.
To daughter Lydia Valentine £6. To daughter Hannah Baldwin £22
and household goods at 18. To son William Baldwin £14. To son
Thomas £14 at 21.
Executor: Son William.
Witnesses: Thomas Gregg, Joshua Pusey.

RILEY, JOHN. Chichester.
April 12, 1755. Codicil: November 15, 1760. December 4, 1760.
To son William Riley £10 yearly during life to be paid by son
Richard. To daughter Mary Taylor £50 and 2 large silver spoons
and a gold ring. To daughter Elizabeth Riley plantation in
Concord bought of Joseph Way containing 50 acres. All remaining
real and personal to son Richard, who with Thomas Cummings of
Chester are Executors.
Witnesses: John Crawford, Adam Clayton, Hannah Crawford.
Letters to Richard Riley, the other being absent.
Codicil gives to daughter Elizabeth £180 in place of the land
which had been sold.

Witnesses to Codicil: William Crabb, John Wall.

WOOD, JOSEPH.
November 21, 1760. Chichester.
Adm. to Edward Whiteker.

REES, MORRIS. Uwchlan.
June 25, 1760. December 4, 1760.
Directs body to be buried at Uwchland grave yard. Provides for wife Catherine. To granddaughter Margaret Hudson of Caernarvon, Lancaster County, £15 at 21. To grandson Morris Hudson £15 at 21. To daughters Elizabeth Lloyd of East Nantmeal and Anne Evans of Caernarvon, Lancaster County, all remainder of estate real and personal. £5 to be paid to the overseers of Uwchlan Meeting to repair grave yard.
Executors: Elizabeth Lloyd and Anne Evans.
Witnesses: Joseph Phillip, John Roberts, David John.

TRIMBLE, JAMES. Middletown.
May 26, 1760. December 6, 1760.
Mentions his mother Margaret. To brother Thomas £50. To sister Margaret £20. To brother Samuel all land left me by my father.
Executors: John Scott Esq. and mother.
Letters to Margaret Trimble, the other being absent.
Witnesses: Hugh Linn, Charles Linn.

WARBURTON, RUTH. Middletown.
July 30, 1760. December 10, 1760.
To my son Henry, son of Henry and Ruth Tompson, all personal estate during life with reversion to my sister's children Robert, Samuel and Martha, children of Joseph and Mary Butler living in Brooms Grove Wister Shier. To servant girl Elizabeth Folley £5 when of age 18. To John Rittew's 4 children John, Mary, William and Aaron £2 each.
Executor: John Rittew.
Witnesses: Richard Noblet, John Rittew, Jr., Elioner Rittew.

LEWIS, WILLIAM.
December 8, 1760. Haverford.
Adm. to Charles Jones &
Daniel Williams.

RAWSON, JOHN.
December 15, 1760. Chichester.
Adm. to James Rowan.

PRESTON, HANNAH alias LEWIS.
December 8, 1760. Chester.
Adm. to Jonas Preston.

PUSEY, MARY.
8/22/1760. September 1, 1760. December 15, 1760.
Memorandum, on the 22nd of 8 mo. 1760, then Mary Pusey Sr. desired that some persons should be present to hear what she had to say and we whose names are hereunder written being present, she the aforesaid Mary said that she left two parts to her daughters and one part to her sons and furthermore said she was sensible which we believed she was and she requested that we should take a memorandum of what she said.

Letters C.T.A. to Ellis Pusey.
Witnesses: Samuel Morton, Sr., John Pusey, Sr.

JACKSON, JOSEPH. Londongrove.
9/5/1760. December 15, 1760.
To wife Susanna profits of real estate until sons come of age, then 1/2 to her absolutely and the remaining 1/2 to children equally except daughter Rachel, also £200. To son in law John Jordan £3. To daughter Rachel, wife of John Jordan £200. To son Ephraim 106 acres of the north end of plantation purchased of John Jackson, also 1/4 of mill. To son John plantation that John Jordan now lives on which formerly belonged to Richard Bennett containing 50 acres, also 112 acres of leased land adjoining and 1/4 mill and £150. To son Josiah south end of above mentioned tract and 1/4 of mill. To son Samuel plantation where I now dwell containing about 150 acres and 1/4 of mill at 21, paying £70 to daughter Sarah. To son in law James Jackson £3 and to his wife, my daughter Mary £60. To daughter Hannah £120. To daughter Susanna £120 at 18. To daughter Alice £120 at 18. To daughter Sarah £140 at 18.
Executors: Wife Susanna and neighbor Samuel Morton.
Witnesses: Richard Flower, James Willson, Isaac Jackson.

NETHERMARDT, CONRADT. Ridley.
January 24, 1759. December 17, 1760.
Provides for wife Christian. Remainder of real estate to my children, viz., son Luke and daughters Mary, Elizabeth and Rebecca. Son to take the land at appraised value on condition that he do not sell any part of said lands to Charles Granttum or John Knowles or any of the name or family or to any person for them. Also mentions Sarah, daughter of son Mathias.
Executors: Son Luke and friend John Justis.
Witnesses: John Morton, Samuel McCoy, Jonathan Brady.
* Conrad Niedermardt naturalized April 10[?], 1741.

BROWN, THOMAS. Thornbury. Being advanced in years.
November 30, 1760. December 23, 1760.
To brother George Brown of Whitington in Staffordshire, England interest at £100 during life. To each of the children of my brother in law and sister, Joseph and Elizabeth Deakon £5. To said sister Elizabeth £5. To cousin Robert Deakon of Philadelphia, joiner, and to his wife Catharin all remainder of estate.
Executors: Cousin Robert Deakon and James Day of Springfield.
Witnesses: Richard Cheyney, John Harper, Joseph Moore.

MARIS, GEORGE. Springfield.
June 9, 1757. December 24, 1760.
To son James 5 shillings. To son Jesse lot of ground in Chester near the meeting house and £40. To daughter Alice Lewis £40. To daughter Susanna Hall £25. To son John £50. To son Caleb £50. To daughter Ann Maris £50. To son Isaac west end of plantation. To son Jehu the remainder of plantation including buildings, subject to provision for his mother. To wife Ann £100 and all

remainder of estate.
Executors: Wife and sons Jesse and Jehu.
Witnesses: James Bartram, Isaac Howell, Elizabeth Bartram.

YOUNG, ANNE alias OTTEY.
December 23, 1760. Middletown.
Adm. to Daniel Young.

CLAYTON, SUSANNA. Chichester. Tayloress.
December 17, 1760. December 26, 1760.
To brother Joseph Clayton all my land in Chichester and 1/2 of my money which is in my aunt Abigail Whiteley's hands. To sister Margaret the 1/2 of said money. To Sarah Mahan, Abigail wife of Richard Clayton, and Hannah Cracker wearing apparel. All remainder to sister Margaret.
Executor: Brother Joseph.
Witnesses: Moses Moore, Rachel Padrick, John Power.

DUNN, WILLIAM. West Caln.
December 1, 1760. January 7, 1761.
To son William £40 when of age. To daughter Sarah £40 to be put in trust when 8 years old. To daughter Ann £40 to be put in trust at age 8. To son James £40 to be put in trust at age 8. All remainder to wife Jean, also executrix.
Witnesses: Thomas Dunn, John Guthery.

COX, LAWRENCE. Willistown.
8/18/1760. January 12, 1761.
To wife Sarah and son John Cox plantation where I now live in trust for payment of debts and legacies. To wife Sarah £130. To daughter Rachel Cox £55 at 18. To daughters Hannah and Jane £50 each at 18. To daughter Mary Hains £30. To son John £15. Remainder on death of wife to Rachel, Hannah and Jane.
Executors: Wife and son John.
Witnesses: Isaac Massey, Jacob Norbury, Thomas Massey.

GRANTUM, CHARLES, JR. Darby.
May 27, 1760. January 23, 1761.
Now Lieutenant under Capt. John Bryan in Provincial Service intending to march to the Westward, to 2 brothers George and Jacob Grantum, all estate of every description, also Executors.
Witnesses: Joseph Fordham, Patrick Hayes, George Morton, Rebecca Morton.

DUCKWORTH, WILLIAM. Frederick County, Virginia.
January 10, 1761. January 30, 1761.
To wife Eailes plantation in Frederick County, Virginia, that I now dwell on and all remainder of estate real and personal in Frederick County. To my 5 children, viz., Uriah, Aaron, Sarah, Grace and Rodey Duckworth all estate in Trenttown, New Jersey, share and share alike. Letters to Allice Duckworth, the other being absent.
Executors: Wife Eailse and friend Hugh West in Frederick County, Virginia.
Witnesses: John Kerlin, James Sinkler.

BEVAN, AUBREY. Chester Borough.
October 15, 1751. February 20, 1761.
To wife Anne and daughter Mary Bevan brick messuage and land in Chester where I now dwell commonly known as Pennsylvania Arms in trust to be divided on death of wife among children, Mary, Tacy, Davis and Anne, Annie to have £50 more than the others.
Executors: Wife and daughter Mary.
Letters to Mary, the other being deceased in the lifetime of Testator.
Witnesses: Benjamin Davis, Samuel Howell.

GARDNER, HENRY.
February 24, 1761. Whiteland.
Adm. to Peter Valleau.

PRYOR, JAMES. New Garden.
2/1/1761. February 24, 1761.
To son Solomon Dixon £10 for maintaining my mother. To son Silas all wearing apparel and to be put apprentice to the trade of a carpenter. To wife Elizabeth, executrix, remainder of estate.
Witnesses: Thomas Hutton, Nehemiah Hutton, William Phillips.

THOMAS, LEWIS. Darby.
2/16/1761. March 3, 1761.
To son John Thomas £60. To my 3 other sons Nathan, Lewis and Isaac £60 at 21. To daughter Mary £40 at 21 or marriage, also household goods. Remainder equally divided.
Executors: Cousin John Thomas of Blockley and Abraham Johnson of Darby.
Witnesses: John Sellers, William Garrett, John Hayes.

COOK, THOMAS. New London.
January 21, 1761. March 9, 1761.
To son Joseph Cook all the land I now possess 100 acres and stock of household furnishing and what money is due me. Provides for wife (not named). To daughter Mary, son John, daughters Elizabeth and Jean 5 shillings each.
Executor: son Joseph
Letters to Joseph Cook.
Witnesses: James McCanles, John Ross.
* Mary married David Wiley.

HAMILTON, JOHN. West Nantmeal.
November 25, 1759. March 10, 1761.
Provides for wife Janet. To son James all remainder of movables and plantation during his lifetime and at his decease to his children. To son John £24. To daughter Janet Hamilton £3. To daughter Margaret Hamilton £3.
Executors: Sons James and John.
Witnesses: Charles Cummings, James Mareshl.

HUBBERT, THOMAS. Whiteland.
January 1, 1761. March 16, 1761.
Provides for wife Rachel. Provides for education of children

mentioning Thomas and gives them the land I now live on. To
daughter Mary £300 at 18.
Executors: Brother Stephen and friend John Templeton.
Letters to Rachel Hubbert, the executors named having renounced.
Witnesses: James Hunter, John Blatchford, John Rees.
* Rachel was daughter of Joseph Phipps, and married 2nd Owen
Aston. They kept the White Horse Tavern.

COPPOCK, BARTHOLOMEW. Marple.
2/9/1761. March 17, 1761.
To son in law Seth Pancoast plantation in Marple containing 188
acres paying £160: that is, £50 to daughter Rebecca Fell, £60 to
daughter Sarah Sharpless, £40 to daughter Margaret Camm and £10
to grandson Bartholomew Coppock. To son Moses 5 shillings. To
daughters Rebecca, Margaret and Esther household goods and
wearing apparel. Remainder to daughter Esther Pancoast.
Executors: 3 sons in law William Fell, Daniel Sharpless and Seth
Pancoast.
Witnesses: Matthew Hall, James Maris, Aaron Vernon, Jr.

DOUGHERTY, GEORGE. West Fallowfield.
November 19, 1760. March 21, 1761.
Leaves all estate to mother Cathrin and sisters Sarah and Cathrin
Docherty including a legacy from his father now in possession of
brother Owen Docherty in the Parish of Magiligan, County of
Londonderry.
Executors: Mother and sisters.
Letters to Sarah Dougherty.
Witnesses: James McCormick, Margaret Maguire, Thomas Maguire.

BRINTON, WILLIAM. Concord.
1/27/1759. March 23, 1761.
Provides for wife Cisly. To grandson Joseph Walter, son of
Joseph and Jane, messuage in Concord containing by estimate 100
acres when he is 21, he paying to his brother James £5 and to his
sisters Hannah, Elizabeth and Phebe £5 each and to Robert and
John Chamberlin £5. To son in law Joseph Walter 5 shillings and
to his wife, my only daughter Jane dishes that was her mother's.
To granddaughter Hannah Walter case of drawers. Remainder to
wife Cisly.
Executrix: Wife Cisly.
Witnesses: Robert Mendenhall, Abraham Johnson, Stephen Hall.

BAILEY, ALEXANDER. Willistown.
April 11, 1758. March 23, 1761.
2 parts of estate to brother William Bayley and one part to
friend and kinsman Giles Feagan.
Executor: Joseph James.
Witnesses: Benjamin Hibberd, Richard Jones, Ludwig Bender.

JONES, JANE.
March 24, 1761. Goshen.
Adm. to Evan Jones.

CALDWELL, ANN. East Nottingham.
August 21, 1759. March 25, 1761.
To brother Andrew Sim £10. To Samuel son of brother Andrew £10.
To William son of brother Andrew £3. To Andrew son of brother
Andrew, £20 when of age. To Ann Sim, daughter of Andrew £30. To
Jean Sim, daughter of Andrew £20. To James Wharrey Sr., West
Nottingham £15. To James Wharrey Jr., £10 and one great pot. To
Mary Wharrey £10. To John Caldwell, son to my brother in law Dan
£10. To Jennett Solsberry of Philadelphia £3. To John Sim, son
of brother John. To James son of George McCollough £4. To
William Karr of Octorara £6.16.
Executors: Hugh Thompson, James Wharrey.
Witnesses: Patrick McCullough, William Porter.

TOWNSEND, HANNAH, widow of James. Birmingham.
December 6, 1753. March 30, 1761.
To daughter Hannah Curry £40 and household goods. To daughter
Isabel, wife of George Baily £12. Remainder if any to 3
surviving daughters.
Executrix: Daughter Hannah Curry.
Witnesses: John Chads, John Stuart, John Taylor.

TANNER, MARY, widow of Philip. East Nottingham.
November 5, 1759. April 3, 1761.
To son Philip Tanner 5 shillings and the Geneva Bible. To son
Joseph 5 shillings. To daughter Hannah, wife of William Henry
furniture. To daughter in law Elizabeth and her daughter Mary
wearing apparel. To son James, wife Mary the same. To daughter
Rachel 5 shillings. To grandson Philip Tanner all right and
title to my land now rented by his Uncle James at 21. £11.8.3 in
John Crosier's hands to daughter Rebecca's children. Remainder
to daughter Hannah's children, Philip to have a double portion.
I give the middle sized pot for James' eldest daughter Mary and
Philip Henry his Bible, the Bible he reads on at school.
Executors: Sons Philip and James.
Letters to Philip, the other renouncing.
Witnesses: John Hathorn, John Hill, Jr., Sarah Best, Patrick
Power.

ALEXANDER, JAMES.
March 25, 1761. London Britain.
Adm. to Mary Alexander.

DAVIES, JONATHAN.
April 14, 1760. April 6, 1761.
To son David plantation on which John Nealy now dwells. Place
whereon I now live to be sold. Provides for wife (not named).
To David a watch and wearing apparel. David to pay £30 each to
the other children Rachel, Mary and Priscilla and to Jonathan £60
at 21. Reference to Testator's father, David Davies.
Executors: Ellis Davies, Amos Davies and Esther Davies.
Letters to Ellis and Amos Davies, the other renouncing.
Witnesses: John Nealy, Jeremiah Jarman, Thomas Worrall.

TAYLOR, ISRAEL. April 7, 1761. Thornbury. Adm. to Thomas
Taylor. Sureties Samuel Mendenhall, Samuel Raine. Elizabeth
Taylor the widow, and Isaac, the eldest brother renounce
administration. Witnesses: Richard Parks, Jacob Taylor, April 7,
1761.

KIRK, ROGER. West Nottingham.
6/30/1759. April 14, 1761. Died 3/28/1761.
Directs body to be buried in Friends Burying Ground in East
Nottingham. Provides for wife Elizabeth including tract of land
in East Nottingham containing 100 acres purchased of Daniel
Brown, also Mulatto girl Phillis, negro girl Jenny, negro man
Harry and negro boy Tobe. To son Timothy £5 and to his wife Ann
£5. To son William 10 acres, part of plantation whereon I now
dwell, also £5 and to his wife Mary £5. To daughter Elizabeth
Woodward £30 and to her husband, Thomas £5. To Mathew
Aughiltree, husband to my daughter Deborah deceased 5 shillings.
To daughter Rebecca Cook £40 and mulatto girl Violet and to her
husband John Cook £5. To son Samuel plantation where I now
dwell, also stock. To grandson Roger Kirk, son of Timothy tract
of land in East and West Nottingham containing 150 acres. To
grandson Nathaniel Kirk, son of William 1/4 of lot of land in
Charlestown on North East River, the other 1/4 of do to grandson
Samuel Woodward. To granddaughter Rebecca Woodward furniture.
To grandchildren Jacob, William, Elizabeth, Katherine and Joseph
Wollison, children of Joseph and Deborah Wollison deceased £10
each when of age. All remainder to wife Elizabeth, also
Executrix.
Witnesses: Elisha Hughes, Benjamin Chandler, Alexander McCaskey.

WORRALL, THOMAS, son of John. Ridley.
February 22, 1761. April 21, 1761.
To youngest brother Edward all personal estate and plantation in
Upper Providence containing 70 acres conveyed to me by my father
paying legacies. To brother Joseph's eldest son, Peter Worral £5
at 21. To brother John £10 and all he now owes me. To sister
Ruth Lean £10 and to her 3 children, viz., William, Edward and
Ruth Lean £5 at 21. To sister Eleanor's oldest son Jonathan
Worrall £5 at 21. To mother Ruth Worrall 40 shillings a year
during her life.
Executors: Mother and brother Edward.
Witnesses: John Sharpless, Thomas Sharpless, William Swaffer.

STARR, JOHN. Chester.
3/27/1761. May 9, 1761.
Divides estate between brothers Thomas, Isaac, William, Jacob,
Samuel and Moses with contingent legacy to the 2 children of
sister Mary Parvin.
Executor: Brother Isaac Starr.
Witnesses: Mary Lea, Priscilla Ashbridge.

YEARSLEY, JACOB.
April 11, 1761. Westtown.
Adm. to Susanna Yearsley.
Daughter of Robert Chamberlin and Cicely; had daughter Hannah who

married Thomas Howell, Mary who married Richard Thornbury, Ann who married James Clark, Phebe who married James Simcock, Rachel, Jacob who married Rachel.

BOURNE, THOMAS. West Marlborough.
11/30/1746/7. May 26, 1761.
To brothers Jacob and George Bourn all my land in Colbert [Calvert] County, Maryland. To 3 sisters Ann, Susanna and Sarah all rents now due on said land and remainder of estate.
Executor: Uncle George Maris.
Letters C.T.A. to Nathaniel Pennock (who married the Testator's sister, Sarah), George Maris being deceased.
Witnesses: Joseph Taylor, Jesse Taylor.

THOMSON, JOSHUA. Late of Ridley, now Gloucester County, New Jersey.
May 3, 1761. May 28, 1761.
To son John £5. To daughter Mary Levis £5. To son Joshua 1 shilling sterling "and he is not to have any more of my estate." To son Thomas £5. To son Daniel £5. To daughters Abigail Hoof and Sarah Thomson £10 each. To daughter Margaret Reed £10. To son Nathan £10. To grandson Joseph Thomson 1 shilling sterling and no more in right of his father, my son Mordecai deceased.
Executors: Son John and son in law Samuel Levis.
Witnesses: Charles Grantum, John Morton.

THOMAS, DAVID. Easttown.
June 1, 1761. June 11, 1761.
To mother Elizabeth Hingham profits of all my real estate during her life. To brother William Thomas of Bucks County, all real estate at mother's death.
Executors: Mother and brother William.
Witnesses: David Reece, Samuel Caley, Caleb Reece.

MEYER, ADAM.
May 28, 1761. E. Nantmeal.
Adm. to Jacob Meyer.

BOON, SWAN.
May 29, 1761. Darby.
Adm. to Rebecca Boon.
Orphans' Court 20 Sept. 1763. On petition William Boon over 14, George Grantham is appointed guardian of William, Mary, Rebecca and Swan Boon, children of Swan deceased.

DOWNARD, WILLIAM.
June 13, 1761. New London.
Adm. to Anne Downard.

DICKS, ABRAHAM.
June 15, 1761. Ridley.
Adm. to Margaret Dicks & John Crosby.

FREECE, JOSHUA.
June 15, 1761. Willistown.
Adm. to George Freece.

BYERS, JOSEPH. East Caln.
June 5, 1761. June 20, 1761.
To 2 eldest sons John and Samuel tract of land whereon I lately lived in Charlestown when eldest son is 21, paying 1/3 of appraised value to son Joseph when he is 21. To daughter Margaret £50 at 18. Provides for wife Ann and education of

children who are "to be taught to read the English Bible well, write and cyffer to the Rule of three." Brother Samuel Byers and brother in law Joseph to be guardian to my children.
Executors: Wife Ann and friend David John of Charlestown.
Witnesses: Joseph Williams, John Buyers, John Griffith.

CHANDLER, THOMAS. Birmingham.
10/8/1753. June 25, 1761.
Provides for wife Mary. Watch, large Bible and desk to Thomas Chandler, son of brother William. To my sister Ann Jones and her 2 daughters and grandson Henry Chads £15 to be divided. To John Chandler, son of brother George £15. To Isaac son of brother George £20. To Ann, Mary and Moses, children of brother William £15 to be divided. To Mary, daughter of Thomas and Hannah Chandler £5. To George Chandler, son of brother George 5 shillings. To Thomas Chandler, son of brother William plantation where I now live subject to wife's interest, also residuary legatee and Executor.
Witnesses: Jonathan Langley, Thomas Gibson, Richard Baker.

JOHNSON, JAMES.
12/2/1758. July 6, 1761.
To John Butterfield and Hannah his wife £1 each. To daughter Abigail White £2 and to her husband Thomas White £1. To wife Ruth plantation in West Nottingham for support and education of younger children. On her death or marriage to be sold and proceeds divided among my 8 children, viz., Hannah Butterfield, Abigail White, Sarah, Margaret, Mary, Ruth, Rachel and Susanna Johnson as they come of age.
Executors: Wife Ruth and William Knight.
Witnesses: George Sayer, William Crookshank, Elisha Brown.

MC MICHAN, JAMES. Uwchlan.
June 30, 1761. July 8, 1761.
To mother Sarah McMichan £100. To brother Samuel McMichan all my right to a certain tract of land in Fanett Township, Cumberland County, where I have lately improved. Remainder to 2 sisters Mary and Ginnett McMichan and brother Andrew.
Executors: Brother Samuel and friend John Culbertson, Esq.
Witnesses: Thomas Evans, Joseph Vaughan, Myrick Davies.

MATTHEWS, JOHN. West Bradford.
July 7, 1761. July 24, 1761.
All estate real and personal to be equally divided between "my brothers and sisters children."
Executors: Brother Thomas' son, Oliver Matthews and Nathaniel Way, Jr.
Witnesses: James Alen, Richard Baker, James Marshall.

ARMENT, WILLIAM. Concord.
10/8/1757. July 24, 1761.
To son John all the land I live on in Concord containing 50 acres providing maintenance for his mother during life. To son William all wearing apparel. To son in law Jacob Mote and wife Sarah £5. Mentions he 4 grandchildren Thomas, William, John and Jacob

Arment.
Executors: Son John and friend Nathaniel Newlin Sr.
Witnesses: John Palmer, Sr. John Palmer, Jr., William Smith.

DAVID, THOMAS. Vincent.
April 8, 1761. July 30, 1761.
Provides for wife Mary. To daughter Mary £5. To son David £100. To son George £80. To daughter Elizabeth £30.
Executors: Wife Mary and son George.
Letters to George, the other renouncing.
Witnesses: John Fitzsimons, John Martin, David Thomas.

MALONE, PATRICK. Upper Providence.
January 27, 1758. August 5, 1761.
To son John all wearing apparel and 1/2 of my money. To daughter in law Mary Martin the other 1/2 of my money and all household goods and as my son John has gone a privateering I bequeath his portion to daughter in law Mary Martin if he does not personally appear and demand it. To brother Henry Malone 1 shilling sterling. To sister Jean Malone 1 shilling sterling. To sister Isabel 1 shilling.
Executors: William Lindsay and Mary Martin.
Letters to Mary Martin, the other renouncing.
Witnesses: James Lindsay, William Lindsay.

MC COY, HENRY.
August 5, 1761. London Britain.
Adm. to John McCoy.

FITZSIMMONS, JAMES.
August 14, 1761. Vincent. Britain.
Adm. to Margaret & George Fitzsimmons.

ROUSE, CHARLES.
August 19, 1761. Aston.
Adm. to Patience Rouse.

MILLER, ROBERT.
August 25, 1761. East Caln.
Adm. to Warrick Miller.

JURY, RICHARD.
August 25, 1761. London
Adm. to Mary Jury.

DOUGLAS, MARY.
August 26, 1761. Londongrove.
Adm. to Thomas Clarke.

CLAYPOOLE, NATHANIEL. Easttown.
6/14/1761. August 27, 1761.
Provides for wife Kathrine. To 2 sons Thomas and James plantation I now live on in Easttown, also all my rights and interests in Philadelphia subject to the payment of 5 shillings to each of my daughters, viz., Elizabeth, Ann, Elishe, Jane, Martha, Kathrine and Mary.
Executors: Wife and son Thomas.
Witnesses: Isaac Minshall, William King, George Smedley, Jr.

JENKIN, GWEN, widow. Whiteland.
2/26/1760. August 27, 1761.
To daughter Mary, wife of William Beale furniture and wearing apparel. To grandson David Jenkin £15 at 21. To granddaughter Hannah Jenkin £13. To granddaughter Mary Jenkin £15 at 18. To Gwen Jenkin £15 at 18. To grandson Thomas Beal £10. To grandson

William Beale £10. To grandson John Beal £10 at 21. To grandson David Beal £10 at 21. To grandson Joshua Beal £10 at 21. To granddaughter Susanna Beal £10. To granddaughter Mary Beal £10 at 18. To granddaughter Eddey Beal £10 at 18. To Mary Anderson the girl that lived with me, my best iron pot.
Executor: Son in law William Beal.
Witnesses: John Todhunter, Cadwallader Jones.

HARRIS, DANIEL. East Marlborough.
1/21/1761. September 15, 1761.
To brother Evin Harris 5 shillings and remainder of estate to mother Elizabeth Webster.
Executor: Friend Edward Swayne.
Witnesses: John Wilson, Isaac Swayne.

JACKSON, JOHN.
September 23, 1761. Chichester.
Adm. to Jacob Richards.

ALCOTT, THOMAS.
October 15, 1761. E. Caln.
Adm. to Anne Alcott.

BAILY, DAVID.
September 24, 1761. E.Fallowfield.
Nottingham.
Adm. to Sarah & Samuel Baily.

GARTRILL, JOHN.
October 21, 1761. W.
Adm. to William Allen & Jacob Haines.

MILLER, BRICE.
October 1, 1761. W. Nottingham.
Adm. to William Reynolds.

BURNS, ROBERT.
Nov. 11, 1761. W. Fallowfield.
Adm. to George & Robert Burns.

LAMPLUGH, JOHN. October 5, 1761. Chichester. Shipwright.
Adm. to William Lamplugh. Sureties John Cloud, Samuel Armor, Widow Elizabeth renounces adm. same date. Inventory by John Crawford & Samuel Armor Oct. 8, 1761.

WILSON, JOHN. Birmingham.
9/19/1759. November 24, 1761.
Provides for wife Hannah according to the terms of marriage contract. To son John 3 shillings, 5 pence out of each £ of my estate. To daughter Ruth Lewis 3 shillings per £ of my estate. To daughter Hannah Mendenhall 3/5 per £ of my estate. To son James remainder of estate real and personal.
Executors: Son in law Benjamin Mendenhall and William Harvey, Sr.
Witnesses: Adam Redd, Ann Redd, Jesse Mendenhall.

BARNARD, ISAAC. Aston.
August 17, 1761. December 3, 1761.
To only son James messuage in Aston where Andrew Jack now lives during life and in default of heirs to my brother Thomas. To daughter Hannah £40 at 18. Provides for wife Isable. To son James all other real estate. Remainder of personal including bond in hands of Archibald Dick to brother Thomas.
Executors: Thomas Barnet and Richard Dutton.
Letters to Barnard, the other renouncing.
Witnesses: Benjamin Weldon, John Loan, James Brown.

STARRATT, JAMES.
June 7, 1761. December 19, 1761.
To oldest son William part of the tract of land he now lives on containing 272 acres and to second son John the other part of said tract containing 274 acres in East Nantmeal. To daughter Jean Starratt £400. To young son James the plantation in West Nantmeal containing 250 acres and this plantation I now live on in Springfield Manor and remainder of personal estate paying legacies and maintaining wife during widowhood.
Executrix: Wife Jean.
Witnesses: James Dunning, Rachel Liggett, John Gardner.

HEALD, THOMAS.
November 26, 1761. Goshen.
Adm. to Ellis Davies.

FEW, JOSEPH.
November 30, 1761. W. Bradford.
Adm. to Joseph Buffington & wife Mary.

MARTIN, JOHN.
December 8, 1761. Birmingham.
Adm. to Hannah Martin.

MECHEM, FRANCIS.
December 8, 1761. Goshen.
Adm. to John Mechem.

WELDON, ELIZABETH.
December 8, 1761. Chichester.
Adm. to John Crawford.

MC VEA, THOMAS.
Dec. 31, 1761. E. Fallowfield
Adm. to James Mc Vea & Miles Mc Swaine.

BOYD, WILLIAM. Sadsbury.
January 13, 1762. January 27, 1762.
Orders tombstone for grave of self and first wife. Provides for wife Elizabeth. To son Alexander £100. To son John 15 pistoles. To daughter Martha Stuart £50. To daughter Janet Boyd £100. To daughters Mary, Ann and Hannah Boyd £100 each. To son William £200. To daughter Elizabeth Boyd £100. Executors to sell 400 acres off the south end of plantation, remainder equally divided.
Executors: Brother James Boyd and wife Elizabeth.
Witnesses: Andrew Sterling, Alexander Simrall, Robert Meser.

KIRK, ROGER. West Nottingham.
12/28/1761. February 4, 1762.
To eldest daughter Abigail Corbally and to each of my other 5 daughters, viz., Jane, Elizabeth, Mary, Hannah and Sarah Kirk £3.10 each. To daughter Rachel Serjeant 5 shillings having given her portion already. To daughter Margaret £5.10 and maintenance while she remains unmarried. To son John plantation where I now dwell at 21. Tract of land purchased of Thomas Brown to son Sampson Kirk at 21. Also makes provision for young sons Henry and William.
Executor: Son Timothy.
Trustee: William Churchman, of Nottingham, to see this will faithfully performed.
Witnesses: William Kirk, Thomas Brown, Benjamin Jacobs.

WORRALL, THOMAS.
January 5, 1762. Goshen.
Adm. to Ellis Davies.

KENDALL, BENJAMIN.
Feb 4, 1762. W. Nottingham.
Adm. to Mordecai James.

RICHARDS, RACHEL.
January 28, 1762. Chichester.
Adm. to Jacob Richards.

SMITH, PETER.
February 6, 1762. Thornbury.
Adm. to George Pierce.

FLOWER, RICHARD. Chichester.
January 24, 1762. February 10, 1762.
To son John east end of mansion house. To son Richard the west end of mansion house. To 2 daughters Rachel and Mary lott of ground behind St. Martin's Church. To daughter Jemima lot of ground purchased of John Kerlin with all my right of lotts from my father, John Flower deceased. Provides for wife Hannah.
Executors: Wife, brother John Flower and Richard Riley.
Witnesses: John Marshall, William Crabb, Mary Crabb.

HUBBERT, STEPHEN. Tredyffrin.
December 30, 1761. Codicil: January 31, 1762. March 1, 1762.
Provides £7 per annum for father and mother during their lives. To cousin John Campble £100 at 21 and to his sister Mary Campble £25 at 18. To sister Mary Richison £20. To cousin Samuel Richison £5 at 21. To Thomas Hubbert my brother's son £100 at 21 and to his sister Mary Hubbert £25 at 18. Plantation where I now live to sister Elizabeth davis and her son, Thomas Davis on her death, also tract of land bought of John Boggs containing 35 acres. Reversionary legacy to cousin Sidney Davis.
Executrix: Sister Elizabeth Davis.
Witnesses: Joseph Collins, Lewis Gronow, Enoch Walker.

HORNE, BENJAMIN. Haverford.
3/1/1762. March 15, 1762.
To wife Elizabeth all estate for bringing up and educating my 2 children, viz., Abigail and Ruth Horne, until they come of age.
Executors: Wife and brother William Horne.
Witnesses: Allen Poolke, Benjamin Simcock, Rachel Taylor.

MANSELL, WILLIAM.
February 23, 1762. Newlin.
Adm. to George Pierce.

COLLINS, ANDREW.
March 15, 1762. Chichester.
Adm. to John Mather.

KERLIN, PETER.
February 23, 1762. Concord. Adm. to Joseph Kerlin.

HOLLIDAY, ROBERT. New Garden.
March 2, 1762. March 17, 1762.
Provides for wife Hannah and mentions her 2 sons Samuel and James Dobins. To daughter Phebe Holliday £30 and all her own mother's clothes. To son Jacob wearing apparel. To daughter Sarah £15. Jeremiah Starr to be guardian for children. Remainder to son Jacob.
Executor: Samuel Miller, Sr.
Witnesses: Morris Thomas, Samuel Miller, Jr., James Rowen.

BUFFINGTON, JOHN, bachelor. Newlin.
February 18, 1762. March 25, 1762.
To brother Thomas Buffington my plantation in West Bradford containing 120 acres now in tenure of Joseph Martin, also

personal estate. To sister Mary Cremer 5 shillings. To sister
Sarah Buffington 5 shillings.
Executor: Brother Thomas.
Witnesses: George Martin, tanner, and George Martin.

ROWLAND, JAMES.
January 8, 1762. March 26, 1762.
To wife Jean the benefit of the plantation and stock until "her
son John comes to the years of minority which is 21 years" when I
allow him the said plantation. To daughter Jean Smith and my
wife's youngest daughter £20 when of age. To son Hugh Rowland my
watch and use of the still. To son William Rowland, son Robert
Rowland and daughter Agnes Andrew 5 shillings each.
Executrix: Wife.
Witnesses: Samuel Ewing, Robert McMasen, John Ewing.

TAYLOR, PHILIP. Thornbury.
March 17, 1762. March 29, 1762.
To sons Stephen and John Taylor all wearing apparel. To wife
Mary all remainder of estate for the bringing up of the minor
children, not named, also Executrix.
Witnesses: James Dilworth, Anthony Baldwin.

EDWARDS, CATHERINE.
March 17, 1762. W. Caln.
Adm. to Joseph Parker, Jr.

CLENDENAN, WILLIAM.
April 19, 1762. Uwchlan.
Adm. to Eleanor Clendenan &
William Elliott.

CULBERTSON, ROBERT. Kennett.
March 21, 1762. May 3, 1762.
To wife Jean 1/3 of all estate real and personal absolutely. To
son Samuel £20 and all he now owes me and negro lad James on
condition that he shall take my wife Jane and all his sisters
living at my decease into Cumberland County and take care of them
until my wife's decease and his sisters marriage. To son in law
Alexander Porter 5 shillings. To each of my grandchildren by my
daughter Elizabeth Porter 5 shillings. To daughters Jean, Mary,
Martha, Isabella and Sarah Culbertson all remainder of estate to
be divided and paid to each of them on day of their marriage.
Executors: Wife Jean and son Samuel.
Witnesses: Joseph Bennett, Joseph Musgrave, George Craghead.
Letters to Jean, the other renouncing.

WEBB, NATHAN. Concord.
1/15/1762. May 3, 1762.
To mother Rachel Cross all estate real and personal.
Executors: William Cross, my father in law and mother, Rachel
Cross.
Witnesses: John Burnet, Samuel Talkinton, Joseph Nicklin.

PARKER, ELISHA.
May 15, 1762. New Garden.
Adm. to Sebbellah Parker.

MC KEE, JAMES.
May 26, 1762. E. Nottingham.
Adm. to Jane McKee.

THOMAS, JAMES. May 17, 1762. Radnor. Adm. to Amos Thomas.

THOMAS, MARY. Newtown.
January 4, 1750. May 26, 1762.
To nieces Mary and Jane Dunham and Julian Thomas household goods. To brother Davis Thomas' 4 children, viz., Julian, Rebecca, Margaret and Elizabeth Thomas, my cow. To nephew Azariah Thomas 40 shillings. To nephews Samuel and Ezekiel Thomas all that is due me from their father Ezekiel Thomas deceased. Remainder divided among nephew David Dunham, his sisters Mary and Jane and my brother David Thomas.
Executor: David Thomas.
Witnesses: Jacob Thomas, Hezekiah Thomas, Elizabeth Wayne.

HOLLAND, JOHN. Whiteland.
5/22/1762. June 12, 1762.
To nephew Ezekiel, son of John Bowen and Hannah his late wife, my sister, plantation on which I lately lived containing 239 acres in Whiteland now occupied by John McCord subject to the interest of my step mother Sarah Holland and following legacies. To niece Esther Bowen £40 at 21. To Hannah and Ruth Bowen £40 each at 21. Also to Daniel and Joshua Bowen £40 each at 21. To nephew John Bowen, second son of John and Hannah deceased, tract of land in Goshen containing 100 acres which my father John Holland conveyed to me by Deed of May 3, 1752 paying legacies to each of his brothers and sisters above named £10. All remainder personal estate to sister Hannah Bowen.
Executors: Thomas Hoopes and John Todhunter.
Witnesses: John McCord, Richard Jones, Agnes Dunwoodies.

HENDERSON, ANDREW. New London.
May 27, 1762. June 28, 1762.
All estate to be sold and equally divided amongst wife and children, viz., sons John, William, Thomas and Andrew Henderson and daughter Elizabeth Henderson. Share of daughter to be in wife Elizabeth's hands for her support and education.
Executors: Brother John Henderson and Joseph Moore.
Guardian: My uncle Thomas McKean in the Valley.
Witnesses: Joseph Allison, Edward Henderson, John Scott.

HOGG, GEORGE.
June 9, 1762. Aston.
Adm. to John Chamberlin.

SMITH, MARGARET.
June 9, 1762.
Adm. to Emanuel Grubb.

ROSS, JAMES.
June 22, 1762. W. Nantmeal.
Adm. to Dorcas Ross & Francis Gardner.

BAILEY, ALEXANDER.
July 14, 1762.
Adm. to William Baily.

EVANS, LEWIS. June 16, 1762. Vincent. Adm. to Sarah & Daniel Evans Jr.

SCARLET, SHADRACH. Londongrove.
3/19/1760. July 31, 1762.
All estate to be sold and divided into 10 equal parts and divided

as follows: To sister Phebe Allen 2 parts. To cousin Hannah
Allen 1 part. To cousin Emey Allen one part. To cousin Ann
Allen one part. To cousin John Allen one part. To cousin Samuel
Allen one part. To Phebe Allen, daughter to sister Alice, one
part. To sister Ann Linvil one part. To William Linvil her son
one part.
Executors: Uncle Nathaniel Scarlet and cousin Joshua Pusey.
Letters to Scarlet, Pusey being deceased.
Witnesses: John Greenfield, Joseph Lawson, John Allen.

THATCHER, RICHARD. Kennett.
7/29/1762. August 24, 1762.
Son David to have £30 left by my mother Sarah Thatcher with
interest at 21 and 5 shillings of my estate. Remainder to be in
the hands of wife Abigail for bringing up the younger children,
on her death or marriage to be divided among my 7 children, viz.,
Hannah, Sarah, Deborah, Susanna, Levy, Abigail and Oliver
Thatcher. Executors: Wife Abigail and William Harvey.
Letters to Harvey, the other renouncing.
Witnesses: Benjamin Taylor, William Cloud, Thomas Carleton.

HENDRICKSEN, JOHN.
July 15, 1762. Ridley.
Adm. d.b.n. to Swan Culin.
Andrew Culin married the
widow of John Hendrickson
and they exhibited accounts
in 1760.

TAYLOR, JOHN, JR.
August 14, 1762. Thornbury.
Adm. to John Peirce.

CUMMINS, WILLIAM.
August 25, 1762. W.
Fallowfield. Adm. to Mary
Cummins.

MATHER, PETER.
August 3, 1762. Charlestown.
Adm. to Sarah & Peter Mather.

HIBBERD, MOSES.
July 20, 1762. Darby.
Adm. to Sarah Hibberd.

GRUBB, NATHANIEL. Willistown.
May 17, 1760. September 4, 1762.
Real estate in Philadelphia consisting of 3 houses, one lot to be
sold. To daughter Charity Calvert £50. To daughter Margaret
Vernon £50. To daughter Ann Singelear £50. To daughter Phebe
Worrall £50. To daughter Mary Grubb £100. To daughter Frances
Grubb £100. To grandson Jesse Grubb £50 at 21. To son Samuel
that part of plantation on east side of Crum Creek except mills
and land belonging, now under lease, to Thomas Harris. To son
Nathaniel that part of plantation on west side of Crum Creek. To
above 2 sons mill and land belonging when they come of age.
Executors: Son Samuel and John Fairlamb and Joseph James.
Letters to Samuel Grubb, the others renouncing.
Witnesses: Mordecai Moore, Joseph James.

COBOURN, THOMAS. Chester Township.
October 8, 1762. October 20, 1762.
To son Caleb plantation where I now dwell which was left me by my
father Thomas Cobourn containing about 100 acres, also part of
tract purchased of William Jefferis containing about 14 acres
providing during life for wife Elizabeth Cobourn. To son Thomas

tract purchased of William Jefferis containing 55 acres (except
above 14), also tract purchased of my father containing about 55
acres, also a part of tract left me by my father containing about
(reserved in the devise to son Caleb). To 5 daughters, viz.,
Rachel, Susanna, Elizabeth, Mary and Lydia £5 each.
Executor: Son Caleb residuary legatee.
Witnesses: Thomas Phillips, John Lewis, E. Price.

MC FETERS, JOHN.
September 7, 1762. W. Marlborough.
Adm. to Jane McFeters & Samuel
Scott.

EVANS, RICHARD.
October 20, 1762. Tredyffrin.
Adm. to Joel & Joshua Evans.

HOPE, JOHN.
October 1, 1762. Kennett.
Adm. to Amos Hope.

SMITH, WILLIAM.
October 25, 1762. Birmingham.
Adm. to Sarah Smith & Ralph
Pyle.

BRYAN, THOMAS.
October 6, 1762. Londongrove.
Adm. to Mary Bryan.

FRANCIS, JOSEPH. Whiteland.
October 11, 1762. October 30, 1762.
To father Rees Francis and mother Lettice Francis £300. To wife
Mary Francis £200. To 2 infant children £250 when of mature age.
Executors: Kinsman James David and Henry Atherton.
Letters to David, the other renouncing.
Witnesses: Edward Pearce, Joseph Lewis.

BROWN, JEREMIAH, JR.
November 17, 1762. November 29, 1762.
Provides for wife Esther, half of estate and choice of negroes.
To daughter Rachel, wife of John Lewden 1/2 of estate real and
personal, the other 1/2 to wife during widowhood.
Executors: Son in law John Lewden and wife Esther.
Witnesses: Timothy Kirk, William Cole, John Hull.

HAYES, JOHN. West Marlborough.
8/30/1762. December 10, 1762.
To 4 sons David, William, Jesse, and Abram Hayes all my lands to
be divided allowing David 2 shares. Provides for wife Hannah.
To eldest daughter Ann £50. To youngest daughter Hannah £50 at
18. Remainder equally divided.
Executors: Henry Chalfant and Mordecai Hayes, my brother.
Letters to Hayes, the other renouncing.
Witnesses: Andrew McCoy, Mary Pusey, William Hayes.

OLDHAM, RACHEL. East Nottingham.
5/23/1761. December 13, 1762.
To son Simon Taylor 5 shillings. To son Joshua Littler 5
shillings. All remainder of estate real and personal to
granddaughter Rachel, wife of Elisha Brown, and Thomas Barrett to
be divided.
Executors: Thomas Barrett and Elisha Brown.
Witnesses: Mordecai James, David Brown, Micajah James.

LLEWELLIN, JOHN.
October 30, 1762. Easttown.
Adm. to Rebecca Llewellin &
Joseph Tucker.

MC KEE, JOHN.
November 1, 1762. East Caln.
Adm. to Richard Downing.

FERRIS, JAMES.
November 12, 1762. Nottingham.
Adm. to John Ferris.

MURPHY, BRYAN.
November 23, 1762. Ridley.
Adm. to Anne Murphy.

HOPE, ENOCH.
November 20, 1762. Kennett.
Adm. to Amos Hope.

TORTON, DANIEL, JR.
December 9, 1762. Ridley.
Adm. to Daniel Torton.

YARNALL, AARON.
November 13, 1762. Willistown. Adm. to Amos Yarnall.

WILLIAMS, WILLIAM. Darby.
December 1, 1758. December 24, 1762.
"Being at this time inclined and preparing to go to Europe," to father William Williams £150. To sister Rachel Williams £200. To sister Mary Williams but £150 considering she was advanced £50 from estate of my uncle Edmund Williams. Lot of land in Darby to Ann Steel, daughter of James Steel by my sister Ann, his late wife deceased, at 21. Remainder of estate to brother Thomas Williams. Joseph Bonsall and John Pearson of Darby to be guardians of my brother and sisters, also Executors. Letters to Pearson.
Witnesses: Joseph Fordham, John Rudulph, William Wood.

MC PHERSON, JOHN. Sadsbury.
November 23, 1762. January 11, 1763.
Provides for wife (not named). To son Alexander the plantation where I now live. To son Robert plantation whereon he now dwells. To said 2 sons tract of land purchased of Samuel Williams until such time as my son John appears and demands it. To daughter in law Sarah £10.
Executors: Wife and sons Alexander and Robert.
Letters to sons, wife Jean renouncing.
Witnesses: Alexander Sumrall and James Simrall.

DIXON, JOSEPH, weaver.
January 6, 1763. New Garden.
Adm. to Sarah Dixon, see p. 148.
Weaver. Children William,
Joseph, Mary, Rachel (m. Samuel
Hurford), Ruth, Sarah &
Catherine. Joseph died in his
minority.

FRANCIS, REES.
January 21, 1763. Whiteland.
Adm. to John Towers.

PEARSON, THOMAS. Darby.
1/4/1763. January 31, 1763.
To daughter Ann, wife of Davis Morris £186 making with what I have advanced her £250. To son James £30 making with what he owes me £250. To son John, tanyard with land there unto belonging and lot adjoining in Darby, also lot bought of estate

of Job Harvey, tanning and currying tools - paying to my estate
£100. To daughter Sarah £250. To daughters Susanna, Mary,
Hannah, and Elizabeth £250 each. To father Benjamin Pearson the
house wherein he now lives in Darby during life. To son Thomas
messuage where I dwell in Darby with lots of land adjacent, at 21
or decease of my wife. Provides for wife Hannah.
Executors: Wife and sons James and John.
Witnesses: Joseph Fordham, Jesse Bonsall, Isaac Pearson.

HOLLINGSWORTH, JAMES. Kennett.
2/2/1763. March 5, 1763.
Estate to be sold. 1/3 of proceeds to wife Mary. To 2 sons
Valentine and Abner 2 shares of remainder at 21. Thomas
Carleton, Jr. to be their guardian. Remainder of estate to 7
daughters, viz., Betty, Ann, Sarah, Susanna, Mary, Hannah and
Rebecca to be divided at 18.
Executor: Friend Aaron Evans.
Letters to Aaron Baker, sole Executor named in will.
Witnesses: Adam Redd, William West, Thomas Harlan.

CULIN, SARAH.
February 5, 1763. Ridley.
Adm. to William Culin.

CALDWELL, JANE.
Feb. 22, 1763. W.Nottingham.
Adm. to David Patten.

LAWRENCE, SARAH, spinster. Haverford.
12/14/1762. March 15, 1763.
To daughters Rachel James and Sarah Griffith all wearing apparel.
To son Daniel Lawrence and wife Elizabeth £15 and to their 4
children 10 shillings each. To daughter Rachel James £10 and
money due me in hands of cousin Daniel Williams. To daughter
Sarah Griffith 20 shillings and to her 3 children, 3 shillings
each in the hands of their father Amos Griffith. To
granddaughter Sarah James £10. To son David Lawrence's,
deceased, 5 children 10 shillings each. To Hannah James 10
shillings. To grandson Samuel James 10 shillings. To son
William Lawrence all remainder of estate, also Executor.
Witnesses: John Gracy, Jeremiah Ellis, Samuel Humphrey.

GIHEN, ROBERT. Concord.
2/26/1763. March 15, 1763.
To the use of Brandywine Meeting £10. To friend David Morrison
£20. Remainder of estate to the children of John Gihen, Joseph
Gihen and Mary Smith to be equally divided.
Executor: David Morrison.
Witnesses: Nathaniel Newlin, John Piper, James Morrison, Thomas
McCall.

STUBBS, THOMAS. Concord.
8/3/1760. Codicil: February 25, 1763. March 16, 1763.
Executors to sell plantation in Concord containing 87 acres. All
estate to be equally divided between my 9 children, Daniel,
Thomas, John and Joseph Stubbs and daughters Esther Carson, Mary
Attmoor, Elizabeth Addoms, Ann and Sarah Stubbs.
Executors: Sons Daniel and Joseph.
Witnesses: Robert Mendenhall, William Walter, Henry Myer.

SLATER, GEORGE. East Nottingham.
8/15/1759. March 25, 1763.
Provides for wife Sarah. To son John all my land except 100 acres, also stock and farming utensils. 100 acres to be sold and proceeds divided among my daughters, viz., Mary wife of Robert Sheppard, Sarah wife of Samuel England, Hannah wife of Messer Brown, and Lydia wife of Isaac Brown, a legacy being first paid to the female children of son John, £10 each at 18.
Executors: Son in law Samuel England and George Churchman Jr.
Witnesses: Thomas Barrett, William Churchman, Nathan Brown.

FRYER, THOMAS. Thornbury.
10/27/1762. April 5, 1763.
To son George 7 shillings 6 and great coat. To son Thomas horse loom and tackling. To daughter Jane Brumhall 7 shillings 6. To brother William Fryer remainder of wearing apparel, if living. All remainder to wife Ann, also Executrix.
Witnesses: Jacob Pyle, Israel Pyle, John Brinton.

CHAMBERLIN, BENJAMIN. Aston.
3/23/1763. April 25, 1763.
To sons of sister Hannah, wife of Robert Pennell. To Joseph 10 shillings and gun. To Thomas 20 shillings. To Mary 40 shillings. To Susanna, Abigail and Lydia 20 shillings each. All remainder of estate to wife Elizabeth, who with father Joseph Chamberlin are Executors.
Witnesses: John Hall, Isaac Chamberlin, Abraham Martin.

GREGORY, ANNE.
March 26, 1763. Haverford.
Adm. to John Gregory.

LLOYD, THOMAS.
April 11, 1763. E. Nantmeal.
Adm. to Elizabeth & Thomas Lloyd.

TURNER, MOSES.
April 2, 1763. Oxford.
Adm. to John Shee.

BOWEN, HOWELL.
April 11, 1763. Marple.
Adm. to Joel Willis & Charles Linn.

FLEMING, JAMES.
April 8, 1763. E. Fallowfield.
Adm. to Anne Fleming & Robert Withrow.

PEARSON, JOHN. Darby.
April 11, 1763. May 10, 1763.
To eldest son Samuel 5 shillings. To daughter Margaret Pearson 5 shillings. To son John, son Benjamin, daughter Rebecca, son George, son Jonathan 5 shillings each. All remainder real and personal to wife Sarah to bring up my 2 youngest children, also Executrix.
Witnesses: Joseph Fordham, John Rudulph, Jonathan Wilkinson.

MORRIS, FRANCIS. Londonderry. Blacksmith.
April 30, 1763. Codicil: May 10, 1763. May 30, 1763.
To wife Mary £40 and horse. To granddaughter Mary Campbell £10 at 6 years of age. To daughter Rebecca Campbell £5. To daughter Jean now in Ireland £20 with reversion to Elizabeth Moore, her aunt if she have no children. To brother John and his heirs £15.

To sister in law Rebecca Boggs £2.10. To son Francis all
remainder of estate. It is my will that Philip Clayton be free
next Christmas if he pleases.
Executors: Friend Ellis Pusey and son Francis.
Codicil increases wife's legacy to £90 and reduces the others.
Letters to Ellis Pusey.
Witnesses: John Baily, David Buchanan, James Pague, Thomas
Maguire.

BOGGS, FRANCIS.
May 11, 1763. E. Fallowfield.
Adm. to Agnes & William Boggs.

DIXON, JOSEPH.
May 31, 1763. New Garden.
Adm. to William Dixon.

HILL, ALEXANDER.
May 21, 1763. Aston.
Adm. to Elizabeth Hill.

DIXON, SARAH.
May 31, 1763. New Garden.
Adm. to William Dixon.

LINCHFIELD, FRANCIS. May 30, 1763. Londongrove. Adm. to Margaret
Linchfield.

CRAWFORD, MARY, relict of James. East Nottingham.
May 12, 1763. June 1, 1763.
To sons James and Andrew 1/3 part of 150 acres of plantation. To
son Josias the remainder of land and all moveable estate. To son
John 4 acres of land besides 3 acres he hath already cleared. To
son Alexander £23. To my daughter all clothes except one
petticoat to my daughter in law Anexander, my son's wife.
Executor: Son Josias.
Witnesses: John Fulton, Andrew Boyd, John Knox.

PHIPPS, JOSEPH, SR. Uwchlan.
7/27/1754. December 1762. Letters June 3, 1763.
To son Samuel 5 shillings. To son Joseph 5 shillings. To son
Nathan 5 shillings. To son John 5 shillings. To daughter Sarah
Houlston 20 shillings. To Mary Phipps my wife £18. To son
George £14 at 21. Remainder of personal estate equally divided
between wife Mary and son George. To wife Mary tract of land
containing 100 acres part of a tract purchased of David Lloyd
during life and at her decease to son George. To son George
tract of land in Uwchlan containing 111 acres purchased of Samuel
John, also tract of 30 acres adjoining purchased of Ralph Helsby,
also plantation where I now live to be given up to him at 21
years of age. To Uwchlan Meeting of people called Quakers £10.
Executors: Wife Mary and friends Thomas Downing.
Trustees: Samuel Lightfoot Sr. and Thomas Halhouse (Milhous) of
Pikeland.
Letters to Mary Phipps.
Witnesses: Samuel John, Griffith John, Robert John.

HARAH, WILLIAM. West Nottingham.
March 28, 1763. June 3, 1763.
Provides for wife Agnes. To son Patrick big Bible. Remainder of
estate to be sold and divided between son Patrick and daughter
Agnes, Patrick to have £20 more than Agnes.
Executors: Wife and father Patrick Harah.

Overseer: Brother Charles.
Witnesses: David Paten, Thomas Paten, Moses Irwin.

OWEN, HUGH. Vincent.
January 20, 1763. June 6, 1763.
Provides for wife Sarah. To William Kirk 15 shillings in trust for repairing Nantmeal Meeting House. To sons Evan, Mordecai and Abraham and daughter Elizabeth all remainder of estate when of legal age.
Executors: Brother in law Mordecai Williams and nephew William Owen.
Witnesses: William Stanfield, Samuel Stanfield, Simon Meredith.

MARTIN, THOMAS. Middletown.
12/31/1762. August 8, 1763.
Provides for daughter Ann while she remains unmarried, also £100. To daughter Martha Pennell 5 shillings. Remainder of personal estate to daughter Mary Dutton, daughter Ann Martin, sons Jonathan and Abraham and children of late daughter Alice Beson in equal shares. To eldest son Jonathan messuage whereon I now dwell in Middletown containing 220 acres paying legacies. To daughter Mary Dutton £50. To daughter Ann Martin £50. To children of daughter Alice Beson £50. Remainder to son Jonathan who with son Abraham are Executors.
Witnesses: John Fairlamb, Caleb Harrison, Fredrick. Fairlamb.

VERNON, JOSEPH.
June 7, 1763. N. Providence.
Adm. to Nathaniel Vernon.

MC CALL, MARY.
July 15, 1763. Londongrove.
Adm. to Thomas McCall.

DUTTON, RUTH.
June 15, 1763. Aston.
Adm. to Archibald Watson.

SMITH, THOMAS.
August 1, 1763. Tredyffrin.
Adm. to Israel Davis.

JEFFERIS, GEORGE. East Bradford. Carpenter.
June 3, 1763. August 29, 1763.
Provides for wife Lydia including plantation during widowhood and then to 2 sons George and James. To daughter Mary, wife of John Thomson 5 shillings. To daughter Jane, wife of John Siddins 5 shillings. To daughter Alice, wife of Samuel Erely 5 shillings. To daughters Lydia, Martha, Joanna, and Rachel 5 shillings each.
Executors: Wife Lydia and Samuel Coope.
Witnesses: Jason Cloud, Abraham Cloud, Benjamin Hawley, Jr.

COULSON, THOMAS. West Nottingham.
January 23, 1761. August 30, 1763.
Provides for wife Martha. To son John Coulson plantation where I now live, also stock. To sons Thomas and William plantation in West Nottingham joining to Octorara Creek containing 200 acres and £5 each. To son Joseph plantation in York County whereon he now lives, also £5. To son Samuel plantation in Little Britain, Lancaster County, already given him and £5. To daughter Sarah Rich £5. To son Isaac £5. To youngest daughter Elizabeth Coulson £60, also negro woman Joan.
Executors: Wife Martha and son Thomas.

Witnesses: William Allen, Robert Givan, Joseph Brown.

MORGAN, THOMAS. Vincent.
August 26, 1763. September 16, 1763.
To John Bound married to my daughter Anne £10. To Samuel Martin married to daughter Esther £10. To son Jacob Morgan 1/3 of plantation and movables. To son Thomas 1/3 of the same. To daughter Hannah Morgan £10. To daughter Mary Morgan £10. To son William the remainder of plantation and movables, also time of servant Joseph Foely.
Executors: Sons in law John Bound and Samuel Martin and son Thomas.
Witnesses: James Evans, Thomas Owens, Jr.

HARRIS, JOHN.
August 30, 1763. W. Nottingham.
Adm. to Phebe Harris.

COLLINS, JOSEPH.
September 6, 1763. Tredyffrin.
Adm. to Jonathan Gilbert.

MEEK, JOHN. West Nottingham.
December 27, 1762. October 1, 1763.
To sons John and Andrew and to daughters Mary, Jean and Rebecca Meek each 1/9 of all estate. To daughters Agnes and Nelley Meek 2/9 of estate, when of age.
Executor: James Maxwell.
Guardian: Adam Meek.
Witnesses: James Dougherty, James Davison.

GRIFFITH, WILLIAM. Edgmont.
September 20, 1762. October 1, 1763.
To son Joseph plantation in Edgmont containing 135 acres commonly known by name of Kingsmans Land. To wife Susanna plantation in Edgmont containing 100 acres bought of Thomas Goodwin during widowhood, at her decease to be sold and proceeds divided. To daughter Susanna Griffith £60, remainder to sons William and Joseph. To daughter Alice Cornock 5 shillings. Remainder to wife.
Executors: Son William and friends Francis Yarnall and Joseph Pratt.
Witnesses: Jacob Carter, Adam Grubb, E. Price.

HAINES, JOSEPH. West Nottingham.
10/27/1762. October 7, 1763.
Provides for wife Elizabeth. To son William all my title to tract of land where he is now settled esteemed 245 acres, also £20. To son Nathan plantation where he now lives in Frederick County, Maryland, part of a tract purchased of William Kersly called Cornwell and an addition, also £10. To son Daniel plantation where he now lives in Frederick County, Maryland, purchased of Walter Moore, also £10. To son Isaac 200 acres of the north end of the land whereon I now live, also £50. To son Job plantation whereon I now dwell and remainder of said lott with reversion to son William. To son Joseph 1 shilling sterling. To daughter Deborah Haines £100. To daughter Ruth Miller £5. To daughter Ann Sidwell £10. To daughter Dorothy Beeson 5 shillings. To granddaughter Patience Miller £10. All

remainder of estate to son Job at 21.
Executors: Wife Elizabeth and son Job, son William assistant.
Witnesses: Joseph Williams, John Butterfield, Sr. John Butterfield.

GRAHAM, JAMES. London Britain.
October 13, 1763. October 22, 1763.
To son Henry £50 and 1/3 benefit of the "Lace if he'l come and work along with these 3 boys." To son Charles £20. To daughter Elizabeth £10. To daughter Mary £35. To son James £20. To son William £20. All remainder equally divided betwixt wife Mary and John and George and Joseph and Sarah and Ann and "I leave the three little boys each a colt."
Executors: Wife Mary and James Kennedy.
Witnesses: John Dickie, Thomas Dugless.

MATHER, JOHN, JR. Chester. Attorney.
September 6, 1763. November 3, 1763.
To sister Rebecca Vanleer my gold ring. Executors to sell all estate and proceed put to interest for use of son James.
Executors: Plunket Fleeson of Philadelphia, and William Atlee of Lancaster.
Witnesses: Margaret Mather, Joseph Mather.

MOORE, DANIEL. West Nantmeal.
January 1, 1756. November 4, 1763.
Provides for wife Elizabeth. To eldest son Daniel 100 acres of land where he now dwells. To son John remainder of my land and implements of husbandry. To son Moses, daughter Ann and daughter Sarah 5 shillings each.
Executors: Wife and son John.
Letters to John Moore, the other renouncing.
Witnesses: Robert Brown, Nathan Moore.

THORNBURY, THOMAS.
October 10, 1763. W. Bradford.
Adm. to George Stalker.

SHUSTER, ANDREW.
October 29, 1763. Chichester.
Adm. to James Cole.

ASHBRIDGE, AMOS.
October 11, 1763. Darby.
Adm. to Hannah Ashbridge.
Sureties Joseph Ashbridge and Joseph Pratt. Brief inventory. Evidently not a married man.

MC DOWELL, JOSEPH.
November 3, 1763. New Garden.
Adm. to John Carpenter.

PENNOCK, WILLIAM.
October 24, 1763. E. Marlborough. Adm. to Alice & Moses Pennock.

GREGG, DINAH, widow. Kennett.
3/8/1763. November 8, 1763.
To son Michael Gregg £5. To son Thomas £5. To deceased daughter Mary Richards children £5. Remainder of estate to 4 daughters, Lydia wife of Thomas Carleton, Dinah wife of Christopher Wilson, Amy wife of James Wilson and Abigail wife of George Sharp and son Stephen Gregg. To son John my riding mare.

Executor: Son in law Thomas Carleton.
Witnesses: Thomas Harlan, Abigail Flower.

CULBERTSON, JAMES. West Nottingham.
October 14, 1763. November 15, 1763.
To brother Samuel Culbertson 5 shillings. To brother Robert and sisters Jean Culbertson and Sarah Brackingreg and Martha Miller and Rebecca Park, an equal share of all my real and personal estate.
Executor: Brother Robert.
Witnesses: William Allen, John Kirkpatrick.

PYLE, AMOS.
November 3, 1763. W. Marlborough.
Adm. to Abner Cloud.

WILLSON, JOHN.
November 28, 1763. Oxford.
Adm. to Hugh Luckie.

CULIN, GEORGE, JR.
November 14, 1763. Ridley.
Adm. to Swan Culin.
Gibson.

GIBSON, THOMAS.
Nov. 29, 1763. W. Fallowfield.
Adm. to Mary and Andrew

MOORE, JAMES. New London.
June 9, 1763. November 29, 1763.
To Elizabeth Carter £20. To James Moore son of my son John £50. To Catharine Moore, daughter of son John £10 when of age. To son William's 2 sons, James and Samuel £10 each. To my son by the law John Moore's 6 children, viz., James, Alexander, John, Henry, Elizabeth and Martha £10 when of age. To Mathew Porterfield's children, viz., James, Denney, Nelly and Elizabeth Porterfield £10 each when of age. To son John Moore £30. To son William £20. To daughter Elizabeth £40. To daughter Martha Porterfield £20. Remainder divided among my 2 sons and 2 daughters.
Executors: David Wiley and John Scott.
Witnesses: Joseph Cook, Peter Gubby.

BONSALL, JOSEPH. Darby.
December 8, 1763. December 19, 1763.
Provides for wife Sarah. To 4 daughters Sarah, Mary, Jane and Amy silver spoons. To granddaughter Hannah Harry silver spoons because she is called after my former wife. To grandson Bonsal Harry silver spoons because he is named after me. To daughter Amy £25. In consideration of the good behavior of my son in law Jacob Bonsall £50, but if he should die in his minority then to my 4 daughters. I acquit my son in law Aubrey Harry of 1/2 of what he is charged with in my book and Patrick Kelley of what he is charged with. To 4 daughters dwelling house and 2 lotts which I bought of Enoch Bonsall after death of wife.
Executors: Brother in law William Horne and kinsman David Gibson and Isaac Pearson.
Letters to Gibson and Pearson.
Witnesses: Benjamin Lobb, Josiah Bunting, John Pearson.

LARKIN, WILLIAM. December 19, 1763. Bethel. Adm. to Jane Larkin.

LEWIS, ISAAC, SR. Uwchlan.
September 27, 1762. December 22, 1763.
To son Isaac £50. To daughter Mary, wife of Evan Miles £20. To daughter Anne, wife of Thomas Green 5 shillings having had her portion. To daughter Margaret, wife of Joseph Phipps £15. To son Henry 5 shillings having had a deed for the most valuable part of my lands. My said 2 sons and 3 daughters having at this time 23 living children, I give to each of said 23 grandchildren 10 shillings. To Uwchlan Meeting for building or repairing grave yard wall £3. To wife Anne all my right in plantation where I live during life.
Executor: Son Isaac.
Witnesses: David Beatty, Samuel Halliday.

ARNOLD, THOMAS. West Bradford.
November 7, 1763. February 1, 1764.
To wife Ann plantation I now live on in West Bradford containing about 30 acres and all personal estate. To only daughter Sarah 6 pewter plates and dishes that was formerly her mothers.
Executor: Joseph Martin.
Witnesses: George Martin, John Smith.
* Thomas Arnold married Hannah Eavenson 10/30/1714 and Ann Rattew 11/14/1729.

ARNOLD, ANN. West Bradford.
1/26/1764. February 1, 1764.
To friend Joseph Martin all my estate as the same is specified in my husband Thomas Arnold's will, also Executor.
Witnesses: Richard Buffington, Margaret Erwin, James Kenny.

HAINS, JOHN. Greenwich, Gloucester County, New Jersey.
1/12/1754. March 16, 1754.
To son David Hains 5 shillings. To grandson John, son of said David all my land in Goshen in Pennsylvania. Provides for wife Jane. To son William all the plantation whereon I now dwell and all remainder of estate providing for wife during life.
Executors: Wife and son William.
Witnesses: William Gerrard, Thomas Robson, Joseph Land.

JONES, HENRY.
December 24, 1763. East Caln.
Adm. to Ann Jones.

MALIN, WILLIAM.
February 1, 1764. Willistown.
Adm. to Thomas Malin.

COURTNEY, ROBERT.
January 6, 1764. Vincent.
Adm. to Frances Courtney.

LOUGHEAD, ROBERT.
February 9, 1764. Oxford.
Adm. to Jane & James Loughead.

BRIGGS, RICHARD. Upper Providence. Cordtwiner.
November 4, 1762. February 13, 1764.
To wife Mary and son Thomas Briggs all real estate during her life and at her death to Thomas, paying to son John £10. Also to Richard, Agabus, Elizabeth and William Briggs and my daughter Mary Briggs £10 each as they arrive to the age of 21.
Executors: Wife and son Thomas.

Witnesses: Thomas Nuzum, John Moore, Richard Nuzum.

YARNALL, PHILIP. Edgmont.
9/21/1763. February 28, 1764.
To sister Grace's son, Philip Bonsal £5. To brother David Yarnall £10 and 1/2 wearing apparel and to his daughter, Lydia 40 shillings at 18. To brother Abraham £10 and 1/2 wearing apparel and to his children, viz., Rachel, Abner, Mary, Uriah and Ezekiel 20 shillings each. To my sister Dorothy's son Philip Yarnall £5 and to her daughter Jane 20 shillings when of age. Remainder divided between brothers and sisters, David and Abraham Yarnall, Jane Griffith, Elizabeth Yarnall, Esther Yarnall, Dorothy Yarnall and Mary Yarnall.
Executors: Brother David and brother in law John Griffith.
Witnesses: George Ashbridge, Isaac Williams, Thomas Morgan.

ALLISON, JOSEPH.
February 17, 1764. New London.
Adm. to Elizabeth and Robert Allison.

MC KEE, ALEXANDER.
September 3, 1748. February 29, 1764.
To Rev. Mr. Samuel Finley, my present Pastor, 20 shillings. To wife Martha the full half of my whole estate and all right and claim she ever had to the plantation which her former husband possessed shall be continued to her youngest son William Craig at his mother's disposal. To children of James Leeper and his wife, my daughter Margaret, 1/2 of remainder of estate, their son Alexander to have 1/3 thereof and the rest of their children the remainder. To children of Thomas Thompson and his wife, my daughter Martha, all remainder of estate, their son Alexander to have 1/2 of it.
Executors: Wife Martha and son James Leeper.
Letters to Leeper.
Witnesses: Abraham Scott, James Evans.

ROMAN, JOSHUA, SR. East Caln.
February 7, 1764. March 5, 1764.
To sons Joseph and Absalom 10 shillings each. To 2 sons Joshua and Benjamin real estate which I may be possessed of at my death. Rents to the use of 2 daughters Rachel and Sarah until said sons are 21. Samuel Filson to have use of quarry and lime kiln for 2 years from this date.
Executors: "Trusty and lawful wife" and Richard Downing.
Letters to Rachel Roman, the other renouncing.
Witnesses: Samuel Filson, William Purdy.

KITTERA, JAMES. West Fallowfield.
January 31, 1763. March 6, 1764.
Provides for wife Margaret. To niece Elizabeth Fulton and her children £30. To Margaret daughter of James Leeke £6 when of age. To Margaret Stuart £10. To Thomas Kittera 1/3 of estate at death of wife and the other 2/3 to Susanna Willson and Mary Ann Kinard. Executors: Wife Margaret and Thomas Kittera and John

Park, Sr. to be Executor along with them.
Letters to 2 first named, Park renouncing.
Witnesses: Robert Messers, John Keyl, James Allison.

BRADLEY, GRISSELL.
March 1, 1764. Uwchlan.
Adm. to John Hitchin.

WORRALL, GEORGE.
March 12, 1764. Easttown.
Adm. to Priscilla Worrall.

NOBLITT, RICHARD.
March 12, 1764. Middletown. Adm. to William Smedley.

THOMAS, JOHN. Uwchlan.
February 29, 1764. March 12, 1764.
To brother David Thomas of West Nantmeal all my goods and chattels, also my part of an estate in Uwchlan (Youghland), paying legacies. To brother Thomas Thomas and sister Anne, wife of David Williams 5 shillings each.
Executor: David Thomas.
Witnesses: Jacob Alexander, Joseph Darlinton.

CRISWELL, JOHN. West Nottingham.
June 4, 1761. March 26, 1764.
Provides for wife Jane. To sons James and William plantation whereon I now live to be divided at 21. Remainder of estate to be divided between 3 daughters Margaret, Rachel and Mary Criswell.
Executors: Brother in law and wife Jane.
Witnesses: John Gartril, William Criswell.

HEANEY, HUGH. East Fallowfield.
January 11, 1764. March 30, 1764.
Executor to sell plantation I now live on. To wife Margaret 1/3 of all estate. To son Hugh £5. To 3 daughters Isabella Cummings, Jane McIlvaine and Margaret Heaney all remainder to be divided.
Executor: Friend Thomas Coates.
Witnesses: Caleb Kirk, Moses Coates, Jr. Thomas Pimm.

JOHNSON, FRANCIS.
March 20, 1764. L. Chichester.
Adm. to Elizabeth Johnson & Archibald Dick.

HAGUE, JOHN.
March 27, 1764. Kennett.
Adm. to William Hague.

BRISBAN, SAMUEL.
March 29, 1764. E. Nottingham.
Adm. to Elizabeth Brisban.

STEVENSON, WILLIAM.
March 22, 1764. N. Providence.
Adm. to Robert Stevenson.

BEESON, MARY.
March 23, 1764. U. Chichester.
Adm. to Martin Carter. She was a legatee of John Beeson in sum of £5. Inventory - £47.9.6.

HOWELL, ISRAEL. Cordwainer. Late of Philadelphia.
12/30/1763. April 5, 1764.
Provides for wife Mary. To son Stephen £50 at 21. To daughter

Esther £40 together with the money in her Uncle Francis Swain's hands at 18. To my mother Sarah Surman £10. Remainder to wife and 2 children with reversion to brothers and sisters in law, viz., William, Francis, Thomas and Samuel Swain, Mary Pusey and Ann Webb.
Executors: Wife Mary and brother in law William Swain.
Witnesses: John Thomson, James Yarnall, Elisha Jones.

EYRE, WILLIAM. Bethel.
August 24, 1763. April 6, 1764.
Provides for wife Mary. To son Lewis plantation purchased of Joseph Wood in Upper Chichester containing about 45 acres, also £100. To son William plantation where I now live in Bethel containing about 200 acres. To son Robert plantation in Chichester purchased of John Fairlamb, Esq., containing 100 acres. To son John messuage and lot of ground in Boro of Chester purchased of John Fairlamb, Esq., also £20. To daughter Jane, wife of Robert Wilson, £10. To son Isaac £200. To daughter Ann Eyre £100. To son in law Joseph Askew 5 shillings. To grandchildren, viz., John, William and Parker Askew £5 each at 21.
Executors: Wife Mary and sons Lewis and William.
Witnesses: Adam Clayton, Joseph Buffington, John Power.

GIBSON, JOSEPH. West Nantmeal.
March 27, 1764. April 16, 1764.
To wife Alice 1/3 of all estate. To daughter Ann Clark £50. To son Isaac £40. To daughter Rebecca £60. To son Joseph £40. To son Thomas £40. To son John £90 with 3 acres of wheat. To son James £40. To son Moses £70. To granddaughter Alice Clark £5.
Executors: Sons Isaac and John.
Witnesses: William Nisbet, Robert Brown.

MILLARD, THOMAS. April 5, 1764. Coventry. Adm. to Lydia Millard.

BOURGOIN, JOSEPH. East Bradford. Husbandman.
March 4, 1764. April 19, 1764.
To wife all estate during widowhood, then to be divided as follows: To daughter Sarah and son Joseph £10 each. To daughter Tamar (married John Beale) £10. To son James 10 acres of land adjoining John Baldwin's and timber sufficient to build him a house. To daughter Susanna £10. To daughter Hannah £30. To son John £10. To granddaughter Asenath, daughter of daughter Sarah £2. Remainder equally divided. Son John to be put to a trade at 16 and daughter Hannah to be put to a trade at 16. 80 acres of land to be sold to pay debts.
Executors: Wife Hannah and daughter Sarah Burgoin.
Witnesses: John Ingram, William Ingram, John Gray.
Joseph Burgoin and Hannah Woolman, 2/10/1735, 1st Presbyterian Church in Philadelphia. Joseph Burgoign and Hannah Price, November 30, 1737, Christ Church in Philadelphia.
John Burgoyne, Jr., attorney at law, Cincinnati, Ohio, writes January 10, 1876 to J. Smith Futhey to know of his ancestry: says his great grandfather was Joseph Burgoyne of Chester County;

that his grandfather John married Ann McNeel, daughter of Dominic and Anne McNeel in Chester County and moved to Loudon County, Virginia.

CUMING, WILLIAM. West Nottingham.
March 12, 1764. April 25, 1764.
Wife Agnes provided for and gives £50 to each daughter and £10 over the rest to daughter Esther and £100 to each son to be put to interest for schooling. The clock to son James and bookcase to son Samuel and daughter Esther is to get a bill of sale of Bell, negro girl from Mrs. Morris in Philadelphia for her own use and as for Charley the niger boy is to be kept for the use of the house and if son Joseph is alive till my wife leaves this world of troubles the he is to fall to him. To daughter Elizabeth a chest of drawers. Testators signature proven by William Buchanan, aged 56 years, who was acquainted with Testator for 34 years and John Crawford, aged 44, who was acquainted with William Cumings for 22 years.
Executors: Wife and James Evins and Joseph Fraser of Lancaster, County.
Letters to wife Agnes and John Fraser.

EVANS, AMOS. April 24, 1764. Radnor. Adm. to Elizabeth Evans.

TAYLOR, MORDECAI. Springfield. Innkeeper.
March 11, 1764. April 30, 1764.
All estate to be sold. Provides for wife Ann. To son George 5 shillings. To daughter Hannah, wife of Nathan Thomson £10. To daughter Jane, wife of John Markward what my Executor thinks she stands in need of. All remainder to sons Benjamin, John, Jesse and Isaac to be equally divided.
Executors: William Fell and John Morris.
Witnesses: James Rhoads, Benanuel Lownes, George Grantham.

HEACOCK, JONATHAN. Marple.
4/14/1753. May 9, 1764.
Executors to make deed to son Joseph for £50 according to article of agreement. Remainder of land in Marple to wife Anne during life and on her death to son Joseph, he paying £120. Remainder of estate equally divided among 5 of my children, viz., John, Jonathan and William Heacock, Mary Penrose and Morgan.
Executors: Son John and friend John Lewis.
Witnesses: Rebecca Fell, William Fell, Seth Pancoast.

HUNT, ROGER, ESQ. May 1, 1764. East Caln. Adm. to William Hunt.

MARTIN, LLEWELYN. Charlestown.
January 21, 1740/41. May 9, 1764.
To wife Elizabeth and son Mathias all real and personal estate until said son is 21 paying legacies. To eldest daughter Anne Martin sufficient to make a legacy from her grandfather £20. To daughter Hannah Martin sufficient to make her legacy £15. To daughter Ethliw Martin £10 at 12 years. To daughter Mary £6 at 10. To daughter Martha £8 at 10. Testator's signature proven by

Lewis Martin, his brother and Richard Richardson of Whiteland,
John Griffith of Charlestown and David John of Charlestown.
Executors: Wife Elizabeth and son Mathias.
Guardians: Brother Lewis Martin and Thomas John of ye Glandy and
David Emanuel to Guardians and Assistants.
Witnesses: Emanuel Jones, James John, John Thomas.

TAYLOR, JOHN. Westtown.
June 10, 1761. May 16, 1764.
To wife Phebe plantation I now live on in Westtown containing 50
acres during widowhood. At her decease or marriage to son Thomas.
To son Thomas the other 50 acres now in his tenour over and above
the 100 acres I have already given him. to 3 grandsons, viz.,
Titus, Thomas and Caleb Taylor £10 each at 21. Remainder to wife
Phebe, also with son Thomas, executors.
Witnesses: William Hawley, Lawrence Townsend, William Johnson.

PENNELL, JOHN. East Caln.
March 3, 1761. May 16, 1764.
To sons Joshua and John Pennell 5 shillings each. All remainder
of estate to wife Mary Pennell, also executrix.
Letters C.T.A. to John Lewis, the Executrix being deceased.
Witnesses: Thomas Downing, Rachel Lewis, Thomas Pim.

ALEXANDER, JOHN.
January 13, 1762. May 17, 1764.
To daughter Rebecca Emmit £5. To wife Susanna all remainder of
estate real and personal, also Executrix. Theophilus Alexander
makes oath that he wrote the will at the request of Testator,
January 13, 1762.
Witnesses: Amos Alexander, Joseph Cannon, John Jordan, John
McKnitt Alexander.

HUBBERT, THOMAS.   GRAHAM, HENRY.
May 19, 1764. Tredyffrin.   May 17, 1764. London Britain.
Adm. to Elizabeth Davis.

TIDBALL, JOHN. West Nottingham.
April 19, 1764. May 21, 1764.
To Mother £10 yearly during life. To son Thomas £20 left by my
brother Joseph. 1/3 of remainder to wife and remainder to be
equally divided amongst my children, viz., Thomas, Margaret,
Abraham, Joseph, Sarah and James.
Executors: Wife and brother William.
Letters to Elizabeth and William Tidball.
Witnesses: Robert Marques, Samuel Scott.

BOYD, JAMES. Sadsbury.
February 15, 1764. May 29, 1764.
Provides for wife Jane. To son Andrew the mill and premises
where he now lives in North London and East Nottingham. To sons
Daniel and Robert 5 shillings each having had their part. To
sons Matthew and George all estate real and personal in Sadsbury
paying legacies. To daughter Hannah £50. To daughter Mary £100
when married.

Executors: Wife Jean and son Andrew.
Witnesses: James Cochran, Jr., Math. Henderson, William Boyd.

MUIRHEAD, JAMES. West Nottingham.
March 4, 1764. June 29, 1764.
To Aunt Agnes Rogers of Parish of Rapho, County Donegal, Ireland, £5. To Aunt Isabel Kirk of same place £5. All remainder to father James Muirhead of same place if living with reversion to the latter children of my father, viz., John, Thomas, William and Margaret Muirhead.
Executor: Friend Michael Randel.
Witnesses: Andrew Wallock, James Wharrey, Micajah James.

TAYLOR, THOMAS.
May 22, 1764. Ridley.
Adm. to Rebecca Taylor &
Luke Nethermark.

LLOYD, JOHN.
May 30, 1764. Willistown.
Adm. to Erasmus Lloyd.

BEATON, DANIEL. May 29, 1764. Charlestown. Adm. to Mary Beaton.

JAMES, JOHN. Vincent.
May 21, 1764. June 11, 1764.
To wife Lettice 1/2 of all estate during life and at her decease to son John James. To daughter Elenor, wife of David Davies £40. To son William tract of land he now lives on. To son in law Jeremiah Price that was married to my daughter Mary 10 shillings. To son in law George David that was married to my daughter Elizabeth 10 shillings and to his son Thomas £10 at 21, also to their sons John, George and Ephraim David £10 each at 21. To son John the other 1/2 of plantation I now live upon. Also to wife and son John time of my servants Jane Allison and William Carter.
Executors: Sons William and John.
Witnesses: Owen Thomas, Rees Evan, David Thomas.

YARNALL, THOMAS. Edgmont.
6/7/1764. June 16, 1764.
To son William plantation where I now dwell containing 100 acres, he paying to daughter Margaret Yarnall £12 yearly during her life and house room, also £20 at 18. All remainder of estate to 3 sons, Job, Caleb and Joseph.
Executors: Brother Nathan Yarnall and friend Thomas Minshall.
Witnesses: George Smedley, Cadwallader Evans, George Miller.

JENKIN, RICHARD.
June 15, 1764. Chester.
Adm. to Jane Jenkin.

MARSHALL, JOSEPH.
August 1, 1764. W. Bradford.
Adm. to Levis Pennock.

1764, 6 mo., 13th. Thomas Minshall, Nathan Yarnall Executors of Thomas Yarnall deceased to making his coffin with six handles £2.10.6. (William Smedley's account book)

WEBB, WILLIAM. Kennett.
8/22/1763. August 6, 1764.
Provides for wife Elizabeth. To son William £5. To son Stephen

plantation whereon I now dwell with land adjoining purchased of Thomas Fisher containing in the whole 327 acres, giving to granddaughter Rebecca, daughter of son William, a heifer at 10 years of age. To son Ezekiel plantation in East Marlborough purchased of Abraham Parker's Executor containing about 75 acres at 21, also £200. To daughter Rebecca, wife of Benjamin Taylor, Jr. £5. To daughter Jane Webb £100 at 18. To grandson Joseph Taylor £5 at 14. To grandson William Taylor £10 at 14.
Executors: Wife and son Stephen.
Witnesses: John Hoopes, Phebe Carter, Joseph Pierce.

KIRK, SAMUEL. West Nottingham.
August 22, 1763. August 28, 1764.
To brother Timothy Kirk £5. To cousin Joseph Kirk horse. To cousin Abner Kirk all the land South of the great road at my mother's decease and when he is 21. To cousin Samuel Woodward all land North of road at my mother's decease. To cousin Timothy Kirk all shop tools. To cousin Roger Kirk all my books. To cousin Joseph Woolison chest. To cousin Jacob Kirk my desk. To cousin Thomas Woodward mare and saddle. To cousin William Cook all wearing apparel. To cousin Rebecca Woodward all my sheep. To cousin Mary Woodward a cow. To cousin Elizabeth Woolison bed and bedding. To mother Elizabeth Kirk negro wench June.
Executor: Brother Thomas Woodward.
Witnesses: James Maxwell, Andrew Willson, Isabella Maxwell.

BAILY, THOMAS. August 18, 1764. Newlin. Adm. to John Baily.

JOHNSON, WILLIAM. Haverford.
May 6, 1755. August 28, 1764.
To son John Johnson plantation whereon he now dwells in Haverford containing 114 acres paying legacies. To daughter Rachel £2.10. To son William £10 at 18. To daughter Martha £5 at 16. To son David £10 at 18. To son Samuel plantation whereon I now dwell containing 76 acres paying legacies to brothers and sisters, also all remainder of personal estate and providing for wife Mary during life.
Executors: Sons John and Samuel.
Witnesses: Jesly [Justy?] Giger, Thomas Simon, Benjamin Hayes.

WILKIN, GEORGE. Sadsbury.
January 15, 1763. August 29, 1764.
Provides for wife Eloner. To son Leonard 15 shillings. To daughter Elizabeth 10 shillings. To son William £50. To daughter Hannah £25. To daughter Eloner £25. To son John messuage I now live on in Sadsbury.
Executors: Wife and son William.
Letters to William, the other renouncing.
Witnesses: James Fleming, John Fleming.

TATNALL, ANNE. Ridley.
7/28/1760. August 30, 1764.
To Darby Monthly Meeting £10. To Anne Foulke, daughter of sister Dorothy Leister £10. All remainder to child or children of daughter Elizabeth Knowles to be divided at 18.

Executor: Son in law John Knowles.
Witnesses: George Grantum, Robert Crozer, Hannah Crozer.

CAMPBELL, WILLIAM. West Caln.
August 21, 1764. September 20, 1764.
To mother Ann Hendry living in Parish of McCaskey in Ireland 1/2 of estate and the other 1/2 to my brother Alexander Campbell of same place.
Executors: Cousin George Campbell and James Keys, Senr. Letters to Campbell, the other renouncing.
Witnesses: William Fulton, James Kys, Jr., William Clark.

HILL, JOHN, SR. East Nottingham.
May 7, 1764. Codicil: August 1, 1764. October 1, 1764.
Provides for wife Margaret including use of house where Jonathan Hill now lives. To youngest daughter Jane £10 at 18. To son Samuel bay mare and house Bible. To son in law Robert Grimes £3. To youngest son Thomas remainder of plantation and personal estate.
Executors: John Hathorn and brother Samuel Hill.
Witnesses: William Kear, John Canan.

DAVIES, JANE, widow. Goshen.
7/26/1764. October 1, 1764.
To son Ellis clock and case. To son Amos Davis £20 and to his daughter Hannah furniture. To daughter Priscilla, wife of Joseph Ashbridge £10. To daughter in law Ann Davies wearing apparel. To granddaughter Mary Ashbridge furniture. To daughter Susanna Hoopes and daughter Jane Pratt, books. To grandson Jonathan Davies walnut desk.
Executors: Son Ellis Davies and son in law Joseph Ashbridge.
Overseers: Brother Richard Jones and George Ashbridge.
Witnesses: Richard Jones, Sarah Davies.

CURREY, ARCHIBALD.
September 27, 1764. Darby.
Adm. to Gilbert Weeks.

MC KEE, JAMES.
October 1, 1764. W. Nantmeal.
Adm. to Joseph McKee.

MC KAGHAN, DANIEL.
October 1, 1764. Uwchlan.
Adm. to James Duncan.

STARRETT, ROBERT.
Oct 1, 1764. W. Nottingham.
Adm. to Mary Starrett.

CALDWELL, ELIZABETH. Newtown.
8/14/1759. October 1, 1764.
To son James McClelan 5 shillings. To son Samuel £1.13.4 and Bible. To daughter Rebecca McMichael £2. To daughter Mary Caldwell £2. To son in law William McClelan £1. To daughter in law Jane Miller £1. To daughter in law Isabel Hunter £1. All remainder to sons Robert, Thomas and Samuel McClelan and daughters Elizabeth McCrey, Rebecca McMichael, and Mary Caldwell.
Executor: Son Samuel McClelan.
Witnesses: Isaac Cochran, John Cochran, James Lindsay.

DAVIS, ABRAHAM. East Bradford.
January 20, 1762. October 1, 1764.

Provides for wife Susanna. To son John Davis 5 shillings. To 3 daughters Mary Townsend, Alice Guest and Hannah Chapman £5 each. To sons James and Joseph all remainder of personal estate.
Executors: Wife Susanna and son Joseph.
Witnesses: James Dilworth, Charles Dilworth, George Brinton.

THOMAS, ELEANOR, widow of Owen. Vincent.
December 7, 1761. October 9, 1764.
To son David Thomas £20. To son Morris £1.17.6. To son Owen £1.7.6. To daughter Sarah Evans, wife of Abner £20. To daughter Elizabeth, wife of Joseph Thomas £20. To daughter Mary Jury £20. To grandchild Eleanor Evans, daughter of Abner bed and bedding. To Eleanor, daughter of Joseph Thomas £2.10. To grandchild Eleanor Jury £2.10.
Executor: Son David Thomas.
Letters C.T.A. to Joseph Thomas, executor named having renounced.
Witnesses: David Jenkin, Joseph Jenkin.

SMITH, WALTER.
October 4, 1764. Chester.
Adm. to Robert Erwin &
William Marlow.

SHARPLESS, JOSEPH, JR.
October 6, 1764. Middletown.
Adm. to Benjamin Sharpless &
Benjamin Sharpless, Jr.

PIERSOLL, BRIDGET. West Nantmeal.
December 27, 1762. October 15, 1764.
To daughter Rachel Morgan wearing apparel. To daughter Elizabeth Davis all my pewter and to daughter Martha Hunter 15 gallon pot. To daughter Mary Douglas walnut chest and to her daughter Bridget £10. Remainder to 4 daughters except 5 shillings to son Richard Piersoll.
Executors: Capt. Jacob Morgan and Robert Brown.
Witnesses: Joseph Darlinton, Robert Darlinton.

WILLIAMS, ELLIS. Goshen.
8/28/1764. October 20, 1764.
Provides for wife Lydia to have 10 acres next [to] Jonathan Ashbridge. Remainder of estate divided. Sons Jesse, Ellis, Isaac and Nathan to have £10 each more than daughters Jane and Lydia. Also makes provision for "the child my wife is now big of."
Executors: Wife Lydia and Randle Malon.
Witnesses: James Garrett, John Griffith.

FRANCIS. LETTICE, widow. Whiteland.
December 11, 1762. November 16, 1764.
To daughter Margaret, wife of John Towers £80. To daughter Anne, wife of John Parry £20. To Pierce Frasher eldest son of daughter Anne £10. To son John 1 shilling. The above legacies to be paid out of the £300 given to my husband Rees Frances and myself.
Executor: Friend James Davis of Tredyffrin.
Witnesses: Samson Davis, Thomas John.

HOWELL, ISAAC.
October 16, 1764. Marple.
Adm. to Mary Howell.

PHILLIPS, THOMAS.
November 14, 1764. Darby.
Adm. to Thomas Phillips.

WHITE, NICHOLAS. Whiteland.
February 29, 1764. November 19, 1764.
to son Uriah White £50 and to his children £50 to be divided when
of age. To son Thomas £10. To daughter Elizabeth Smith £5. To
son in law George Smith £30 to be in full for all charges he may
have against me and to the children of George and Elizabeth Smith
£40 to be divided as they come of age. To son in law William
Garrett and his wife, my daughter Mary 1/2 remainder of estate,
the other 1/2 to their children when of age, also Executors.
Witnesses: Richard Richison, Joseph Rea.

KYLE, ROBERT.
June 9, 1764. November 27, 1764.
To nephew Robert Dingwall £40. To cousin James Finley, Sr. horse
saddle and to his son William silver buckles. To cousin Elenor
Marques all remainder of estate.
Executors: Cousin James Finley and James Evans.
Letters to Evans, the other having renounced.
Witnesses: William Patton, David Beard.

MILLER, SAMUEL. New Garden.
November 1, 1764. November 27, 1764.
Provides for wife Margaret. To cousin Samuel Miller's son Joseph
£10 at 21 with reversion to his sister Rebecca. To nephew
Samuel, son of late brother Joseph Miller, all lands and all
remainder of personal estate subject to wife's life interest,
also Executor.
Witnesses: Moses Starr, Samuel Moor, Jeremiah Starr.

HARRY, STEPHEN. December 3, 1764. E. Marlborough. Adm. to Evan
Harry.

LOGAN, THOMAS. New London. December 11, 1764. Adm. to Margaret
Logan, John Fulton & John Hathorn.

CHARLTON, ISABELLA. Londonderry.
December 14, 1754. December 17, 1764.
To son John Charlton £9. To daughter Margaret and son Henry
Charlton 5 shillings each. To son Thomas plantation I live on in
Faggs Manor. To daughter Lettice Charlton all remainder of
personal estate.
Executors: Son Thomas and daughter Lettice.
Letters to Thomas.
Witnesses: Hugh Luckie, Joseph Parkinson, Thomas Richardson.

GEST, SIMON. Concord.
November 2, 1764. December 29, 1764.
Provides for wife Mary. To son John Gest plantation I now live
on in Concord which my father bought of Mathias Kirlin containing
106 acres with 20 acres to be taken off my other tract of land
and silver watch that was that of his grandfather, John Gest. To
son Thomas remainder of land in Concord containing 280 acres at
21. Both sons to be bound apprentices at 16. Son John to be
brought and educated under the care of his grandfather John
Salkeld until he is 16. If sons die with heirs, real estate to

Uncle Henry Gest and children of Uncle James by his wife Phebe.
Executors: Wife Mary and Robert Mendenhall.
Witnesses: Moses Palmer, Joseph Kirlin, John Reynolds.

BLACKWELL, ELIZABETH, widow. Bethel..
March 4, 1762. January 23, 1765.
To son Stephen Foulke 5 shillings having done sufficiently for
him in my lifetime. To each of my grandchildren, the children of
daughter Sarah Babb deceased, 1 shilling. To great granddaughter
Elizabeth Foulk, daughter of grandson John Foulk, case of drawers
at 18. Remainder to grandson John Foulk, also Executor.
Witnesses: Nathanel Cloud, Robert Cloud, Mary Scott.

HOLLIS, GEORGE.
December 25, 1764. Birmingham.
Adm. to John Gray.

PYLE, SAMUEL.
February 26, 1765. Bethel.
Adm. to Sarah Pyle.

RICE, EDWARD.
January 17, 1765. Bethel.
Adm. to Judith Rice.

EDMUNDS, THOMAS.
February 26, 1765. New London.
Adm. to Mary Edmunds.

TAYLOR, SAMUEL. East Bradford.
2/8/1765. February 27, 1765.
To brother Isaac Taylor messuage in East Bradford containing
about 76 acres at 21, paying to each of his brothers, Abraham and
John Taylor £60. To friend Deborah Scarlet, daughter of
Nathaniel £10. To mother Deborah Taylor all remainder of estate.
Executors: Uncles Abraham and Thomas Darlington.
Witnesses: John Brinton, Caleb Woodrow, Joseph Pierce.

GIBSON, CHRISTIAN, widow of John. West Marlborough.
8/20/1764. February 27, 1765.
To son Thomas Gibson all bonds, notes and cash except as
hereafter devised. To granddaughter Elizabeth Chandler bond of
£14 due from James Wilson, household goods and mare. To grandson
John Gibson £20 and clock at 21. To my 4 other grandchildren,
Joshua, Lydia, Elizabeth and Nathaniel Gibson £20 each to be kept
by their father until of age. To cousin Rachel, daughter of
Bancroft and Ruth Woodcock £3. To friend Susanna Carleton £2.
To my ancient friend Deborah Clarke £1. To son Thomas and Hannah
his wife all remainder.
Executor: Son Thomas.
Witnesses: Elizabeth Ring, Christopher Hollingsworth, Nathaniel
Ring, Jr.

BATEMAN, JOHN. Vincent.
January 8, 1765. March 9, 1765.
To wife Anne 1/2 of clear estate. To daughter Catharine, wife of
David Evan 5 shillings. To daughter Anne, wife of Elis Elis 5
shillings. To son in law Andrew Geirce that was married to my
daughter Susanna 5 shillings if he will come and demand it. To
daughter Mary, wife of John Fitzsimmons 5 shillings. To son
Henry 10 shillings. To daughter Margaret, wife of James Evan 5
shillings. To daughter Martha, wife of Abraham Hammer 5

shillings. To son John 5 shillings. To son William other 1/2 of
clear estate. To daughter Sarah Bateman 5 shillings. To son
Thomas £5. to daughter Hannah Bateman £3.
Executors: Wife Anne and son William.
Witnesses: John Phillips, Morris Evan, John Martin.

NICHOLIN, JOSEPH. Concord.
10/5/1758. March 9, 1765.
To wife Susanna plantation whereon I now dwell in Concord bought
of Morgan Jones deceased during life and to be disposed of by
will as she shall think proper. Also my plantation in Concord
bought of Elizabeth Parks, widow. To daughter Mary, wife of John
Davis of Birmingham 5 shillings. To daughter Patience, wife of
Edward Bennett of Thornbury 5 shillings. To wife Susanna all
remainder of estate during life and at her death to be divided
between my daughter Rachel, wife of William Cross of Concord and
Susanna Webb, my granddaughter, daughter of Benjamin Webb of
Kennett.
Executors: Wife and son in law William Cross.
Letters to Cross, the other being deceased.
Witnesses: Joseph Chamberlin, John Hall, Samuel Rutter.

MADDOCK, HENRY. Springfield.
February 28, 1765. March 12, 1765.
To father James Maddock wearing apparel. Real estate being 1/2
plantation in Springfield on which I now dwell to Executors in
trust for use of mother Susanna Maddock during life and at her
death to my brothers and sister, Isaac, Jacob, Jesse and Rebecca
to be equally divided.
Executors: John Morton, Esq. and James Crozer.
Witnesses: James McCollough, William Price.

MACWILLIAMS, SARAH.
March 9, 1765. March 14, 1765.
Directs body to be buried in husband's grave and tombstones
erected. To son William silver buckles and chest. To son John 5
shillings. Remainder divided into 3 parts, 2 of which I give to
daughter Mary and the other to my kinswoman Esabella Stockman.
Executors: John Hanthorn and Archibald Job.
Witnesses: Robert Hervie, Sampson Moor.

WALL, JOHN. Goshen.
3/14/1764. March 15, 1765.
To son Edward Wall plantation whereon I now live in Goshen
containing 105 acres, he paying to the heirs of son William £5,
also 20 shillings each. To daughter Anne, wife of Benjamin
Elliot 20 shillings. To daughter Mary, wife of John Carr 20
shillings. To 2 granddaughters Ann and Mary Wall, daughters of
son Joseph deceased 20 shillings. All remainder to son Edward
for support of him and his wife and children.
Executor: Friend and neighbor Isaac Haines, Jr.
Witnesses: William Bane, Enoch Eachus, Nathaniel Moore.

TAYLOR, JOSIAH. Kennett.
1/16/1765. March 19, 1765.

Provides for wife Jane. To daughter Sarah Hall furniture. To daughter Mary furniture. To son Caleb plantation where I now dwell at 21, paying following legacies. To son Abraham £20. To son John £20. To daughters Mary and Jane £7.10 each.
Executors: Francis Swayne and son John.
Letters to Swayne, the other renouncing.
Witnesses: Daniel Mercer, Joseph Taylor, Stephen White.

LETTIMUR, ARTHUR. London, Britain.
April 2, 1764. March 20, 1765.
To son Robert, clothes. To son George, clothes and "my forged griddle or plank." To wife £20 and "liquise the half of the pewter and the other 1/2 to cousin Pally Dargan." To sons Robert, James and George and John McCamond, Emmson Bond all my land together with all money and bonds to be sold and equally divided.
Executor: Son James. Son in law John McCamond, assistant.
Witnesses: James Kennedy, John Dickie.

JOHN, DAVID. Charlestown. Labourer.
February 22, 1765. April 3, 1765.
To father £10 and horse and saddle till my brother Benjamin is of age. To brother Daniel wearing apparel. To brother Thomas my watch. Remainder among my 3 elder brothers John, Thomas and Daniel.
Executor: Father Thomas John.
Witnesses: John Allan, Abel Griffith, John Griffith.

MYER, HENRY.
April 3, 1765. Aston.
Adm. to John Cox.

JACKSON, SAMUEL. Oxford.
November 29, 1764. April 5, 1765.
To son Paul Jackson 10 shillings. To son Samuel 200 acres of land lying most convenient to the dwelling house subject to wife Rachel's interests. To daughter Mary, son David, daughter Rachel each a child's portion of my estate, daughter Rachel to be put to school until 10 years of age.
Executors: Son in law Samuel Dickie and son Samuel.
Witnesses: George McCollough, Adam Cooper.

RICHARD, EDWARD. Ashe. Township.
January 12, 1764. April 22, 1765.
Directs body to be interred in burial ground of St. Paul's Church, Chester, by my deceased wife Elizabeth. Provides for wife Margaret. My little plantation adjoining Daniel Brown to be sold and proceeds divided among my 7 daughters, Sarah, Rachel, Rebecca, Elizabeth, Susanna, Catherine and Martha. Also plantation at ye Hook to be sold and divided as above. To Church Wardens when I am interred £3. To son Jacob Richards plantation which I lived on in Ash Township, also smith tools.
Executors: John Fairlamb, Esq. and son Jacob.
Witnesses: George Craig, John Smith, Ann Smith.

COWPLAND, CALEB. Chester Borough.
12/15/1758. April 26, 1765.
To Caleb son of John and Agnes Lowns £300. To Joseph, son of do £150 to be at interest until they are 21. To James Cowpland £50. To Edward Pancost, my first cousin, £50. To brother in law John Lowns wearing apparel and books. All remainder to brother Jonathan Cowpland. Any surplus over £1000 to be given to the poor of Chester and for a school in Borough of Chester.
Executors: Brother Jonathan and Henry Graham and William Swaffer.
Letters to Cowpland, the others renouncing.
Witnesses: John Eyre, Thomas Pedrick, James Young.

FELL, EDWARD.
April 11, 1765. Marple.

KELLEY, THOMAS. West Caln. Weaver.
March 1, 1765. April 26, 1765.
To Alexander Brown married to my daughter Janet £12 to be paid out of that £100 bound if it can be recovered of John Walker or his estate. To daughter Jean £10. To daughter Frances £15. To daughter Mary £15, to William Roger married to daughter Margaret £12. To son Mathew £10 "if he comes back again." Remainder to son Alexander which is £26.
Executors: William Crawford and William Lyon.
Witnesses: John Thompson, James Stevenson.

GRAHAM, ARTHUR. West Nantmeal.
February 13, 1765. April 29, 1765.
Provides for wife Jean. To son James £5. To 5 sons, Arthur, John, Michael, Jared and Daniel an equal share of all estate after payment of legacies. To daughter Mary £20. To daughter Margaret £50 and negro woman Bette. To daughter Helinor £50. To daughter Sarah a warrant right of land joining land I made over to son James on north side. To daughter Jean £50. Sons under age to be bound to trades.
Executors: George Irwin, James Hanna and James Hair.
Witnesses: Joseph Kennedy, Moses Scott, Jarett Graham, Michael Graham.

BELL, WILLIAM. April 29, 1765. Vincent. Adm. to William & Edward Bell.

MENDENHALL, AARON. Caln.
10/27/1764. May 4, 1765.
To son Aaron £5. To daughter Lydia £200. To son James 5 shillings. To son John 5 shillings. Remainder to wife during widowhood and then to be divided between daughters Elizabeth and Rose.
Executor: Son in law Caleb Kirk.
Witnesses: Thomas Coates, Thomas Stalker, Benjamin Davis.

LAW, MARTHA. East Nottingham.
April 16, 1765. May 23, 1765.
To James Hudder's children by his first wife Rachel £30, viz., to

John £10, to Martha £10, to Mary £10. To Robert Law's daughter
Martha £5. To my Uncle's daughter Mary Wilson £5. To Robert
Law's wife, to James Wilson's wife, to Finley McGrew's wife,
Robert Wilson's wife and to Elizabeth Carmichael wearing apparel.
Remainder to be divided among my sister's daughters, viz.,
Martha, Margaret, Katren Shaws in County Tyrone, Ireland.
Executors: William Willson of Oxford and John Fultorn, clothier
of East Nottingham.
Witnesses: Robert Wilson, James Hudders.

SMEDLEY, SARAH, widow. Willistown.
2/25/1765. May 28, 1765.
To son Thomas Smedley £60. To grandson Abiah Taylor £5.
Remainder to be equally divided among sons and daughters, viz.,
Francis, John, George, and Sarah Minshall. Mulatto woman Nell
and her 2 children to be free at my death.
Executors: Sons John and George.
Witnesses: Isaac Garrett, Joshua Hoopes.

YARNALL, ISAAC.
May 6, 1765. Edgmont.
Adm. to Mary Yarnall &
Abel Green.

BOONE, REBECCA.
May 27, 1765. Darby.
Adm. to Peter Matson.

PAINTER, JOHN. Birmingham.
November 17, 1764. May 30, 1765.
Provides for wife Sarah. To son Samuel plantation given me by my
father Samuel. Also my plantation in Birmingham purchased of
William Thatcher. To 2 daughters Sarah and Lydia plantation in
Ashtown and Chester which was my first wife Agnes Painter's and
purchased by me from Thomas Painter and £50 each.
Executors: Wife Sarah and Andrew Yeatman.
Witnesses: Jonathan Thatcher, Gideon Gilpin, Isaac Widdos.

DONNELL, JAMES. New London.
August 27, 1764. June 11, 1765.
To wife Annas all estate during life and at her death to be
disposed of among my children at her discretion. I ordered my
servant John Mahan to remain with my wife until his time be done
if he proves a good boy. If he behaves other ways I order him to
be sold.
Executrix: Wife Annas.
Witnesses: James Clinton, Alexander Geddes.

GEORGE, THOMAS. Springfield.
July 18, 1765. July 22, 1765.
To son Thomas 5 shillings. To daughter Isabel, wife of Matthew
Hopkins of York County, 5 shillings. To daughter Jane, wife of
William Maxwell 5 shillings. To daughter Mary, wife of Thomas
Cahoon of Kent County, 5 shillings. To daughter Ann, wife of
Joseph George of Chester County, 5 shillings. To daughter
Martha, wife of Henry McClelland 5 shillings. To daughter
Margaret, wife of Hugh Maxwell of Chester County, 5 shillings.
All remainder to wife Mary and son William.
Executors: Wife and friend Charles Linn.

Witnesses: Daniel Rees, Hugh Linn, Henry Dexter.

CHURCH, PAUL. June 3, 1765. West Nantmeal. Adm. to Dorcas Church.

CARTER, JOSEPH.
May 14, 1765. July 23, 1765.
Land bought of John Richards to be sold and mortgage paid. Remainder of money to cousin Jasack Carter, also bond of £60 James Cole owes me. To brother Edward Carter wearing apparel and £10. To brother Robert bond he owes me and my watch. To brother Samuel all he owes me and my desk. To sister Hannah Foroh bed and bedding.
Executors: Hugh Linn and James Cale.
Letters to Linn, the other having renounced.
Witnesses: James Cole and Oliver Farra.

GLASSFORD, HENRY. Kent County, Maryland.
November 5, 1767. July 13, 1768.
To wife Elizabeth 1/3 of tract of land in Kent County, Maryland. Remainder 2/3 to niece Margaret Glasford now living in Ireland and remainder 1/3 on death of wife. £6 per year for 10 years to the Congregation of Presbyterians in Kent County. To 2 nephews Henry Glasford and James Wilson tract of land in Chester County. Plantation whereon Henry Culley now lives on East branch of North East to be sold and of the money I give to Henry Cully £50 and Michael Askins' children 30 shillings each and their mother £5. To cousins Henry and Elizabeth, children of my cousin John Glasford, £10 and Sarah the child of said John £5. To brother Joseph Glasford remainder of said money. To Mary, wife of Aquilla Page £10. To Elizabeth Cry £5. To Jane Black all remainder of estate.
Executor: James Black.
Witnesses: Aquilla Page, John Wallace, William Rogers.

CARUTHERS, ALEXANDER. West Fallowfield.
October 4, 1764. July 29, 1765.
Provides for wife Margaret. To son John messuage that I now possess and 1/2 cattle. To son James £30 and 1/2 cattle. To grandson Alexander £10 at 21. To grandson James £5 when of age. To granddaughter Margaret furniture. To grandson David table. To granddaughter Jean 2 sheep.
Executors: Son John and James Gilleland.
Witnesses: Michal Finley, Elijah Criswell, William Boyd.

TREGO, SUSANNA. Upper Providence.
7/22/1764. August 23, 1765.
To mother Ann Trego all land and right of land in Upper Providence descended to me from my father and all other estate, also Executrix.
Witnesses: Nathan Taylor, Rachel Evans, George Miller.

WEBB, BENJAMIN. Kennett.
7/22/1765. Codicil: 8/2/1765. August 26, 1765.
All real estate to be sold. Provides for wife. To son James

large Bible. To brother Daniel wearing apparel. Remainder equally divided among my 4 children, viz., James, Rachel, Alice, and Elizabeth Webb, son James having 2 shares.
Executors: Wife Jane and brother in law Aaron Musgrove. John Smith and Moses Brinton to be their assistants.
Witnesses: James Brinton, James Bennett, Robert Fisher.

DUTTON, KINGSMAN.
July 29, 1765. U. Chichester.
Adm. to Anne Dutton.

JOHNSTON, ALEXANDER.
August 28, 1765. Goshen.
Adm. to Alice Johnston.

EMMITT, DAVID.
July 31, 1765. E. Nottingham.
Adm. to Isabelle Emmitt.

STERLING, ANDREW, REV.
Sept. 7, 1765. W. Marlborough.
Adm. to Thomas Kerr.

LANE, BENJAMIN. August 21, 1765. Goshen. Adm. to James Massey & John Smedley.

BAILY, GEORGE. Radnor.
January 11, 1765. September 28, 1765.
Plantation whereon I now live in Radnor containing 82 acres to be sold. To wife Isabella £200. To grandson George Harry £10 at 21. Remainder divided between 3 daughters Hannah, Betty and Dinah.
Executor: Son in law Amos Harry.
Witnesses: John Davis, Mordecai Morgan, Mary Morgan.

FARRAN, PHILIP. West Fallowfield.
January 22, 1765. October 1, 1765.
2/3 of whole estate to wife Margaret and son Michael and 1/3 to daughter Mary, £20 being taken from her share for son John.
Executors: William Noble and Dorrinton Boyle.
Letters to Noble.
Witnesses: Thomas Elder, Charles Kelley.

PEDRICK, RACHEL. Chichester. Widow.
December 15, 1764. March 18, 1765. Letters October 1.
To 3 children, viz., John, Adam and Rachel all real estate as Tenants in Common. To daughter Rachel wearing apparel and pair gold sleeve buttons. To son Adam my other pair gold sleeve buttons. Remainder of personal divided.
Executor: Brother Adam Grubb.
Witnesses: Richd. Riley, Samuel Grubb, Hannah Flower.

WORRALL, BENJAMIN. Marple.
August 5, 1765. October 3, 1765.
Provides for wife Phebe. To son Amos all my land called by the name of *William Wintons* containing 44 acres when he is 21. All rest of land divided between my other 3 sons, viz., Nathan, John and Aaron when youngest comes of age. To daughter Elizabeth furniture. Remainder divided between all my daughters as they come to age.
Executors: Wife and son Amos.
Witnesses: James Worrall, William Burn, Edward Hewes.

SANFORD, ROBERT. West Caln.
September 6, 1765. October 8, 1765.
Provides for wife Anne. To my children, Abraham, Isaac, Jacob, Jean, Elizabeth, Anne and Patience after death of my wife an equal share of all my estate. To son Samuel 5 shillings.
Executors: Alexander Simrall and John Cochran.
Witnesses: Thomas Simrall, James Cochran, Elizabeth Cochran.

MC CAY, WILLIAM. Springfield.
April 25, 1759. October 21, 1765.
All estate to 4 sons, viz., John, William, Thomas and Galbreath, £20 to be taken from Galbreath's share and given to John Galbreath to pay for his maintenance until he is of age.
Executors: Brothers in law John Galbreath and James McCollough.
Witnesses: Jesse Maris, Alban Roberts.

GATIS, JAMES.
October 10, 1765. New London.
Adm. to Martha Gatis.

WITHY, JOHN.
October 22, 1765. Chester.
Adm. to Mary Withy & George Gray.

HUMPHREY, MARY. Darby.
September 7, 1765. October 24, 1765.
To son Daniel clock and desk. To son Richard lot of land bought of Samuel Bethel. To son John, house and lot of ground in which I now live and lot adjoining which formerly belonged to my mother, also another lot adjoining devised to me by my late husband when he comes of age, paying £15 each to sons Daniel and Richard. £20 each to daughters Martha and Mary. Wearing apparel to daughters. Executors: Sons Daniel and Richard.
Letters to Daniel.
Witnesses: Joshua Pearson, Jesse Bonsall, William Parker.

DAVIS, JONATHAN.
May 28, 1765. October 30, 1765.
Provides for wife Susanna including land in Coventry and Vincent Townships to her and heirs and assigns forever. To son John plantation whereon I now live with stock at age of 20. All profits of estate to wife to maintain and educate children, viz., John, Sarah, Hannah, and Mary during their infancy. To my 3 daughters £100 each at 18. Refers to tract of land in Tredyffrin which he obtained with his wife.
Executors: Wife and brother David Davis and brother in James Davis.
Witnesses: Andrew Todd, William Lewhelin, John Griffith.
* Taxed in Charlestown 1753-1764. 250 H. See will of John Davis III 1 & 2. No. 3593. See will of Susanna Evans III 370.

SLOAN, WILLIAM. Chichester. Weaver.
September 10, 1765. December 11, 1765.
To nephew John Moore £15, wearing apparel and silver buckles at 21. To my niece Margaret Moore, sister of John £15 and household goods at 18. To sister Margaret Steel £5. To nephew Charles Ferguson walnut desk if he shall live to return from sea. To

sister Mary, wife of Moses Moore during life the use of my gold
ring and at her death to her daughter Margaret. Remainder to
sister Mary Moore, also with John Crawford Executors.
Witnesses: John Crawford, John Marshall, Samuel Armor.

PATRICK, JOHN. October 29, 1765. E. Nottingham. Adm. to Abigail
& Samuel Patrick.

SCOTT, JOHN. East Nottingham.
December 5, 1765. December 23, 1765.
Provides for wife Agnes. To my 4 children, viz., Thomas, Jean,
Mary and Samuel 2/3 of personal estate and all houses, lands to
be divided. Thomas to have 2 shares.
Executors: Brother Philip Scott.
Witnesses: John Hathorn, Samuel Hindman, James Scott.

SMEDLEY, GEORGE, JR. Willistown.
8/21/1765. December 24, 1765.
Provides for wife Hannah. To daughter Hannah Smedley £50 at 18.
To eldest son Jeffrey that part of my plantation which lies on
the west side of the road from Grubbs Mill to Lancaster Road, at
21. To younger sons Joshua and Francis the other part of my land
lying on the east side of said road. To father George Smedley
£10. To brother Joshua all my right to plantation Moses Meredith
lives on in Edgmont. Remainder for schooling and clothing
younger children. Executors: Brother Joshua, Uncle Benjamin
Hibberd and friend George Miller.
Letters to Joshua Smedley, the others refusing.
Witnesses: Benjamin Hibberd, Jr., Caleb Hibberd.

REYNOLDS, ELIZABETH, widow. Chichester.
12/16/1765. January 10, 1766.
All estate to sons Benjamin, John, Samuel, Francis and daughters
Lydia Talbot and Christian Hoopes and children of Henry Reynolds
deceased and Prudence Dutton deceased in equal 1/8 shares.
Executors: Son Benjamin and John Hoopes.
Letters to Benjamin.
Witnesses: John Talbot, Sarah Worrel, Archibald Sherer.

GRIFFITH, MAURICE. Willistown.
September 24, 1765. February 15, 1766.
Provides for wife Mary. To nephew Benjamin Griffith after wife's
decease 100 acres of the plantation whereon I now dwell including
house and improvements together with my pew in St. Peter's Church
paying 20 shillings yearly to the minister forever. To Rachel
Lewis my wife's kinswoman remainder of plantation during life and
at her decease to her son Joel Lewis. To brother William
Griffith in Caermarthenshire 10 shillings if demanded. To Joel
Lewis, son of Rachel Lewis £10. To nephew John Williams, son of
Isaac Williams of Caermarthenshire £10 if demanded. To Lydia
Lewis, daughter of Rachel Lewis £5 at 18. To Hannah Owen,
daughter of Rachel Lewis £5 at 18. To sister Eleanor Williams 10
shillings. To Vestry of St. Peter's Church in Great Valley £20
for building wall round the grave yard. To the Minister that
shall bury me and my wife £5. Remainder to daughters of sister

Eleanor Williams. Executors: Rev. William Currie, Randle Malin and Joseph Williams.
Witnesses: John Gronow, Lewis Gronow, Ezekiel Bowen.
Letters to Malin and Williams, the other renouncing.

O'MULLEN, ROBERT. East Nottingham. Weaver.
September 26, 1765. February 24, 1766.
To daughter Marthew all that remains of my worldly goods.
Executors: James Tood, Gaven Morrison.
Letters to Tood.
Witnesses: John Morrison, Molly Tood.

LAWRENCE, HENRY. Haverford. Blacksmith.
8/23/1762. February 24, 1766.
To daughter Jane Lewis £10. To daughter Mary Jones £20. To 5 grandchildren Mordecai, Joseph, Joshua, Samuel and Mary Lawrence 20 shillings each. To 7 grandchildren Abner, Rachel, Henry, Mary, Enos, Lewis and Hannah Lewis 20 shillings. Provides for daughters Margaret, Ellen and Hannah Lawrence while they remain unmarried. To son Henry messuage where I now live containing about 200 acres paying to my aforesaid daughters £400. All remainder to 3 daughters Margaret, Ellen and Hannah Lawrence, also Executors.
Trustees: Son Henry, son in law David Lewis, cousins Daniel Williams and William Lawrence and friend Samuel Humphreys.
Witnesses: Edward Humphreys, William Lawrence.

POWELL, JOHN. Marple.
February 7, 1766. February 26, 1766.
Provides for mother, wife and 2 children Mary and John until grown up. Plantation to be sold if necessary. If not sold, to son John at 21 paying to his sister Mary £80. Remainder divided among wife Ellen and 2 children.
Executors: James Rhoads and Henry Lawrence.
Witnesses: John Neilson, James Powell, James Maris.

YEARSLEY, NATHAN. Thornbury.
1/18/1766. March 11, 1766.
Provides for wife Susanna. To son Jacob Yearsley plantation in Thornbury and Westtown containing about 200 acres at 21. To daughter Elizabeth Yearsley £100 at 21. To daughter Sarah £100 at 21. If children die without issue, real estate to John Yearsley, son of brother Thomas.
Executors: Brother Isaac, brother in law Jacob Wright and Thomas Taylor of Westtown.
Witnesses: Nathaniel Eavenson, George Eavenson, Lawrence Townsend.

FAIRLAMB, JOHN. Middletown.
February 2, 1766. March 25, 1766.
Provides for wife Susanna. To son Nicholas part of plantation lying between Edgmont Road and Chester Creek. To son Frederick the part of plantation lying between Edgmont Road and Ridley Creek, also £20. To sons Samuel and John £300 each. To each of 5 daughters Catherine, Anne, Susanna, Eleanor and Mary £150.

Executors: Henry Hale Graham and son Frederick.
H. H. Graham to be guardian of children.
Witnesses: John Cox, Frederick Engle, Joshua Cowpland.

EVANS, THOMAS. Goshen.
October 5, 1765. Codicil: June 20, 1765. March 25, 1766.
To daughter Margaret, wife of William Bane, clock and case and £50. To son David Evans £10. To daughter Esther, wife of Enoch Eachus £50. All remainder to 2 daughters Margaret and Esther. Codicil reduces David's legacy to 1 shilling and gives the £10 to daughter Esther Eachus.
Executors: John and Thomas Hoopes of Goshen.
Witnesses: Nathaniel Moore, John Speakman, Richard Jones.
Witnesses to Codicil: Richard Jones, Ann Hankey.

ROSS, MOSES. Oxford.
May 11, 1766. May 22, 1766.
Provides for wife Rosanna. To daughter Rebecca, wife of John Walker, 2 bonds of John Walker's £20 each. To daughter Sarah, wife of John Porter £10. To daughter Ann, wife of Samuel Crow £1 with the writings of plantation Samuel Crow now lives on to be delivered up to said daughter Ann. To daughter Mary, wife of Andrew Noble £20. To daughter Hannah £100 1/2 at 17. To son Joseph all real and personal estate paying legacies. Mentions his step son Hugh Bones.
Executors: John Smith, Sr. and John Ross.
Witnesses: George McCullough, Andrew Reed, Robert Smith.

WILSON, HANNAH. Birmingham.
3/14/1764. May 26, 1766.
To Elizabeth Willis, daughter of James Harlan £5. To Ann Harlan, daughter of James £10. To Solomon Harlan, son of James £10. To Henry Harlan, son of James £10. To the youngest son of James £10. To Susanna Harlan, daughter of James £10. To the children of Ezekiel Harlan £50 to be divided.
Executor: James Wilson.
Letters C.T.A. to Benjamin Mendenhall, the Executor named being absent beyond the sea.
Witnesses: Hannah Mendenhall, James Knightley.

YARNALL, DOROTHY.
May 10, 1766. Edgmont.
Adm. to Ephraim Yarnall.

SMEDLEY, WILLIAM.
May 14, 1766. Middletown.
Adm. to Elizabeth Smedley.

WRATH, WILLIAM.
May 14, 1766. Ridley.
Adm. to Rebecca Wrath.

FLEMING, JOHN.
May 28, 1766. Oxford.
Adm. to Jennett Fleming & James Fleming. Sureties David Fleming & Alexander Gibson. Inventory £170.9. Widow Jennet and children James, Agnes, Margaret, Sarah & Jane. Inquisition.

HARLAN, THOMAS. May 28, 1766. Kennett. Adm. to Mary Harlan & Joel Baily.

MORTON, SAMUEL. Londongrove.
10/14/1765. June 28, 1766.
To daughter Margaret and her husband John Hadley £5. To son Samuel Morton £50. To daughter Mary Morton £100. To 2 sons William and Thomas all real estate paying legacies.
Executors: Sons William and Thomas.
Witnesses: John Jackson, Joshia Jackson.

HUNTER, HANNAH, widow. Middletown.
February 10, 1757. June 2, 1766.
To Aaron Baker, son of daughter Elizabeth £2. To Mary Howell, daughter of daughter Elizabeth £2. To Richard Baker, son of daughter Elizabeth £2. To Hannah Davis, daughter of John Baker £2. To Joseph Baker, son of John Baker £2. To Hannah Peirce, daughter of Henry Peirce £2. To Henry Peirce, son of Henry Peirce £2. To Rachel Peirce, daughter of Henry Peirce £2 and to the 2 other sons of said Henry Peirce, William and John £2 each at 21. To William Moore, son of Charles Moore £2 at 21. To Hannah Moore, daughter of Charles Moore £2 and to the 2 other daughters of said Charles Moore, Margaret and Rachel Moore £2 each at 18. To Philip Moore, son of Charles Moore £2. All remainder to 2 daughters Elizabeth Moore and Sarah Peirce, also Executors.
Witnesses: Samuel Sharpless, Thomas Grissell.

NORBURY, RACHEL, spinster. Chester.
March 15, 1766. June 2, 1766.
To nephew Jacob Norbury, niece Mary wife of William Key, niece Sarah wife of Thomas Pedrick £5 each. All remainder of estate real or personal to son William Herriot to be put into the hands of Jacob Howell and his wife Ann as Trustees.
Executor: Abraham Martin.
Witnesses: Joshua Cowpland, Elisha Price.

TALLEY, REBECCA.
May 28, 1766.
Adm. to William Talley.

PARKER, JOSEPH.
May 31, 1766. Chester.
Adm. to Mary Norris.

STRINGER, JOSEPH. West Fallowfield.
March 8, 1766. June 5, 1766.
To brother William Stringer all personal estate until his son Joseph shall be of age when I give to my said nephew and namesake Joseph Stringer all my lands paying to his sisters Sarah McKim £10, Eleanor Stringer £10 and Martha Stringer £10 with reversion successively to his brothers William, George and John.
Executors: Brother William Stringer and James Glendening.
Witnesses: William Robb, John Huston, Mary Huston.

ELDER, JAMES. New London.
January 9, 1766. June 18, 1766.
To daughter Martha Elder £50. To brother Robert Elder £10. To John Scott £10. Remainder to brother John Elder's children.
Executor: Brother Robert if alive, otherwise John Fleming.
Witnesses: James Elder, Thomas Scott, Elizabeth Hamilton.

WEBSTER, ELIZABETH. East Marlboro.
2/12/1762. June 18, 1766.
To son Evan Harry 10 shillings. To son Thomas Webster furniture.
To daughters Ann Hutton and Hannah Chalfin household goods and
wearing apparel. To daughter Mary Green 5 shillings. To
granddaughter Phebe Hutton 5 shillings.
Executors: John Hutton and James Chalfin.
Witnesses: William Swayne, Isaac Swayne.

HOWELL, BENJAMIN.
June 7, 1766. Chichester.
Adm. to Rebecca Howell.

FILLSON, SAMUEL.
June 9, 1766. E. Fallowfield.
Adm. to Robert Fillson.

REYNOLDS, HENRY.
June 12, 1766. Chichester.
Adm. to Sarah Reynolds.

TORTON, DANIEL.
June 17, 1766. Ridley.
Adm. to Letitia Torton,
Lawrence Garrett & Thomas
Thomas Smith.

COLVIN, JOHN.
June 17, 1766. E. Nottingham.
Adm. to Elizabeth & Robert
Colvin.

FEW, ISAAC. East Bradford. Weaver.
2/12/1764. June 20, 1766.
To sons Richard and Joseph, daughter Dorcas Wollerton, sons
Isaac, and Benjamin 10 shillings each. To son James all
remainder of estate subject to maintenance of wife Jean and son
Isaac as long as they live.
Executors: Wife Jean and son in law James Wollerton.
Witnesses: Benjamin Hawley, Jr., John Wollerton, James Kenny.

WARK, WILLIAM. London Britain. Clothier.
July 14, 1766. July 29, 1766.
To wife Elizabeth Wark £20 and bed and bedding. All remainder to
sister Rebecca Gilbreath.
Executor: Evan Evans.
Witnesses: Hugh Houston, Robert Ramsey.

PUSEY, JOHN. Londongrove.
3/19/1766. August 1, 1766.
Provides for wife Catherine. To son John Pusey plantation
whereon I now dwell containing about 100 acres. To daughter
Lydia, wife of Joel Baily 5 shillings having already provided for
her. To son George £2. To daughter Jane Pusey £5. To son
Nathan £40. To daughter Susanna £5 at 18.
Executor: Cousin Joshua Pusey.
Witnesses: Thomas Harlan, William Baily, Benjamin Wilson.

BALDWIN, WILLIAM.
July 1, 1766. W. Bradford.
Adm. to James Marshall.
Widow Ruth renouncing in
his favor June 30, 1766.
Wit: Joel Baily & Richard
Baker. Sureties James
Marshall & George Gilpin.

HARVEY, DAVID.
July 23, 1766. E. Nottingham.
Adm. to John Warnock.

PUSEY, JAMES.
July 31, 1766. Londongrove.
Adm. to Joshua Pusey.

Inv. £12.18.6. Appraisers George Carter & Joel Baily, affd. July 2, 1766. Advance on sales £6.10.3. Nothing left.

LINN, HUGH, JR.
August 7, 1766.
Adm. to Anne Linn.

LOUGHRIDGE, JOHN. July 23, 1766. East Nottingham. Adm. to Elizabeth Loughridge.

HAYES, JOHN. Oxford.
July 31, 1766. August 8, 1766.
Provides for wife Margaret. To daughter Mary, wife of James Dickey 20 shillings. To son David 200 acres of land paying £100 to my Executors. To daughter Elizabeth, wife of Walter Hood £10. To daughter Hannah, wife of William Baley £10. To daughter Ann £50. To daughter Mary £50. To son John all remainder of estate real and personal.
Executors: William Bunting, Sr. and Walter Hood.
Witnesses: John Smith, Robert Smith, John Arnatt.

TARBET, HUGH. Oxford.
January 13, 1763. August 13, 1766.
Provides for wife Katherine. To son John Tarbet £10 and large Bible. To daughter Jane, wife of James Read £5. To daughter Ealse, wife of John Faron £5. To daughter Katherine £5 and cow. To son Hugh tract of land in Oxford containing 150 acres adjoining John Love, William Robb and David Brooks and £3. Remainder divided among children, viz., David, Margaret, Elizabeth, Allen, Jannet, and Robert Tarbet.
Executors: Dorrinton Boyle, David Simpson and Hugh Tarbet.
Witnesses: John Poston, Matthew Young, James Dunn.

WILLSON, THOMAS. West Fallowfield.
January 28, 1764. August 22, 1766.
Provides for wife Elizabeth and possible children. To brother Joseph plantation whereon he now lives subject as above. Letters to Joseph Wilson, the other being deceased.
Executors: Andrew Stirling and brother Joseph.
Witnesses: William Boggs, Robert Hamilton, Alexander Dunlap.

RICE, JUDITH.
August 12, 1766. Bethel.
Adm. to Humphrey Johnson.

MACE, GEORGE.
August 15, 1766. Middletown.
Adm. to Susanna Mace.

FLOWER, THOMAS.
August 14, 1766. Chichester.
Adm. to Prudence Flower & Richard Riley.

MASSEY, LEWIS.
August 18, 1766.
Adm. to James Massey.

CUMMINGS, THOMAS. Chester Borough.
August 30, 1754. August 22, 1766.
To wife Alice all estate real and personal, also Executrix.
Witnesses: John Larner, Elisha Price, Henry Hale Graham.

WILLIAMS, EDWARD. Easttown.
November 27, 1762. August 25, 1766.

Provides for wife Jane. To son William £15. To daughter Mary £2.10. To son Edward £80. To daughter Elizabeth £15. To grandson Simon Meredith £2, said Simon to abide with my Executor until 16. To son Griffith Williams 100 acres of land in Easttown where I now live and remainder of personal estate, also Executor.
Assistants: William Godfree and Edward Jones.
Witnesses: Thomas Rowland, Isaac Hughes, Griffith James.

SMITH, JOHN. Uwchlan.
February 12, 1761. Codicil: January 16, 1764. May 26, August 26, 1766.
To son James 5 shillings having given him his portion. To son John wearing apparel having given him his portion. To son Abraham 5 shillings having given him his portion. To Robert 5 shillings having given him his portion. To Isaac 5 shillings having given him his portion. To daughter Elizabeth Graham 5 shillings having given her her portion. To daughter Susanna Armstrong 5 shillings having given her her portion. To daughter Mary Lewis 5 shillings having given her her portion. To daughter Sarah Smith 5 shillings having given her her portion. Provides for wife Susanna. On her death remainder divided among James, John, Abraham and Isaac and daughters Susanna, Mary and Sarah.
Executors: Sons John and Abraham.
Witnesses: William Denny, Samuel Denny, David Denny, James Creswell, John Dunwoody.

DURROUGH, BARTHOLOMEW.
August 26, 1766. E. Nottingham.
Adm. to Jane Durrough.

ELDRIDGE, JAMES.
August 26, 1766. Uwchlan.
Adm. to John Jacobs, Jr.

THOMAS, EDWARD. East Caln.
6/11/1766. August 27, 1766.
House and lot in Reading to be sold as conveyed to my by William Iddings. To brothers George and William, sister Ann and brother Ellis Thomas £10 each as they come of age. All remainder towards erecting and supporting a Free School amongst Friends.
Executors: George Churchman of East Nottingham and John Milhouse of Pikeland.
Witnesses: William Baldwin, Adam Richard, Samuel Johnson.

WEATHERBY, BENJAMIN. Tredyffrin. Innkeeper.
August 20, 1766. September 1, 1766.
Provides for wife. Executors to sell land in East Caln and house and lot in Wilmington, Delaware, bought of George Ogden, also 65 acres part of that purchased of John Fairlamb sheriff, formerly the property of Anthony Wayne deceased. Money to be equally divided amongst wife and children now living, viz., Whitehead, Samuel, David, George, William, Benjamin, Septimus and Richard. Remainder of real estate to be sold on death of wife and divided as above.
Executors: Son Whitehead and brother in law Barnhard Van Leer, Doctor, and friend Isaac Wayne.
Witnesses: Joshua Evans, Samuel Turbet.

MORRISON, WILLIAM.
June 4, 1766. September 5, 1766.
To Mary Price £10. To William Price horse. To Thomas and John Price £20. To Daniel Price £15. To Abjagh Price £25. To Vell Price £5.
Executor: Daniel Price.
Witnesses: Job Dicks, William Price.

CARSON, MARY.
August 28, 1766.
Adm. to James McMichen, Jr.

HOLLYWOOD, FRANCIS.
September 8, 1766. Ridley.
Adm. to John Bryan.

PERGRIN, THOMAS.
September 1, 1766. Charlestown.
Adm. to Issac Wayne.

BLACKBURN, JAMES.
Sept. 12, 1766. W. Nottingham.
Adm. to Mary & Ephraim Blackburn.

HALL, MATTHEW. Marple.
9/8/1766. September 18, 1766.
To son David Hall plantation where I now dwell in Marple purchased of Abel Janney, he paying to daughter Margery Warner £6 per annum during the lifetime of her husband and £100 to her or heirs at his death. Also paying to daughter Sarah Pearson £100. To son Mahlon my plantation in Blockley whereon he now lives purchased of Veronica Warner, widow, also 10 acres of woodland in same township. To Mary, wife of John Mitchner £10. Remainder equally divided among sons David and Mahlon, daughters Margery and Sarah.
Executors: Sons David and Mahlon.
Witnesses: William Fell, Seth Pancoast, Nathaniel Holland.

HINDE, JAMES. Darby.
8/28/1766. September 19, 1766.
To brother John Hinde, wearing apparel. To brother Roger 5 shillings if he comes to demand it. To brother John £60 to be paid by my 2 sisters Mary Hinde and Elizabeth Horne. To brother John's 3 children, Rachel, Hannah and Elizabeth £5 each at 18. To sister Elizabeth Horne's daughters Abigail and Benjamina £5 each at 18. To 2 sisters Mary Hinde and Elizabeth Horne my lands and plantation in Darby on which I now live paying legacies.
Executors: Friends William Horne and Abraham Bonsall.
Witnesses: John Serrill, Benjamin Lobb, Jr., Anthony Howks.

LEWIS, ABEL.
September 18, 1766. Radnor.
Adm. to Elizabeth Lewis.

BONSALL, ISAAC.
September 19, 1766. Darby.
Adm. to Joshua Bonsall.

COCHRAN, JAMES. West Fallowfield.
May 21, 1766. September 20, 1766.
To daughter Ann, wife of Rev. John Roan, and granddaughter Isabel, daughter of son Robert deceased, and to 2 sons John and Stephen 1 shilling each having heretofore advanced them. To son James 100 acres of land adjoining land whereon I now live. Plantation where I now live to be sold and proceeds divided 1/2 to daughter Jane, 1/4 to son George and remaining 1/4 to son

James.
Executors: George and Jean Cochran.
Letters to George Cochran. June 3, 1769. Letters to George Cochran, Alexander Mitchell and Jane his wife (late Jane Cochran).
Witnesses: James McCormick, John Caruthers.

TOWNSEND, JOSEPH. East Bradford.
5/18/1765. September 22, 1766.
Provides for wife Martha including plantation whereon I lately dwelt in East Bradford containing about 185 acres and all personal estate during life, she to maintain my son William during her life. After her decease the plantation to son John except 64 acres he paying £12 yearly to my son William. To daughter Mary Woodward and her husband Henry 32 acres of land whereon they now dwell during their lives, after their death to their son Henry. To daughter Hannah Ryant 32 acres of land adjoining the above. To son Joseph deceased estate his bond for £100. Remainder divided.
Executors: Wife Martha and son John.
Letters to John, the other renouncing.
Witnesses: Phineas Eachus, Alexander Forman, David Ferris.

LEWIS, JOHN. West Nantmeal.
March 31, 1762. October 14, 1766.
To wife Christian Lewis all estate absolutely, paying £5 to granddaughter Elizabeth Rypole at 23.
Executrix: Wife Christian.
Witnesses: Abel Griffith, Robert Brown.

HARRISON, CALEB. Middletown.
7/22/1753. October 4, 1766.
Provides for wife Hannah. To eldest son Caleb my messuage in Middletown on death of wife, paying legacies as follows: To son John the £50 he owes me. To daughter Hannah maintenance while unmarried and £100 at marriage. To grandson Joseph Harrison £33.6.8 at 21. To grandson Richard Harrison £33.6.8 at 21. To grandson John Harrison £33.6.8 at 21.
Executors: Wife, son Caleb and friend John Fairlamb.
Letters to Caleb, the other being deceased.
Witnesses: Jonathan Martin, John Hurford, Samuel Parks, Susanna Fairlamb.

GRANTHAM, GEORGE. Ridley.
September 16, 1766. October 10, 1766.
Directs body to be buried "at the Church burying ground in Kingsess." To wife Margaret all personal estate and 10 acres of meadow in Darby, also 15 acres of upland bought of Andrew Boon her heirs and assigns. The landed estate in Ridley where I now dwell which devolves to me at death of my father, I give to be equally divided among my children at 21. Requests father to allow his wife to live on plantation without rent until children come of age.
Executrix: Wife Margaret.
Witnesses: Jacob Fritz, Lydia Grantham, Elizabeth Knowles.

INDEX

161

-A-
ABRAHAM, James, 89
  Noah, 89
ADAMS, James, 26
  Jane, 1
  Mary, 26
  Robert, 26
ADDOMS, Elizabeth, 125
AILES, Amos, 79
  Ann, 79
  Hannah, 79
  Mary, 79
  Rebecca, 79
  Stephen, 79
  William, 79
ALBIN, Elizabeth, 28
  Hannah, 28
  James, 27, 28
  Jane, 27
  Mary, 28
ALCOTT, Anne, 117
  Thomas, 117
ALEN, James, 115
ALEXANDER, Amos, 137
  Francis, 69
  Jacob, 134
  James, 112
  John, 26, 97, 137
  John McKnitt, 137
  Mary, 112
  Theophilus, 137
  William, 77
  Zacheus, 106
ALFORD, Elizabeth, 88
ALISON, Francis, 13, 19
ALLAN, John, 145
ALLCOT, Anne, 34
ALLEN, Agnes, 24
  Alice, 122
  Ann, 122
  David, 24
  Emey, 122
  Ester, 80
  Esther, 89
  Hannah, 122
  Isaac, 89

James, 80, 84, 89
  John, 36, 62, 79, 80, 89, 122
  Patience, 89
  Phebe, 62, 122
  Samuel, 26, 38, 80, 122
  William, 65, 80, 89, 117, 129, 131
ALLISON, Alex, 89
  Alexander, 3
  Christian, 3
  Dorcas, 89
  Elizabeth, 72, 133
  James, 134
  Jane, 138
  Joseph, 121, 133
  Robert, 61, 133
ANDERSON,
  Elizabeth, 19
  Mary, 117
ANDREW, Agnes, 120
  Robert, 89
  William, 66
ARCHER, Adam, 11, 45, 59
  Ellin, 59
  Gertrude, 11
  Jacob, 11, 30
  Martha, 11
  Mary, 11, 45
ARCHIBALD,
  Patrick, 22
ARMENT, Jacob, 115
  John, 115, 116
  Thomas, 115
  William, 115
ARMITT, Elizabeth, 11
  Joesph, 11
  Mary, 11
ARMOR, Samuel, 117, 151
ARMOUR, Elizabeth, 67
  William, 80
ARMSTRONG, James, 49
  John, 49
  Lancelot, 49

Susanna, 27, 157
  William, 16, 49
ARNATT, John, 156
ARNOLD, Ann, 132
  Mary, 57
  Sarah, 57
  Thomas, 132
ASH, Alice, 15
  Ann, 24
  Anne, 20
  John, 20
  Joshua, 15, 20, 25, 95
ASHBRIDGE, Aaron, 78
  Amos, 130
  Ellis, 141
  George, 133, 140
  Hannah, 58, 130
  Isaac, 141
  Jane, 141
  Jesse, 141
  Jonathan, 141
  Joseph, 58, 71, 130, 140
  Mary, 140
  Nathan, 141
  Priscilla, 58, 113
ASHE, Caleb, 95
  Edward, 95
  Elizabeth, 95
  Joshua, 95
  Mary, 95
  Matthew, 95
  Samuel, 95
  Thomas, 95
ASHTON, Abraham, 41, 57, 99
  Owen, 111
ASKEW, Elizabeth, 99
  John, 99, 135
  Joseph, 99, 135
  Lazarus, 99
  Mabel, 99
  Parker, 135
  Sarah, 99
  William, 99, 135
ASKINS, Michael, 148
ASTON, Elizabeth, 3

Hannah, 3
Peter, 3, 4
ATHERTON, Abigail, 4
　Caleb, 102
　Henry, 19, 56, 63, 102, 123
　Thomas, 105
ATLEE, William, 130
ATTMOOR, Mary, 125
AUGHILTREE,
　Deborah, 113
　Mathew, 113

-B-
BABB, John, 92
　Sarah, 143
　Thomas, 92
BACKHOUSE, Allen, 68
　Anne, 27, 68
　Isabella, 68
　Richard, 27, 68
BAILEY, Alexander, 111, 121
　William, 121
BAILY, Betty, 149
　Daniel, 78
　David, 117
　Dinah, 149
　George, 112, 149
　Gravener, 92
　Hannah, 11, 149
　Isaac, 69, 78, 85
　Isabel, 112
　Joel, 66, 153, 155, 156
　John, 127
　Lydia, 155
　Mary, 11
　Samuel, 117
　Sarah, 11, 117
　Thomas, 139
　William, 106, 155
BAKER, Aaron, 54, 92, 96, 125, 154
　Ann, 32
　David, 32
　Elizabeth, 154
　Jesse, 32
　John, 154

Joseph, 3, 35, 85, 154
Joshua, 96
Josph, 85
Lettice, 85
Lydia, 32
Mary, 17, 37, 89, 92
Moses, 85
Nehemiah, 30
Richard, 115, 154, 155
BALDEN, Johyn, 67
BALDWIN, Ann, 103
　Anthony, 103, 120
　Elizabeth, 54, 103, 106
　George, 103
　Hannah, 54, 103, 106
　John, 12, 99, 103, 135
　Joseph, 103
　Lydia, 54
　Margery, 103
　Martha, 103
　Mary, 54
　Robert, 103
　Sarah, 103
　Thomas, 54, 103, 106
　William, 15, 54, 106, 155, 157
BALEY, Hannah, 156
　John, 8
　Wiliam, 156
BANE, Alexander, 44
　Margaret, 153
　Mary, 57
　William, 144, 153
BANKSON, Hannah, 67
　Jacob, 67
BARBER, John, 102
　Robert, 102
　Susanna, 10
BARCLAY, James, 20
BARNARD, Hannah, 117
　Isaac, 117
　Isable, 117
　James, 117

Jeremiah, 2
Jude, 14
Judith, 2
Thomas, 86, 117
BARNES, Emanuel, 6
　Frances, 50
　James, 50
　Joseph, 50
　Mary, 50
BARNET, Thomas, 117
BARNETT, Abraham, 90
　John, 90
　Robert, 91
　William, 90
BARRETT, Hannah, 64
　Mary, 94
　Thomas, 64, 88, 123, 126
BARRON, Richard, 27
BARRY, A., 18
　James, 31
BARTON, James, 4
　Joseph, 4
　Lydia, 12
　Mary, 4
BARTRAM, Ann, 17, 18
　Elizabeth, 109
　James, 50, 109
　John, 17, 78
　Sarah, 78
BATE, Ann, 25
　George, 25
　Hannah, 25
　John, 25
　Richard, 25
　Sarah, 25
BATEMAN, Anne, 143
　Catharine, 143
　Hannah, 144
　Henry, 143
　John, 143, 144
　Sarah, 144
　Thomas, 144
　William, 144
BATTEN, James, 30
　Mary, 42
BATTIN, John, 29, 72
　Rachel, 60
　Richard, 34

Samuel, 60
BAYLEY, Sarah, 94
  Thomas, 94
  William, 111
BEAL, David, 117
  Eddey, 117
  John, 117
  Joshua, 117
  Mary, 117
  Susanna, 117
  Thomas, 116
  William, 117
BEALE, John, 135
  Mary, 116
  Tamar, 135
  William, 58, 87,
    116, 117
BEAN, Mary, 8
  Nathan, 8
  William, 2
BEARD, David, 142
BEATEY, Francis,
  60
BEATON, Daniel,
  37, 138
  Mary, 138
  Samuel, 73
BEATTY, David, 6,
  132
  Francis, 40
  George, 13
  Martha, 13
  Rebecca, 6
  Robert, 6
  William, 6, 13,
    40
BEATY, Abraham, 6
  David, 6
  Robert, 6
  Samuel, 106
BEELER, Josph, 4
BEESON, Charity,
  98
  Dorothy, 129
  John, 134
  Mary, 134
BELL, Edward, 146
  Humphrey, 100
  Jean, 68
  John, 52
  Joseph, 68
  Mary, 68
  Richard, 69
  William, 146
BENDER, Ludwig,
    111
BENNET, Deborah,
  15
BENNETT, Edward,
  40, 63, 144
  Elizabeth, 28
  Esther, 47
  Hannah, 94
  Jacob, 36
  James, 27, 28,
    98, 149
  John, 39
  Joseph, 36, 120
  Mary, 15, 16, 98
  Patience, 144
  Richard, 108
  Titus, 82
  William, 16, 56
BENNING, Samuel,
  71
BENSON, John, 8
BENTLEY, Jeffrey,
  5, 94
  John, 5
  Joseph, 94
  Mary, 94
BESON, Alice, 128
BEST, Sarah, 112
BETHEL, Samuel,
  150
BETTLE, Ann, 39
  Samuel, 4, 25,
    39
BETTY, Agnes, 29
  Edward, 29
  Jane (Jean), 28
  John, 29
  Margaret, 28
  Susanna, 29
  William, 13
BEVAN, Anne, 110
  Annie, 110
  Aubrey, 17, 40,
    45, 110
  Davis, 110
  Mary, 110
  Tacy, 110
BEVERLY, Jane, 33,
  66
  Mary, 33, 66
  Samuel, 33, 66
BEZER, Edward, 31,
  70
  Jane, 31, 95
  John, 5, 31, 70
Richard, 31, 70
William, 70
BICKERDIKE,
  Esther, 95
BIGGARD, William,
  91
BISHOP, Charles,
  47
  John, 47
  Joseph, 101
  Mary, 101
  Patience, 47
BITTLE, Ann, 64
  Martha, 70
BLACK, Elizabeth,
  41
  Henry, 10
  James, 41, 148
  Jane, 148
  Jean, 82
  John, 63, 91
  Mitchell, 82
  Samuel, 41
  Sarah, 10
BLACKBURN,
  Ephraim, 158
  Hugh, 105
  James, 158
  Mary, 158
BLACKMAN, Rebecca,
  19
BLACKSHALL,
  Richard, 33, 66
BLACKWELL,
  Elizabeth, 143
  Hugh, 40
BLAIR, Elizabeth,
  35
  Frances, 35
  Francina, 35
  Hannah, 35
  Isaac, 35
  James, 8
  John, 88
  Martha, 35
  Mary, 35
  Samuel, 35
  Sarah, 35
  Susanna, 35
  William, 8, 35
  William
    Lawrence, 35
BLAKE, Deborah, 11
BLAKELY, Charles,
  13

163

BLATCHFORD, John,
    111
BLAUFOY, John, 59
BLELOCK, James, 60
BLOWIT, Sarah, 51
BLUNDELL, Robert,
    5
BLUNSTON, Michael,
    78
    Phebe, 19
BLUNTON, Michael,
    78
BOAKE, Abel, 34
    Amos, 34
    Ann, 34
    Sarah, 34
BOGG, William, 37
BOGGS, Agnes, 127
    Francis, 33, 127
    John, 7, 15, 39,
    119
    Margaret, 39, 46
    Martha, 7
    Rebecca, 104,
    127
    William, 96,
    127, 156
BOND, Emmson, 145
    James, 67
    Mary, 88
    Phineas, 22
    Richard, 88
BONES, Hugh, 153
BONSAL, Enoch, 25
    Grace, 133
    Isaac, 25
    Philip, 133
BONSALL, Abraham,
    19, 22, 158
    Amy, 131
    Elizabeth, 24
    Enoch, 131
    Isaac, 158
    Jane, 131
    Jesse, 125, 150
    Joseph, 25, 42,
    124, 131
    Joshua, 158
    Mary, 131
    Obadiah, 61
    Philip, 84
    Rebecca, 61
    Sarah, 81, 131
    Vincent, 81
BOON, Andrew, 159

Hannah, 80
Mary, 73, 114
Rebecca, 114
Samuel, 73
Swan, 114
William, 114
BOONE, Rebeca, 147
BOOTH, Joseph, 40,
    92
    William, 29
BOSS, John, 5
BOUCHANON,
    Gilbert, 97
BOUCHER, Mary, 27
BOUND, Anne, 129
    John, 129
BOURGOIN, Asenath,
    135
    Hannah, 135
    James, 135
    John, 135
    Joseph, 135
    Sarah, 135
    Susanna, 135
    Tamar, 135
BOURN, Ann, 114
    George, 114
    Sarah, 114
    Susann, 114
BOURNE, Jacob, 114
    Thomas, 114
BOWEN, Anne, 70
    Benjamin, 68,
    101
    Daniel, 121
    Esther, 121
    Ezekiel, 70,
    121, 152
    Hannah, 93, 121
    Howell, 126
    John, 70, 71,
    93, 121
    Jonathan, 70
    Joshua, 121
    Ruth, 121
    William, 70
BOWLS, Ann, 26
    Barbara, 26
    Eleanor, 26
    Elizabeth, 26
    Jane, 26
    John, 26
    Kety, 26
    Mary, 26
    Thomas, 26

William, 26
BOYD, Adam, 27
    Alexander, 55,
    118
    Andrew, 127,
    137, 138
    Ann, 118
    Daniel, 89, 137
    Elizabeth, 118
    Francis, 55
    George, 137
    Hannah, 118, 137
    Hugh, 55
    James, 69, 89,
    101, 118, 137
    Jane, 137
    Janet, 118
    Jean, 138
    John, 14, 29,
    118
    Lettice, 29
    Margaret, 55
    Mary, 62, 118,
    137
    Matthew, 137
    Robert, 29, 137
    Thomas, 68
    William, 14, 59,
    61, 88, 97,
    101, 118, 138,
    148
BOYES, Robert, 41
BOYLE, Abigail,
    101
    Alexander, 101
    Dorinton, 101
    Dorrinton, 149,
    156
    Margaret, 101
    Mary, 101
    Robert, 101
BRABSTON, Hannah,
    87
BRACKENRIG, David,
    88
    John, 88
BRACKINGREG,
    Sarah, 131
BRADLEY, Enoch,
    100
    Grissell, 134
    John, 57
BRADY, Jonathan,
    108
BRALLY, John, 50

BRATTEN, James, 91
BRENTON, Jane, 2
  John, 2
  Joseph, 2
  William, 2
BRIDGES, Francis, 1
BRIGGS, Agabus, 132
  Elizabeth, 132
  John, 132
  Mary, 132
  Richard, 132
  Thomas, 132
  William, 132
BRINNAN, John, 22
BRINTON, Caleb, 39
  Cisly, 111
  David, 4
  Edward, 4, 22, 30, 35, 39, 51, 55, 64, 67, 79
  George, 39, 141
  Hannah, 4, 39
  Jacob, 4, 81
  James, 149
  Jane, 39, 64, 111
  John, 4, 39, 126, 143
  Joseph, 22, 39
  Lydia, 4
  Margaret, 100
  Mary, 39
  Moses, 149
  Phebe, 39
  William, 25, 39, 64, 111
BRISBAN,
  Elizabeth, 134
  Samuel, 134
BROOKES, David, 81
BROOKS, David, 156
  Elizabeth, 48
  Hannah, 8
  Jane, 25
  John, 48
  Martin, 25
BROOM, Daniel, 105
BROUSTER, Ann, 85
  John, 85
BROWN, Alexander, 66, 146
  Charles, 75
  Daniel, 8, 64, 113, 145
  David, 123
  Elisha, 115, 123
  Elizabeth, 1
  Esther, 100, 123
  George, 66, 89, 108
  Hannah, 1, 65, 100, 126
  Isaac, 126
  Jacob, 10
  James, 117
  Jane, 94
  Janet, 146
  Jean, 66
  Jeremiah, 100, 101, 123
  John, 35, 94
  Joseph, 1, 129
  Joshua, 10, 72, 89, 100, 101
  Katherine, 1
  Lydia, 126
  Margaret, 10, 89
  Martha, 75
  Mary, 1, 66
  Messer, 126
  Nathan, 126
  Phebe, 10
  Rachel, 123
  Robert, 36, 47, 53, 74, 130, 135, 141, 159
  Samuel, 1
  Sarah, 49, 101
  Susanna, 64
  Thomas, 80, 108, 118
  William, 1, 10, 16, 38, 49, 66
BROWNBACK,
  Garrett, 52
BROWNE, Nathaniel, 103
BRUFF, Patrick, 96
BRUMHALL, Jane, 126
BRYAN, John, 109, 158
  Mary, 123
  Thomas, 7, 12, 56, 123
BUCHANAN, Andrew, 37
  David, 83, 127
  Elizabeth, 83
  Gilbert, 16
  John, 83
  William, 20, 136
BUCHANON, Walter, 81
BUCKLEY, Adam, 5
BUFFINGTON, Ealse, 14
  Isaac, 98
  John, 119
  Joseph, 4, 56, 98, 100, 118, 135
  Mary, 118
  Phebe, 13
  Richard, 132
  Sarah, 120
  Thomas, 119
  William, 13
BULGER, Richard, 6
BULLER, Richard, 91
BUNTIN, Samuel, 31
BUNTING, Hana, 78
  Hannah, 78
  John, 19
  Joshia, 78
  Josiah, 78, 131
  Martha, 78
  Samuel, 12, 19, 29, 78, 95
  Sarah, 19, 78
  William, 156
BURGESS, Hannah, 19
BURGOIN, James, 69
  John, 69
  Joseph, 54, 69
  Susanna, 69
  Tamer, 69
BURGOYNE, John, 135, 136
  Joseph, 135
BURKE, Patrick, 20
BURN, William, 149
BURNET, John, 98, 120
BURNS, George, 117
  Robert, 117
BURSTON, John, 11
BUTCHER,
  Elizabeth, 62
  Hannah, 62
  Margaret, 62

Mary, 62
Rachel, 62
Sarah, 62
Susanna, 62
Zachariah, 34, 62
BUTLER, Joseph, 107
Martha, 107
Noble, 76
Robert, 107
Samuel, 107
BUTTERFIELD,
Hannah, 115
John, 115, 130
BUTTLER, Hannah, 94
John, 94, 95
Samuel, 94
BUYERS, Andrew, 77
John, 115
Samuel, 77
BYER, Ann, 114
John, 114
Joseph, 114
Margaret, 114
Samuel, 114
BYERS, Ann, 115
Joseph, 115
Samuel, 115

-C-
CADWALLER, Moses, 84
CADWELLADER,
Sarah, 12
CAHOON, Mary, 147
Thomas, 147
CALBREATH, Isabel, 90
CALDWELL, Ann, 31, 42, 45, 112
Dan, 112
Elizabeth, 82, 140
Henry, 82
James, 140
Jane, 69, 125
John, 69, 75, 76, 112
Joseph, 75
Mary, 140
Priscilla, 75
Robert, 18, 77
Samuel, 140

William, 13, 69, 77
CALE, James, 148
CALEY, Samuel, 114
CALLWELL, Ann, 62
Martha, 62
CALVERT, Charity, 122
Daniel, 54, 88, 104
Hannah, 57
John, 57
Sarah, 100
CALWELL, Abraham, 62
Dann, 62
James, 62
John, 62
William, 62
CAM, Henry, 19, 80
Margaret, 19, 80
CAMM, Margaret, 111
CAMPBELL,
Alexander, 140
Charles, 85
Elizabeth, 25
George, 140
James, 25, 85
Jean, 126
John, 68, 105
Martha, 85
Mary, 126
Michael, 85
Rachel, 85
Rebecca, 126
William, 85, 140
CAMPBLE, John, 119
Mary, 119
CANAN, John, 140
CANBY, Hannah, 89
Theophilus, 89
CANNON, Joseph, 137
CARLETON, Ann, 125
Betty, 125
Hannah, 125
Lydia, 130
Mary, 125
Rebecca, 125
Sarah, 125
Susanna, 125, 143
Thomas, 9, 27, 29, 78, 88,

122, 125, 130, 131
CARMICHAEL,
Elizabeth, 147
CARPENTER, John, 130
CARR, John, 144
Mary, 144
CARRITHERS, James, 14
John, 14
CARSON, Elizabeth, 52
Ester, 77
Esther, 125
George, 91
James, 49
Jean, 77
John, 91
Mary, 48, 158
Patrick, 77
Richard, 91
Robert, 91
William, 76
CARTER, Abraham, 75
David, 75
Edward, 98, 148
Elizabeth, 131
George, 6, 29, 87, 95, 156
Hannah, 98
Isaac, 98
Jacob, 27, 28, 129
Jasack, 148
John, 6, 33, 98
Joseph, 98, 148
Lydia, 75
Martin, 134
Mary, 6, 75
Phebe, 139
Robert, 33, 148
Samuel, 98, 148
William, 138
CARTMAN, Dinah, 11
CARUTHERS,
Alexander, 148
David, 148
James, 148
Jean, 148
John, 148, 159
Margaret, 148
CASSEDY, Bryan, 5
CASTER, Rachel, 22

CATER, Elizabeth,
  84
CATHCART,
  Elizabeth, 53
  Robert, 53
CHADS, Elizabeth,
  106
  Henry, 115
  John, 37, 42,
  45, 61, 66,
  106, 112
CHAFFIN, Robert,
  46
CHALFANT,
  Elizabeth, 65
  Henry, 91, 123
  Robert, 94
  Sarah, 106
CHALFIN, Hannah,
  155
CHAMBERLAIN, Ann,
  37
  Benjamin, 37
  Isaac, 37
  Jeremiah, 88
  John, 37
  Joseph, 37
  William, 37
CHAMBERLIN,
  Abigail, 126
  Benjamin, 126
  Cicely, 113
  Elizabeth, 126
  Isaac, 126
  John, 111, 121
  Jonas, 39
  Joseph, 17, 35,
    73, 126, 144
  Lydia, 126
  Mary, 37, 126
  Robert, 37, 82,
    111, 113
  Susanna, 126
  Thomas, 126
CHAMBERS, Joseph,
  60
  William, 43
CHANDLEE, Cotty,
  32
  Sarah, 32
CHANDLER, Ann, 115
  Benjamin, 113
  Elizabeth, 53,
    143
  George, 31, 70,
    115
  Isaac, 115
  James, 53
  John, 49, 115
  Mary, 115
  Moses, 115
  Ruth, 31, 70
  Susanna, 49
  Thomas, 115
  William, 49, 115
CHAPMAN,
  Elizabeth, 74
  George, 74
  Gilley, 74
  Hannah, 141
  Jean, 74
  John, 74
  Joseph, 74
  Lucy, 74
  Mary, 74
  Thomas, 74
  William, 74
CHARLTON, Henry,
  142
  Isabela, 142
  John, 142
  Lettice, 142
  Margaret, 142
  Thomas, 142
CHEYNEY, Ann, 99
  Richard, 108
  Thomas, 89
CHURCH, Dorcas,
  148
  Paul, 148
CHURCHMAN, George,
  64, 89, 94,
  126, 157
  William, 64,
  118, 126
CIDDELL, Seret, 5
CLARK, Alice, 135
  Ann, 114, 135
  Gabriel, 4, 92
  Henry, 1
  James, 114
  Jane, 104
  John, 9, 33
  Mary, 1, 67
  Richard, 25, 67
  William, 30
CLARKE, Deborah,
  143
  Thomas, 116
CLAYPOOLE, Ann,
  116
  Elishe, 116
  Elizabeth, 116
  James, 116
  Jane, 116
  Kathrine, 116
  Martha, 116
  Mary, 116
  Nathaniel, 116
  Thomas, 116
CLAYTON, Adam, 63,
  106, 135
  Ann, 100
  David, 63, 92
  Edward, 6, 100
  Hannah, 63, 75
  John, 100
  Joseph, 109
  Joshua, 100
  Margaret, 75,
    109
  Mary, 8, 17, 75
  Patience, 75
  Philip, 127
  Phipps, 75
  Sarah, 75, 100
  Susanna, 100,
    109
  Thomas, 63
  William, 8, 17,
    75, 100
CLENDENAN,
  Eleanor, 120
  William, 120
CLENDENIN, Thomas,
  86
CLETON, Mary, 4
CLIFFE, Benjamin,
  22
CLINGAN, William,
  76, 91, 92
CLINTON, James,
  147
  Margret, 24
  William, 5, 13,
    24, 45, 63
CLOUD, Abigail, 85
  Abner, 85, 131
  Abraham, 128
  Jason, 34, 128
  Jeremiah, 81
  John, 70, 117
  Joseph, 12, 30,
    85
  Lydia, 33

167

Mary, 42
Mordecai, 85, 106
Nathaniel, 143
Robert, 143
Thomas, 33
William, 85, 122
COATES, Elizabeth, 17
Moses, 134
Samuel, 17
Thomas, 134, 146
COBOURN, Caleb, 122, 123
Elizabeth, 122, 123
Joseph, 33
Lydia, 123
Mary, 123
Rachel, 123
Susanna, 123
Thomas, 122, 123
COCHRAN, Ann, 158
David, 14
Elizabeth, 150
George, 158, 159
Isaac, 140
Isabel, 158
Jacob, 53
James, 9, 14, 138, 150, 158, 159
Jane, 158, 159
Jean, 159
Jennett, 90
John, 140, 150, 158
Robert, 90, 158
Stephen, 14, 158
COCK, Ann, 39
Benjamin, 22
COEBURN, Thomas, 20
COLBERSON, John, 23
COLE, Ellis, 84
James, 130, 148
Prudence, 84
Rebecca, 84
William, 83, 84, 123
COLES, Lydia, 84
COLGAN, William, 74
COLLEN, Margaret, 63
Roday, 63
COLLETT, James, 40
Jane, 40
Jane Bazella, 40
Jeremiah, 40
Joseph, 40
Mary, 40
William, 40
COLLIER, Isaac, 34, 71
James, 34
Ruth, 71
COLLINS, Andrew, 32, 119
Ann, 3
Hannah, 32, 44
Henry, 3, 8, 44
John, 3
Joseph, 3, 8, 44, 119, 129
Mary, 3, 44
Patrick, 41
Peter, 13
COLSON, Tamer, 89
COLVIN, Elizabeth, 155
John, 155
Robert, 155
COMMONS, James, 12
COMSTON, Henry, 24
Mary, 24
CONN, Samuel, 32
CONNELL,
 Elizabeth, 77
 George, 77
CONNER, Charles, 29
CONNOLY, Rachel, 57
COOK, Cathrine, 14
Dinah, 87
Elinor, 87
Elizabeth, 14, 110
Jean, 14, 110
John, 87, 113
Joseph, 110, 131
Mary, 110
Rebecca, 113
Roger, 72
Stephen, 87
Thomas, 110
William, 14, 139
COOPE, Samuel, 128
COOPER, Adam, 145
John, 62
William, 4, 47
COPLAND, George, 93
COPPOCK,
 Batholomew, 111
 Esther, 111
 Margaret, 111
 Moses, 111
 Rebecca, 111
CORBALLY, Abigail, 118
 Elizabeth, 118
 Hannah, 118
 Jane, 118
 Mary, 118
 Sarah, 118
CORBET, Mary, 64
CORBIT, Mary, 39
CORNOCK, Alice, 129
 Thomas, 27
 William, 27
CORREY, George, 49
 John, 79
 Samuel, 79
CORSBUE, William, 88
CORSBY, William, 59
COULSON,
 Elizabeth, 128
 Isaac, 128
 John, 128
 Joseph, 128
 Martha, 128
 Samuel, 128
 Tamer, 80
 Thomas, 1, 128
 William, 128
COUNCILL, Hannah, 95
 John, 95
 Sarah, 95
COURTNEY, Frances, 132
 Robert, 132
COWAN, Anne, 79
 Esther, 80
 Hugh, 38
 James, 37
 Jean, 37
 Joseph, 37
 Keatren, 38

COWDEN, Joseph, 97
Matthew, 8, 13
COWPLAND, Caleb,
  57, 76, 79, 146
James, 146
Jonathan, 79,
  146
Joseph, 146
Joshua, 153, 154
Sarah, 76, 78
COX, Andrew, 101
Elizabeth, 101
Hannah, 109
Jane, 109
John, 101, 109,
  145, 153
Lawrance, 35
Lawrence, 109
Martha, 101
Mary, 101
Peter, 101
Rachel, 109
Rebecca, 15, 101
Sarah, 109
CRABB, Mary, 119
William, 107,
  119
CRACKER, Hannah,
  109
CRAFORD, Aaron, 5
CRAGHEAD, George,
  120
CRAIG, George, 145
William, 133
CRANSTON,
  Elizabeth, 67
William, 67
CRAWFORD,
  Alexander, 127
Andrew, 127
Anexander, 127
Hannah, 106
James, 21, 127
John, 9, 56,
  102, 106, 117,
  118, 127, 136,
  151
Josias, 127
Martha, 72
Mary, 21, 127
William, 102,
  146
CREMER, Mary, 120
CRESWELL, Hannah,
  104

Isabella, 104
James, 104, 157
Jane, 104
John, 104
Joseph, 104
Mary, 104
Rachel, 104
Robert, 44, 104
CRISWELL, Elijah,
  148
Elizabeth, 97
George, 104
James, 97, 99,
  134
Jane, 99, 134
John, 134
Margaret, 134
Mary, 134
Rachel, 134
Robert, 99, 104
William, 134
CROOK, Thomas, 59
CROOKSHANK,
  William, 115
CROSBY, Eleanor,
  28
John, 11, 28,
  43, 114
Richard, 28
Samuel, 28
Susanna, 28
CROSIER,
  Elizabeth, 46
Esther, 46
James, 46
John, 33, 46,
  112
Mary, 46
Rachel, 46
CROSLEY, Charles,
  10, 23
Hannah, 23
James, 23
John, 23
Samuel, 23
CROSS, Rachel,
  120, 144
William, 120,
  144
CROSWELL, Robert,
  77
CROW, Ann, 153
Samuel, 153
CROXSON, Mary, 49
Samuel, 49

CROZER, Hannah,
  140
James, 10, 144
Robert, 140
CRUCKSHANK, John,
  64
CRY, Elizabeth,
  148
William, 14
CULBERSON, John,
  26
CULBERTSON,
  Isabella, 120
James, 74, 131
Jane, 120
Jean, 120, 131
John, 14, 72,
  82, 115
Kettren, 14
Martha, 120
Mary, 120
Robert, 120, 131
Samuel, 14, 76,
  120, 131
Sarah, 120
William, 14
CULIN, Abraham, 96
Andrew, 122
Daniel, 14, 32,
  96
Elizabeth, 96
George, 15, 59,
  96, 131
Jonas, 14
Margaret, 96
Martha, 96
Samuel, 96
Sarah, 125
Swan, 96, 122,
  131
William, 96, 125
CULLEY, Henry, 148
CULLIPHER,
  William, 90
CULLIVER,
  Benjamin, 17
Catherine, 17
Richard, 5
CUMING, Agnes, 136
Elizabeth, 136
Esther, 136
James, 136
Joseph, 136
Samuel, 136
William, 62, 65,

136
CUMINGS, Thomas, 73
CUMMIN, William, 13
CUMMINGS, Alice, 31, 156
 Charles, 110
 Elizabeth, 31, 68
 Hannah, 31
 Isabella, 134
 Jane, 5
 John, 12
 Mary, 31
 Thomas, 25, 28, 31, 68, 106, 156
CUMMINS, Mary, 122
 William, 122
CUNNINGHAM, Elizabeth, 20
CURREY, Archibald, 140
CURRIE, William, 152
CURRY, George, 12
 Hannah, 112
 Thomas, 76
CUTHBERT, John, 28

-D-
DAILY, Sarah, 91
DALZIEL, James, 16
DANIEL, Hannah, 88
 Hugh, 88
 Isabella, 90
 James, 88
 Jane, 14
 John, 14, 88, 90
 Mary, 88
 Samuel, 88
DARGAN, Pally, 145
DARKE, Martha, 105
 Samuel, 105
DARLINGTON,
 Abraham, 35, 143
 Elizabeth, 35
 Joseph, 12
 Mary, 12
 Rachel, 35
 Rebecca, 35
 Thomas, 143
DARLINTON, John, 27, 74
 Joseph, 74, 134, 141
 Mary, 74
 Meredith, 74
 Robert, 59, 74, 141
 William, 23, 27, 74
DAUCHARTY,
 Richard, 45
DAVID, Ann, 19
 Benjamin, 145
 Bridget, 23
 Daniel, 145
 David, 116
 Edward, 10, 23
 Elizabeth, 116, 138
 Ephraim, 138
 Esther, 10
 George, 116, 138
 Hannah, 19
 Isaac, 42, 64, 65
 James, 21, 123
 Jane, 71
 Jenkin, 6
 Jenness, 10
 John, 22, 23, 138, 145
 Joshua, 22
 Llewellyin, 64
 Llewellyn, 37, 41
 Margaret, 64
 Maris, 21
 Mary, 19, 23, 116
 Phebe, 10
 Priscilla, 10
 Ruth, 64
 Samuel, 10, 19, 22, 23
 Sarah, 10
 Stephen, 19
 Thomas, 19, 71, 116, 145
DAVIDSON, John, 82
DAVIES, Amos, 58, 112, 140
 Ann, 140
 David, 4, 21, 43, 58, 112, 138
 Elenor, 138
 Elizabeth, 43
 Ellis, 4, 58, 112, 118, 140
 Esther, 112
 Hannah, 140
 Jane, 140
 Jonathan, 58, 89, 112, 140
 Mary, 112
 Myrick, 43, 115
 Philip, 43
 Priscilla, 112
 Rachel, 112
 Richard, 4, 58
 Sarah, 42, 140
DAVIS, Abner, 71
 Abraham, 140
 Amos, 69
 Ann, 92
 Anne, 93
 B., 17, 40
 Benjamin, 73, 92, 110, 146
 Benton, 74
 Bethell, 73
 Catharine, 93
 David, 37, 57, 60, 63, 93, 150
 Dinah, 96
 Elijah, 39
 Elizabeth, 42, 93, 119, 137, 141
 Hannah, 106, 150, 154
 Isaac, 35, 42, 43, 90
 Israel, 128
 Jacob, 42
 James, 4, 5, 11, 41, 51, 60, 71, 93, 141, 150
 Jane, 57, 93
 Jennett, 5
 Joan, 5
 John, 4, 5, 11, 19, 20, 21, 29, 64, 71, 90, 93, 141, 144, 149, 150
 Jonathan, 150
 Joseph, 20, 29, 33, 61, 77, 92, 93, 94, 106,

141
Lewis, 11, 20,
  29, 66, 93
Margaret, 5, 93
Mary, 11, 20,
  29, 42, 60, 71,
  92, 93, 144,
  150
Methuselah, 42
Myrick, 92
Nathan, 92
Rachel, 93
Rebecca, 19, 29
Robert, 26, 96
Rose, 92
Sampson, 90, 93
Samson, 5, 71,
  141
Samuel, 40
Sarah, 20, 29,
  93, 150
Sidney, 42
Susanna, 141,
  150
Thomas, 5, 71,
  93, 119
William, 64
DAVISON, James,
  129
John, 99
DAWSON, Abraham,
  101
Isaac, 101
Jacob, 101
Mary, 101
Richard, 101
Thomas, 101
DAY, James, 104,
  108
John, 41
DAYSARD, William,
  61
DAYSERT, John, 61
DEAKON, Catharin,
  108
Elizabeth, 108
Joseph, 108
Robert, 108
DEAN, Alexander, 7
Benjamin, 7
Hannah, 13
John, 7
Joseph, 7, 40
Mary, 13
Sarah, 7

William, 7, 23,
  60
DEEBLE, George, 23
Delaware
  (Wilmington),
  9, 80, 157
DELL, Mary, 26
Sarah, 26
Thomas, 3, 26
DELLZEL, James, 25
DELY, John, 55
DENNIS, Edward, 94
Jane, 76
John, 76
Sarah, 94
Thomas, 94
DENNY, David, 62,
  157
Samuel, 157
William, 20, 157
DERRICK, Richard,
  87
DEVONISH,
  Elizabeth, 31
DEVONSHIRE, Alice,
  22
DEXTER, Henry, 148
DICK, Archibald,
  86, 117, 134
Mary, 86
DICKEN, Martha, 24
DICKEY, James, 156
John, 33
Mary, 156
Rebecca, 33
William, 92
DICKIE, Elizabeth,
  5
John, 5, 73,
  130, 145
Margaret, 36, 96
Moses, 10, 36
Samuel, 145
William, 36
DICKINSON, Joseph,
  53
Margaret, 53
DICKS, Abraham,
  102, 114
Anne, 102
Jane, 103
Job, 102, 158
Joseph, 102
Margaret, 114
Nathan, 103

Peter, 57, 102
Roger, 102
Sarah, 10, 103
DILLON, Richard,
  26
DILWORTH, Charles,
  141
Hannah, 35, 45
James, 22, 39,
  45, 55, 61, 64,
  82, 98, 120,
  141
John, 35, 45
William, 43
DITTON, Richard,
  86
DIX, Elizabeth,
  102
Esther, 35
Joseph, 35
Mary, 102
Nathan, 35, 102
Peter, 35
Sarah, 35, 102
DIXON, Catherine,
  124
Elizabeth, 110
Joseph, 124, 127
Mary, 124
Ruth, 124
Sarah, 124, 127
Silas, 110
Solomon, 110
William, 124,
  127
DOAGREY, Cattrin,
  14
DOAKE, Henry, 45
Mary, 45
DOCHERTY, Owen,
  111
DODDSON, Ann, 100
Eleanor, 100
John, 100
Michael, 100
DONALDSON, Arthur,
  76
Margaret, 76
William, 73, 76
DONNALY, Arthur,
  92
DONNEL, James, 13
DONNELL, Annas,
  147
James, 147

DOUGHERTY,
  Cathrin, 111
  Edmund, 81
  George, 111
  James, 129
  Jane, 90
  Mary, 7, 81
  Richard, 7
  Sarah, 111
  Susanna, 106
DOUGLAS, Mary,
  116, 141
DOUGLASS, Adam, 47
  James, 47
  Thomas, 76
DOWNARD, Anne, 114
  William, 114
DOWNING, John, 100
  Richard, 124,
  133
  Thomas, 7, 127,
  137
DOYLE, Susanna, 33
DUCKWORTH, Aaron,
  109
  Allice, 109
  Eailes, 109
  Grace, 109
  Rodey, 109
  Sarah, 109
  Uriah, 109
  William, 109
DUGLESS, Thomas,
  130
DUNCAN, James, 140
DUNHAM, Jane, 121
  Mary, 121
DUNKIN, Samuel, 6
DUNLAP, Alexander,
  156
DUNN, Ann, 109
  James, 109, 156
  Jean, 109
  Sarah, 109
  Thomas, 109
  William, 109
DUNNING, James,
  118
DUNWOODIES, Agnes,
  121
DUNWOODY, John,
  157
DURROUGH,
  Bartholomew,
  157

Jane, 157
DUTTON, Anne, 149
  David, 86
  Edward, 47
  Elizabeth, 14
  Hannah, 18, 28
  Jacob, 18
  Jennett, 52
  John, 14, 75, 86
  Kingsman, 149
  Mary, 128
  Prudence, 92,
  151
  Richard, 14, 49,
  86, 117
  Robert, 28
  Ruth, 128
  Susanna, 28
DYSANT, Rachel,
  104

-E-
EACHUS, Daniel,
  77, 98
  Enoch, 77, 144,
  153
  Esther, 153
  John, 7, 77
  Phineas, 159
  Robert, 7, 77
  William, 58, 77
EAVENSON, George,
  152
  Hannah, 132
  Jemima, 53
  Nathaniel, 152
  Richard, 53, 61,
  82
EDGAR, Margaret,
  10
  Robert, 10
EDGE, Abigail, 79
  Ann, 73
  Anne, 29
  George, 29
  John, 73
  Mary, 73
  Sarah, 73
EDMESTON, David,
  7, 26
  Elizabth, 71
  Hugh, 7, 71
  James, 71
  Jane, 7
  John, 7, 71

Margaret, 71
  Martha, 7
  Mary, 7
  William, 7, 71
EDMISTON, William,
  62
EDMONDS, Thomas,
  46, 87
EDMONSON, Rosanne,
  53
EDMUNDS, Mary, 143
  Thomas, 3, 143
EDMUNSON, Jean, 53
EDWARD, John, 12
EDWARDS, Amos, 17
  Catherine, 120
  John, 17, 104
  Joseph, 17
  Mary, 17
  Moses, 17
  Thomas, 32
  William, 103
ELDER, James, 89,
  154
  John, 154
  Martha, 154
  Robert, 154
  Thomas, 149
ELDRIDGE, James,
  157
ELIS, Anne, 143
  Elis, 143
ELLIOT, Anne, 144
  Benjamin, 144
  Christopher, 11
  Gerall, 11
ELLIOTT, Anne, 82
  Enoch, 12
  James, 52, 85
  John, 82
  Margaret, 52, 82
  Morris, 85
  Peter, 85
  Robert, 82
  Sarah, 85
  William, 120
ELLIS, Ann, 48
  Benjamin, 48
  David, 55
  Ellis, 48
  Hannah, 48, 73
  Humphrey, 55
  Jeremiah, 55,
  125
  Jesse, 55

Jonathan, 55
Margaret, 55
Margret, 28
Mary, 48
Rachel, 48
Rebecca, 48
Sublimus, 55
Thomas, 48, 55
William, 48
EMANUEL, David, 137
EMMIT, Abraham, 6, 72, 97
Abram, 106
David, 106
John, 106
Josias, 72, 106
Rebecca, 106, 137
Samuel, 106
EMMITT, David, 149
Isabelle, 149
England, 2, 45, 59, 94, 108
ENGLAND, Samuel, 126
Sarah, 126
ENGLE, Frederick, 153
ENGLISH, Andrew, 14, 15
Elizabeth, 14, 15
James, 14
Jane, 14
John, 14
ENTRIKEN, Mary, 46
Samuel, 46
ENTRIKIN, George, 44
Mary, 44
ERELY, Alice, 128
Samuel, 128
ERWIN, Ann, 85
Margaret, 132
Robert, 141
EVAN, Ann, 63, 100
David, 100, 143
James, 100, 143
Jenkin, 100
John, 1, 100
Margaret, 143
Mary, 82
Morris, 144
Owen, 90

Rachel, 148
Rees, 138
Thomas, 22, 83
William, 100
EVANS, Abner, 141
Amey, 1
Amos, 28, 136
Ann, 68
Anne, 107
Cad., 32
Cadwallader, 17, 68, 91, 138
Cadwaller, 30
Daniel, 121
David, 22, 153
Elinor, 76
Elizabeth, 74, 136
Evan, 4, 23, 46, 155
George, 43
Griffith, 46
Hannah, 28, 58
Hugh, 63
Isabel, 41
James, 26, 41, 129, 133, 142
Jane, 1, 24
Jean, 41
Joel, 58, 103, 123
John, 1, 24, 28, 41, 43
Jonathan, 70
Joshua, 58, 103, 123, 157
Lea, 28
Lewis, 121
Margaret, 41
Mary, 28, 58, 85
Morris, 60
Rachel, 28
Rebecca, 22
Richard, 4, 58, 123
Robert, 41
Sarah, 121, 141
Stephen, 21, 27
Susanna, 150
Thomas, 4, 24, 44, 76, 115, 153
William, 21, 58, 70, 103
EVENSON,

173

Nathaniel, 34
EVERARDS, Dr., 15
EVINS, James, 136
EWING, Alexander, 41
Anne, 41, 102
James, 102
John, 41, 54, 120
Robert, 54
Samuel, 120
Susanna, 54
EYRE, Isaac, 135
John, 95, 135, 146
Lewis, 135
Mary, 135
Robert, 135
William, 135

-F-
FAIRLAMB, Anne, 152
Catharine, 28
Catherine, 152
Eleanor, 152
Frederick, 152, 153
Fredrick, 128
John, 25, 28, 87, 122, 128, 135, 145, 152, 157, 159
Mary, 152
Nicholas, 152
Samuel, 152
Susanna, 152, 159
FAL, E., 60
FARLOW, William, 33
FARON, Ealse, 156
John, 156
FARR, Edward, 69
FARRA, Abraham, 94
James, 94
Joseph, 94
Mary, 94
Oliver, 148
Samuel, 94
William, 94
FARRAN, John, 149
Margaret, 149
Mary, 149
Michael, 149

Philip, 149
FARTON, John, 93
FAWKES, John, 84
  Richard, 70, 84
FEAGAN, Giles, 111
FEAGON, Giles, 96
FEARNAN, Edward, 68
  Elizabeth, 68
  Francis, 68
  Margaret, 68
  Margery, 68
  Solomon, 68
FELL, Edward, 146
  Mary, 6
  Rebecca, 111, 136
  William, 10, 18, 46, 80, 111, 136, 158
FERGUS, John, 91
FERGUSON, Charles, 150
FERRI, David, 159
FERRIS, James, 124
  John, 124
FEW, Benjamin, 155
  Dorcas, 70
  Isaac, 155
  James, 55, 155
  Jean, 155
  Joseph, 118, 155
  Richard, 155
FIELD, Sarah, 7
FILLSON (Felson),
  Davison, 32
  Jane, 32
  John, 32, 33
  Margaret, 32
  Robert, 155
  Samuel, 155
  William, 32, 33
FILSON, Davison, 33, 37
  John, 33
  Samuel, 99, 133
FILSONS, John, 32
  Robert, 33
FINDLEY, Jean, 55
  Robert, 55
FINLEY, Catharine, 14
  James, 105, 142
  John, 21, 47
  Margaret, 21

Michal, 148
Samuel, 133
William, 14
FINLY, Samuel, 35
FINNEY, Jane, 33
  Robert, 6, 33, 61
  William, 33
FISHER, Ezekiel, 139
  Henry, 73
  Rebecca, 139
  Robert, 149
  Thomas, 93, 139
  William, 139
FITZSIMMONS,
  Felix, 72
  George, 116
  James, 116
  John, 116, 143
  Margaret, 116
  Mary, 143
  Rachel, 72
FLEESON, Plunket, 130
FLEMEN, Anne
  Catherine, 11
FLEMING, Agnes, 153
  Ann, 126
  David, 153
  George, 30
  Henry, 25
  James, 30, 126, 139, 153
  Jane, 153
  Jennett, 153
  John, 103, 139, 153, 154
  Joseph, 77
  Margaret, 153
  Robert, 104
  Sarah, 25, 153
  William, 103
FLETCHER, Mary, 55
  Richard, 55
FLOWER, Abigail, 12, 56, 131
  Dinah, 56
  Hannah, 119, 149
  Jemima, 119
  John, 119
  Mary, 119
  Prudence, 156
  Rachel, 119

Richard, 7, 12, 49, 56, 67, 108, 119
  Thomas, 56, 156
FLOYD, Samuel, 93
FOELY, Joseph, 129
FOLLEY, Elizabeth, 107
FORD, Benjamin, 52
  John, 75
  Prudence, 75
FORDHAM, Joseph, 109, 124, 125, 126
FORMAN, Alexander, 159
FOROH, Hannah, 148
FOULK, Elizabeth, 143
  John, 143
  Stephen, 91
FOULKE, Anne, 139
  Stephen, 143
FOX, George, 14
FRANCES, Rees, 141
FRANCIS, John, 141
  Joseph, 123
  Lettice, 123
  Mary, 123
  Rees, 123
  Richard, 10
FRASER, John, 136
  Joseph, 136
FRASHER, Anne, 141
  Pierce, 141
FRAZER, Miriam, 29
FRAZIER, Aaron, 29
  Alexander, 29
  James, 29
  John, 29
  Moses, 29
FREAM, David, 91
FRED, Benjamin, 36
  John, 21
  Joseph, 76
  Katherine, 41
  Mary, 41
  Nicholas, 41
  Sarah, 41
  Susanna, 21
FREDD, Ann, 41
  Benjamin, 41
  Deborah, 41
  John, 41
  Joseph, 25, 41

Nicholas, 25
FREDERICK, Henry, 24
FREECE, George, 114
Joshua, 114
FREED (FREECE),
  Anne, 34
FREEMAN,
  Elizabeth, 2, 13
  John, 2, 13
  Nathan, 13
  Nathaniel, 2, 14
  Samuel, 2, 13
  Susannah, 13
FRITZ, Jacob, 159
FRYER, Ann, 126
  George, 126
  Thomas, 126
  William, 126
FULLERTON,
  Humphrey, 89
  Robert, 89
  William, 89
FULTON, Elizabeth, 133
  John, 127, 142
  Mary, 97
  Robert, 97
  William, 140
FULTORN, John, 147
FUTHEY, J. Smith, 135

-G-
GALBREATH, John, 150
GALLOWAY, Grace, 95
GALT, Samuel, 47
GAMBLE, Andrew, 97
GANTRIL, John, 72
GARDNER, Francis, 121
  Henry, 110
  James, 26
  John, 26, 118
GARRATT, Ellis, 64
GARRET, Lawrence, 58
  Lydia, 58
  Mary, 58
  Rebecca, 58
GARRETT, Amos, 83

Enoch, 83
George, 64
Isaac, 83, 147
James, 141
Joseph, 3, 5
Lawrence, 32, 155
Lydia, 73
Mary, 64, 83, 142
Nathan, 20
Rebecca, 32
Thomas, 63, 64
William, 63, 78, 110, 142
GARRETTSON, Mary, 29
GARTRIL, John, 1, 65, 80, 134
GARTRILL, John, 44, 117
GATCHELL, Elisha, 100
  Rachel, 100
GATIS, James, 150
  Martha, 150
GATLIVE, James, 34
  Rees, 34
GAY, John, 81
  Margaret, 81
  Matthew, 81
GEDDES, Alexander, 85, 147
GEIRCE, Andrew, 143
  Susanna, 143
GEORGE, Amey, 1
  Ann, 147
  Edward H., 1
  George, 1, 71
  John, 1
  Joseph, 147
  Richard, 1
  Thomas, 147
  William, 147
GERRARD, William, 132
GEST, Daniel, 39, 64
  Henry, 143
  Jean, 44
  John, 30, 44, 54, 104, 142
  Mary, 142, 143
  Phebe, 143

175

Simon, 104, 142
Thomas, 142
GIBBONS, Abraham, 51
  Ann, 44, 51
  Charity, 44
  Jacob, 51
  James, 51
  John, 51
  Joseph, 34, 44, 51, 83, 91
  Mary, 51
GIBONS, Jane, 51
  Thomas, 51
  William, 51
GIBSON, Alexander, 153
  Alice, 33, 135
  Andrew, 131
  Christian, 53, 143
  David, 131
  Elizabeth, 143
  Hannah, 57, 143
  Isaac, 135
  James, 135
  John, 53, 135, 143
  Joseph, 135
  Joshua, 143
  Lydia, 143
  Mary, 131
  Moses, 135
  Nathaniel, 143
  Rebecca, 135
  Thomas, 53, 57, 115, 131, 135, 143
GIGER, Eve
  Margaret, 13
  Jesly, 139
GIHEN, John, 125
  Joseph, 125
  Robert, 125
GIHON, Elizabeth, 30
  Thomas, 30
GILBERT, Jonathan, 129
GILBRAITH, John, 65
GILBREATH,
  Rebecca, 155
GILLELAND, James, 148

GILLES, James, 62
GILLESPIE,
  Alexander, 97
  David, 97
  John, 97
  Mary, 97
  Ruth, 97
  Samuel, 97
  William, 97
GILLESPY, William, 9
GILLILAND, James, 16, 35
GILPIN, George, 23, 71, 155
  Gideon, 147
  Hannah, 71, 82
  Joseph, 62, 81, 83
  Mary, 81
  Samuel, 45, 62
  Thomas, 30
GIREY, Andrew, 78
GIVAN, Robert, 129
GLASFORD, John, 148
  Joseph, 148
  Margaret, 148
  Sarah, 148
GLASGOW, William, 72
GLASSFORD,
  Elizabeth, 148
  Henry, 148
GLEAVE, Elizabeth, 46, 77
  Isaac, 46
  John, 46
GLENDENING, James, 154
GLENDINNING,
  James, 93
GODFREE, William, 157
GOFF, Anne, 42
  Edward, 42, 43
  Frances, 42
  John, 43
  Mary, 42, 43
  Sarah, 42
  William, 43
GOFORTH, Mary, 78
GOFREY, Thomas, 21
GOHEEN, Anne, 32
  John, 32

GOLLIFER, John, 80
GOOD, Mary, 15
GOODWIN, Thomas, 35, 88, 129
GORMAN, Daniel, 90
  David, 35
GORRELL, James, 7
GORSUCH, Charles, 84
GRACY, John, 125
GRAHAM, Ann, 130
  Arthur, 146
  Charles, 130
  Daniel, 146
  Elizabeth, 130, 157
  George, 130
  H. H., 19, 26, 73, 99, 103
  Helinor, 146
  Henry, 130, 137, 146
  Henry Hale, 153, 156
  James, 49, 130, 146
  Jared, 146
  Jarett, 146
  Jean, 146
  John, 130, 146
  Joseph, 130
  Margaret, 146
  Mary, 130, 146
  Michael, 146
  Sarah, 130, 146
  William, 38, 130
GRANT, John, 32
GRANTHAM, George, 114, 136, 159
  Lydia, 159
  Margaret, 159
GRANTTUM, Charles, 108
GRANTUM,
  Catherine, 58
  Charles, 15, 25, 32, 58, 59, 92, 109, 114
  Elizabeth, 92
  George, 15, 59, 71, 109, 140
  Jacob, 59, 109
GRAY, George, 150
  John, 135, 143
  Thomas, 53

GREAG, Dinah, 14
  Thomas, 14
GREEN, Abel, 32, 90, 100, 147
  Anne, 132
  Betty, 9
  Edward, 90
  Hannah, 100
  Henry, 9, 38
  Jane, 100
  Mary, 155
  Robert, 53
  Thomas, 23, 132
GREENFIELD, John, 122
GREGG, Ann, 81
  Dinah, 130
  John, 56, 130
  Michael, 130
  Stephen, 130
  Thomas, 106, 130
GREGORY, Anne, 126
  Edward, 2
  John, 2, 126
  Margaret, 62
  Martha, 2
  Mary, 2
  William, 2, 62
GRIFFITH, Abel, 145, 159
  Amos, 125
  Benjamin, 151
  Benoni, 102
  Catharine, 102
  Daniel, 37, 65, 102
  David, 37
  Ezekiel, 102
  Hannah, 102
  Hosea, 37
  Jane, 133
  John, 19, 37, 65, 102, 115, 133, 137, 141, 145, 150
  Joseph, 129
  Mary, 19, 37, 151
  Maurice, 151
  Nathan, 102
  Rebecca, 19
  Sarah, 125
  Susanna, 129
  Timothy, 37
  William, 69, 98,

129, 151
GRIFFITHS, Abel,
 105
 Amos, 105
 Dan, 105
 Evan, 105
 Griffith, 105
 Gwin, 105
 John, 105
 Levi, 105
 Rebecca, 105
 William, 105
GRIFIN, Thomas, 4
GRIMES, Robert,
 140
GRISELL, Thomas,
 35
GRISSELL, Thomas,
 154
GRISTE, John, 37
 Susanna, 37
GRIZELL, Edward,
 43
 Mary, 43
 Thomas, 43
GRONOW, John, 152
 Lewis, 119, 152
GROVE, Martha, 31
 Sarah, 31
GROWDEN, Hannah,
 95
 Lawrence, 95
GRUBB, Adam, 129,
 149
 Curtis, 98
 Emanuel, 121
 Frances, 122
 Hannah, 17, 98
 Henry, 75, 98
 Jesse, 122
 John, 98
 Lydia, 25
 Mary, 47, 98,
 122
 Nathaniel, 42,
 98, 103, 122
 Peter, 17, 98
 Rachel, 50
 Rebecca, 25
 Samuel, 5, 47,
 98, 103, 122,
 149
GUBBY, Peter, 131
GUEST, Alice, 141
 Hannah, 57

Thomas, 3
GUTHERY, John, 109
GWIN, John, 11
GWYN, Hannah, 90

-H-
HACKET, David, 21
HACKETT, Agnes, 63
 Elizabeth, 63
 John, 33, 63
 Mary, 63
HADLEY, John, 154
 Margaret, 154
 Phebe, 98
HADLY, Joshua, 41
 Sarah, 41
HAGUE, John, 134
 William, 134
HAINES, Daniel,
 129
 David, 54
 Deborah, 129
 Elizabeth, 129,
 130
 Isaac, 129
 Jacob, 117
 Job, 129, 130
 Joseph, 129
 Josiah, 58
 Mary, 54
 Nathan, 129
 William, 129,
 130
HAINS, David, 132
 Isaac, 44
 Jane, 132
 John, 132
 Mary, 109
 William, 132
HAIR, James, 146
HALCOMBE, Jacob,
 73
HALE, Frances, 14
HALHOUSE
 (MILHOUS),
 Thomas, 127
HALL, Alexander,
 65
 Alice, 65
 Caleb, 108
 David, 158
 Elizabeth, 54,
 92
 George, 81, 84

Hezekiah, 54
 Jane, 65
 John, 46, 54,
 81, 103, 108,
 126, 144
 Joseph, 43
 Mahlon, 158
 Margery, 158
 Mary, 81
 Matthew, 80,
 111, 158
 Richard, 65
 Samuel, 95
 Sarah, 145, 158
 Stephen, 111
 Susanna, 108
 William, 93
HALLIDAY, Robert,
 41
 Samuel, 132
HAMBLETON, James,
 94
 Margaret, 94
 William, 94
HAMILL, James, 64
 John, 53
 Robert, 37, 96
HAMILTON,
 Catherine, 61
 Elizabeth, 154
 James, 61, 110
 Janet, 110
 Jean, 61
 John, 7, 61, 110
 Margaret, 110
 Robert, 32, 91,
 156
 William, 80
HAMMER, Abraham,
 143
 Martha, 143
HAMPTON, Benjamin,
 30
HANKEY, Ann, 153
HANNA, James, 146
 John, 49
 William, 77
HANNAWAY, Thomas,
 99
HANNUM, John, 66,
 67, 79
HANSON, Jonathan,
 84
 Susanna, 13
HANTHORN, John,

144
HARAH, Agnes, 127
  Charles, 127
  Patrick, 127
  William, 127
HARDING, Francis,
  39
  John, 92
HARIS, Thomas, 122
HARKNESS, David,
  67
HARLAN, Aaron, 72
  Abigail, 42, 85
  Amos, 21
  Ann, 153
  Anne, 33
  Betty, 72
  Caleb, 56
  David, 21, 77
  Edith, 22
  Elizabeth, 21,
    24, 72
  Ezekiel, 54, 153
  George, 21, 24
  Hannah, 33, 85
  Henry, 153
  Isaac, 33
  James, 153
  Joshua, 29
  Mary, 72
  Michael, 77
  Samuel, 90
  Sarah, 72, 85
  Silas, 21
  Solomon, 153
  Stephen, 56
  Susanna, 153
  Thomas, 27, 42,
    45, 47, 56, 66,
    96, 125, 131,
    153, 155
  William, 42
HARMAN, Mary, 15
HARMON, Elizabeth,
  47
HARPER, Alexander,
  105
  Ann, 95
  Charles, 105
  James, 105
  John, 4, 105,
    108
HARRIS, Daniel,
  117
  Elizabeth, 1
  Evan, 55
  Evin, 117
  George, 30, 43
  Hannah, 1
  James, 47
  John, 1, 129
  Phebe, 129
  Rachel, 1
  Richard, 1
  Samuel, 52
  Sarah, 1
  Susanna, 1
  Thomas, 1, 42,
    96
  William, 1
HARRISON, Caleb,
  26, 128, 159
  Hannah, 159
  John, 2, 159
  Joseph, 159
  Rachel, 20
  Richard, 159
  Sarah, 17, 54
  Thomas, 17, 20
HARRY, Amos, 81,
  149
  Aubrey, 131
  Benjamin, 98
  Bonsall, 131
  Daniel, 42
  Dina, 81
  Elizabeth, 98
  Elizabth, 98
  Ester, 81
  Evan, 81, 142,
    155
  George, 149
  Hannah, 131
  Hugh, 81, 98
  Jacob, 131
  James, 98
  Jesse, 98
  Nathan, 98
  Olive, 81
  Silas, 81
  Stephen, 98, 142
  Thomas, 98
  William, 81
HARVEY, Alice, 64
  Amos, 55, 61,
    106
  Benjamin, 31
  David, 155
  Elizabeth, 31
  Hannah, 17, 55
  Henry, 72
  Isaac, 31, 55,
    106
  James, 55
  Job, 30, 31, 125
  Joseph, 31, 64
  Josiah, 31
  Keziah, 106
  Kezie, 61
  Margaret, 31
  Martha, 83
  Mary, 31, 64
  Rebecca, 30
  Susanna, 64
  William, 9, 55,
    69, 117, 122
HASELET, Samuel,
  54
HASELGROVE, John,
  21
HASLAM, Richard,
  105
HASSELETT, Robert,
  21
HASTINGS,
  Elizabeth, 79
  Hannah, 79
  Henry, 79
  James, 79
  Phebe, 79
  Rebecca, 79
HATHORN, John, 34,
  67, 112, 140,
  142, 151
HATTON, Elizabeth,
  83, 87
  James, 83
  John, 83, 87
  Peter, 83, 90
  Sarah, 54
HAVARD, David, 85
  John, 85
HAWLEY, Benjamin,
  6, 15, 32, 35,
  70, 95, 128,
  155
  William, 137
HAYE, Ann, 156
  John, 156
  Mary, 156
HAYES, Abram, 123
  Ann, 106, 123
  Benjamin, 139
  David, 123, 156
  Hannah, 77, 89,

123
Henry, 54, 77,
  106
Isaac, 89
James, 77
Jane, 3, 44
Jesse, 123
John, 21, 97,
  110, 123, 156
Joseph, 3
Lydia, 77
Margaret, 156
Mary, 77
Mordecai, 123
Nathan, 77
Patrick, 109
Rachel, 77
Samuel, 77
Sarah, 21, 77
Stephen, 21, 79
William, 123
HAYS, John, 21
Stephen, 55
HAYWOOD, Mary, 90
HEACOCK, Anne, 136
John, 136
Jonathan, 136
Joseph, 136
Wililam, 136
HEALD, Elizabeth,
  2
Jacob, 22
John, 2, 59, 72
Joseph, 22
Rachel, 5
Samuel, 5
Thomas, 59, 118
HEALL, Thomas, 89
HEANEY, Hugh, 134
Ruth, 77
HEASTINGS, Henry,
  46
HELEM, Mary, 43
HELSBY, Ralph, 127
HEMPHILL, John, 65
HENDERS, John, 23
HENDERSON,
  Alexander, 12
  Andrew, 121
  Daniel, 12, 74,
  82, 89, 101
  Edward, 121
  Elizabeth, 121
  Janett, 69
  John, 69, 121

Matthew (Math.),
  89, 138
Thomas, 121
William, 74, 121
HENDRICKS,
  Frances, 31
  Tobias, 31, 70
HENDRICKSEN, John,
  122
HENDRICKSON,
  Andrew, 43
  Catherine, 3
  Israel, 43
  John, 3, 43
  Matthias, 43
  Maudlin, 43
  Susanna, 43
HENDRY, Ann, 140
HENRY, Hannah, 33,
  112
  James, 82
  William, 33, 112
HENZLEY, Charles,
  88
HERRIOT, William,
  154
HERVIE, Robert,
  144
HERY, Isabella, 60
  Jane, 60
HEWES, Aaron, 22,
  49, 86
  Caleb, 22, 25
  Edward, 149
  Hannah, 25
  Isaac, 22, 25
  Jacob, 86
  John, 22, 25,
  49, 70, 86
  Lydia, 22
  Mary, 22, 25, 86
  Rebecca, 49
  Samuel, 16, 22,
  25, 86
  William, 22, 25,
  49, 63, 86
HIBBARD, Anne, 20
  Esther, 24
  Jacob, 20
HIBBERD, Aaron, 73
  Abraham, 53, 73,
  83
  Ann, 74
  Benjamin, 24,
  35, 53, 111,

151
  Caleb, 151
  Daniel, 73
  Deborah, 73
  Hezekiah, 24
  Isaac, 24
  Jacob, 24
  John, 24, 73,
  74, 83
  Joseph, 24
  Moses, 54, 122
  Phineas, 83
  Phinehas, 73
  Rachel, 73
  Samuel, 73
  Sarah, 24, 54,
  122
HICKMAN, Ann, 99
  Benjamin, 99
  Francis, 51, 93,
  99
  John, 99
HIETT, Ann, 36
  Elizabeth, 36
  Katherine, 36
  Sarah, 36
  Thomas, 36
HIGET, Peter, 5
HIGHET, Frances,
  24
  Peter, 24
HILL, Alexander,
  127
  Christian, 89
  Elizabeth, 98,
  127
  Jane, 140
  John, 112, 140
  Jonathan, 140
  Margaret, 140
  Samuel, 10, 140
  Thomas, 140
  William, 98
HINDE, Elizabeth,
  158
  Hannah, 158
  James, 22, 158
  John, 158
  Mary, 158
  Rachel, 158
  Roger, 158
HINDMAN, Samuel,
  151
HINDS, Mary, 19
HINGHAM,

Elizabeth, 114
HITCHIN, John, 134
HOAPP, Thomas
   Hope, 38
HOARE, John, 68
HOCKLEY, Henry, 46
HODGSKINS, James, 38
HOE, Ann, 66
HOGG, George, 121
HOGSON, George, 25
   Mary, 25
HOLIS, Henry, 46
HOLLAND, John, 71, 121
   Nathaniel, 158
   Sarah, 121
HOLLIDAY, Hannah, 119
   Jacob, 119
   Phebe, 119
   Robert, 119
   Sarah, 119
HOLLINGSWORTH,
   Abner, 125
   Ann, 72
   Betty, 42, 72
   Christopher, 143
   Enoch, 9, 38, 42, 72
   Hannah, 9, 42
   Isaac, 70
   Jacob, 38, 40
   James, 29, 71, 72, 88, 125
   Jehu, 38, 42
   John, 9
   Judith, 31, 70
   Samuel, 9, 38
   Sarah, 72
   Susanna, 31, 40
   Thomas, 70
   Valentine, 71, 72, 125
HOLLIS, George, 143
   Henry, 95
HOLLYWOOD,
   Francis, 158
HOLMAN, Charles, 12
   Eleanor, 12
HOLSTON,
   Elizabeth, 66
HOLTON, Martha, 57

Nathaniel, 57
Samuel, 57
HOOD, Elizabeth, 156
   Walter, 156
HOOF, Abigail, 114
HOOPES, Christian, 151
   Daniel, 8
   John, 22, 139, 151, 153
   Joshua, 147
   Susanna, 58, 140
   Thomas, 121, 153
HOOPS, Mary, 100
HOPE, Amos, 21, 123, 124
   Elizabeth, 21
   Enoch, 124
   John, 21, 123
   Mary, 24
   Rachel, 72
   Richard, 101
   Thomas, 21, 24
HOPKINS, Isabel, 147
   Matthew, 147
HOPPS, Martha, 4
HOPTON, Esther, 40
   John, 40
HORNE, Abigail, 119, 158
   Benjamin, 119
   Benjamina, 158
   Elizabeth, 119, 158
   Ruth, 119
   William, 19, 20, 119, 131, 158
HORNER, Elizabeth, 29
HOSKINS, Joseph, 31
HOULDEN, Jane, 4
   Thomas, 4
HOULSTON, Sarah, 127
HOUSE, Amos, 66
   James, 66, 96
   Mary, 66
HOUSTON, Hugh, 155
   Joseph, 74
HOWARD, Hannah, 104
   Henry, 104

John, 104
Peter, 104
Rebecca, 104
Richard, 104
HOWEL, Ann, 38
HOWELL, Ann, 154
   Benjamin, 12, 75, 86, 155
   David, 38, 50, 75, 93, 100
   Elizabeth, 38, 75, 154
   Esther, 135
   Ezekiel, 65
   Griffith, 93
   Hannah, 75, 114
   Howell, 38
   Isaac, 35, 50, 86, 109, 141
   Israel, 134
   Jacob, 31, 50, 86, 88, 154
   James, 71
   Jonathan, 32
   Joseph, 38
   Magdalen, 64, 67
   Martha, 75
   Mary, 75, 86, 134, 141, 154
   Owen, 67
   Rebecca, 155
   Reece, 38
   Samuel, 50, 69, 74, 110
   Sarah, 75
   Stephen, 134
   Susanna, 50
   Thomas, 50, 75, 114
   William, 50, 75
HOWKS, Anthony, 158
HUBBARD, Margret, 43
HUBBERT, Mary, 111, 119
   Rachel, 110, 111
   Stephen, 111, 119
   Thomas, 110, 111, 119, 137
HUDDER, James, 146
   Rachel, 146
HUDDERS, James, 147

HUDSON, Margaret, 107
　Morris, 107
　William, 37, 61
HUEY, Gennett, 54
　James, 55
　John, 68
　Mary, 55
　William, 54
HUGH, Isaac, 56
　Margaret, 134
HUGHES, Alexander, 38
　Elisha, 113
　Isaac, 48, 157
　Jean, 38
　John, 16, 38
　Jonathan, 42
　Margaret, 38
　Rebecca, 38
HUGHS, James, 38
　Sarah, 101
HULL, John, 123
HUMPHREY, Daniel, 83, 150
　Edward, 83
　John, 27, 83, 150
　Martha, 83, 150
　Mary, 83, 150
　Richard, 83, 150
　Samuel, 125
　Solomon, 83
HUMPHREYS, Edward, 152
　Samuel, 152
HUNT, John, 19, 61
　Joseph, 49
　Mary, 31, 55
　Roger, 136
　William, 136
HUNTER, Alexander, 35
　Ann, 37
　Elizabeth, 37
　Hannah, 35, 37, 57, 154
　Isabel, 140
　James, 28, 37, 40, 111
　John, 37
　Margaret, 37
　Martha, 141
　Mary, 37, 41
　Thomas, 41

William, 57, 78, 104
HURDMAN, John, 25
HURFORD, John, 159
　Rachel, 124
　Samuel, 124
HUSTON, Frances, 103
　Henry, 103
　Jeannet, 103
　John, 154
　Leveness, 103
　Mary, 154
HUTCHESON, James, 2
HUTCHISON, James, 21
　John, 82
　Robert, 21
HUTCHMAN, William, 44
HUTTON, Ann, 155
　Hannah, 36
　John, 36, 155
　Nehemiah, 110
　Phebe, 155
　Thomas, 36, 110
HYATT, Thomas, 6
HYNMAN, Robert, 7

-I-
IDDINGS, Margaret, 47, 48
　Richard, 47, 48
　William, 157
INGHAM, Elizabeth, 93
　Thomas, 93
INGLISH, Matthew, 12
INGRAM, John, 135
　William, 135
Ireland, 4, 7, 13, 14, 26, 62, 74, 77, 88, 89, 101, 103, 105, 126, 138, 140, 147, 148
IRWIN, Alexander, 11
　Archibald, 11
　George, 11, 146
　Jane, 11
　Jerret, 11
　John, 11

Letitia, 11
　Mary, 11, 75
　Mercy, 11
　Moses, 128
　Robert, 11
　Samuel, 46, 75
　Sarah, 11
　Theophilus, 59
　Thomas, 75
　William, 11, 75
IVORY, Judith, 65

-J-
JACK, Andrew, 117
JACKSON, Alice, 108
　Ann, 65, 89
　Catherine, 33
　David, 145
　Ephraim, 108
　Hannah, 108
　Henry, 72, 104
　Isaac, 9, 33, 72, 80, 87, 102, 108
　James, 9, 33, 108
　John, 33, 51, 65, 80, 108, 117, 154
　Jonathan, 51, 65, 89
　Joseph, 108
　Joshia, 154
　Josiah, 108
　Mary, 32, 108, 145
　Nehemiah, 72
　Paul, 145
　Rachel, 108, 145
　Samuel, 62, 69, 108, 145
　Sarah, 41, 108
　Susanna, 72, 108
　Thomas, 33, 65
　William, 9, 33, 79
JACOBS, Benjamin, 118
　John, 157
JAMES, Aaron, 3, 29
　Anne, 27
　Benjamin, 34
　Elizabeth, 3, 58

Evan, 51
Griffith, 157
Hannah, 3, 29,
  58, 125
John, 27, 138
Jonathan, 3, 43
Joseph, 3, 34,
  53, 58, 96, 98,
  111, 122
Lettice, 138
Magdalen, 58
Margaret, 51
Martha, 3
Mary, 34
Mary Earl, 3
Micajah, 123,
  138
Mordecai, 118,
  123
Rachel, 58, 125
Samuel, 3, 24,
  53, 56, 57, 58,
  125
Sarah, 58, 125
Thomas, 3, 34
William, 138
JAMESON, David, 90
JANEY, Abel, 158
JANNEY, Abel, 45,
  51
JARMAN, Jeremiah,
  112
John, 18
JEFFERIES, Hannah,
  70
JEFFERIS, Abigail,
  6
  Benjamin, 6
  Elizabeth, 6
  Emmor, 6
  George, 128
  James, 6, 128
  Joanna, 128
  Lydia, 128
  Martha, 128
  Nathaniel, 98
  Rachel, 128
  Robert, 22
  William, 122,
    123
JENKIN, David,
  116, 141
  Gwen, 116
  Hannah, 116
  Jane, 138

John, 87
Joseph, 141
Richard, 138
JENKINS, Ann, 36
  Hannah
    (Joannah), 36
  James, 36
  Jane, 36
  Jonathan, 40
  Mary, 41
  Nathaniel, 21,
    36
  Rebecca, 57
  Rowland, 36
  William, 40
JESSE, Walter, 42
JOB, Archibald,
  144
JOBSON, Samuel, 78
JOHN, Daniel, 41,
  76
  David, 41, 65,
    107, 115, 137
  Eleanor, 58
  Elias, 58
  Evan, 46
  Given, 84
  Griffith, 3, 51,
    103, 127
  Henry, 51
  Jacob, 41, 76
  James, 41, 76,
    137
  John, 41
  Margaret, 41
  Owen, 46
  Rebecca, 46
  Robert, 103, 127
  Samuel, 21, 24,
    51, 58, 105,
    127
  Sarah, 46
  Thomas, 46, 51,
    137, 141
  William, 46, 51
JOHNSON, Abraham,
  104, 111
  Ann, 16
  Catherine, 70
  David, 17, 85,
    139
  Elizabeth, 134
  Francis, 16, 134
  Humphrey, 16,
    17, 156

Isaac, 22
James, 115
John, 139
Joshua, 102
Margaret, 85,
  87, 115
Martha, 139
Mary, 115, 139
Rachel, 16, 115,
  139
Robert, 65, 70,
  79, 85, 99, 104
Ruth, 115
Samuel, 139, 157
Sarah, 115
Susanna, 115
William, 137,
  139
JOHNSTON, Alex, 61
  Alexander, 62,
    149
  Alice, 149
  Andrew, 23
  Ann, 23
  John, 23, 90
  Margaret, 82
  Mary, 23
  Michael, 13
JONES, Amos, 90
  Ann, 115, 132
  Benjamin, 60
  Cadwallader, 4,
    12, 84, 117
  Charles, 107
  David, 60, 63,
    90
  Edward, 5, 38,
    157
  Elisha, 135
  Ellen, 11
  Emanuel, 137
  Esther, 60
  Evan, 44, 56,
    84, 100, 111
  Griffith, 90
  Henry, 132
  Jane, 111
  Jenkin, 63
  Joanna, 90
  John, 42, 48,
    50, 78, 88, 98
  Joseph, 38, 50,
    88
  Levi, 90
  Malachi, 37

Mary, 39, 152
Morgan, 144
Peter, 58
Richard, 8, 18,
  35, 39, 44, 58,
  64, 68, 78, 79,
  88, 111, 121,
  140, 153
Sarah, 44
Thomas, 5, 43,
  71
William, 17, 37,
  90, 98
JORDAN, John, 108,
  137
Joseph, 68
Rachel, 68, 108
JURY, Eleanor, 141
Mary, 116, 141
Richard, 116
JUSTICE, Daniel,
  101
JUSTIS, John, 108

-K-
KARR, William, 112
KEAR, William, 140
KEECH, Sarah, 2
  William, 2
KEETCH, Sarah, 2
KELLEY, Charles,
  149
Frances, 146
James, 29
Jean, 146
Mary, 146
Matthew, 146
Patrick, 131
Thomas, 146
KELTON, Elizabeth,
  49
James, 49
Margaret, 49
Nancy, 49
Robert, 49
KENDAL, Grace, 104
KENDALL, Benjamin,
  118
KENNEDY, Bryan, 10
David, 21
James, 13, 68,
  130, 145
Joseph, 146
KENNY, James, 132,
  155

KER, Thomas, 82
KERK, Jane, 52
Mary, 55
Rachel, 55
KERLIN, Ann, 15
John, 15, 45,
  49, 50, 75, 86,
  91, 109, 119
Joseph, 119
Matthias, 45
Peter, 119
KERNS, Elizabeth,
  65
Elizabth, 65
KERR, Daniel, 57
Jennett, 60
John, 60
Robert, 57
Thomas, 57, 149
KERSLY, William,
  129
KERSON, Robert, 6
KEY, Allen, 85
Ann, 5, 85
Elizabeth, 5, 85
Martha, 59
Mary, 154
Moses, 5
Rebecca, 85
Robert, 5
William, 5, 85,
  154
KEYL, John, 134
William, 14
KEYS, Jame, 140
KIDD, James, 41
KILCREASE, James,
  27
KILGREIST,
  Elizabeth, 21
KILLCREASE,
  Elizabeth, 20
James, 20
KILPATRICK,
  Robert, 9
KIMBER, Predy, 45
Richard, 45
Sarah, 46
KIMMINGS, Martha,
  52
KIMSON, Samuel, 25
Susanna, 25
KINARD, Mary Ann,
  133
KING, George, 2,

  24
James, 1, 2
Mirick, 25
Sarah, 2
William, 116
KINKEAD, John, 103
KINNISON, William,
  78
KIRGAN, Ann, 32
Hugh, 32
Jacob, 32
John, 6, 32
Mary, 32
Sarah, 32
William, 32
KIRK, Abner, 139
Ann, 101, 113
Caleb, 134, 146
Elizabeth, 113,
  139
Henry, 118
Isaac, 31
Isabel, 138
Jacob, 139
John, 17, 118
Joseph, 139
Margaret, 118
Mary, 113
Nathaniel, 113
Robert, 113
Roger, 113, 118,
  139
Sampson, 118
Samuel, 113, 139
Timothy, 1, 101,
  113, 118, 123,
  139
William, 17,
  113, 118, 128
KIRKEAD, John, 60
KIRKPATRICK, Hugh,
  26
John, 131
KIRLIN, Joseph,
  143
Matihas, 142
KISSICK, John, 71
KITLER, George, 86
KITTERA, James,
  133
Margaret, 133
Thomas, 133
KNIGHT, Elizabeth,
  8
William, 1, 101,

115
KNIGHTLEY, James, 153
KNOWLES,
  Elizabeth, 139, 159
  John, 86, 108, 140
KNOX, John, 127
KYLE, Dingwall, 142
  Robert, 142
  William, 142
KYLL, Robert, 41
KYS, James, 140

-L-

LADELY, Margaret, 77
LAMPLUGH, Abigail, 70
  Elizabeth, 16, 117
  Jacob, 31, 70
  John, 31, 70, 117
  Martha, 70
  Mary, 70
  Nathaniel, 31, 70
  Samuel, 31, 70, 86
  Susanna, 70
  William, 31, 70, 86, 117
LAND, Joseph, 132
LANDERS, Samuel, 71
LANE, Benjamin, 149
LANG, Martha, 72
  Tobias, 72
LANGLEY, Jonathan, 115
LAPSLY, Jean, 75
  John, 75
  Martha, 75
  Thomas, 75
  William, 75
LARKEN, Margaret, 14
LARKIN, Jane, 131
  William, 131
LARNER, John, 156
LAROW, George, 101

LATIMORE, Edward, 71
LATTA, John, 60
LAUGHLIN,
  Elizabeth, 88
  Hugh, 88
  James, 88
  Margaret, 88
  William, 88
LAW, James, 147
  John, 147
  Joseph, 97
  Martha, 146, 147
  Mary, 147
  Robert, 147
LAWRENCE, Daniel, 125
  David, 58, 125
  Elizabeth, 17, 125
  Ellen, 152
  Hannah, 152
  Henry, 152
  Joseph, 152
  Joshua, 152
  Margaret, 152
  Mary, 152
  Mordecai, 152
  Nathan, 17
  Samuel, 152
  Sarah, 20, 125
  Thomas, 20
  William, 125, 152
LAWSON, John, 106
  Joseph, 122
LEA, Abigail, 73
  Anne, 87
  Hannah, 87
  Isaac, 10, 16, 87
  John, 73, 87
  Joseph, 73
  Mary, 73, 87, 113
  Thomas, 87
LEAN, Edward, 113
  Ruth, 113
  William, 113
LEANARD, Richard, 63
LEARD, James, 38
  Mary, 106
LECKEY, Margaret, 82

LEE, William, 2, 13, 98
LEEKE, James, 133
  Margaret, 133
LEEPER, Aleander, 133
  James, 133
  Margaret, 133
LEGGETT, George, 37
LEISTER, Dorothy, 139
LEMON (OR PEARASS),
  Elizabeth, 74
  Mary, 74
  William, 74
LENNON, Ann, 50
  Thomas, 51
LEONARD, Benjamin, 65
  Olive, 79
LEPER, Andrew, 44
LESLIE, William, 7
LETTEMORE, Edward, 16
LETTICE, Francis, 141
LETTIMUR, Arthur, 145
  George, 145
  James, 145
  John, 145
  Robert, 145
LEVIN, William, 27
LEVIS, Hannah, 81
  John, 20, 29, 81
  Joseph, 81
  Mary, 114
  Rebecca, 20, 29
  Samuel, 9, 19, 29, 64, 81, 114
  William, 9, 57
LEWDEN, John, 123
  Rachel, 123
LEWHELIN, William, 150
LEWIS, Abel, 28, 158
  Abner, 152
  Abraham, 85
  Agnes, 74
  Alice, 108
  Anne, 132
  Christian, 159

David, 28, 73, 74, 152
Elizabeth, 3, 28, 158
Enos, 152
Evan, 28
Gabriel, 73
Hannah, 58, 75, 107, 152
Henry, 1, 132, 152
Isaac, 110, 132
Jabez, 73, 75
Jane, 53, 152
Joel, 151
John, 5, 28, 34, 47, 62, 64, 104, 110, 123, 136, 137, 159
Jonathan, 50
Joseph, 3, 35, 53, 104, 123
Joshua, 76
Josiah, 84
Katherine, 28
Lewis, 69, 73, 74, 110, 152
Lydia, 151
Margaret, 12
Mary, 50, 54, 110, 152, 157
May, 28
Mordecai, 50
Nathan, 8, 12, 42, 74, 110
Nathaniel, 39
Phineas, 83
Phinehas, 18, 38, 73, 74
Rachel, 28, 79, 137, 151, 152
Robert, 39, 79
Ruth, 117
Samuel, 28, 47, 57
Susanna, 75
Thomas, 110
William, 48, 50, 53, 55, 57, 58, 69, 70, 74, 75, 104, 107
LIGGETT, Ann, 99
George, 99
John, 99
Margaret, 99
Mary, 99
Rachel, 99, 118
Rebecca, 99
Ruth, 99
William, 90
LIGHTFOOT,
Benjamin, 50
Michael, 36
Samuel, 50, 62, 71, 84, 127
Thomas, 62
LINARD, Richard, 87
LINCHFIELD,
Francis, 127
Margaret, 127
LINDLAY, Simon, 99
LINDLEY,
Catharine, 99
Deborah, 99
Eleanor, 99
James, 99
John, 99
Jonathan, 99
Ruth, 99
Thomas, 99
LINDLY, Jonathan, 77
LINDSAY, James, 41, 85, 116, 140
John, 85
William, 82, 116
LINDSEY, James, 15, 52
LINN, Anne, 156
Charles, 23, 78, 107, 126, 147
Hugh, 40, 47, 63, 82, 92, 99, 107, 148, 156
Margaret, 82
Mary, 23
LINSEY, William, 75, 86
LINVIL, Ann, 122
William, 122
LINVILLE, William, 31
LIPARD, Andrew, 27
James, 27
LITTER, Joshua, 64
LITTLE, John, 5
Mary, 95
William, 34, 67
LITTLER, Joshua, 123
LIVERING,
Elizabeth, 90
LLEWELLIN, John, 124
Rebecca, 124
LLEWELLYN, David, 27
William, 27
LLOYD, Anne, 70
David, 95, 127
Elizabeth, 107, 126
Erasmus, 138
Grace, 95
Hannah, 11, 61
Hugh, 61
Humphrey, 43, 76, 95
Isaac, 61
James, 71
John, 138
Mary, 5
Richard, 25, 61
Robert, 61
Thomas, 71, 95, 126
Walter, 70
LOAGUE, James, 32
LOAN, John, 117
LOBB, Benjamin, 22, 131, 158
LOCKHART,
Elizabeth, 59
Jacob, 59
Jane, 59
Jean, 59
Margaret, 59
Mary, 59
Patrick, 59
Robert, 59
Susanna, 59
LOGAN, John, 43
Margaret, 142
Rachel, 85
Thomas, 142
LONG, Francis, 23
John, 4, 23
Joseph, 23
Martha, 25
Rebecca, 23
Thomas, 25
William, 23
LONGAUR, Susanna,

LOO, Elizabeth, 22
    59
LOTTY, Matthew, 27
LOUDON, John, 103
LOUGHEAD, James,
    132
  Jane, 132
  Robert, 132
LOUGHRIDGE,
  Elizabeth, 156
  John, 156
LOVE, Andrew, 48
  Hannah, 68
  John, 156
  Margaret, 48
  Samuel, 68
  William, 13
LOW, Jennet, 95
  Jennett, 45
  John, 45
  Levi, 61
  Thomas, 45
LOWNES, Agnes, 79
  Benanuel, 136
  Benauel, 46
  John, 79
LOWNS, Agnes, 146
  Alice, 100
  Caleb, 146
  John, 146
LUCKIE, Hugh, 131,
    142
LYANN, John, 20
LYON, William, 146

    -M-
MCADOW, James, 67
  John, 24
MCAFFEE, William,
    103
MCBEATH,
  Alexander, 85
MCBRIDE, Jane, 68
MCCADDEN, Ann, 74
  Henry, 91
MCCADDON,
  Elizabeth, 74
  John, 74
  Margaret, 74
  Mary, 74
  Richard, 74
MCCALL, James, 68
  Mary, 128
  Thomas, 125, 128
MCCAMANT, Isaac,

    66
  James, 66
  William, 66
MCCAMOND, John,
    145
MCCANDLIS,
  Elizabeth, 49
  James, 49
MCCANLES, James,
    110
MCCARTY, John, 3
MCCASKEY,
  Alexander, 113
  Frederick, 69
MCCAY, Galbreath,
    150
  John, 150
  Patrick, 29
  Thomas, 150
  William, 46, 150
MCCLAIN, Samuel,
    27
MCCLASKEY,
  Barbara, 52
  Elizabeth, 52
  James, 52
  Joseph, 52
MCCLEAN, Samuel,
    78
MCCLEAVE, George,
    13
MCCLELAN, James,
    82
  Martha, 82
  Robert, 140
  Samuel, 82
  Thomas, 140
  William, 140
MCCLELEN, John, 2
  William, 2
MCCLELLAN, Samuel,
    100
MCCLELLAND, Henry,
    147
  Martha, 147
MCCLENACHAN,
  Robert, 6
MCCLENNAN, Mary,
    34
  William, 34
MCCLINTOCK, Mary,
    69
MCCLUGHAN, Hugh,
    83
MCCLURE, Esther,

    62
  James, 62
  Jean, 62
  John, 62
  Mary, 62
  Rebecca, 51
  Robert, 62
  Samuel, 62
MCCLUSKEY, David,
    59
  Elizabeth, 59
  Ester, 59
  Jean, 59
  Joseph, 59
  Mary, 59
MCCOLLOCK, George,
    13
  Isabella, 13
  Martha, 13
  Mary, 13
  William, 13
MCCOLLOUGH,
  George, 112,
    145
  James, 112, 144,
    150
MCCOMONS,
  Elizabeth, 36
  Robert, 36
MCCONALL, Sarah,
    27
  William, 27
MCCONNELL,
  Alexander, 81
  Frances, 82
  Francis, 12, 67
  Jean, 81
MCCORD, John, 84,
    121
  Rose, 55
MCCORMICK, James,
    14, 97, 111,
    159
MCCOSKRY, James,
    73
MCCOY, Andrew, 85,
    90, 123
  Henry, 116
  John, 116
  Mary, 85
  Samuel, 108
MCCRACKEN,
  Archibald, 63
  Hannah, 63
MCCREA, William,

36
MCCREY, Elizabeth,
  140
MCCUE, Abraham, 94
  Alice, 95
  Ann, 94
  Anthony, 94
  Elizabeth, 94
  John, 94
  Mary, 94
  Samuel, 94, 95
  Thomas, 94
MCCULLOUGH, Agnes,
  62
  George, 47, 49,
  153
  James, 8, 21, 62
  Martha, 21
  Patrick, 112
MCCUNE, John, 68
MCDONALD,
  Jeremiah, 4
  Thomas, 4
MCDOUGALL,
  Matthew, 45
MCDOW, Agnes, 44
  Andrew, 44
  John, 44
MCDOWELL,
  Archibald, 67
  Catherine, 7
  John, 7
  Joseph, 63, 130
  William, 7, 22
MACE, George, 156
  Susanna, 156
MCFADNER, James,
  10
MCFARLIN, Ann, 66
MCFETERS, Jane,
  123
  John, 123
MCGEE, Margaret,
  13
  Nathaniel, 13
MCGREW, Finley,
  16, 19, 147
MCGUIRE, Hugh, 25
MCILHENNY, James,
  57
  Mary, 57
MCILVAINE, Jane,
  134
MCKAGHAN, Daniel,
  140

MCKEAN, Anne, 39
  Thomas, 48, 121
  William, 39
MCKEE, Alexander,
  133
  James, 120, 140
  Jane, 120
  John, 53, 124
  Joseph, 140
  Martha, 133
  Robert, 62
MACKENTYRE, John,
  5
MCKIM, Sarah, 154
  William, 55
MCKINLEY,
  Elizabeth, 99
  George, 99
MCKISACK, Arthur,
  97
MCKNIGHT, Charles,
  60
  David, 60
  Hugh, 60
  James, 60
  John, 60
  Thomas, 60
  William, 60, 89
MCKOWN, Richard,
  81
MCKOWNE, Daniel,
  12
MACKY, Robert, 75
MCLAUGHLIN, Ann,
  82
  Dennis, 20
  James, 81
  John, 81, 93
  Lawrence, 20
  Michael, 81
  William, 81, 82
MCLEAN, Hugh, 19
  Rachel, 72
MCLOGHLIN,
  Matthew, 39
MCLONE, Agnes, 39
  Margaret, 57
MCMASEN, Robert,
  120
MCMICHAEL,
  Charles, 29, 78
  Elizabeth, 78
  James, 102
  Jane, 78
  John, 102

187

  Martha, 78
  Rebecca, 78
  Robert, 78
  Walter, 78
MCMICHAN, Andrew,
  115
  Ginnett, 115
  James, 115
  Mary, 115
  Samuel, 115
  Sarah, 115
MCMICHELL, James,
  10
  John, 8, 10
  Priscilla, 10
MCMICHEN, James,
  158
MCMINN, John, 98
MCMULLAN, Robert,
  34
MCMULLEN, Deborah,
  4
MCNEEL, Ann, 136
  Anne, 136
  Dominic, 136
MCNEELY, Joseph, 7
MCNEIL, Elizabeth,
  47
MCPHERSON,
  Alexander, 124
  Daniel, 66
  Jean, 124
  John, 60, 124
  Robert, 124
  Sarah, 124
MCSPARRAN,
  Archibald, 36
  James, 36
MCSWAINE, Miles,
  118
MCSWINE, James, 89
MCVEA, James, 118
  Thomas, 118
MCWHENY, William,
  34
MCWHORTER,
  Margret, 46
MACWILLIAMS/MCWILL
  IAMS, John, 144
  Mary, 144
  Sarah, 67, 144
  William, 67, 144
MACY, Thomas, 48
MADDEN, John, 3
MADDOCK, Benjamin,

102
Deborah, 35
Henry, 144
Isaac, 144
Jacob, 144
James, 144
Jesse, 144
Joseph, 35
Mordecai, 55
Nathan, 35
Rebecca, 144
Susanna, 144
MAGUIRE, Margaret,
  111
  Thomas, 54, 92,
    111, 127
MAHAN, John, 147
  Sarah, 109
MALCHOR, John, 42
MALIN, Elizabeth,
  23
  Jacob, 23
  Randal, 36, 56,
    69
  Randle, 152
  Thomas, 132
  William, 23, 132
MALLAN, Elizabeth,
  3
  Mary, 3
  Sarah, 3
  Thomas, 3
MALON, Randle, 141
MALONE, Henry, 116
  Isabel, 116
  Jean, 116
  John, 116
  Patrick, 116
MANSELL, William,
  119
MARESHL, James,
  110
MARIS, Alice, 6
  Ann, 80, 108,
    109
  Elizabeth, 80
  George, 6, 46,
    108, 114
  Hannah, 6
  Isaac, 108
  James, 46, 85,
    108, 111, 152
  Jane, 46
  Jehu, 108, 109
  Jesse, 6, 80,
    108, 109, 150
  Jonathan, 10, 18
  Joseph, 50, 64,
    80
  Mary, 80
  Samuel, 80
MARKWARD, Jane,
  136
  John, 136
MARLOW, William,
  141
MARQUES, Elenor,
  142
  Robert, 137
MARSH, Elizabeth,
  92
  George, 4
  Gravener, 92
  Henry, 92
  John, 4
  Jonathan, 4, 12
  Joshua, 4
  Margaret, 92
  Mary, 12
  Peter, 4
  Sarah, 92
  William, 92
MARSHALL, Abraham,
  6, 20, 31
  Abram, 29
  Ann, 18, 31
  Benjamin, 18, 83
  Edith, 91
  Eleanor, 20
  Elizabeth, 29
  Hannah, 18, 29,
    31
  Humphry, 31
  Isaac, 8
  Jacob, 21
  James, 14, 29,
    31, 56, 115,
    155
  Johanna, 20
  John, 18, 20,
    21, 31, 56,
    119, 151
  Joseph, 31, 138
  Joshua, 81
  Martha, 18, 20
  Mary, 18, 20,
    29, 31
  Rachel, 6, 29
  Ruth, 31, 155
  Samuel, 29
  Susanna, 20
  Thomas, 17, 18,
    20, 91
MARTEN, Elizabeth,
  76
  Thomas, 76
MARTIN, Abraham,
  20, 85, 126,
    128, 154
  Ann, 128
  Anne, 136
  Betty, 13
  Elizabeth, 136,
    137
  Esther, 129
  Ethliw, 136
  George, 79, 98,
    120, 132
  Hannah, 118, 136
  John, 60, 116,
    118, 144
  Jonathan, 20,
    128, 159
  Joseph, 119, 132
  Lewis, 137
  Llewelyn, 136
  Lydia, 13
  Martha, 136
  Mary, 13, 116,
    136
  Mathias, 136,
    137
  Samuel, 129
  Sarah, 84
  Thomas, 12, 76,
    84, 128
MARTINE, Hugh, 91
Maryland, 56, 61,
  68, 84, 100,
  114, 129, 148
MARY, Thomas, 153
MASCALL,
  Elizabeth, 31
  William, 31
MASSEY, Ann, 73
  Hannah, 6
  Isaac, 74, 109
  James, 6, 149,
    156
  Lewis, 156
  Mordecai, 6
  Rebecca, 6, 30
  Sarah, 10
  Thomas, 6, 8,
    10, 74, 100,

104, 109
MATHER, James, 20, 130
  John, 3, 12, 119, 130
  Joseph, 130
  Margaret, 130
  Peter, 122
  Sarah, 122
MATHIES, David, 93
MATLOCK, Joseph, 87
  Nathan, 7
MATSON, Hannah, 6
  John, 6
  Peter, 147
MATTHEWS, John, 115
  Oliver, 115
  Thomas, 115
MAXWELL, Hugh, 147
  Isabella, 139
  James, 129, 139
  Jane, 147
  John, 29
  Margaret, 147
  William, 50, 147
MAY, Robert, 6, 37
  William, 12
MAYES, Jane, 32
  William, 32
MEAK, Anne, 55
MEARS, Hannah, 72
  James, 72
  Martha, 72
  Mary, 72
  Samuel, 72
  Susanna, 72
MEAS, John, 19, 33
MECHEM, Francis, 18, 118
  John, 118
MECHIM, Francis, 91
  John, 91
MECLEMONS, William, 13
MEEK, Adam, 129
  Agnes, 129
  Andrew, 129
  Jean, 129
  John, 129
  Mary, 129
  Nelley, 129
  Rebecca, 129

MELCHIOR,
  Elizabeth, 60
  William, 60
MENAUGH, George, 6
MENDENHALL, Aaron, 146
  Abigail, 81
  Alice, 18
  Ann, 9, 17, 18, 42
  Benjamin, 9, 17, 117, 153
  Caleb, 18
  Elizabeth, 146
  Esther, 17, 100
  Hannah, 9, 17, 117, 153
  Isaac, 9, 17
  James, 146
  Jesse, 9, 17, 117
  John, 18, 146
  Joseph, 9, 17
  Joshua, 17
  Lydia, 17, 146
  Martha, 17
  Mary, 17
  Moses, 18
  Nathan, 17
  Phebe, 17, 18
  Philip, 18
  Rebecca, 18
  Robert, 17, 18, 90, 111, 125, 143
  Rose, 146
  Ruth, 9, 18
  Samuel, 17, 113
  Sarah, 38
  Stephen, 9, 17
MENOUGH, John, 45
MERCER, Ann, 42, 45
  Daniel, 77, 145
  Joseph, 84
  Thomas, 51, 77
MEREDITH, Alice, 63
  Ann, 63
  Daniel, 63
  David, 57, 63
  Eleanor, 63
  Elijah, 63
  Esther, 63
  George, 63

189

  Hannah, 63
  John, 57, 64
  Joseph, 57
  Margaret, 70
  Mary, 68
  Moses, 68, 84, 151
  Samuel, 11, 52
  Sarah, 57, 63
  Simon, 157
  William, 57, 63
MERES, Ann, 31
MERIS, John, 48
MERSHEL, William, 55
MESER, Robert, 118
MESSERS, Robert, 134
MEYER, Adam, 114
  Jacob, 114
MICKLE, Ann, 66
  Anne, 33
  Jane, 33, 66
  John, 33, 66
  Mary, 33, 66
  Robert, 5
  Sarah, 33, 66
MILES, Enos, 51
  Evan, 132
  Nathaniel, 51
  Sarah, 53
MILHOUS, Thomas, 127
MILHOUSE, John, 157
MILLAR, Patrick, 27
MILLARD, Lydia, 135
  Thomas, 135
MILLER, Ann, 28
  Benjamin, 41, 91
  Brice, 117
  George, 10, 47, 78, 104, 138, 148, 151
  James, 6, 9, 33, 36, 39, 41, 66, 80
  Jane, 140
  Jesse, 41, 66
  John, 101
  Joseph, 142
  Katherine, 41
  Margaret, 142

Martha, 78, 131
Patience, 129
Rachel, 41
Rebecca, 80, 142
Robert, 16, 116
Ruth, 129
Samuel, 41, 48,
 119, 142
Thomas, 41
Warren, 116
MILLESON, Grace,
 44
 James, 6, 44, 79
MILLS, Mary, 11
MINER, Thomas, 19
MINOR, Thomas, 61
MINSHALL, Aaron,
 70
 Agnes, 16, 19
 Griffith, 70
 Isaac, 19, 116
 Jane, 16, 19
 John, 19, 70, 78
 Mary, 78
 Moses, 16, 19,
  70
 Rebecca, 19
 Samuel, 19
 Sarah, 19, 70,
  78, 147
 Thomas, 16, 19,
  70, 138
MITCHELL, Agnes,
 82
 Alexander, 159
 Elizabeth, 82,
  100
 George, 82
 Isabella, 85
 James, 11
 John, 82
 Joseph, 82
 Margery, 82
 Samuel, 82
 William, 82
MITCHINER, John,
 158
 Mary, 158
MODLEN, John, 28
MOLLOY, Elinor, 11
 William, 106
MOLLY, William, 97
MONEY, Ann, 38
 James, 38
 Joseph, 38

Neal, 38
Samuel, 38
MONTGOMERY, Mary,
 101
 Michael, 7
 Robert, 7
MOOBERY, Barbary,
 80
MOODE, Alexander,
 36
 Rebecca, 36
MOOR, Charles, 43
 John, 29, 30, 49
 Sampson, 144
 Samuel, 142
 William, 30
MOORE, Alexander,
 131
 Amos, 93
 Andrew, 48
 Ann, 130
 Anne, 33
 Catherine, 131
 Charles, 26, 35,
  42, 63, 154
 Daniel, 22, 130
 David, 48
 Edward, 10
 Elizabeth, 42,
  63, 93, 126,
  130, 131, 154
 Gayen, 91
 Hannah, 42, 154
 Henry, 131
 James, 29, 34,
  42, 48, 131
 John, 19, 21,
  22, 26, 34, 42,
  48, 78, 86, 91,
  130, 131, 133,
  150
 Joseph, 42, 48,
  69, 108, 121
 Margaret, 26,
  150, 151, 154
 Martha, 131
 Mary, 18, 151
 Mordecai, 100,
  122
 Moses, 109, 130,
  151
 Nathan, 42, 130
 Nathaniel, 44,
  144, 153
 Philip, 154

Rachel, 19, 26,
 48, 154
Rebecca, 22, 26
Rees, 21
Richard, 21, 86
Robert, 48, 71
Rose, 92
Samuel, 131
Sarah, 42, 48,
 130
Susanna, 22, 42
Thomas, 22, 27,
 42
Walter, 129
William, 13, 22,
 30, 42, 48,
 131, 154
MORDOCH, Jean, 88
MORGAN, ----, 136
 Anne, 56
 David, 10, 56
 Eleanor, 58
 Elizabeth, 5
 Evan, 90
 Francis, 47
 Hannah, 129
 Jacob, 71, 129,
  141
 John, 56, 69, 71
 Joseph, 56
 Lydia, 69
 Magdalen, 58
 Mary, 69, 129,
  149
 Mordecai, 149
 Moses, 56
 Rachel, 141
 Robert, 55
 Samuel, 23, 58,
  69
 Sarah, 56, 58,
  71, 102
 Susanna, 56
 Thomas, 5, 16,
  69, 71, 129,
  133
 William, 129
MORRALL, Mary, 29
MORRION, Gaven,
 152
MORRIS, Ann, 124
 Davis, 124
 Elizabeth, 103
 Francis, 126,
  127

Hannah, 103
Jane, 103
John, 50, 103,
 126, 136
Jonathan, 102
Mary, 30, 103,
 126
Mordecai, 30
Mrs., 136
Phebe, 103
Richard, 30
Robert, 103
Thomas, 58
William, 30
MORRISON,
 Alexander, 14
 David, 125
 Guyan, 83
 Hugh, 49
 James, 90, 125
 John, 61
 William, 158
MORTON, Andrew, 59
 George, 109
 Jacob, 45
 John, 11, 32,
  45, 66, 86, 96,
  108, 114, 144
 Lydia, 58, 59
 Margaret, 58, 59
 Mary, 154
 Morton, 58, 59
 Rebecca, 59, 109
 Samuel, 33, 108,
  154
 Thomas, 154
 William, 154
MOSS, Mary, 104
MOTE, Jacob, 115
 Sarah, 115
MOULDER, Benjamin,
 16
 Mary, 84
 Sarah, 25
MOUNDER, Benjamin,
 67
MOWBERRY, Barbara,
 8
 Robert, 8
 William, 8
MUCKLEDUFF,
 Joseph, 27
 Samuel, 27
MUIRHEAD, James,
 138

John, 138
Margaret, 138
Thomas, 138
William, 138
MURPHY, Anne, 124
 Bryan, 124
 Hannah, 84
 James, 84
MUSGRAVE, Aaron,
 52
 Abraham, 78
 Abram, 80
 John, 52
 Joseph, 120
 Moses, 52
MUSGROVE, Aaron,
 149
MYER, Henry, 125,
 145
MYLLS, George, 7
 Henry, 7
 Jean, 7
 Mary, 7
 William, 7

-N-
NAYLE, Deborah, 35
 Henry, 104
NEAL, Henry, 38,
 39, 99
NEALS, Thomas, 63
NEALY, John, 112
NEAVE, Samuel, 29
NEELD, Elias, 30
NEGROES (Blacks
 with single
 name only),
 Bell, 136
 Bella, 35
 Bette, 146
 Black Jack, 27
 Charley, 136
 Esther, 101
 Hannah, 76
 Harry, 51, 113
 Jack, 101
 James, 120
 Jane, 85
 Jenny, 113
 Joan, 128
 June, 139
 Lonnon, 101
 Nell, 147
 Phillis, 113
 Ruth, 85

Sarah, 43
Summer, 93
Tobe, 113
Violet, 113
Will, 95
NEILS, John, 106
NEILSON, John, 152
NETHERMARDT,
 Christian, 108
 Conradt, 108
 Elizabeth, 108
 Luke, 108
 Mary, 108
 Mathias, 108
 Rebecca, 108
 Sarah, 108
NETHERMARK, Luke,
 138
New Jersey, 11,
 80, 109, 114,
 132
NEWBOROUGH, John,
 55
NEWLAND, John, 23
NEWLIN, John, 37,
 45
 Mary, 45
 Nathaniel, 30,
  116, 125
NICHOLIN, Joseph,
 144
 Susanna, 144
NICHOLSON,
 Elizabeth, 95
 Richard, 74
NICKELSON, John,
 44
NICKLIN, George,
 40
 Joseph, 40, 120
 Mary, 40
NICOLS, Elizabeth,
 28
NIEDERMARDT,
 Conrad, 108
NISBET, William,
 135
NIZBET, John, 14
NOBLE, Andrew, 153
 Mary, 153
 William, 149
NOBLET, Richard,
 107
NOBLIT, Richard,
 91

NOBLITT, Richard, 134
NORBURY, Elizabth, 8
  Jacob, 109, 154
  Rachel, 154
NORRIS, Charles, 95
  Mary, 95, 154
NORTON, John, 95
NOSSETT, Jane, 51
  Peter, 51
NOX, Andrew, 7
NUTT, Anna, 59
  Rebecca, 59
  Samuel, 59
NUZUM, Richard, 133
  Thomas, 133

-O-
O CUNNING, Agnes, 93
  Henry, 93
  John, 93
  Margaret, 93
OAAR, Samuel, 5
OCHELTREE, James, 97
  Katherine, 97
O'CONNOR, Thomas, 36
OGDEN, Alice, 77
  David, 12
  George, 157
  Hannah, 104
  Samuel, 12
  Stephen, 104
OGELBAY, James, 46
  Jean, 47
  John, 47
  Sarah, 46, 47
OLDHAM, Edward, 15
  Mary, 15, 24, 62, 64
  Rachel, 62, 64, 123
  Robert, 15, 62
  Sarah, 64
  Thomas, 24, 64
  William, 64
OLIVER, John, 19
O'MULLEN, Marthew, 152
  Robert, 152

ONEAL, Susanna, 71
ORIN, Benjamin, 104
O'SKILLEN, Hannah, 71
  Morris, 71
OTLAY, John, 61
OTTEY, Ann, 48
  Christopher, 48
  Jane, 48
  John, 48
  Philip, 48
  Phillip, 30
  Richard, 48
  Sarah, 30, 48
  Thomas, 48
OTTY, Hannah, 34
OWEN, Abraham, 128
  Anne, 42
  Elizabeth, 128
  Evan, 128
  George, 39, 40, 46
  Hannah, 151
  Hugh, 128
  John, 39
  Mordecai, 128
  Rebecca, 39, 40, 46
  Sarah, 128
  Susanna, 40, 46
  William, 42, 128
OWENS, Owen, 36
  Thomas, 129

-P-
PACKER, John, 2, 21, 36
  Jonathan, 36
  William, 2
PADRICH, Rachel, 109
PADRICK, John, 49
PAGE, Aquilla, 148
  Mary, 148
PAGUE, James, 127
PAINE, Hannah, 38
  William, 38
PAINTER, Agnes, 147
  Ann, 61
  Betty, 23, 106
  Elizabeth, 61, 106
  Grace, 23

  Hannah, 23
  John, 61, 147
  Lydia, 147
  Mary, 61
  Patience, 61
  Samuel, 23, 61, 82, 147
  Sarah, 147
  Thomas, 23, 147
PALMER, Henry, 96
  Isaac, 96
  John, 17, 116
  Martha, 54
  Moses, 54, 143
PANCOAST, Edward, 146
  Esther, 111
  Seth, 80, 111, 136, 158
PARK, George, 82
  John, 134
  Joseph, 14, 74, 82
  Rebecca, 131
  William, 14
PARKE, Hannah, 83
  Jacob, 83
  Jane, 38, 79, 83
  Jonathan, 18
  Rebecca, 18, 83
  Robert, 83
  Sarah, 83
  Thomas, 18, 34, 79, 83
PARKER, Abraham, 33, 45, 139
  Ann, 20, 29, 64
  Eleanor, 45
  Elisha, 120
  Elizabeth, 45
  Jo., 12, 16, 26
  John, 45
  Joseph, 95, 99, 120, 154
  Kezia, 45
  Lydia, 45
  Mary, 45
  Sebbellah, 120
  Thomas, 38
  William, 20, 29, 51, 83, 150
PARKINS, Hannah, 15
PARKINSON, Joseph, 142

PARKS, Elizabeth,
  144
  Mary, 81
  Richard, 81, 113
  Samuel, 159
PARRY, Anne, 141
  Elizabeth, 5
  Llewellin, 3
PARVIN, Mary, 62,
  113
  Thomas, 50, 75
PASCHALL, John, 61
PASSMORE, George,
  91
  Hannah, 104
  Mary, 88
PATEN, David, 128
  Thomas, 128
PATRICK, Abigail,
  151
  John, 151
  Samuel, 151
PATTEN, Andrew, 60
  David, 125
  Elizabeth, 60
  Jean, 60
  John, 60
  Joseph, 60
  Rebecca, 60
  Robert, 60
  Thomas, 60, 68
PATTERSON, Arthur,
  72
  Charity, 72
  Elizabeth, 18
  Isabella, 72
  John, 18, 33
  Mary, 72
  Robert, 105
  Samuel, 18, 46
  Thomas, 18
  William, 18
PATTIN, Rebecca, 5
PATTON, David, 50
  Rebecca, 85
  Richard, 85
  William, 142
PEAK, John, 50
PEARCE, Edward,
  123
PEARSOLL, John, 77
  Sarah, 77
PEARSON, Benjamin,
  51, 125, 126
  Elizabeth, 125
  Esther, 6
  George, 126
  Hannah, 19, 125
  Isa, 93
  Isaac, 21, 24,
   31, 46, 95,
   125, 131
  James, 124, 125
  John, 25, 73,
   95, 124, 125,
   126, 131
  Jonathan, 126
  Joshua, 150
  Margaret, 126
  Mary, 125
  Rebecca, 126
  Robert, 51
  Samuel, 126
  Sarah, 125, 126,
   158
  Susanna, 125
  Thomas, 19, 20,
   31, 93, 124
PEDRICK, Adam, 84,
  149
  John, 75, 84,
   149
  Rachel, 84, 149
  Sarah, 154
  Thomas, 69, 84,
   146
PEIRCE, Caleb, 18,
   30, 42, 51, 81
  George, 42, 69
  Hannah, 154
  Henry, 17, 35,
   66, 154
  Isaac, 42
  John, 40, 66,
   122, 154
  Joseph, 42, 64
  Joshua, 42
  Mary, 18, 69
  Rachel, 42, 154
  Sarah, 66, 154
  William, 66, 154
PEMBERTON, Isaac,
  95
  Rachel, 95
PENNELL, Abraham,
  73
  Edith, 73
  Elizabeth, 73
  Hamath, 73
  Hannah, 37, 50,
   73, 126
  James, 73
  Jemima, 73
  John, 31, 137
  Joseph, 68, 73
  Joshua, 50, 137
  Martha, 128
  Mary, 25, 31,
   73, 137
  Nathan, 73
  Rachel, 73, 77
  Rebecca, 73
  Robert, 29, 37,
   73, 126
  Ruth, 73
  Samuel, 73, 77
  Susanna, 73
  Thomas, 25, 73
  Timothy, 73
  William, 31, 73
PENNOCK, Alice,
  130
  Levis, 138
  Moses, 130
  Nathaniel, 114
  Sarah, 114
  William, 130
PENNY, William, 90
PENROSE, Mary, 136
PEOPLES, Martha,
  32
PERGRIN, Thomas,
  158
PERKINS, Caleb, 66
PERRY, John, 65
  Margaret, 65
PETERS, John, 15,
   53, 54
  William, 15, 54
PETERSON,
  Catherine, 11
  Jonas, 71
  Mary, 106
  Susanna, 71
PETTEL, Martha, 95
PETTERS, Elinor, 5
  John, 15
  Reese, 15
PETTERSON,
  Isabella, 13
  James, 13, 62,
   82
  Jane, 13
  Mary, 13
  Robert, 13

PHILIP, Margaret, 10
PHILIPS, Henry, 40
  Sarah, 40
PHILLIP, Joseph, 107
  Owen, 5
PHILLIPS, Evan, 8
  Grace, 5
  John, 4, 5, 144
  Margaret, 8
  Susanna, 70
  Thomas, 123, 141
  William, 8, 110
PHILSON, John, 37
PHIPPS, Ann, 75
  George, 127
  John, 59, 127
  Jonathan, 75
  Joseph, 59, 111, 127, 132
  Margaret, 132
  Mary, 75, 127
  Nathan, 59, 127
  Prudence, 75
  Rachel, 111
  Samuel, 18, 127
  Sarah, 75
PIERCE, George, 119
  John, 81
  Joseph, 89, 139, 143
PIERSOL, Bridget, 47
  Elizabeth, 47
  Martha, 47
  Mary, 47
  Rachel, 47
  Richard, 47
PIERSOLL, Bridget, 141
  John, 47
  Richard, 141
PIGGOTT, Samuel, 24
PILKINTON, Edward, 43
  Thomas, 43
PIM, Ann, 51
  Hannah, 94
  James, 51
  Jane, 51
  Richard, 83, 94
  Thomas, 38, 83, 137
  William, 18, 38
PIMM, Thomas, 134
PIN, Ann, 38
  Richard, 38
  Thomas, 38
  William, 38
PIPER, John, 125
PLAIN, Mary, 48
PLUMMER, Phebe, 87
POAK, Grisel, 20
POOLEG, George, 11
POOLKE, Allen, 119
PORTER, Alexander, 120
  Andrew, 87
  Ann, 18
  Charles, 87
  Elizabeth, 18, 120
  Hugh, 18
  James, 6, 11, 46, 50
  John, 18, 47, 57, 153
  Margaret, 44
  Mary, 18
  Matthew, 13
  Reese, 18
  Robert, 44
  Sarah, 153
  Violet, 18, 46
  William, 11, 13, 18, 112
PORTERFIELD,
  Denney, 131
  Elizabeth, 131
  James, 131
  John, 29
  Josias, 106
  Mathew, 131
  Nelly, 131
  William, 106
POSTON, John, 156
POWELL, Abigail, 30
  David, 36, 41
  Edward, 41
  Elizabeth, 30
  Ellen, 152
  James, 152
  John, 41, 152
  Joseph, 41
  Katherine, 41
  Mary, 152
  Patience, 18
  Robert, 30
  Susanna, 36
POWER, Jane, 40
  John, 17, 70, 75, 86, 109, 135
  Patrick, 112
  Robert, 40
  Sarah, 86
PRATT, Alice, 69
  Ann, 69
  Jane, 58, 140
  Joseph, 27, 30, 68, 69, 129, 130
  Mary, 69
  Rose, 69
  Sarah, 69
PRESTON, Hannah, 107
  Jonas, 107
PRICE, Abigail, 100
  Abjagh, 158
  Daniel, 158
  E., 89, 123, 129
  Elisha, 69, 101, 154, 156
  Hannah, 69, 135
  Jeremiah, 138
  John, 43, 69, 158
  Mary, 138, 158
  Rees, 24
  Reese, 18
  Sarah, 69
  Thomas, 43, 69, 158
  Vell, 158
  William, 18, 144, 158
PRICHARD, Anthony, 1
PRISE, Thomas, 32
PRITCHARD, Daniel, 3
PRITCHET, John, 53
PRITCHETT, Phebe, 27
  Thomas, 104
  William, 104
PRYOR, James, 110
PUGH, Agnes, 94
  Dinah, 12

Elizabeth, 106
Enos, 12
Hugh, 12, 84
John, 12, 94
Jonathan, 8
Joseph, 24
Rebecca, 12
Samuel, 24
William, 94
PUMROY, Benjamin, 12
PURDY, Susanna, 38
William, 18, 133
PUSEY, Caleb, 33, 65
Catherine, 155
David, 65
Elizabeth, 65
Ellis, 102, 108, 127
George, 155
Hannah, 102
James, 65, 155
Jane, 155
John, 54, 79, 87, 92, 108, 155
Joshua, 54, 55, 79, 92, 102, 106, 122, 155
Lewis, 102
Lydia, 102
Mary, 54, 102, 107, 123, 135
Nathan, 155
Phebe, 102
Prudence, 65
Robert, 65
Susanna, 155
Thomas, 65, 80
William, 102
PYLE, Adam, 52, 54, 91
Amos, 36, 131
Ann, 53, 54
Anne, 36
Betty, 22
Caleb, 36
Deborah, 79
Ebenezer, 37, 40, 43
Elianor, 42
Esther, 53, 54, 91
Hannah, 53, 54, 91
Isaac, 52, 54, 91
Israel, 37, 40, 126
Jacob, 37, 40, 126
James, 8
Jane, 35
Job, 36
John, 4, 22, 36, 37, 40, 106
Joseph, 9, 31, 40, 52, 54, 106
Martha, 53, 54, 91
Mary, 37, 40, 87
Moses, 40, 65, 80
Nathaniel, 91
Nicholas, 22, 51, 63
Rachel, 53
Ralph, 90, 106, 123
Robert, 52, 54, 79
Ruth, 79
Samuel, 22, 47, 143
Sarah, 22, 31, 35, 53, 106, 143
Sarah Ann, 22
Saray, 8
Stephen, 37, 40
Susanna, 37, 40
Susannah, 43
William, 37, 40, 106
PYOTT, Deborah, 19
John, 19

-Q-
QUAINTANCE, Damson, 13
QUIN, William, 43

-R-
RAFESNIDER, Arnst, 32
Frederick, 32, 39
RAIN, John, 60
Mary, 60

Rachel, 63
RAINE, Samuel, 113
RALSTON, Robert, 100
RAMBO, Michael, 14
Moses, 73
RAMSAY, David, 24, 35
RAMSEY, David, 61, 88, 97
John, 89
Nathaniel, 24
Robert, 155
Susanna, 69, 89
William, 69
RANDALL, Rachel, 102
RANDEL, Michael, 138
RANKIN, James, 97
William, 77
RAPSON, Henry, 71
RAWSON, John, 49, 75, 107
RAY, Mary, 105
Robert, 105
REA, Joseph, 142
READ, George, 75
James, 156
Jane, 156
Thomas, 75, 92
William, 105
READING, Jane, 1
Matthew, 1
REDD, Adam, 117, 125
Ann, 117
REECE, Caleb, 114
David, 78, 114
John, 42
Lewis, 58
Thomas, 5
REED, Adam, 97
Andrew, 153
Margaret, 114
Martha, 97
William, 28
REES, Catherine, 107
Daniel, 148
Francis, 124
James, 24, 76
Jane, 46, 76
John, 28, 37, 46, 111

Lewis, 71
Morris, 76, 107
REESS, Jane, 46
REGESTER, David, 32
  Hannah, 75
  John, 75
  Robert, 32
  William, 32
REGISTER, Jane, 49
  Robert, 49
RENICK, Catherine, 79, 80
  Henry, 79, 80
RENNOLDS, Deboroh, 25
  James, 25
REYNOLDS,
  Alexander, 43
  Benjamin, 86, 92, 151
  Christiana, 92
  Elizabeth, 92, 151
  Francis, 21, 91, 151
  Henry, 1, 68, 92, 151, 155
  John, 92, 143, 151
  Lydia, 92
  Richard, 12
  Samuel, 56, 92, 151
  Sarah, 155
  William, 1, 68, 117
RHOADES, Benjamin, 30
  Elizabeth, 46
  James, 30, 46
  Jean, 30
  John, 30
RHOADS, Abigail, 30
  Elizabeth, 36, 39
  James, 6, 39, 40, 80, 136, 152
  John, 6, 36
RICE, Daniel, 80
  Edward, 143
  Judith, 143, 156
  Nicholas, 80

RICH, Anne, 72
  Elizabeth, 72
  Hannah, 72
  John, 72
  Joseph, 72
  Martha, 72
  Mary, 72
  Peter, 72
  Rachel, 72
  Samuel, 72
  Sarah, 29, 72, 128
  Stephen, 72
RICHARD, Adam, 157
  Catherine, 145
  Edward, 145
  Elizabeth, 145
  Jacob, 145
  Jones, 74
  Margaret, 145
  Martha, 145
  Rachel, 145
  Rebecca, 145
  Sarah, 145
  Susanna, 145
RICHARDS, Jacob, 99, 117, 119
  John, 148
  Jonathan, 63
  Joseph, 8, 10, 63
  Lydia, 63
  Mary, 41, 63, 130
  Rachel, 119
  Samuel, 60
RICHARDSON,
  Francis, 95
  Joseph, 95
  Patience, 95
  Richard, 137
  Thomas, 142
  William, 79
RICHEY, John, 16
RICHISON, Mary, 119
  Richard, 3, 28, 142
  Samuel, 119
RIDDLE, John, 57
RIES, Daniel, 66
RIGG, Ann, 3
  Clement, 3
  Elizabeth, 3
  Mary, 3

Richard, 3
Robert, 3
Sarah, 3
RILEY, Edward, 7
  Elizabeth, 106
  John, 25, 28, 53, 62, 63, 67, 106
  Richard, 62, 106, 119, 149, 156
  William, 106
RING, Benjamin, 26, 57
  Elizabeth, 143
  Lydia, 57
  Nathaniel, 57, 143
RISK, Humphrey, 9
RITTEW, Aaron, 107
  Elioner, 107
  John, 107
  Mary, 107
  William, 107
ROACH, Israel, 2
  William, 2
ROADS, Elizabeth, 19
ROAN, John, 158
ROBB, William, 154, 156
ROBERTS, Alban, 150
  Aubrey, 12
  Awbrey, 49, 76
  John, 76, 107
  Mary, 28, 74
  Rachel, 28
  Ruth, 49
ROBERTSON, Isabel, 24
  John, 24
  Thomas, 24
  William, 24, 88
ROBESON, Jean, 16
  Jonathan, 59
  Mary, 16
  Samuel, 16
ROBINETT, Allen, 74, 87
  Allin, 87
  Joseph, 87
  Lydia, 87
  Prudence, 87
  Rachel, 87

ROBINSON, Eleanor, 106
Genet, 16
John, 8
Joseph, 52
Mary, 51
Michael, 51
Rachel, 18
Richard, 52
Robert, 69
Sarah, 53
William, 18, 90
ROBISON, Benjamin, 22
Janet, 105
John, 105
ROBSON, Thomas, 132
ROGER, Margaret, 146
William, 146
ROGERS, Agnes, 138
Alexander, 60, 76, 79, 91, 105
Elizabeth, 8
Hannah, 52
John, 8
Joseph, 52
Mary, 52
Priscilla, 8
Rowland, 8, 86
Susanna, 8
Thomas, 8, 79
William, 8, 105, 148
ROMAN, Absalom, 133
Benjamin, 133
Jacob, 12
Joshua, 133
Mary, 12
Rachel, 133
ROMANO, Rachel, 54
ROSS, Dorcas, 121
Hannah, 153
Isabel, 97
James, 91, 121
Jane, 65
John, 49, 77, 90, 91, 97, 110, 153
Joseph, 153
Margaret, 90
Moses, 82, 91, 153

Robert, 26
Rosanna, 153
William, 62
ROSWELL, Joseph, 3
ROUSE, Charles, 116
Patience, 116
ROUTH, Francis, 8
ROWAN, Andrew, 105
Elizabeth, 76
James, 107
Mary, 105
Michael, 105
William, 76
ROWEN, James, 119
ROWLAND, Hugh, 120
James, 120
Jean, 55, 120
Robert, 120
Thomas, 4, 95, 157
William, 120
ROWLES, Lacy, 64
Mary, 64
RUDDELL, Deborah, 8
RUDULPH, John, 61, 83, 124, 126
RUSSELL,
Alexander, 45
Edward, 87, 99
Henry, 13
John, 38
Martha, 97
Robert, 89
RUSTON, Anne, 41
James, 41
Job, 35, 77
RUTH, Francis, 17
RUTTER, Samuel, 144
RYANT, Hannah, 159
RYPOLE, Elizabeth, 159

-S-

SALKELD, Agnes, 16
Daniel, 19
David, 16, 88
John, 19, 89, 142
Sarah, 89
Thomas, 16, 18
William, 16, 19
SAMUEL, Hugh, 80

John, 38, 80
SANDERLIN, David, 11
SANFORD, Abraham, 150
Anne, 150
Elizabeth, 150
Isaac, 150
Jacob, 150
Jean, 150
Patience, 150
Robert, 150
Samuel, 150
SANKEY, Giles, 24
William, 24
SAVAGE, Samuel, 59
SAYER, George, 115
SCARLET, Deborah, 143
Nathaniel, 122
Shadrach, 121
SCIVINGTON, James, 64
Martha, 64
SCOT, Thomas, 26
SCOTHORN, Joseph, 20, 29
SCOTT, Abraham, 20, 71, 133
Agnes, 151
Ann, 61
Eleanor, 94
Hugh, 20
James, 55, 81, 151
Jane, 20, 76
Jean, 151
John, 32, 69, 76, 107, 121, 131, 151, 154
Josiah, 20, 61
Lydia, 32
Mary, 143, 151
Moses, 146
Nathan, 32
Philip, 151
Providence, 61
Samuel, 20, 50, 137, 151
Sarah, 20
Thomas, 20, 76, 94, 151, 154
SEED, Abigail, 56
Adam, 56
Edward, 56

George, 56
James, 56
Mary, 56
Richard, 56
SELLERS, Esther,
  54
  John, 21, 110
  Luke, 54
  Samuel, 29, 54
  Thomas, 54
  William, 54
SERJEANT, Rache,
  118
SERRILL, James, 34
  John, 158
SEVILL, Alice, 80
  Isaac, 3
  James, 80
SHANKS, Samuel, 62
  Sarah, 62
  Widow, 65
SHARP, Abigail,
  130
  Alexander, 76,
    77
  Andrew, 77
  Deborah, 41
  Edward, 77
  George, 130
  John, 51
  Samuel, 63
  Thomas, 97
SHARPLESS,
  Abigail, 35
  Abige, 35
  Abraham, 35, 40
  Ann, 40
  Benjamin, 141
  Daniel, 105, 111
  Elizabeth, 10
  Hannah, 5, 60,
    85
  Jacob, 35, 60
  James, 10, 51
  Job, 10
  John, 26, 41,
    57, 85, 103,
    105, 113
  Joseph, 37, 73,
    141
  Joshua, 10
  Lete, 85
  Martha, 60
  Mary, 10, 37, 51
  Nathan, 60

Nathaniel, 10
Philip P., 2
Rebecca, 10
Samuel, 35, 37,
  154
Sarah, 105, 111
Thomas, 113
William, 35
SHAW, Mary, 16,
  19, 22
SHAWS, Katren, 147
  Margaret, 147
  Martha, 147
SHEE, John, 126
SHEERER, Ann, 26
  David, 26
  Elizabeth, 96
  Francis, 26
  Hugh, 96
  John, 26
  Mary, 26
SHELDON, Ann, 43
  Jonathan, 43
  Joseph, 43
  Mary, 43
  Richard, 43
  William, 43
SHENTON, Hannah,
  20
  Rachel, 20
SHEPPARD, Ann, 88
  James, 88
  John, 88
  Mary, 126
  Robert, 88, 126
  Samuel, 88
  William, 87, 88
SHERER, Archibald,
  151
SHEWARD, Ruth, 57
  Samuel, 57
  Thomas, 14
SHIELD, Mary, 11
SHIELDS,
  Archibald, 97
  Cathrin, 97
  Daniel, 82
  Elizabeth, 77
  Hannah, 97
  Joseph, 97
  Martha, 97
  Mary, 77
  Mathew, 82
  Robert, 97
  Thomas, 97

William, 77, 97
SHIPLEY,
  Elizabeth, 81
SHORT, John, 63
SHUSTER, Andrew,
  130
SHUTE, Atwood, 29
SIDDINS, Jane, 128
  John, 128
SIDEWALL, Hugh, 56
SIDWELL, Abraham,
  56
  Ann, 129
  Anne, 56
  Henry, 56
  Jacob, 56
  John, 56
  Joseph, 56
  Mary, 56
  Richard, 55
SILL, James, 40
  John, 40
  Joseph, 30, 43
SILLEKER, William,
  48
SIM, Andrew, 112
  Ann, 112
  Jean, 112
  John, 112
  Samuel, 112
  William, 60, 112
SIMCOCK, Banjamin,
  119
  Elizabeth, 11
  James, 114
  Phebe, 114
SIMM, Andrew, 62
SIMON, Thomas, 139
SIMONS, Elinor, 53
  Richard, 53
  Susanna, 53
  William, 53
SIMPSON, David,
  156
  George, 12
  Josias, 8
  Mary, 8
  Rebecca, 8
  Sarah, 8
  William, 12
  Zebulon, 12
SIMRALL,
  Alexander, 118,
    150
  James, 124

Thomas, 93, 150
SIMSON, Allen, 67,
  97
  Cataren, 67
  David, 67
  Ellis, 67
  James, 97
  John, 67, 97
  Margaret, 67
  Robert, 67
  William James,
  67
SINGELEAR, Ann,
  122
SINKLER, Ann, 93
  George, 38, 73,
  93
  James, 101, 109
  John, 73, 93
  Samuel, 93
  William, 73
SITTON, Matthew,
  77
SKETCHLEY, John,
  11, 30, 45
  Mary, 11, 45
  Richard, 45
SLACK, John, 53
SLATER, George,
  126
  John, 88, 126
  Sarah, 126
SLEMONS, Thomas,
  98
SLOAN, William,
  150
SLYCER, Mary, 1
SMART, Ann, 44
SMEDLEY,
  Elizabeth, 153
  Francis, 49, 78,
  147, 151
  George, 17, 57,
  58, 70, 78,
  100, 116, 138,
  147, 151
  Hannah, 151
  Jeffrey, 151
  John, 78, 147,
  149
  Joshua, 151
  Mary, 17
  Sarah, 78, 147
  Thomas, 78, 147
  William, 43,
  134, 153
SMILEY, Robert, 34
SMITH, Abraham,
  36, 157
  Abram, 97
  Ann, 34, 96, 145
  Anne, 34, 36
  Charles, 66
  Elizabeth, 92,
  102, 142
  Esther, 97
  George, 142
  Hannah, 1, 16,
  20, 29
  Isaac, 157
  Isabel, 97
  James, 9, 16,
  96, 98, 157
  Jean, 9, 120
  Jenah, 9
  John, 9, 10, 16,
  19, 34, 42, 78,
  81, 90, 97,
  102, 132, 145,
  149, 153, 156,
  157
  Jonathan, 9
  Joseph, 5, 46,
  67, 97
  Joshua, 16
  Margaret, 34,
  121
  Martha, 97
  Mary, 92, 125
  Peter, 119
  Rachel, 92
  Rebecca, 16
  Robert, 9, 97,
  98, 153, 156,
  157
  Samuel, 34, 92,
  93
  Sarah, 123
  Susanna, 157
  Thomas, 89, 128,
  155
  Tristin, 16
  Walter, 141
  William, 9, 11,
  34, 38, 116,
  123
SMYLEY, William,
  10
SNARGRASS, Hannah,
  72
Joseph, 72
SNODDY, Samuel, 13
SOLSBERRY,
  Jennett, 112
SOREL, Susanna, 4
SORSBY, William,
  94
SPARRAN,
  Archibald, 22
SPEAKMAN, John,
  153
  Micajah, 30, 83
SPEAR, Ann, 61
  John, 61
  Mary, 61
SPLAN, Morris, 14
STACKHOUS, Caleb,
  79
STALKER, George,
  130
  Rebecca, 18
  Thomas, 146
STANFIELD, Mary,
  101
STANNINGS, Mary,
  25
STANSON, Susanna,
  3
STARR, Alice, 33
  Isaac, 33, 50,
  58, 62, 113
  Jacob, 62, 113
  Jeremiah, 33,
  119, 142
  John, 50, 62,
  113
  Jremiah, 25
  Margaret, 50, 62
  Mary, 33, 50,
  56, 58
  Moses, 33, 50,
  62, 113, 142
  Rebecca, 33
  Samuel, 50, 62,
  113
  Thomas, 50, 62,
  113
  William, 50, 62,
  113
STARRATT, James,
  118
  Jean, 118
  John, 118
  William, 118
STARRET, Robert,

72
STARRETT, Mary, 140
Robert, 140
STEADWELL,
  Ebenezer, 14
STEDMAN, Richard, 10
STEDWELL,
  Ebenezer, 43
STEEL, Andrew, 84
Ann, 97, 124
Anne, 75
Elizabeth, 97
Frances, 97
Isabel, 101
James, 26, 75, 97, 124
Jean, 96
John, 7, 104
Joseph, 97
Margaret, 150
Ninian, 97
Robert, 96, 101
Ruth, 96
Samuel, 19, 96, 97
Sarah, 84
STEEN, James, 49
Jane, 49
John, 49
Mary, 49
Sarah, 49
STEPHEN, David, 11
Hannah, 11
STEPHENS, David, 105
James, 72
Priscilla, 72
STEPHENSON,
  Grisel, 16
Jean, 65
John, 16
STERLING, Andrew, 37, 82, 85, 96, 118, 149
Dorcas, 85
STEVENS,
  Elizabeth, 39
Robert, 39
STEVENSON, James, 146
Robert, 134
William, 134
STEWART, John, 13

STINSON, Francis, 21
Robert, 12
STIRLING, Andrew, 156
STOCKMAN, Esaella, 144
STRINGER, Eleanor, 154
George, 154
John, 103, 154
Joseph, 154
Martha, 154
William, 154
STRODE, Deborah, 67, 76
Elizabeth, 100
George, 15, 76
Mary, 15, 16
Richard, 15, 76
William, 67, 76
STROUD, James, 86
Joseph, 86
Mary, 86
Rachel, 86
Thomas, 86
STUART, Agnes, 45
James, 45
Jean, 45
John, 45, 112
Margaret, 45, 133
Martha, 118
Mary, 45
Robert, 45
William, 45
STUBBS, Ann, 125
Daniel, 125
John, 125
Joseph, 125
Sarah, 125
Thomas, 13, 103, 125
STURGEON, William, 72
SULLIVAN, Denis, 81
SUMRALL,
  Alexander, 124
SURMAN, Sarah, 135
SWAFER, William, 102
SWAFFER, William, 57, 71, 102, 113, 146

SWAIN, Caleb, 38
Deborah, 38
Esther, 35, 38
Francis, 35, 38, 135
Joshua, 38
Nancy, 38
Samuel, 135
Sarah, 38
Thomas, 135
William, 135
SWAINE, Anne, 26
Elizabeth, 26
Samuel, 26
Thomas, 26
SWAYNE, Caleb, 83
Edward, 55, 84, 117
Francis, 145
Isaac, 117, 155
Joshua, 83, 93
William, 65, 89, 155
SWENEY, Barnaby, 86

-T-
TALBOT, Benjamin, 18
John, 54, 151
Joseph, 35
Lydia, 151
TALKINTON, Joseph, 3
Samuel, 120
TALLEY, Rebecca, 154
William, 154
TANNER, Elizabeth, 112
James, 33, 112
Joseph, 33, 112
Mary, 33, 112
Philip, 33, 112
Rachel, 112
Rebecca, 112
TARBERT, Elinor, 62
John, 62
TARBET, Allen, 156
David, 156
Elizabeth, 156
Hugh, 156
Jannet, 156
John, 156

Katherine, 156
Margaret, 156
Robert, 156
TASSEY, Alexander, 75
Mary, 75
TATE, Ann, 91
TATNALL, Anne, 139
TAYLOR, Abiah, 78, 87, 147
  Abraham, 87, 143, 145
  Ann, 136
  Benjamin, 10, 11, 12, 122, 139
  Caleb, 137, 145
  Christopher, 11
  Deborah, 86, 87, 143
  Elizabeth, 10, 66, 77, 87, 113
  George, 46, 136
  Hannah, 46, 84
  Irarel, 113
  Isaac, 10, 87, 143
  Israel, 89
  Jacob, 113
  Jane, 103, 145
  Jesse, 84, 114
  John, 2, 3, 4, 7, 10, 11, 22, 30, 55, 60, 66, 67, 71, 79, 87, 90, 99, 112, 120, 122, 137, 143, 145
  Joseph, 10, 11, 57, 66, 84, 114, 139, 145
  Josiah, 10, 144
  Mary, 58, 66, 87, 106, 120, 145
  Mordecai, 6, 65, 103, 136
  Nathan, 148
  Peter, 57, 103, 105
  Phebe, 35, 137
  Philip, 58, 103, 120
  Rachel, 87, 119
  Rebecca, 7, 138, 139
  Robert, 18, 103
  Ruth, 28, 90
  Samuel, 11, 86, 87, 143
  Sarah, 10, 11, 12, 66
  Simeon, 35
  Simon, 123
  Stephen, 120
  Thomas, 7, 11, 66, 113, 137, 138, 152
  Titus, 137
  William, 139
TEMPLE, Jane, 39
  William, 21
TEMPLETON, Jane, 75
  John, 111
  Matthew, 75
THATCHER, Abigail, 27, 122
  David, 27, 122
  Deborah, 122
  Hannah, 42, 122
  Jonathan, 23, 25, 35, 61, 147
  Levy, 122
  Mary, 35
  Oliver, 122
  Richard, 23, 25, 27, 61, 81, 122
  Sarah, 17, 27, 122
  Susanna, 122
  William, 147
  Zerubable, 17
THOMAS, Abraham, 8
  Amos, 121
  Ann, 8, 157
  Azariah, 121
  Benjamin, 28
  David, 5, 20, 38, 48, 50, 114, 116, 121, 134, 138, 141
  Davis, 121
  Dinah, 8
  Edward, 157
  Eleanor, 141
  Elizabeth, 121, 141
  Elizabth, 8
  Ellis, 157
  Evan, 8
  Ezekiel, 50, 121
  George, 56, 157
  Grace, 56
  Hannah, 56
  Hezekiah, 53, 121
  Isaac, 8, 88
  Jacob, 48, 53, 121
  James, 121
  Jeffry, 94
  Jemima, 8, 9
  John, 5, 21, 63, 84, 94, 134, 137
  Joseph, 8, 141
  Julian, 121
  Lewis, 20, 54
  Lydia, 56
  Margaret, 121
  Mary, 10, 28, 121
  Morris, 8, 63, 119, 141
  Nathan, 8, 9
  Oliver, 11
  Owen, 5, 94, 138, 141
  Phebe, 50, 56
  Philip, 20, 48
  Priscilla, 8, 53
  Rebecca, 84, 121
  Richard, 3, 5, 24, 36, 56
  Samuel, 8, 50, 121
  Sarah, 11, 28, 53
  Solomon, 53
  Tamer, 8
  Thamar, 28, 53
  Theophilus, 100
  Thomas, 10, 23, 28, 48, 53, 134
  William, 8, 10, 28, 53, 114, 157
THOMPSON,
  Alexander, 133
  Abraham, 4
  Arthur, 25
  Hannah, 80
  Hugh, 112
  John, 27, 146

Margaret, 59
Martha, 105, 133
Mary, 24
Mordecai, 80
Robert, 61
Thomas, 59, 133
William, 12
THOMSON,
  Alexander, 19
  Daniel, 114
  Esther, 16
  Hannah, 136
  James, 19
  John, 16, 19,
    114, 128, 135
  Joseph, 114
  Joshua, 45, 114
  Martha, 16
  Mary, 17
  Mordecai, 64,
    114
  Moses, 17
  Nathan, 114, 136
  Robert, 19
  Ruth, 19
  Samuel, 15, 19,
    47
  Sarah, 114
  Thomas, 114
  William, 16, 19
THOPTSON, John, 49
THORNBOROUGH,
  Alice, 69
  Hannah, 95
  Robert, 90
  Ruth, 90
  Sarah, 69
  Susanna, 90
  Thomas, 70
THORNBURY, Mary,
  114
  Richard, 114
  Ruth, 98
  Thomas, 130
TIDBAL, Elizabeth,
  20
TIDBALL, Abraham,
  137
  Elizabeth, 137
  James, 137
  John, 137
  Joseph, 137
  Margaret, 137
  Sarah, 137
  Thomas, 137

William, 137
TIPPIN, George, 56
TODD, Andrew, 150
TODHUNTER, John,
  32, 34, 56,
  117, 121
  Margaret, 4
TOILLY, Catherine,
  54
TOMLINSON, Mary,
  67, 87
  Othniel, 67
TOMPSON, Henry,
  107
  Ruth, 107
TOOD, James, 152
TOOL, Bartholomew,
  71
TORTON, Andrew,
  15, 45
  Ann, 15
  Daniel, 15, 32,
    58, 124, 155
  Hans, 15, 32
  John, 15
  Letitia, 32, 58,
    155
  Margaret, 32, 59
  Martha, 15
  Mary, 15
  Rodde, 15
  Susannah, 15
TOWERS, John, 124,
  141
  Margaret, 141
TOWNSEND,
  Benjamin, 22
  Deborah, 88
  Esther, 22
  Francis, 22
  Hannah, 112
  John, 2, 34, 60,
    69, 88, 159
  Joseph, 22, 159
  Lawrence, 137,
    152
  Lydia, 22
  Martha, 159
  Mary, 141
  Rebecca, 88
  William, 159
TRAVERS, Arthur,
  10
TRAYHORN, Abigail,
  104

Adam, 104
Barshaba, 104
Elizabeth, 104
Israel, 104
Mary, 104
Ruth, 104
TREGO, Ann, 148
  Anne, 40
  Joseph, 47
  Peter, 40
  Susanna, 148
TREVILLER, Thomas,
  58
TRIMBLE, Hugh, 47,
  78, 97
  James, 56, 97,
    103, 107
  Margaret, 97,
    107
  Samuel, 97, 107
  Thomas, 97, 107
  William, 17, 35,
    37
TRUMAN, Thomas, 92
TRUSTLE, Jacob, 69
TURBET, Samuel,
  157
TURNER, Elizabeth,
  12
  George, 70
  Jean, 23
  John, 23
  Joseph, 124
  Mary, 13
  Moses, 126
TURTON, Andrew, 15
TUSTIN, Anne, 54
TWEED, Agnes, 62
  George, 62
  Robert, 62
TYBOUT, Andrew, 50

-U-
UNDERWOOD, Hannah,
  44
  Joseph, 44
  Ruth, 79
URIAN, Andrew, 47,
  58
  Benjamin, 47
  Margaret, 47

-V-
VALENTINE, Lydia,
  106

Mary, 18
Robert, 83
VALLEAU, Peter, 110
VAN LEER,
  Barnhard, 157
VANAMAN, John, 52
VANLEER, Bernard, 9
  George, 9
  John George, 9
  Rebecca, 9, 130
VAUGHAN, Emma, 23, 24
  Isaac, 23, 24
  John, 23
  Jonathan, 23
  Joseph, 23, 24, 115
  Joshua, 23
  Margaret, 23
VAUGHN, John, 55
  Thomas, 55
VERNON, Aaron, 56, 111
  Abigail, 57, 70
  Abraham, 17
  Ann, 2, 18
  Elizabeth, 9
  Isaac, 14, 72
  Jacob, 9, 81
  Jonathan, 12, 57
  Joseph, 10, 41, 57, 128
  Lettice, 5
  Lydia, 17, 57
  Margaret, 56, 57, 122
  Mary, 72
  Mordecai, 57
  Moses, 57
  Nathan, 70
  Nathaniel, 57, 128
  Richard, 72
  Ruth, 72
  Thomas, 57, 99
  Virginia, 13, 27, 55, 105, 109, 136
VOGEN (VOGAN),
  James, 46
  Jean, 46
  William, 46

-W-
WADDEL, William, 82
WADDLE, Rachel, 85
WADE, Robert, 95
  Sarah, 95
WALKER, Alexander, 44, 45
  Anne, 92
  Daniel, 21
  Enoch, 19, 119
  George, 92
  Isaac, 21
  James, 92
  Jane, 26
  John, 73, 146, 153
  Rebecca, 153
  Robert, 44
  William, 92
WALL, Ann, 144
  Edward, 144
  John, 24, 76, 107, 144
  Joseph, 24, 144
  Mary, 144
  William, 144
WALLACE, John, 148
  Margaret, 77
  Sarah, 12
  Thomas, 12
WALLOCK, Andrew, 138
WALN, Mary, 50
  Richard, 50
WALTER, Abraham, 84
  Elizabeth, 111
  Esther, 84
  Hannah, 111
  James, 8, 72, 111
  Jane, 111
  Joseph, 111
  Lydia, 72, 84
  Phebe, 111
  Sarah, 84
  Thomas, 27
  William, 125
WARBURTON, Robert, 91
  Ruth, 91, 107
  William, 91
WARK, Elizabeth, 155

William, 155
WARNER, Margery, 158
  Veronica, 158
WARNOCK, John, 155
WATER, Thomas, 21
WATKIN, Aaron, 5
WATKINS, Robert, 1
WATSON, Archibald, 128
  John, 46
  William, 60
WAY, Benjamin, 82
  Isaac, 82
  Jacob, 55
  James, 38, 58
  John, 21, 82, 91
  Joseph, 106
  Mary, 58, 82, 89, 91
  Nathaniel, 115
  Robert, 91
  William, 91
WAYNE, Anthony, 60, 157
  Elizabeth, 48, 60, 121
  Humphrey, 48, 60
  Isaac, 74, 95, 157
  Issac, 158
  John, 58
  Priscilla, 47
  Sarah, 58
  Thomas, 74
WEARE, Daniel, 2
  John, 2
WEATHERBY,
  Benjamin, 157
  David, 157
  George, 157
  Richard, 157
  Samuel, 157
  Septimus, 157
  Whitehead, 157
  William, 157
WEATHERMAN,
  William, 49
WEBB, Alice, 149
  Ann, 135
  Benjamin, 144, 148
  Constant, 54
  Daniel, 25, 33, 47, 149

203

204

Elizabeth, 54,
  92, 138, 149
Ezekiel, 47
Faithful, 54
George, 54
James, 149
Jane, 54, 92,
  139
Mary, 25
Nathan, 120
Rachel, 149
Rebecca, 47
Samuel, 54
Stephen, 47, 139
Susanna, 144
William, 47, 54,
  138
WEBBER, Jacob, 51,
  93
WEBSTER,
  Elizabeth, 55,
  117, 155
  John, 55
  Thomas, 55, 155
  William, 55
WEEKS, Gilbert,
  140
WEIRE, Elizabeth,
  54, 92
  George, 54
WELCH, Ann, 67
  William, 77
WELDON, Benjamin,
  117
  Elizabeth, 15,
  118
WELLS, Samuel, 50
WELSH, Ann, 67
  George, 65
  James, 65
  Jane, 65
  Mary, 65
  Robert, 65
  William, 65
WENTWORTH, Mary,
  51
WEST, Hugh, 109
  Isaac, 40
  Jane, 40, 46
  John, 74
  William, 125
WESTHERBY, David,
  30
WHARREY, Ann, 62
  James, 62, 112,
  138
  Mary, 112
WHARRY, David, 34
WHARTON, John, 52
WHIGAM, Hannah, 53
  John, 53
WHITE, Abigail,
  115
  Agnes, 77
  Eleanor, 57
  Elizabeth, 102
  John, 14, 68,
  75, 77, 94
  Margaret, 74
  Marget, 74
  Mary, 77
  Matthew, 74
  Nathaniel, 93,
  101
  Nicholas, 142
  Richard, 45
  Robert, 74
  Samuel, 68, 88
  Sarah, 94
  Stephen, 96, 145
  Thomas, 57, 68,
  74, 115, 142
  Uriah, 142
  William, 94
WHITEHILL, James,
  101, 104
  Rachel, 104
WHITEKER, Edward,
  32, 107
  Mary, 87
  Peter, 87
WHITELEY, Abigail,
  109
WHITHILL, James,
  53
WHITKER, Robert,
  15
WHITTAKER, Edward,
  99
WICKERSHAM, Ann,
  77
  Dan, 78
  James, 13, 78,
  98
  John, 41
  Robert, 39
  Thomas, 41
WIDDOS, Isaac, 147
WIDDOW, Isaac, 25
WILEY, David, 77,
  110, 131
  Mary, 110
WILKIN, Elizabeth,
  139
  Eloner, 139
  George, 139
  Hannah, 139
  John, 139
  Leonard, 139
  William, 139
WILKINS, Richard,
  43
  Thomas, 66
WILKINSON,
  Jonathan, 126
  Joseph, 40, 59
WILKISON, Evan, 93
WILLIAM, Anne, 134
  Daniel, 125
  David, 134
  Edward, 78, 156
  Esther, 5
  Joseph, 50, 78
  Margaret, 78
  Robert, 5
WILLIAMS, Abigail,
  101
  Amos, 39, 92
  Ann, 43, 51, 64
  Catherine, 3
  Daniel, 107
  Edmund, 51, 124
  Edward, 157
  Eleanor, 151,
  152
  Elizabeth, 51,
  65, 157
  Ellis, 64, 141
  Esther, 64
  Griffith, 157
  Isaac, 64, 133,
  151
  James, 39
  Jane, 157
  Joan, 28
  John, 12, 52,
  54, 151
  Joseph, 2, 4,
  10, 30, 37, 39,
  65, 101, 115,
  130, 152
  Levi, 43
  Lewis, 64
  Lydia, 141
  Margaret, 65

Mary, 30, 43,
  51, 64, 124,
  157
Mordecai, 128
Rachel, 51, 124
Robert, 64
Ruth Garrett, 64
Samuel, 48, 52,
  124
Simeon, 43
Susanna, 1
Thomas, 3, 51,
  124
William, 28, 43,
  51, 124, 157
WILLIAMSON,
  Daniel, 100
  John, 57, 100
  Joseph, 2
  Mary, 50
  Robert, 62
  Sarah, 100
WILLIS, Elizabeth,
  153
  Joel, 126
WILLISTON,
  Eleanor, 15
WILLSON, Andrew,
  23, 139
  Catharine, 96
  Catherine, 36
  Elizabeth, 36,
  96, 156
  Gideon, 36
  Hugh, 36
  James, 7, 19,
  32, 108
  Jane, 96
  Janet, 36, 96
  Jean, 36
  John, 7, 36, 74,
  89, 96, 131
  Joseph, 36, 96,
  156
  Martha, 7
  Mary, 19, 89
  Matthew, 19
  Robert, 19
  Sarah, 7
  Susanna, 133
  Thomas, 36, 52,
  96, 156
  William, 93, 147
WILSON, Amy, 130
  Andrew, 52, 68,
  69
  Ann, 93
  Barbara, 44
  Benjamin, 155
  Cathrine, 44
  Christopher, 130
  Dinah, 130
  Elizabeth, 52,
  93, 101
  Esther, 44
  George, 69
  Hannah, 44, 117,
  153
  James, 52, 90,
  91, 101, 117,
  130, 143, 148,
  153
  Jane, 135
  Jean, 52
  Jennet, 52
  John, 52, 117
  Joseph, 52, 69,
  91
  Margaret, 52, 93
  Margery, 52
  Martha, 90
  Mary, 52, 69,
  93, 147
  Nicholas, 44
  Robert, 21, 44,
  52, 69, 93,
  135, 147
  Thomas, 44, 69
WINDLE, Alice, 33
  Francis, 39
WITHROW,
  Alexander, 23,
  81
  Robert, 92, 126
WITHY, John, 150
  Mary, 150
WOLLERTON, Dorcas,
  155
  James, 155
  John, 155
WOLLISON, Deborah,
  113
  Elizabeth, 113
  Jacob, 113
  Joseph, 113
  Katherine, 113
  William, 113
WOOD, Ann, 25
  George, 25
  Hannah, 25, 72
  Jane, 25
  Jonathan, 25
  Joseph, 107, 135
  Sarah, 25
  William, 83, 124
WOODCOCK,
  Bancroft, 143
  Rachel, 143
  Ruth, 143
WOODROF, John, 80
WOODROW, Caleb,
  143
  Isaac, 80
  Jane, 41
  Joseph, 80
  Mary, 80
  Simeon, 41
  Simon, 80
  Thomas, 80
WOODS, John, 60
WOODSIDE, Rachel,
  104
WOODWARD, Abigail,
  70, 95
  Amos, 35
  Ann, 6, 35
  Deborah, 44, 95
  Edward, 53, 56,
  57, 70
  Elizabeth, 56,
  70, 80, 113
  George, 56, 57,
  70
  Hannah, 70, 81
  Henry, 15, 16,
  35, 159
  James, 6
  Jane, 6, 56, 70
  John, 15, 35,
  44, 81
  Joseph, 6, 95
  Joseph Bruce, 96
  Margaret, 70
  Martha, 44, 59
  Mary, 15, 16,
  139, 159
  Nayle, 35
  Rachel, 95
  Rebeca, 113
  Rebecca, 139
  Richard, 15, 35,
  44, 95
  Robert, 6
  Samuel, 113, 139
  T., 55, 65, 85,

206

99
Thomas, 15, 79,
 113, 139
William, 6, 44,
 95, 100
WOOLISON,
Elizabeth, 139
Joseph, 139
WOOLLEY, Anne, 103
Sarah, 103
WOOLMAN,
Elizabeth, 89
Hannah, 135
John, 89
WORRAL, Martha,
 105
WORRALL, Aaron,
 149
Amos, 149
Benjamin, 18,
 149
Edward, 105, 113
Eleanor, 113
Elinor, 105
Elizabeth, 149
George, 134
Hannah, 76
James, 18, 149
John, 18, 76,
 105, 113, 149
Jonathan, 18,
 113
Joseph, 18, 105,
 113
Mary, 105
Nathan, 149
Peter, 18, 113
Phebe, 17, 122,
 149
Priscilla, 134
Ruth, 105, 113
Thomas, 105,
 112, 113, 118
WORREL, Sarah, 151
WORRILL, John, 105
WORTH, Ebenezer,
 44, 59, 87
Elizabeth, 6
Samuel, 6, 94
Susanna, 44, 59
Thomas, 6, 16,
 44, 59, 87
WRATH, Rebecca,
 153
William, 153

WRAY, James, 5
WRIGHT, Ann, 76
George, 76
Hannah, 76, 92
Jacob, 152
James, 76
Mary, 65
Moses, 76, 92
William, 16, 76
WYETH, John, 2, 94
Mary, 2
WYLLEY, Abigail, 4
James, 4
Katherine, 4
William, 4

-Y-
YARNALL, Aaron,
 124
Abner, 133
Abraham, 84, 133
Caleb, 138
Daniel, 53, 79
David, 84, 133
Dorothy, 84,
 133, 153
Elizabeth, 84,
 133
Ephraim, 153
Esther, 84, 133
Ezekiel, 133
Francis, 129
Isaac, 89, 147
James, 135
Jane, 84, 133
Job, 138
John, 89
Joseph, 79, 138
Lydia, 133
Margaret, 89,
 138
Mary, 79, 84,
 98, 133, 147
Nathan, 138
Philip, 84, 133
Rachel, 133
Samuel, 17
Sarah, 17
Thomas, 89, 138
Uriah, 133
William, 138
YEARSLEY,
Elizabeth, 152
Isaac, 2
Jacob, 37, 113,
 152
John, 2, 152
Nathan, 2, 34,
 152
Phebe, 59
Rachel, 114
Sarah, 2, 34,
 152
Susanna, 37,
 113, 152
Thomas, 152
YEATMAN, Andrew,
 147
YOUNG, Ann, 27
Anne, 109
Daniel, 109
Elizabeth, 44
James, 146
John, 44
Margaret, 26, 60
Matthew, 45, 156
Robert, 2, 26,
 27, 67
Samuel, 77
William, 25, 27

Other books by F. Edward Wright:

Abstracts of Bucks County, Pennsylvania Wills, 1685-1785
Abstracts of Cumberland County, Pennsylvania Wills, 1750-1785
Abstracts of Cumberland County, Pennsylvania Wills, 1785-1825
Abstracts of Philadelphia County Wills, 1726-1747
Abstracts of Philadelphia County Wills, 1748-1763
Abstracts of Philadelphia County Wills, 1763-1784
Abstracts of Philadelphia County Wills, 1777-1790
Abstracts of Philadelphia County Wills, 1790-1802
Abstracts of Philadelphia County Wills, 1802-1809
Abstracts of Philadelphia County Wills, 1810-1815
Abstracts of Philadelphia County Wills, 1815-1819
Abstracts of Philadelphia County Wills, 1820-1825
Abstracts of Philadelphia County, Pennsylvania Wills, 1682-1726
Abstracts of South Central Pennsylvania Newspapers, Volume 1, 1785-1790
Abstracts of South Central Pennsylvania Newspapers, Volume 3, 1796-1800
Abstracts of the Newspapers of Georgetown and the Federal City, 1789-99
Abstracts of York County, Pennsylvania Wills, 1749-1819
Bucks County, Pennsylvania Church Records of the 17th and 18th Centuries Volume 2: Quaker Records: Falls and Middletown Monthly Meetings
Anna Miller Watring and F. Edward Wright
Caroline County, Maryland Marriages, Births and Deaths, 1850-1880
Citizens of the Eastern Shore of Maryland, 1659-1750
Cumberland County, Pennsylvania Church Records of the 18th Century
Delaware Newspaper Abstracts, Volume 1: 1786-1795
Early Charles County, Maryland Settlers, 1658-1745
Marlene Strawser Bates and F. Edward Wright
Early Church Records of Alexandria City and Fairfax County, Virginia
F. Edward Wright and Wesley E. Pippenger
Early Church Records of New Castle County, Delaware, Volume 1, 1701-1800
Frederick County Militia in the War of 1812
Sallie A. Mallick and F. Edward Wright
Inhabitants of Baltimore County, 1692-1763
Land Records of Sussex County, Delaware, 1769-1782
Land Records of Sussex County, Delaware, 1782-1789
Elaine Hastings Mason and F. Edward Wright
Marriage Licenses of Washington, District of Columbia, 1811-1830
Marriages and Deaths from the Newspapers of Allegany and Washington Counties, Maryland, 1820-1830
Marriages and Deaths from The York Recorder, 1821-1830
Marriages and Deaths in the Newspapers of Frederick and Montgomery Counties, Maryland, 1820-1830

Marriages and Deaths in the Newspapers of Lancaster County, Pennsylvania, 1821-1830
Marriages and Deaths in the Newspapers of Lancaster County, Pennsylvania, 1831-1840
Marriages and Deaths of Cumberland County, [Pennsylvania], 1821-1830
Maryland Calendar of Wills Volume 9: 1744-1749
Maryland Calendar of Wills Volume 10: 1748-1753
Maryland Calendar of Wills Volume 11: 1753-1760
Maryland Calendar of Wills Volume 12: 1759-1764
Maryland Calendar of Wills Volume 13: 1764-1767
Maryland Calendar of Wills Volume 14: 1767-1772
Maryland Calendar of Wills Volume 15: 1772-1774
Maryland Calendar of Wills Volume 16: 1774-1777
Maryland Eastern Shore Newspaper Abstracts, Volume 1: 1790-1805
Maryland Eastern Shore Newspaper Abstracts, Volume 2: 1806-1812
Maryland Eastern Shore Newspaper Abstracts, Volume 3: 1813-1818
Maryland Eastern Shore Newspaper Abstracts, Volume 4: 1819-1824
Maryland Eastern Shore Newspaper Abstracts, Volume 5: Northern Counties, 1825-1829
F. Edward Wright and Irma Harper
Maryland Eastern Shore Newspaper Abstracts, Volume 6: Southern Counties, 1825-1829
Maryland Eastern Shore Newspaper Abstracts, Volume 7: Northern Counties, 1830-1834
Irma Harper and F. Edward Wright
Maryland Eastern Shore Newspaper Abstracts, Volume 8: Southern Counties, 1830-1834
Maryland Militia in the Revolutionary War
S. Eugene Clements and F. Edward Wright
Newspaper Abstracts of Allegany and Washington Counties, 1811-1815
Newspaper Abstracts of Cecil and Harford Counties, [Maryland], 1822-1830
Newspaper Abstracts of Frederick County, [Maryland], 1816-1819
Newspaper Abstracts of Frederick County, 1811-1815
Sketches of Maryland Eastern Shoremen
Tax List of Chester County, Pennsylvania 1768
Tax List of York County, Pennsylvania 1779
Washington County Church Records of the 18th Century, 1768-1800
Western Maryland Newspaper Abstracts, Volume 1: 1786-1798
Western Maryland Newspaper Abstracts, Volume 2: 1799-1805
Western Maryland Newspaper Abstracts, Volume 3: 1806-1810
Wills of Chester County, Pennsylvania, 1766-1778

www.ingramcontent.com/pod-product-compliance
Lightning Source LLC
Chambersburg PA
CBHW062209080426
42734CB00010B/1851